Why Do You Need this New Edition?

If you're wondering why you should buy this new edition of *Discovery: From Sentence to Paragraph*, here are ten good reasons!

1. **Strengthens Writing Skills Mastery** Multiple opportunities in this new edition of *Discovery* allow you to master grammar and writing skills, including a new, unique "Assessment" feature. Use this to evaluate your progress and mastery in four crucial areas of college success: as a writer, a reader, an editor, and a student.

2. **Illustrates and Highlights the Writing Process** This new edition does more to explain the writing process by example. New prewriting models strengthen the continuity and flow to the new Spotlight pieces that end each chapter in Part One. New model paragraphs show each stage of the writing process—from initial ideas to successful final draft—in Chapters 2 through 4.

3. **Boosts Your Confidence** "The Faces of Discovery" feature—brief interviews of twenty students who candidly share their personal struggles with writing and what they have done to overcome those struggles—will help you to overcome various obstacles. All the students profiled attribute their success to the writing skills they mastered using *Discovery*.

4. **Shows What Good Writing Looks Like** Student "Spotlights" in Chapters 1 through 5 showcase what students can achieve through confidence and practice. Throughout the book annotated papers, peer responses, and instructors' comments provide a unique window into each stage of the writing process.

5. **Provides Appealing and Interesting Practice** *Discovery*'s engaging "For Further Exploration" and "Journaling" writing activities ask you to explore topics that are familiar to you—from Facebook and Twitter to exercise and fitness. "Discovering Connections" present additional challenging topics for you to explore through photos, such as global climate change, national public service, and extreme sports.

6. **Explains the Dangers of Plagiarism** Even at this basic level, it is important to understand that claiming another's work as your own is wrong. New introductory material on understanding how to identify and avoid plagiarism has been added to Chapter 4, "Revising."

7. **Emphasizes the Connection between Writing and Reading** *Discovery* concludes with an anthology of six professional and seven student readings, with five of the readings newly chosen for this edition. Each reading provides opportunities for critical thinking and active reading as well as for discussion and writing.

8. **Encourages Inquiry and Discovery** To highlight the inquiry-based approach of the text, the chapter openers contain the following features: "Getting Started Q&A," which highlights the most frequently asked questions about writing and grammar; "Overview," which offers a synopsis of the chapter's major concepts; and "Navigating This Chapter," which provides an at-a-glance view of the chapter's key points.

9. **Shows You Concepts in Action** The revised visual presentation teaches the mind as well as attracts the eye; illustrations of writing and grammatical principles and processes have been revised to better suit the way students visually learn today.

10. **Takes You Beyond the Page** New MyWritingLab (www.mywritinglab.com) prompts at the end of each chapter take you to Pearson's dynamic online learning and assessment system for additional practice.

D1059790

PEARSON

A Conversation with

William J. Kelly

Q. *How does this book guide students along their personal paths to both self- and academic discovery?*

A. One of the things I really like about writing is that it is such a great vehicle for developing and examining ideas on all kinds of subjects. When you write, you learn about yourself, about different academic subjects, and about the world beyond the classroom. *Discovery* is the ideal guide for the journey because it clearly and completely explains and illustrates how to develop and examine your ideas and present them in a proper form.

Q. *Why and how do you think your book can help students overcome their writing fears?*

A. In my life, I've never met anyone who wants to make a mistake, who wants *not* to understand something. The fear that you can't do or make sense of something that you believe others can—that you will fail—can be almost paralyzing. As someone who sometimes struggled in school, often as a result of my own negative attitude, I know that fear well, so I have worked to make sure that *Discovery* will reduce it. The presentation throughout *Discovery* is incremental—step-by-step, bit by bit—so that whether the discussion concerns a stage in the writing process or an explanation of how to avoid an error in usage, the resulting lessons are easier to follow and master.

Q. *What would you say to the student who claims, "I don't need to improve my writing; I'm going to be a computer scientist. I won't need to write"?*

A. I'd tell that student the truth: Writing plays a significant role in the work of *all* professionals. The writing you will do as a computer scientist, an accountant, a medical professional, or a social worker won't necessarily be in the form of paragraphs and essays. But it will still be writing that presents and supports a point, always in complete and correct sentence form. Think of it this way: Writing will be the way that you explain, apply, or transfer the specialized knowledge you have. If your writing skills aren't strong, your professional performance will suffer. It's that simple.

Q. *What is the best advice you can give to students taking a developmental writing course?*

A. Here's my advice: Really mastering something, anything—a musical instrument, an athletic activity, a dance step, a computer game—takes time and hard work. And it takes patience, and patience is the hardest part, especially at the beginning, when it all can seem overwhelming and when it's hard to see or appreciate the progress you've made. The secret to success is to work at being more patient, so that you can tolerate the frustration that learning can entail and complete the practice you need to develop greater skill. *Practice* doesn't really make *perfect.* That's just a saying. But *practice* does make *better,* and that's the ultimate goal when it comes to writing.

Discovery

From Sentence to Paragraph

Fifth Edition

Annotated Instructor's Edition

William J. Kelly
Bristol Community College

Deborah L. Lawton
Bristol Community College

Longman

Boston   Columbus   Indianapolis   New York   San Francisco   Upper Saddle River
Amsterdam   Cape Town   Dubai   London   Madrid   Milan   Munich   Paris   Montreal
Toronto   Delhi   Mexico City   São Paulo   Sydney   Hong Kong   Seoul   Singapore   Taipei   Tokyo

Dedication

To Amy, who is everything a daughter could be, and more. . . .
—D. L. L.

To Flo and Leo Nadeau—my mother- and father-in-law—for their continued, consistent love and support.
—W. J. K.

Acquisitions Editor:	Matthew Wright
Development Editor:	Lai T. Moy
Assistant Editor:	Jessica Kupetz
Editorial Assistant:	Haley Pero
Marketing Manager	Thomas DeMarco
Senior Supplements Editor:	Donna Campion
Senior Media Editor:	Stefanie Liebman
Production Manager:	Eric Jorgensen
Project Coordination Text Design, and Electronic Page Makeup:	Elm Street Publishing Services
Senior Cover Design Manager:	Nancy Danahy
Cover Designer:	Susan Koski Zucker
Cover Image:	Close-up of a sailing ship. Photographer: Tina und Horst Herzig. © LOOK/Getty Images, Inc.
Photo Researcher:	Pearson Image Resource Center/Kathy Ringrose
Image Permission Coordinator:	Jan Marc Quisumbing
Senior Manufacturing Buyer:	Dennis J. Para
Printer and Binder:	Worldcolor, Dubuque
Cover Printer:	Coral Graphics Services, Inc.

For permission to use copyrighted material, grateful acknowledgments is made to the copyright holders on p. 499, which is hereby made part of this copyright page.

Library of Congress Cataloging-in-Publication Data

Kelly, William J. (William Jude), 1953–
    Discovery: from sentence to paragraph / William J. Kelly; Deborah L. Lawton.—5th ed.
    p. cm.
    Includes index.
    ISBN 0-205-65158-5–ISBN 0-205-65159-3
    1. English language—Rhetoric. 2. English language—Grammar—Problems, exercises, etc.
3. College readers. 4. Report writing. I. Lawton, Deborah L. II. Title.
    PE1408.K4735 2009
    808'.042—dc22

                                                                                        2009039696

1 2 3 4 5 6 7 8 9 10—WCD—13 12 11 10

Longman
is an imprint of

www.pearsonhighered.com

ISBN 0-205-65158-5, 978-0-205-65158-0
(Student Edition)
ISBN 0-205-65159-3, 978-0-205-65159-7
(Annotated Instructor's Edition)

Detailed Contents

PART 2
Effective Sentences:
Constructing
Meaning   123

The Faces of Discovery   124

PART 6

Discovering
Connections
through
Reading   449

Preface

Whether it's an actual piece of paper or a virtual one on a computer screen, a blank page is always a discovery waiting to happen. As soon as you generate your first ideas, your exploration into the world of writing begins.

Through writing, you learn about yourself, about the world, and about the people with whom you share it. The process unlocks your creativity and provides the opportunity for you to apply your reserves of knowledge on a variety of subjects. Writing also enables you to exchange information and react to what you learn from others. *Discovery: From Sentence to Paragraph,* Fifth Edition, provides everything you need to negotiate the twists and turns you'll experience on your writing journey.

Three basic premises underlie *Discovery:*

1. **Practice leads to competence and confidence.** It's simple. To improve as a writer and to become comfortable with the writing process, you need to practice writing. *Discovery* encourages this practice by immediately introducing you to each stage of the writing process, and reminding you that the process can be just as familiar and as regular as the writing you do on a daily basis— from text messaging to tweeting on Twitter to posting on Facebook. *Discovery* gets you involved in stimulating writing activities.

2. **Good writing results from sound critical thinking and creativity.** Writing well requires you to know your subject thoroughly and to analyze it from a variety of perspectives. *Discovery* addresses these concerns by providing a multitude of writing activities and assignments to stimulate your critical thinking, creative expression, and self-assessment. In addition, it emphasizes the value of collaboration, encouraging you to work in a meaningful way with others as you develop and refine your work.

3. **Good writing is a happy marriage of content and form.** You succeed as a writer when you communicate your good ideas in a form that is universally accepted and understood by all readers. For this reason, a significant amount of *Discovery* is devoted to basic sentence development and correct use of sentence elements. It presents the guidelines of acceptable written language in a simple, clear, and direct manner, putting mastery of this material within your reach.

Organization of the Text

Discovery's organization makes it easy to develop your skills in a cumulative fashion. Part One, "The Elements of Effective Writing," consists of five chapters that walk you through the various stages of the writing process. Chapter 1 provides an overview of the writing process, emphasizing the importance of *purpose* in writing and knowing your *audience*. The next three chapters cover each stage of the writing process in greater depth: Chapter 2 introduces the five techniques of prewriting and also covers journal writing—another method of developing writing skills. Chapter 3 offers step-by-step guidelines for developing clear and engaging topic and supporting sentences, which you then learn to organize into paragraph form. Chapter 4 illustrates how to assess and improve a first draft, highlighting the importance of revising for unity, coherence, and effective language. At the same time, it emphasizes the importance of feedback from an objective reader and demonstrates how to polish a draft through editing. The fifth and final chapter of Part One serves as a bridge from paragraph to essay writing. This chapter explains each stage of the essay writing process and concludes with an annotated final-draft essay.

The next four parts of *Discovery* build on the lessons of Part One, covering the elements of grammar and usage that can be especially challenging. Through simple explanations, clear examples, and stimulating and thought-provoking writing exercises, activities, and assignments, these chapters emphasize that effective writing is a *synthesis* of content and form.

The five chapters making up Part Two, "Effective Sentences: Constructing Meaning," all focus on how to write correct, effective sentences. Chapter 6 covers the basic architecture of a sentence, and Chapter 7 details ways to recognize and eliminate sentence fragments. Chapters 8 and 9 deal with subordination and coordination, and Chapter 10 shows you how to recognize and eliminate two major sentence errors: comma splices and run-ons.

The five chapters comprising Part Three, "Verbs: Conveying Action and Time," cover various aspects of verb use. Chapter 11 illustrates how to avoid all-too-common errors in subject–verb agreement. Chapters 12 and 13 explain how to form the simple and perfect tenses of regular and irregular verbs. Chapters 14 and 15 discuss other aspects of verb use, such as voice, progressive tenses, and forms of *to be.*

The three chapters constituting Part Four, "Sentence Elements: Striving for Precision," cover the use of nouns, pronouns, and modifiers. Chapter 16 focuses on noun function, proper spelling of plural forms, and the correct use of collective nouns. Chapter 17 concentrates on correct pronoun use, including case, pronoun–antecedent agreement, and sexist language. Chapter 18 illustrates the various forms of adjectives, adverbs, and other modifiers and addresses usage errors such as double negatives and dangling modifiers.

The five chapters making up Part Five, "Consistency Workshop: Aiming for Correctness"—reorganized in this edition for greater logic in presentation—cover matters of mechanics. Chapter 19 explains ways to avoid errors with parallelism, and Chapter 20 deals with common spelling errors and offers strategies to become a better speller. Chapter 21 focuses solely on comma use, while Chapter 22 covers the use of other marks of punctuation. Finally, Chapter 23 discusses guidelines concerning capitalization.

Part Six, "Discovering Connections through Reading," is an anthology of thirteen readings, each followed by sets of questions designed to stimulate critical thinking and inspire additional writing. The introduction to this engaging anthology explains and illustrates active reading, making it clear that this technique is a proven path to greater reading comprehension. It also features a brief, annotated excerpt that illustrates the active reading process. The first six readings are written by professional writers, and the remaining seven readings are by students in response to assignments like those found throughout *Discovery.* These essays are excellent models for close reading and effective writing.

Finally, a practical appendix, "Tips for ESL Writers," supplements the lessons in the text. Although directed at nonnative speakers of English and covering areas of grammar and usage that ESL students generally find confusing, native speakers can also benefit from its content.

Features and Changes in the Text

Discovery's special features are designed to make the journey through the text and toward writing mastery both productive and pleasurable. And with every edition of *Discovery,* our primary goal has been to create a text that is as **accessible, appealing, efficient,** and **practical** as possible. To achieve this aim, we have studied *Discovery* as we use it with our classes, listened to what our students have had to say, and asked colleagues, both locally and across the nation, about ways to continue to refine and improve the text. As a result, the Fifth Edition of *Discovery* contains a number of significant improvements.

To Boost Confidence

- **Faces of Discovery.** What better way to boost writing confidence than by starting each major section of the book with the voices of students just like you? Parts One through Five open with brief interviews of real students who candidly share their personal struggles with writing and what they have done to overcome those struggles.
- **Getting Started Q & A.** We all have fears and concerns about writing that we may not always want to ask out loud. Thus, each chapter opens with the most commonly asked questions about the chapter topic; advice about how to best address these concerns immediately follows.
- **ESL Notes.** Marginal notes that appear throughout the book reference the ESL Appendix, from which all students—whether English is your second language or your first—can benefit.
- **Readings.** Three of the six professional readings are *new* (those by Russell Baker, Annie Dillard, and Charles McGrath), and two of the seven student readings are *new* (those by Soledad A. Munoz-Vilugron and Pranee Vincent).

To Encourage Practice

- **For Further Exploration.** Appearing at the end of each chapter, this feature offers three distinct topics, encouraging you to explore, practice, and complete each stage of the writing process within a single assignment.
- **Discovering Connections.** Also appearing at the end of every chapter, these innovative writing activities rely on both visual and verbal cues to stimulate interest and spark creative associations, imagination, and critical thinking, all of which lead to thoughtful, effective writing. In addition, each assignment contains at least one writing prompt tied to career exploration. Nine of the twenty-*three* assignments are *new* and feature subjects of high interest to students today. These assignments are unmatched in other basic writing texts.
- **Journal writing activities** appear in each chapter, providing an opportunity for discovery about yourself, the world, and other areas of high interest through writing.

To Master Skills

- **Chapter openers.** To highlight the inquiry-based approach of the text and to make the progression through the chapters more logical and easy to follow, the opening features have been reorganized as follows: "Getting Started Q & A," which highlights the most frequently asked questions about writing and grammar; "Overview," which offers a general synopsis of the chapter's major concepts; and "Navigating This Chapter," which gives you an at-a-glance preview of the chapter's key points.

- **Extensive and comprehensive coverage** of the areas of **grammar and usage** that most trouble student writers is provided in Chapters 6–23, including *sentence fragments, comma splices,* and *run-on sentences; verb use; subject–verb agreement; spelling; pronoun–antecedent agreement; modifiers; subordination* and *coordination;* and *punctuation.*

- **Comprehension and Practice** exercises in each chapter call for a demonstration of understanding and application of the principles presented. Almost all are **continuous discourse,** that is, in **paragraph form.** This method of presentation underscores one of the guiding principles of the text: The elements of grammar and usage are a part of writing, not a separate system of rules. Working through these paragraphs, which are on a wide variety of engaging subjects, deepens understanding about the structure of effective topic sentences and support.

- **Challenge** activities in each chapter provide opportunities for critical thinking and writing. Most of them also involve meaningful *collaborative* work.

- **Chapter Quick Checks** (ten sentences long) and **Summary Exercises** (twenty sentences long), cover all the concepts presented in each chapter.

- **Chapter Recaps** at the end of each chapter provide **definitions of new terms** as well as **visual summaries of key concepts.**

- **Appendix: Tips for ESL Writers** presents additional **grammar and usage tips** valuable for both ESL students and native English speakers.

- The **attractive, full-color design,** which includes full-color charts, provides visual stimulation and emphasis of key concepts.

- **Assessment modules.** Innovative, *new* modules located at the end of each part evaluate **progress** and **mastery** in four crucial areas of college success—as a **writer,** as a **reader,** as an **editor,** and as a **student.** These areas are then followed by concrete steps that address any remaining weaknesses.

To Showcase Good Writing

- **Spotlight pieces** in Chapters 1 through 5 (the writing process chapters) feature annotated student writing, modeling what you can achieve with confidence and practice. All five student writings are *new* and are accompanied by a photo of each student writer.

- **Engaging and realistic writing samples, annotated papers, peer responses,** and **instructors' comments** provide a unique window into each stage of the writing process.

- **Anthology of six professional and seven student readings,** with five of the readings newly chosen for this edition, provides opportunities for critical thinking and active reading as well as discussion and writing.

- **Discovering Connections through Writing** activities follow each of the readings in Part Six. These activities include questions and writing assignments that ask you to react to the ideas presented in or raised by the readings.

- **MyWritingLab.** These end-of-chapter cross-references to areas within this interactive online learning system can further supplement what you've learned in the text.

Part One: The Elements of Effective Writing

Chapters 1 through 5, on the writing process, have been completely revised. Some highlights include:

- *New* **prewriting models.** To strengthen the continuity and flow related to the discussion of the writing process, new prewriting models have been added to tie in more closely to the new Spotlight pieces that end each chapter in Part One.
- **A *new* discussion of hybrid (combined) prewriting techniques and checking in** with an objective reader during the prewriting stage now appear in Chapter 2.
- *New* **model paragraphs.** New paragraphs showing each stage of the writing process—from initial ideas to a successful final draft—now appear in Chapters 2, 3 and 4.
- *New* **section on avoiding plagiarism.** Even at this basic level, it is important to understand that claiming another's work as your own is wrong. New basic material on understanding how to identify and avoid plagiarism has been added to Chapter 4, "Revising," as have updates to the **MLA style of documentation**.
- *New* **section on formatting a paper.** New, detailed information on how to properly format a word-processed document now appears in Chapter 4.

Exercises and Activities

In every edition, we try as much as possible to update all exercises and activities throughout the book. Some highlights include:

- **Comprehension and Practice, Challenge, and Other Writing Activities.** The text now covers a wide variety of high-interest subjects, including Facebook, Twitter, and other social networking sites; national public service and civil disobedience; BlackBerries and other smart phones; text messaging; computer gaming; global climate change, acid rain, light pollution, and other environmental issues; exotic activities like Zorbing; exercise, fitness, and extreme sports; astronomy and space exploration; and pop culture issues to engage readers and enhance the mastery of the principles presented.

Visual Presentation

In an effort to make the book as visually appealing as possible, we also wanted to ensure that the visual presentation teaches the mind as well as attracts the eye:

- **Illustrations.** Writing and grammatical principles and processes have been rerendered to better fit the visual way students learn today.
- **Recaps.** These end-of-chapter summaries now more visually demonstrate each chapter's major concepts.

Book-Specific Ancillary Materials

- **Online-Only Instructor's Manual and Test Bank (0-205-65160-7)** includes a wealth of teaching suggestions. Also included are a diagnostic test, tests for each chapter in Parts Two through Five, a comprehensive Mastery Test, sample syllabi, and a full bank of test questions. Instructors simply log onto the Instructor's Resource Center (IRC) to download and print out the tests of their choice.

- **The Pearson Developmental Writing Package.** Pearson is pleased to offer a variety of support materials to help make teaching developmental English easier on teachers and to help students excel in their coursework. Many of our student supplements are available free or at a greatly reduced price when packaged with *Discovery,* Fifth Edition. Contact your local Pearson sales representative for more information on pricing and how to create a package.

- **MyWritingLab.** MyWritingLab is an online learning system that provides improved writing practice through diagnostic assessment and progressive exercises to move students from literal comprehension to critical thinking and writing. With this improved practice model, students develop the skills they need to become better writers. Visit us at **http://www.mywritinglab.com/**.

Acknowledgments

We would like to acknowledge a number of people for their support as we completed this Fifth Edition of *Discovery.* Thanks first to John M. Lannon, University of Massachusetts, Dartmouth, and Robert Schwegler, University of Rhode Island. Their ongoing interest, friendship, and support mean more than they could ever know—and more than we could ever say. We also offer special thanks to Paul Arakelian, University of Rhode Island, for his continued friendship and encouragement.

We also want to thank a number of people here at Bristol Community College. We are deeply grateful for all that our students continue to teach us, including the students who allowed us to use their work and thoughts about writing: Jennifer Bacon, Valeri L. Cappiello, Mi Carnaghan, Guillermo Castro, Nicholas Coleman, Martin Colon, Jr., Nina Coulombe, Joshua Fay, Leslie Ferreira, Marcy Gagnon, Robert Giron, Natalie Gomes, Tyler Hill, Peter LeComte, Brian Levesque, Scott Lopes, Elsa Maldonado, Svetlana Melamedman, Sonya Mendes, Soledad A. Munoz-Vilugron, Vanessa Pareja, Sara Penuel, Samrouay Senghoung, Kathleen Sullivan, Grace Trecarichi, Jason Trenholm, Erin Turcotte, Nadine Verdieu, Pranee Vincent, Russell Wakefield, and David Wilkerson. Thanks also to our colleagues, including Catherine Adamowicz, Debbie Anderson, Denise DiMarzio, David Feeney, Michael Geary, Tom Grady, Jeanne Grandchamp, Farah Habib, Betsey Kemper-French, Diana McGee, Linda Mulready, Jean-Paul Nadeau, Joanne Preston, and Howard Tinberg, for their kind words and genuine interest in our work. Thanks also to Jack Warner, Chief Executive Officer and Chair of the South Dakota Board of Regents of Higher Education, for his encouragement and his friendship. And we are especially indebted to Paul F. Fletcher, professor emeritus of English and retired Dean for Language, Humanities, and Arts at BCC, who, through example, taught us so much about excellence in teaching and respect and compassion for students.

The following talented professionals across the nation offered reviews that helped us shape this edition of *Discovery:* Laura Whitaker Howard, West Central Technical College; Eugene L. Shiro, University of the District of Columbia; Jacklyn R. Pierce, Lake-Sumter Community College; Caren Kessler, Blue Ridge Community College; Patty Rogers, Angelina College; Christopher Z. Twiggs, Florida Community College at Jacksonville; Nicole R. Gould, Palm Beach Community College; Laura F. Kingston, South Seattle Community College; Rebecca Samberg, Housatonic Community College; and William Young, Wilmington University.

A terrific team of professionals at Pearson Longman also deserve our thanks for their contributions to this edition of *Discovery*. Acquisitions Editor Matt Wright's determination to make *Discovery* the best book in its field—and his seemingly unlimited patience—made our work much easier. We also want to single out Development Editor Lai T. Moy for her enthusiasm, vision, and direction relative to every aspect of this revision. We are also extraordinarily grateful to Assistant Editor Jessica Kupetz and Editorial Assistant Haley Pero. Transforming manuscript into text passed to the capable hands of Eric Jorgensen, at Pearson Publishers, and Sue Nodine, Project Editor for Elm Street Publishing Services, who did so much to make our work look so good.

We are also indebted to our family and friends for making *Discovery* possible. Deborah Lawton would like to thank her good friends who have generously shared their time to listen to and encourage her. Cynthia Hahn, Rylan and Cynthia Brenner, Kathleen Hancock, and Liz Alcock have enriched her life with their thoughtfulness. Barbara Wood and Michele Emond exemplify friends who are always there when needed; they have become an extended family. Because of her family's support and love, she has always felt she could reach her goals, both personal and professional. Her parents, siblings, and in-laws have helped her in ways too numerous to mention here. Above all, she is grateful for her husband's and daughter's love and understanding. Kevin and Amy are the heart of her life.

Bill Kelly would like to thank his parents, the late Mary R. and the late Edward F. Kelly, for the lifelong lessons they taught him and his brothers. His parents-in-law, Flo and Leo Nadeau, and his sons-in-law, Timothy Matos and Jeremy Wright, deserve thanks for their love and continued support of him and his work. His children, Nicole Matos and Jacqueline Wright, deserve far more thanks than anyone could ever muster for the extraordinary pleasure they have always provided him. And in a very short time, Alexander Owen Matos has brought amazing joy into his life. Most of all, though, he wants to thank his wife, Michelle Nadeau Kelly, for more than 37 years of unconditional love and support. No words can come close to acknowledging all that she does, all that she means.

WILLIAM J. KELLY
DEBORAH L. LAWTON

About the Authors

William J. Kelly earned his Ph.D. in English from the University of Rhode Island. He also received an M.A. in English from Rhode Island College and a B.A. in English from Southeastern Massachusetts University (now the University of Massachusetts, Dartmouth). A classroom teacher since 1975, he began his career teaching junior high school and high school English in the Fall River (MA) Public Schools. In 1984, he joined the English Department at Bristol Community College and within five years was promoted to full professor. In addition to his teaching at BCC, he enjoyed a three-year stint writing a weekly newspaper column and has presented numerous teacher training workshops and graduate courses in the teaching of writing. In 1997, the Carnegie Foundation for the Advancement of Teaching and the Council for Advancement and Support of Education (CASE) named him Massachusetts Professor of the Year, the first and only time a community college professor in the state has received this prestigious award. He is the author of several other texts, including Pearson Longman's *Odyssey: From Paragraph to Essay; Simple, Clear, Correct: Paragraphs; Simple, Clear, Correct: Essays; Strategy and Structure: Short Readings for Composition;* and *Intersections: Readings for College and Beyond.* A runner for more than 40 years, he is also an avid handball player. He and his wife, Michelle, Assistant Professor of Psychology at Bristol Community College, live in Fall River. They are the parents of two daughters, Nicole C. Matos, Assistant Professor of English at the College of DuPage, and Jacqueline M. Wright, a musician and conductor, currently pursuing further graduate studies in flute performance.

Deborah L. Lawton has been an advocate of the community college mission for more than 20 years. Her professional life at Bristol Community College has included 5 years as a student affairs professional, 7 years as an academic administrator, and more than 20 years as an instructor of writing, literature, and communication. She is currently Professor of English and Coordinator of the Liberal Arts and Sciences Program. She holds an M.A. in English from Western Michigan University, a B.A. in English from the University of Massachusetts, Amherst, and an A.A. in Liberal Arts from Greenfield Community College in Greenfield, Massachusetts. In her spare time, she breeds and exhibits her champion border terriers. She and her husband, Kevin, are residents of Swansea, Massachusetts.

PART 1

The Elements of Effective Writing

What have you found to be the hardest part of writing and how have you learned to deal with it?

The hardest part for me was thinking of something to write and putting it into words to make sense of it. Since I have learned the process of writing, I freewrite to figure out what I want to say first, and then I organize it on paper. And I always reread what I have put down on paper. This system works for me.

Natalie Gomes
Major: **Medical Coding Certificate**
Career Plans: **Upgrade her skills for her current position at an area hospital**

Natalie Gomes and her family came to the United States from the Azores when Natalie was young, and "learning two languages as a child was very difficult. I would have to speak in Portuguese at home to my parents because they did not understand English and then go to school and have to speak English." At age sixteen, Natalie left school to work full time to help her family, but she long regretted her decision. Although she landed a good job at an area hospital, she eventually decided to attend college because she "wanted to improve [her] skills and expand [her] knowledge." College has been a pleasant surprise for Natalie, especially her interactions with her classmates. "I have learned very much from other students and have closely paid attention to their writing skills—for example, their creativity and styles of writing. This whole experience has made me more comfortable with school, thinking if other students can do this, so can I."

Writer's block can be a problem for some students. How do you deal with this problem?

I find that the hardest part of writing is getting started. When I get writer's block, I take a break from writing and relax. Then I start to write again. I have found that talking to other students helps, too.

Martin A. Colon Jr.
Major: **Fire Science**
Career Plans: **To become a firefighter**

Martin A. Colon Jr., whose family is originally from Puerto Rico, "didn't really have any complaints about high school." His life changed during his senior year, however, when he discovered he was going to be a father. "I stood up and took on my responsibility. With the help of God and my family, I am able to provide for my daughter and help raise her." He currently attends college full time and works a heavy part-time schedule as a waiter to supply financial support for his daughter. The oldest of six children, Martin is among the first in his extended family to attend college. He began his college studies as a criminal justice major but has switched to fire science, with the aim of becoming a firefighter. His most important goal is to stay closely involved in the life of his daughter. As Martin proudly points out, "She is a blessing in my life."

Have you found that talking with other writing students about your writing has helped you become a better writer?

Absolutely! Organizing my writing so that it flows is tough, so being able to share my work with other students is very helpful. Having them make constructive criticisms about my work helps me realize the negative and positive sides of my work. When I'm busy writing, maybe I can't see mistakes from my own standpoint. Having someone else point out what I might work on or correct is all I need to succeed as a writer.

While Samrouay Senghoung generally enjoyed high school, she "dreaded going to English class because I was terrified of writing. Worrying where verbs went and making sure that subjects and verbs agreed—all that was also dreadful." For Sam, writing and English itself presented challenges because of her own background: "I am from Laos, but I was never educated there because young girls were not allowed to go to school and learn." Her family left Laos because of war and spent four years in refugee camps in Thailand. Sponsorship by an American family, the Truesdales, brought Sam's family to the United States, where she began her education. She proudly notes that "I am the first of my family to graduate from high school and to attend college." Her academic performance has earned her several honors, including induction into Phi Theta Kappa, the international honor society for the two-year college.

Samrouay Senghoung
Major: **Liberal Arts**
Career Plans: **To become a pharmacist**

Has learning to write helped you become a better thinker? How do you know it has helped?

I think average people think much differently when they write. Part of learning to be a good writer, in my opinion, is to learn how to think and write at the same time. Writing has made my thinking capacity increase over the years. After being out of school for a while, it was like I had to retrain my brain to learn. However, once I did that, I was able to read better, and once I could read better, I could think better. Being able to write has taught me to understand what other people are writing and what they mean.

Jason Trenholm's first year in college didn't unfold as he has hoped. "Coming from a home that did not always put education first made it difficult to make the transition from public high school to college. For me, the responsibility was a bit overwhelming. Having to juggle school, rent, work, and a social life was a lot to absorb all at once." Eventually Jason left school for work, but he soon discovered that his job held no challenge and no possibility for advancement. "After learning the harsh realities of the working world I—with the help of some great people in my life—decided to return to school and continue my education." A loyal Boston Red Sox fan, Jason has now transferred to an area university, continuing to earn great grades as he works toward his goal.

Jason Trenholm
Major: **History**
Career Plans: **To become a professor of history at the university level**

CHAPTER 1
Understanding the Writing Process

GETTING STARTED...

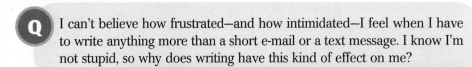

Q I can't believe how frustrated—and how intimidated—I feel when I have to write anything more than a short e-mail or a text message. I know I'm not stupid, so why does writing have this kind of effect on me?

A Writing makes many people feel this way, especially if they lack experience or haven't had previous success in writing. Writing requires critical thinking and close attention to detail and the needs of the **reader**. The good news is that if you can write an e-mail or compose a text message, you can also do the kind of writing that will be required of you in the classroom and in your profession.

Overview: Discovery through Writing

Who could argue with the following simple statement?

> Once you know how to do something well, whether it's completing a task at work, studying for an exam, or playing a musical instrument or sport, you find it even easier to do.

That's exactly how it is with writing. With most tasks, practice increases familiarity and your level of comfort. As a result, you gain the *confidence* you need to develop greater *competence.*

When you begin to focus on writing, you'll also discover that:

- writing is not a product but a **process**, a series of stages called *prewriting, composing,* and *revising.*
- a successful piece of writing doesn't result from a one-time attempt but rather from a series of efforts.
- an effective piece of writing communicates your ideas clearly and directly to a *reader* and fulfills an identifiable *purpose.*

Maybe the most important lesson is that writing is a journey of discovery. On this journey, you will uncover the significance of your ideas and the connections that exist between and among them. You'll also discover and master strategies that will enable you to present your ideas correctly in terms of usage, spelling, and punctuation.

A mastery of writing can do so much for you in the classroom and on the job. Writing well earns you personal success and the respect of your instructors, colleagues, and supervisors. Most important of all, a blank page will no longer seem like a source of intimidation but an invitation to begin a journey of discovery.

Navigating This Chapter In this chapter, you will discover:

- the three stages of the writing process—prewriting, composing, and revising
- the four interacting components of writing—writer, reader, message, and means
- the purposes of writing—to inform, to entertain, and to persuade
- the important connection between reading and writing

The Stages of the Writing Process

When most people watch a person shoot a foul shot, kick a goal, or spike a volley-ball over the net, they may be tempted to think that each action is a single, fluid motion. The truth, however, is that each action is a series of complex, interrelated steps. The same thing is true of writing, which is actually a **process** involving three interrelated stages.

The first stage of the writing process is **prewriting.** When you prewrite, you generate ideas and do preliminary planning. Any approach that enables you to examine a person, situation, idea, or concept more closely and thoroughly can be a good prewriting technique. Reading a book or magazine, a blog or Twitter posting; talking in person or online with friends; observing others live or on a YouTube video; and even thinking are all great prewriting activities. Chapter 2 discusses and illustrates several specific prewriting techniques.

The second stage of the writing process is **composing.** When you compose, you identify a specific focus and isolate and adapt the most promising ideas you have generated during prewriting. Then you transform those ideas into sentences and organize them into a **draft** or preliminary paragraph so that someone else—your reader—can understand them. Chapter 3 covers composing in detail.

The third stage of the writing process is **revising.** When you revise, you *re-see* what you've written in order to develop a more effective, more polished piece of writing. As Chapter 4 explains, a successful piece of writing evolves through different versions. First, you carefully examine or *reassess* the content of a draft, and then you *redraft,* generating new material to fill the gaps you've identified. Finally, you *edit,* making sure that what you have to say appears in full detail and in correct form. This step is especially important. You want to do everything you can to ensure that nothing distracts your reader from your good ideas.

This figure illustrates the writing process:

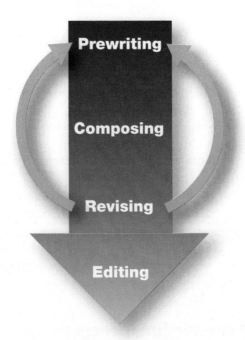

As the figure shows, first you prewrite, then you compose, and then you revise. Notice, however, that the smaller arrows in the illustration flow back from revising to prewriting and then travel on through composing and revising again, finally ending with editing. This flow shows how the writing process is *recursive*—you cycle through the stages, revisiting steps in order to develop the best draft possible. Your ideas on any subject are complex and evolving. You will find, as all writers do, that writing isn't a step-by-step or linear activity. Your ideas don't migrate from your head to a piece of paper or computer screen, from beginning to end, in perfect or complete form. Instead, you will move back and forth through the stages as often as you need to ensure that what you have written truly captures what you are thinking.

COMPREHENSION
AND PRACTICE
1.1

The Stages of the Writing Process

1. How will learning to write well help you achieve success in your courses and beyond the classroom?

   When you write well, you are demonstrating your ability to organize and convey your

   thoughts effectively, which is important for all your classes and will help you earn good

   grades. Writing well will also earn you the respect of supervisors and co-workers,

   and greater opportunities on the job.

2. In your own words, explain the stages of the writing process.

The writing process consists of three stages: prewriting, during which you develop

ideas; composing, during which you identify a focus and your most promising ideas

and convert them into sentences and paragraphs; and revising, during which you

improve and polish the initial draft you have created.

3. How does the revising stage help make your draft better?

During the revising stage, you analyze your draft (reassess) for problems, address

those problems by developing new material to replace the weaknesses (redraft),

and eliminate any remaining errors (edit). The result is a more complete, correct,

polished paper.

CHALLENGE 1.1 Personal Feelings about Writing

1. On the following lines, briefly explain how you feel about writing and why you feel this way. What aspect of writing is easiest for you? What is most difficult?

Answers will vary. Some students may indicate that they like writing. Others,

however, will state that they are uncomfortable with writing, citing concerns with

issues of spelling, grammar, and punctuation, as well as doubts about being able

to express thoughts in writing or about having anything important to say.

collaboration

2. Now compare your responses with a classmate's. What do the two of you have in common? In what ways do your attitudes about writing differ? On a separate sheet of paper, briefly summarize these points.

Answers will vary.

The Dynamics of Writing

As an act of communication, writing differs from speaking in a couple of ways. Writing is more *deliberate*—more fully and carefully thought out—and more *precise*—more intentionally crafted word by word to create just the right effect.

The act of writing involves four basic, interacting components: (1) a **writer,** the person expressing ideas; (2) a **reader** or audience; (3) a **message,** the writer's topic and supporting ideas about it; and (4) the **means** of expressing that message, written language. Here's a visual representation, called the communications triangle:

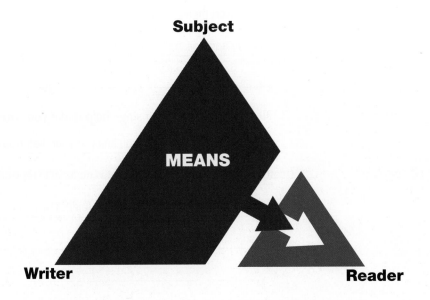

In the figure, the dark blue portion on the left represents what you understand and want to communicate to your *reader.* The examples, explanations, and details encapsulating what you know, expressed in correct word form, constitute the *means.* Your goal, as the arrows indicate, is to use the means to communicate your ideas fully and therefore complete the connection between you and your reader.

Your Reader

ESL Note
See "The Needs of Your Reader," page 496; "Unity," page 496; and "Clarity," page 497, about addressing the reader's needs.

The key to success in writing is to focus on your reader. In some cases, you'll actually know who your reader is. A reader of your sociology paper, for example, would be someone with a basic background in sociology, perhaps your instructor or your classmates. A reader of a formal e-mail about staffing needs at your place of employment would be the company's hiring or scheduling supervisor.

But often you won't know exactly who your reader will be. In these cases, focus on the *average reader,* who is like most of us—she or he knows a little about many subjects, but lacks the details about most of them. For example, let's say you wanted to write about a computer game you have been playing for some time. You may be fairly adept at it now, but the first time you played it, you no doubt made a few mistakes and found some steps complex and confusing. Remember this initial experience as you start to write about the game for your average reader. What aspects did you find most difficult or puzzling? What helped you to understand or deal with these complications? Supply the answers to questions like these and you will meet your average reader's needs.

The Dynamics of Writing

1. In what two ways does writing differ from speaking?

   Writing is more deliberate and more precise than speaking.

2. What are the four components that interact when you write?

   Writer, reader, message, and means

3. List three situations in which you wouldn't necessarily know who your reader is.

   Answers will vary. Possible answers may include a letter of complaint, a note

   requesting information about a product, and a letter of application.

CHALLENGE 1.2 **Attitudes about Writing and Speaking**

1. After examining the communication triangle again (p. 8), think of everything
   you understand about the topic of *e-commerce* (buying, selling, and doing
   business on the Internet). On the following lines, list the three ideas that you
   understand best about this subject and explain them in a way that the average reader would understand.

   Answers will vary.

collaboration

2. Working with a classmate, consider situations in which writing would make it
   easier to communicate a message than speaking would. Then, on a separate
   sheet of paper, list two of the situations you and your classmate identified and
   explain why writing would be the better way to express those ideas.

   Answers will vary.

The Purpose behind Your Writing

People fulfill one of three primary **purposes** or aims when they write: to *inform,*
to *entertain,* or to *persuade.* To inform means to supply information that explains or
clarifies something. A paper discussing the use of wind farms—huge windmills

along ocean shores, mountains, or canyons—as an alternative energy supply would *inform*, as would an article on the increasing popularity of online video sites such as YouTube and Hulu.

To *entertain* means to amuse, captivate, or arouse the reader's interest and emotions. A paragraph about a party at which everything that could go wrong did go wrong would entertain. So would one about encountering a bat flying through your bedroom.

To *persuade* means to sway a reader to consider the validity of a particular point of view. A paragraph urging more people to register as organ donors would persuade. So would a paragraph asserting that the legal driving age across the country should be set at seventeen.

Of course, you will discover a degree of overlap in the three purposes. The entertaining paragraph about the bat in your bedroom could also inform if it explained the proper method for removing a bat that enters a house. The same paper could also persuade if it asserted that bats are beneficial and necessary for a variety of reasons, including insect control, and should be protected rather than killed.

Always take a moment to identify your primary purpose and any secondary purpose. This way, you will be sure that your writing supplies the types of information and examples needed to fulfill that purpose and meet the needs of your reader.

The Relationship between Writing and Reading

Make no mistake about it: A strong relationship exists between writing and reading. People who have read a good deal in their lives often have an easier time with writing. When people read anything—a textbook, a Facebook profile, a novel, or a blog entry, and so on—they are immersed in the world of words. Reading actively, as Part 6, "Discovering Connections through Reading," spells out, leads to a greater understanding of the significance of a piece of writing. When careful readers read actively, they develop a greater **writing awareness.** They see how sentences and paragraphs are formed, notice how ideas are presented and supported, and react to the ideas raised by the writers. Recognizing these elements and strategies is a major step in mastering them yourself.

COMPREHENSION AND PRACTICE 1.3

The Purposes in Writing

1. How does being a better reader help you become a better writer?

When you read carefully, you see how writers present and develop ideas, including

writing correct sentences and paragraphs. This leads to greater writing awareness.

When you are able to identify strategies that writers use, you are better prepared

to use them yourself.

2. Read the following paragraph:

> One of the biggest health crises to confront the United States in modern times is obesity. The situation is so bad that many health care specialists are calling it an epidemic. Some researchers suggest that Americans will actually face a decreased life expectancy over the next several decades if they don't change their dietary and exercise habits. Government statistics show that more than 60 percent of American adults are overweight. Half of this group is classified as obese, meaning that these 59 million people have a dangerously high body mass index (BMI) rating of 30 or more. Scientists consider a healthy BMI rating to be between 18.5 and 24.9. Even more disturbing, recent American Heart Association statistics show that more than 10 percent of American children between ages two and five are overweight, and overall 15 percent of young people under the age of eighteen are classified as overweight. Researchers have pointed to several causes for the rise in the number of overweight and obese people of all ages. The most obvious reason is overeating, especially of fast food, which is often high in fat and sugar and served in oversized portions. Many people also have far more sedentary lifestyles today, with television and computers replacing the more active pastimes and leisure-time activities of past generations. Unless Americans make a concerted effort to change their lifestyles to include less food and more exercise, they face an increased threat to their quality of life, including diabetes, stroke, and heart disease.

What is the primary purpose of this paragraph? On the lines below, briefly explain your answer.

Most students will agree that the primary purpose is to inform the reader about the

health care crisis in the United States resulting from obesity. They will cite as evidence

the various supporting examples illustrating the problem—that almost 60 million

adults are currently obese and need to change their lifestyles or they will face grave

health risks in the future.

3. What other purpose does the above paragraph fulfill? Use the lines below to explain.

Because the paragraph makes a strong case concerning the need for Americans to

adjust their lifestyles to include more exercise and less food, most students will agree

that the passage also persuades. In addition, because it presents the information in

a compelling way, some students will believe that the paragraph also entertains.

The paragraph therefore presents a good opportunity to discuss the overlapping

nature of purpose in writing.

CHALLENGE 1.3   Details Appropriate for the Purpose

collaboration

1. Working with a classmate, choose one of the following subjects, and then list examples you might include for a writing that *entertains,* one that *informs,* and one that *persuades:* video gaming, online social networking, or local politics.

    a. Purpose: to inform

    Answers will vary. If students choose to discuss video gaming, they might explain

    the different types of gaming and gaming devices available—from Xbox to Wii.

    b. Purpose: to entertain

    Answers will vary. Students might tell the story of a funny or embarrassing incident

    on a social networking site they just joined.

    c. Purpose: to persuade

    Answers will vary. Students might assert that individuals need to get involved in

    local politics so that they remain aware of the issues that could affect their futures

    and do what they can to make a difference.

2. Working with a classmate, make a list on a separate sheet of paper about the effects of the increased use of cell phones and BlackBerries.

3. How would you explain the reasons for increased use of mobile communications devices if the purpose of your paper were to entertain? Why would you present the reasons this way?

    Answers will vary. Possible approaches relative to entertaining might involve writing

    about people talking or sending text messages while eating or using a public

    restroom, or about incidents when cell phones rang during inappropriate times,

    for instance, during a funeral or at the movies.

4. Think of any written work that had an impact on your life. On a separate sheet of paper, identify the work and then in a paragraph of five to ten sentences, explain what aspect of the writer's approach affected you the most and why you think it did.

SPOTLIGHT PIECE

PROCESS, DYNAMICS, AND PURPOSE

Here's a brief writing by student Nadine Verdieu. Nadine, a native of Haiti, busily balances school, part-time work, and motherhood. She possesses not only a solid mastery of English, but a fluency in French and Haitian Creole as well. In this paragraph, she discusses an experience with an unreasonable supervisor. Read Nadine's paragraph along with the annotations offering some insight to the process, dynamics, and purposes of writing, and then answer the questions that follow.

Nadine asserts that dealing with a difficult boss is upsetting. Because she is trying to convince her reader, her primary purpose is to persuade.

Highlighted here are key ideas from the prewriting, that Nadine developed and revised for this paragraph.

By providing a specific explanation of this situation and several supporting details, Nadine meets the needs of her reader.

What a Difference a New Boss Can Make

When you have difficulties with your boss, it feels like the worst possible thing that could happen, especially if you like your job. I have first-hand experience in this area from my job at a local gym. I was attracted to the job because the gym had a day-care facility and I have a young son and no one to take care of him while I am at work. I applied for the position, and when I was interviewed, I explained my situation to the manager. He hired me anyway, and he told me that I could bring my son to the day care while I worked. Things went fine for a while. My manager was happy with my work, and everyone at the gym knew my son and me. Then my first manager got fired, and the company replaced him with this awful manager who just seemed to want to pick on me.

He ignored the good evaluations I had received and instead continually questioned why I was allowed to bring my son to day care while other employees couldn't. Eventually, he came to his senses when he recognized the quality of my work. I've been with the company for over two years now, but I don't think I'll ever forget how bad it felt to have a bad relationship with my boss.

COMPREHENSION AND PRACTICE 1.4

Reading Exploration

1. In your view, which of the prewriting details—highlighted in the paragraph—does the best job of explaining and supporting the problems Nadine encountered on the job? What about this detail leads you to this conclusion?

Answers will vary. Students will be split, with some choosing the first example, about her need for childcare, and others choosing the example about her unreasonable boss picking on her and ignoring her good work.

2. As the annotations indicate, the primary purpose in Nadine's essay is to persuade. Now, working with a classmate, consider whether the writing fulfills any other purpose and explain your answer on the lines that follow.

Most students will probably agree that the piece also entertains because it is enjoyable to read. Some may also argue that because it gives readers some background, the essay also informs.

Understanding the Subject through Writing

In her paragraph, Nadine focuses on the complications that ensue when a boss is unfair. Now, on a separate sheet of paper, write a brief passage (50 to 100 words) in which you discuss what you feel a worker needs to do to keep a supervisor happy.

FOR FURTHER EXPLORATION

Consider one of the topics in the bulleted list that follows. Think about what information someone else—the average reader—would need to understand your ideas on the subject and write down those details and examples. Indicate the purpose you might fulfill in writing about the subject you've chosen, and save your work. You may want to develop this material into polished writing later.

- The first day of school
- The person you most remember from your middle school days
- How you expect college will affect your future

DISCOVERING CONNECTIONS

For this assignment, focus on the picture and answer one of the questions that follow (or another that it inspires). Consider your average reader, using the examples in this chapter to guide you. At the same time, jot down what you believe your primary purpose would be if you were to write a paragraph about your thoughts. Save your work for later use.

A. Think about a time when you might have reached a crossroads in your life. What was the situation? How did you deal with it?

B. The landscape in this photo seems barren. If you had a choice, would you prefer to live and work in a seemingly quiet and isolated place like this, or would you prefer life in a more cosmopolitan setting? Why?

RECAP Understanding the Writing Process

Key Terms in This Chapter	Definitions
reader	the audience to whom a paper is directed
the writing process	the series of stages in writing, including prewriting, composing, and revising
prewriting	generating ideas to develop into a piece of writing
composing	selecting and then expressing in sentence and paragraph form some of your prewriting ideas
draft	version of a paper
revising	creating new drafts through reexamining, improving, and polishing your initial version
editing	concentrating on eliminating remaining errors in form
writer	the person expressing ideas through the written word
message	the topic and the supporting examples, details, and explanations that represent your understanding of the topic
means	the written language used to express ideas
purpose	the intent or aim of a paper
writing awareness	a recognition, as you read, of the strategies that other writers have used to make a point

Steps to Writing Effectively

Understand the stages of the writing process: **prewriting, composing,** and **revising.**

Understand how the four elements of writing— **writer, reader, message,** and **means**—interact.

Focus in particular on the **reader.**

Recognize the **purpose** of any writing assignment:

to *inform*—as in a paper explaining how a movie special effect is created

to *entertain*—as in a paper recalling the first time you drove a car

to *persuade*—as in a paper asserting that recycling should be mandatory throughout the United States

Using Discovery Online with MyWritingLab

For more practice understanding the writing process, go to
www.mywritinglab.com.

CHAPTER 2
Prewriting: Developing Ideas

GETTING STARTED . . .

 Q It's not that I don't want to write—I'm just not sure how to begin. What's the best way for me to get started?

 A Like athletes, artists, musicians, dancers, and many others, writers warm up before they perform. For writers, this warm-up is called *prewriting*. Several proven prewriting techniques are available to help you get started. Discovering which strategy works for you will help overcome the frustration you now feel when you face a blank page or computer screen.

Overview: Prewriting

Your writing discovery begins with **prewriting**, the first stage of the writing process. You probably already engage in a number of informal prewriting activities. For example, when you think about a book, an article, or an electronic posting, or have a conversation with someone in person or online, you are exploring the world of ideas. In other words, you are prewriting.

Another informal, but intentional prewriting technique involves asking and answering a series of *discovery questions:*

- What do I already know about this subject?
- Why would someone else want to know about this subject?
- What kinds of details and examples made it easier for me to understand this subject?
- What's the most interesting aspect of this subject?

The answers to these questions can help form a framework for writing.

Prewriting also includes a number of more structured techniques. Each technique helps you uncover and produce ideas that can later be developed into a complete piece of writing. In this chapter, you'll discover the possibilities each of these techniques offers. Then you can decide which technique, or combination of techniques, best suits your individual style.

Navigating This Chapter In this chapter, you will learn how to use the following prewriting techniques:

- freewriting
- brainstorming
- clustering
- branching
- idea mapping
- keeping a journal

Freewriting

Freewriting is a fast-paced and dynamic prewriting technique during which you write down all your ideas on a subject for a set period of time, usually ten minutes or so. You write down every idea that pops into your mind, nonstop. You don't worry about making mistakes, including sentence errors. It's all right if the ideas don't immediately make sense or if you drift away from the subject. If you get stuck and can't think of anything else, write, "I can't think" or make a rhyme for the word you just wrote until something comes to you. If you repeat yourself, it's okay. The only rule in freewriting is to keep writing down ideas.

Freewriting works well on paper or on a computer. If you use a computer and get distracted by seeing the words on the screen, darken it while you are working. Make sure to double-space, as well. That way, after you've printed the material, you'll have room to make changes or add information by hand.

Here's a freewriting on facing a difficult challenge by Scott Lopes; he adapted the ideas developed here for his Spotlight Piece in Chapter 3 (p. 60).

Challenges—I've had to face a lot of them in only 20 years of life, some unbelievably difficult to deal. I just tried to face them down with a stare. My grandfather's death! August 30, 2002. So hard, there was a point where I just broke down. He was so important to me—along with my grandmother, he raised my brother and me. So many feelings went rushing through my head the night he was killed. Sadness, anger, grief. I just wanted to get my hands on that driver, make him pay for what he did. I didn't though. How would that help my grandmother or my brother? I controlled my temper, but it was just hard. My grandfather used to talk to me about stepping up, to be a man. For a while it didn't seem that I could do it—it wasn't possible. But like the commercial "Impossible is nothing" I got through it.

Note that some ideas have been highlighted. Any time you prewrite, mark the ideas that you think have the most potential for being turned into a complete paragraph or essay. Isolate them by highlighting, underlining, or circling them so that they stand out. That way you'll be ready to develop them more fully as you work through the other stages of the writing process.

As you can see, freewriting results in plenty of ideas. Most of the ideas aren't expressed in correct sentences, but that's not a problem. Converting the ideas into sentences will come later in the writing process.

Freewriting Review

1. In your own words, explain freewriting.

   Freewriting is a method of prewriting during which you write down all your ideas on a

   subject for a set period of time, without worrying about mistakes and without stopping.

   _____

2. How does highlighting, underlining, or circling ideas help make freewriting a more effective prewriting technique?

   When you highlight, underline, or circle key ideas, you focus on the most promising

   material that can be fleshed out into a paragraph or essay later.

   _____

3. Take another look at the sample freewriting on facing a difficult challenge on page 18. If you were writing about this topic, which idea or section would you feel most comfortable developing and why?

   Answers will vary, depending on the writer's interests.

   _____

   _____

Freewriting Practice

1. Now it's your turn to try freewriting. On a separate sheet of paper, freewrite for ten minutes on *a difficult challenge* or on one of the following subjects: *volunteerism* or *reality television.*

2. Highlight, underline, or circle the ideas in your freewriting that you want to explore further.

3. Choose the idea that holds the most promise for later development, and write three additional details about it. Save this work for possible later use.

CHALLENGE 2.1 Freewriting Evaluation

collaboration

1. Exchange your freewriting with a classmate. Put a ✓ next to the ideas that make you want to read more. Return the freewriting to the writer, and discuss the areas that seem most promising.

2. On a separate piece of paper, answer the following questions:
   a. What did you like best about freewriting as a prewriting technique?
   b. What did you like least?

Brainstorming

Brainstorming is another proven prewriting strategy. Brainstorming is similar to freewriting in that you write down ideas as you generate them, but brainstorming is a far less expansive activity. When you brainstorm, you concentrate exclusively on one subject, listing only those ideas that directly relate to it. You don't need to set a time limit, although some people feel more comfortable if they do establish one, say fifteen minutes. You can brainstorm with pen and paper or, if you prefer, on a computer. Here is Tyler Hill's brainstorming about a pleasant childhood memory, which he later expanded for the Spotlight Piece at the end of this chapter (see pp. 32–33):

Great Memory-My Infatuation with the Teenage Mutant Ninja Turtles

✓ 5 years old when I first saw them

✓ Saturday morning at 9:30-never missed

✓ Four brother turtles and a rat

✓ Some kind of ooze gave them crime-fighting powers

✓ Had to get to the TV before my younger siblings-they wanted to watch something else

✓ Got my parents to take me to the Civic Center for a live show

✓ Rafael-my favorite-loved his sai blades

✓ Would practice the Ninja moves while I watched

✓ My halloween costume for two years in a row

✓ They fought crime and ate pizza

✓ Still have my Ninja Turtle action figures-so funny now

As with freewriting, highlight, circle, or underline the best brainstorming ideas you generate.

Although you may generate fewer ideas with brainstorming than with freewriting, you will probably still come up with more ideas than you can use. An added advantage with brainstorming is that the connections among the ideas will likely be more direct and obvious. Sometimes, in fact, a brainstorming list can serve as an informal **outline**, plan, or presentation for your first draft.

Brainstorming Review

1. In your own words, explain brainstorming.

   Brainstorming involves picking a subject and listing ideas that come to mind about it.

   _____

   _____

   _____

2. Of the ideas highlighted in the brainstorming about a pleasant childhood memory, which do you think will require the most development or expansion to make sense to a reader? Why?

   Answers will vary. Likely choices will include "Four brother turtles and a rat" and

   "Rafael—my favorite—loved his sai blades." In their current form, these details are too

   vague and confusing to communicate their full meaning to a reader.

   _____

3. What idea or part of the sample brainstorming do you think a reader will find most interesting once it is explained in greater detail? Why?

   Answers will vary, depending on the students' own interest in or knowledge of these

   cartoon characters.

   _____

   _____

Brainstorming Practice

1. Now it's your turn to try brainstorming. On a separate sheet of paper, brainstorm on a *childhood memory* or on one of the following subjects: *television* or *power.*

2. Highlight, underline, or circle the ideas in your brainstorming that you think are worth developing further.

3. Choose the idea that holds the most promise for later development and write three additional details about it. Save your work for possible later use.

CHALLENGE 2.2   Brainstorming Evaluation

collaboration

1. Exchange your brainstorming with a classmate. On your classmate's paper, place a ✓ next to the words or section that you find most interesting. Return it to the writer, and explain why the marked idea interests you.

2. On a separate sheet of paper, answer the following questions:
    a. What did you like best about brainstorming as a prewriting technique?
    b. What did you like least?

Clustering

Clustering is a visual prewriting technique that shows connections among the ideas you generate. This approach frees you from moving across the page from left to right, top to bottom. Instead, you can move in a variety of directions, putting related ideas next to each other, no matter what order they come to you. A clustering is generally easier to do with a pen and paper, but some computer programs allow you to develop one electronically.

To create a clustering, you first write a general topic in the middle of the page and circle it. As related ideas pop into your mind, write them down on the page around your topic and circle each of them. Draw lines to connect ideas that relate to the topic and to each other. As the ideas you list lead to further new ideas and examples, write them down and circle them, again drawing lines to connect them to related ideas.

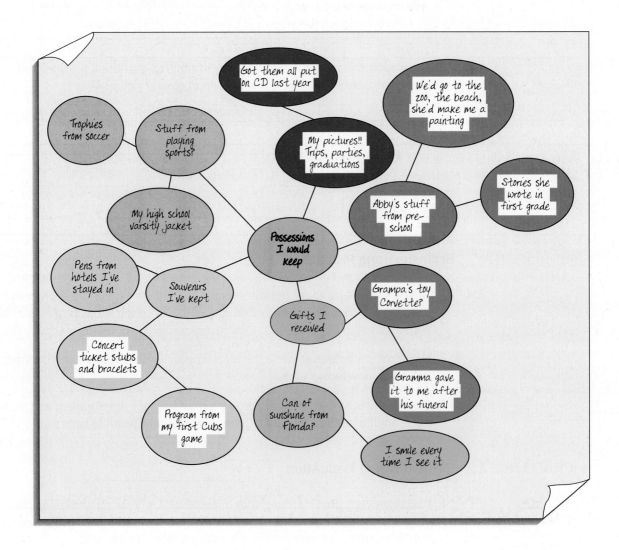

On the previous page is a sample clustering in response to the following question: If you could keep only those personal possessions that could fit in a single shoebox, what would they be?

Remember to highlight, circle, or underline the strongest ideas. As this example demonstrates clustering allows you to follow a broad range of connected ideas as they come to you. In the next two chapters, you will see how the strongest ideas from this clustering are turned into a final draft paragraph.

Clustering Review

1. In your own words, explain how to develop ideas using clustering.

   Write a topic in the middle of a page and circle it. As you think of related ideas, write

   them down and circle them, drawing lines to connect related ideas.

2. What do the various details generated in the sample clustering suggest about the kinds of things this person values or views as significant?

   These details suggest that this person values items with sentimental connections

   rather than monetary worth.

3. In your opinion, which idea or portion of the sample clustering offers the most promise for further development? Explain.

   Answers will vary. Many students will select the highlighted areas.

Clustering Practice

1. Now it's your turn to try clustering. On a separate sheet of paper, create a clustering on *possessions I would keep* or on one of the following topics: *ambition* or *my last birthday*.

2. Highlight, underline, or circle the ideas in your clustering that show potential for development.

3. Choose the idea that holds the most promise for later development and write three additional details about it. Save your work for possible later use.

collaboration

CHALLENGE 2.3   Clustering Evaluation

1. Exchange your clustering with a classmate. Put a ✓ next to the idea or section that interests you most. Explain your choice to your partner as you return his or her paper.

2. On the same page, answer the following questions:

   a. What did you like best about clustering as a prewriting technique?

   b. What did you like least?

   Answers will vary. Some students will like the flexibility that clustering provides.

   Others, however, will feel awkward thinking and writing in a way that is not always

   linear.

Branching

Like clustering, **branching** is another form of visual prewriting. In this case, groupings of related items spread out from left to right. In a way, a branching is like an outline turned on its side. This technique is generally well-suited for pen and paper, but if you are particularly adept with a graphics program, you can create a branching on your computer.

To begin branching, write your topic on the left side of the paper. Then write the ideas that your topic inspires to the right of it, connecting them to the topic with lines. Those subcategories will bring to mind more related thoughts and details. Write these to the right again, letting the list branch out across the paper. On the next page is a branching about a special place by Grace Trecarichi, which she later expanded for her Spotlight Piece in Chapter 4 (pp. 94–95):

Remember to highlight, underline, or circle the most promising of these ideas. As this sample branching shows, one aspect of a subject can lead to many other related ideas and examples, producing several distinctive groups of ideas that can be developed more fully during the other stages of the writing process.

COMPREHENSION AND PRACTICE 2.7

Branching Review

1. In your own words, explain branching.

   Branching is a prewriting technique that involves writing a topic on the left side of a

   paper and writing ideas that stem from it to the right. You continue branching off to the

   right as one idea leads to the next.

2. For the next two questions, look again at the sample branching on a special place (p. 25). Of the highlighted examples, which one do you find most

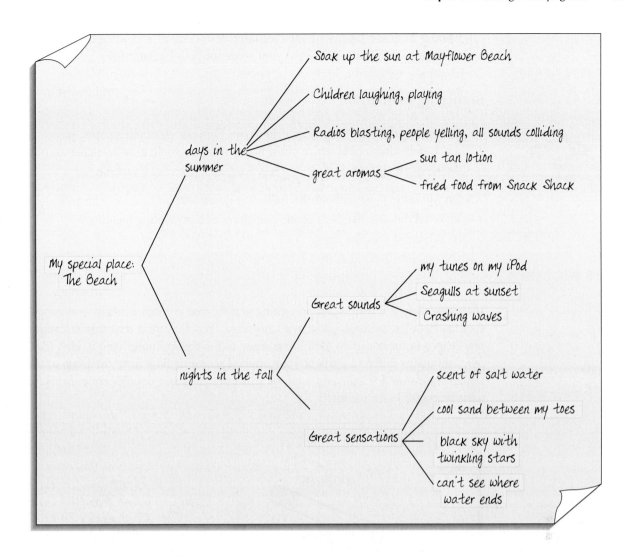

interesting? Which would you like to see explained more fully? Explain your reasoning on the following lines.

Answers will vary, although many students will likely mention one of the sensations,

especially the detail about the sand. Other students may focus on the sounds, keying

in on the crashing waves because of the display of the power of nature.

3. Choose one of the nonhighlighted ideas or sections. Then, on a separate sheet of paper, draw on your own experience and add another two or three details about this point.

Branching Practice

1. Now it's your turn to try branching. On a separate sheet of paper, create a branching on *places that are special to me* or on one of the following subjects: *traveling* or *advertisements*.

2. Highlight, underline, or circle the section or division of your branching that seems most interesting to you.

3. Choose the most promising idea for later development and write three additional details about it. Save your work for possible later use.

Branching Evaluation

collaboration

1. Exchange your branching with a classmate. On your classmate's paper, place a ✓ beside ideas about which you'd like to learn more. Return the paper and discuss your choices.

2. On the same page, answer the following questions:
   a. What did you like best about branching as a prewriting technique?
   b. What did you like least?

Idea Mapping

Idea mapping is a wide-open prewriting activity that combines words and images such as doodles, symbols, sketches, and icons. You may find that this technique produces a number of rich ideas. According to the theory underlying it, idea mapping stimulates different parts of your brain. The words flow from the parts of the brain responsible for logic and analysis while sketches and doodles come from the parts responsible for creativity.

To create an idea map, start anywhere on the page. As your mind travels freely from word to image and back again, write or draw one idea after another. You can emphasize ideas or images by underlining or circling them.

Look at the idea map on the subject of habits on the preceding page. When you finish an idea map, you can translate the images into the words they represent to you. For example, look at the line of figures above "BLEEP!!!" in the upper right corner of the idea map. You might translate these figures into the following words: "People swear so much now—no matter where you are. At a restaurant, in line at the supermarket, people use language they can't even print in the newspaper. It's a bad habit for me, too. I should really watch how I speak." The talking head image might be written as: "Some people just monopolize conversation—they talk on and on, never noticing that other people want to talk, too." These written interpretations of the images can serve as ideas for a piece of writing. Highlight, circle, or underline the words or images that have the most potential. You can then develop them more fully later in the writing process.

COMPREHENSION
AND PRACTICE
2.9

Idea Mapping Review

1. How does idea mapping help you use different areas of your brain?

   The drawings stimulate the creative areas, and the words trigger the logical and

   language areas.

2. How can you use sketches, doodles, or icons to help you develop ideas for writing?

   You translate the images into words and then add these ideas to the others you've

   generated.

3. What images or words on the idea map do you find most interesting? Why?

   Answers will vary.

COMPREHENSION
AND PRACTICE
2.10

Idea Mapping

1. Here's a way to help you discover ideas using different areas of your brain. Play a favorite piece of music. On a separate piece of paper, create an idea map of your thoughts and feelings as you listen. Or, if you prefer, complete an idea map on one of the following subjects: *the environment* or *self-esteem*.

2. Highlight, underline, or circle the words and images of your idea map that you think you can develop further. Translate these images into words.

3. List the most promising idea for later development, and write three additional details about it. Save this work for possible later use.

CHALLENGE 2.5   Idea Mapping Evaluation

collaboration

1. Exchange your idea map with a classmate. On your classmate's paper, place a ✓ beside the portion that you'd most like to see developed. Return the paper to the writer and explain your choice.

2. On the same page, answer the following questions:
   a. What did you like best about idea mapping as a prewriting technique?
   b. What did you like least?

Journal Writing

Journal writing provides vital writing practice and a valuable source of topics. Think of your journal—an entire notebook, a separate section of one of your class notebooks, or an electronic file—as your idea book. Several times a week, in addition to whatever other writing you are doing, write in your journal. Consider the many conversations you have on an average day, either in person, online, through text messages, or while Tweeting. Think of a journal entry as one of those conversations, except that you are writing, at this point anyway, just for yourself.

Keep track of ideas that inspire you, topics you want to explore, and day-to-day experiences you want to examine more closely. Spend at least ten to twenty minutes exploring your subject. Then look back at the material and decide which ideas you might want to discuss further. Highlight, underline, or circle them for future exploration and development.

For those occasions when you don't have a particular subject in mind, consider the following list of topics:

confidence	graduation	superstition
security	frustration	relaxation
family	anticipation	music
reading	pressure	a movie
childhood	hunger	last party attended
accident	a special possession	habit
souvenir	politics	Friday the 13th
pride	an influential person	future
happiness	online social networking	time
depression	dreams	power
ignorance	a first love	the most exciting profession
disappointment	deadlines	an important relationship
first date	fashion	

Here is a journal entry on the subject of *freedom:*

> On holidays like the 4th of July, people talk about freedom. But are people really free? You can't just do anything you want when you want. Like speeding down the highway. You can get arrested and lose your license. How is that freedom? Maybe it's unrealistic to think we can have complete freedom. I guess we do need laws. But not so many. And we are free to do things here that people can't always do in other countries. Criticizing the government—in some other countries, you end up in jail, or dead. You have the freedom to travel anywhere in the country, too, even move anywhere if you have the money to live there. Money—now that's the way to be free. When you have enough money and you live here in the U.S., you have all kinds of freedom. We live in the land of the free, especially if you have plenty of cash.

Don't worry if an entry isn't as complete or grammatically correct as you'd like it to be at first. The best way to improve as a writer is to practice. Journal writing is a great opportunity to develop your skills. Working regularly in your journal is one of the best ways to make writing seem as natural to you as talking and thinking.

The Response Journal

A **response journal** records your reactions to and assessments of specific topics. Although a response journal is good for examining day-to-day events, it is especially valuable for assessing your academic work. Use your response journal at least once a week to write a brief reaction to what was covered in your various classes. By itself, the preparation of these entries certainly provides great writing practice, but it also helps you gain a greater understanding of your subject.

Consider this entry in reaction to a discussion in an introductory psychology class:

> I liked the discussion in class about the part of the brain that causes difficulty with recognizing faces after a stroke—the occipital lobes. Made me think of my grandmother. She had what the doctors called a <u>seeping aneurism</u>, a blood vessel leaking in her brain. After that, she had trouble putting faces and names together. What was weird is that she still recognized voices even if she was confused about the faces. Even weirder, she was right handed but she seemed to forget that she had a right hand. No paralysis—she just never again used her right hand, like she forgot it even existed. The situation was sad, but after today's class about how different parts of the brain work, at least I have a better idea of what happened to my grandmother.

This journal entry recounts what went on during a class discussion, but it also explores the meaning of that experience. If you write a weekly journal entry for each of your courses, you very likely will feel more connected to your classes and better understand the significance of the information.

Journal Writing Review

1. How do journal writing and maintaining a response journal help you develop your skills as a writer?

   Journals offer a chance to practice writing until writing about ideas becomes as

   natural as thinking and talking about them. Regular writing helps students discover

   connections between writing and thinking.

2. Review the entry about freedom on page 29. What is the most effective example or detail? Why do you feel this way?

   Answers will vary. Many students will focus on the material about money as it relates

   to freedom because money provides privileges beyond what average people

   experience.

3. Reread the entry concerning functions of the brain from the response journal on page 29. In your own words, explain why it is significant that the writer learned how different parts of the brain function.

   Learning about the way different parts of the brain function helped the writer to

   understand experiences that happened to her grandmother.

Journal Writing Practice

1. Now it's your turn to try journal writing. In your notebook, write a page on one of the following subjects: *sexism, dieting,* or *learning a skill* (such as driving, dancing, or cooking)

2. Reread your entry, and highlight a section you'd like to explore in greater detail.

3. Look again at the part of your journal entry that you highlighted and on a separate page, write three more details about it. Save this work for possible later use.

Prewriting That's Right for You

Not everyone prefers the same prewriting technique, so ultimately you should choose the approach that best suits your individual style of working and organizing. In addition, you may find that your prewriting approach will change, depending on your writing topic or goal. When a topic concerns something that you know well and have already spent some time thinking about, you might try brainstorming. If the subject is complex and requires some simplifying before you can effectively approach it, you might look to branching.

You might also find that you prefer a **hybrid** prewriting technique: two or more approaches combined. Perhaps you'll find yourself freewriting until you hit upon an idea that interests you. At that point, you switch to clustering or branching to explore multiple dimensions of that idea. Maybe you prefer to combine *discovery* questions such as those on page 17 with brainstorming, letting the questions drive your exploration. Ultimately, the "correct" approach to prewriting is the approach that works for you.

Writing Rituals

It's a simple truth: Writing is an idiosyncratic act, and no two people follow exactly the same routine or approach. As proof, consider your own writing rituals. What time of day do you prefer to write? Where do you prefer to do it? Do you have to work in solitary silence in your room, or do you prefer a public area with sound and activity such as a coffee shop or cafeteria? Do you start with a pen and paper, and, if so, does the type of pen or paper make a difference to you? Or are you most comfortable doing all your work on your computer?

Of course, there are no wrong answers to these questions. Except for tasks like completing in-class essay assignments or test questions, you should plan to work under the conditions that make you must comfortable.

Check-in Time

Regardless of what strategy or combination of strategies you use when you prewrite, you are establishing the foundation for your work. Therefore, once you have finished prewriting, *check in* to see if what you are thinking of writing has merit. Checking in is easy. Share your ideas, in person or online, with someone else—a classmate, a friend, a family member, and so on. Explain what you hope to do, and ask a few basic questions such as:

- Do you see where I am going with this?
- Does the approach I want to take seem reasonable to you?
- Besides what I've indicated, are there other things I might do to develop support—read a particular book or document, see a movie or video, interview somebody?
- Am I overlooking anything obvious?

Checking in at this point is important because it helps you establish if your initial plan for writing seems reasonable; if it isn't, you can make adjustments.

CHALLENGE 2.6 **Prewriting Choice, Personal Writing Rituals, and Checking in**

1. You have had the chance to use all the prewriting techniques discussed in this chapter. On the lines below, briefly explain which technique—or combination of techniques—you prefer and why you think this choice works for you.

   Answers will vary.

   _____

   _____

collaboration

2. Think of the last time you did any extended writing outside the classroom and answer this question: When you write, what rituals do you follow? On a separate sheet of paper, write a brief journal entry about your writing rituals. Then share your entry with a classmate. See what rituals—if any—you have in common.

3. Take another look at the list of check-in questions on page 31. Working with a classmate, develop two additional questions that could help identify whether your initial plans for writing make sense and list them on the following lines.

   Answers will vary.

   _____

   _____

   _____

SPOTLIGHT PIECE   DEVELOPMENT OF PREWRITING IDEAS

Here's a paragraph by Tyler Hill on a pleasant childhood memory. Of all his cousins, Tyler is the first to attend college. He has worked hard to become a better writer because, as he explains, "Being a good writer will gain the respect of not only employers and professors but also of fellow students." Tyler has already been accepted as a transfer student to become a physician assistant, and he was named valedictorian of his graduating class. Read his paragraph and the accompanying annotations, which offer insight to how he effectively developed his prewriting material (see p. 20). Then answer the questions that follow.

My Teenage Mutant Ninja Turtle Childhood

To guide his reader, Tyler indicates his focus—that cartoon heroes captivated his attention when he was a youngster.

When I was young, I had a strange passion for the Teenage Mutant Ninja Turtles. The very first time I saw the Teenage Mutant Ninja Turtles was on a Saturday morning when I was about five years old. I quickly became fascinated with these four brother turtles who stumbled across "ooze" that magically turned them into crime fighters. With the help of a rat, they mastered karate and fought bad guys in New York City, all while being undetected and living in a sewer. These reptilian brothers each had different areas of specialty, and they even had ninja weapons. My favorite, Rafael, carried twin sai blades, dagger-shaped instruments with additional prongs. Every Saturday morning at 9:30, you could find me in front of the tube watching my heroes. I can remember getting up and pretending that I was fighting right alongside them, mimicking the ninja moves I saw on the television. I'm still not sure why I became hooked on these pizza eating, ninja slaying, crime-fighting turtles. I guess I thought that they were the epitome of what superheroes should be. Now they just remind me of how young and free I was then, just like Rafael, my favorite turtle.

Highlighted here are key prewriting ideas that help make his point clear for his reader.

Tyler concludes his paragraph by emphasizing the significance of his childhood recollection.

Reading Exploration

1. As the annotations show, Tyler indicates the focus that grew out of the prewriting material. On the lines below, explain how the other sentences in his paragraph help to explain and support Tyler's focus.

Answers will vary somewhat, but most students will note that the specific details about

the television show, adapted from his prewriting, explain why the characters had such

a hold on his attention.

2. Of the examples and details Tyler uses to support his main idea, which one stands out for you? What about this material leads you to this conclusion? Write your answer on the lines below.

Answers will vary, although many students will cite the material about his watching the

show on Saturday mornings and acting out what he saw on the screen.

Understanding the Subject through Writing

In his paragraph, Tyler recounts a pleasant childhood memory about an animated, but violent, television show. Some people argue that such violence, even if it involves just the actions of cartoon characters, is simply bad for children. On a separate sheet of paper, write a brief passage (50 to 100 words) in which you express your point of view on whether cartoon violence on television or in computer games should be restricted.

FOR FURTHER EXPLORATION

1. Consider one of the following topics. Use your favorite prewriting technique to explore ideas about the subject and think of the purpose you might fulfill in writing about it.

   - The most significant role you play in your life
   - A time when you saw something you wish you hadn't
   - The best way to avoid difficulties or disagreements with coworkers

2. Evaluate your prewriting material, identify a focus, and create a draft paragraph of at least five to ten sentences.

3. Exchange your draft with a writing partner. Using the material in this chapter as a guide, evaluate the draft you receive. Note any problems with the prewriting method used, and return the draft to the writer.

collaboration

4. Revise your draft, eliminating any errors identified by your writing partner.

DISCOVERING CONNECTIONS

Take a look at the following picture. Using your favorite prewriting technique, explore this picture and any one of the questions listed below (or another that the photo inspires). See what you can discover. Consider the purpose you might fulfill, and then, using the idea you have developed, prepare a draft paragraph of at least five to ten sentences.

A. What's the first thought that comes to mind about paleontology as a field of study or career? What does studying or recording the past teach us about the present and the future? What about the power of history makes you feel this way?

B. What do you think the world was like during the age of the dinosaurs? What sights, sounds, and smells dominated the scene during that long-ago time?

RECAP   Prewriting: Developing Ideas

Key Terms in This Chapter	Definitions
prewriting	the first stage of writing during which you generate and develop ideas
freewriting	write everything that comes into your head for a ten-minute period without stopping to edit
brainstorming	list specifically related ideas on a topic
clustering	draw a circle around a topic and then list and circle all ideas that come to mind, drawing lines to connect them
branching	list the topic on the left and write the ideas that develop from the topic to the right, drawing lines to connect them
idea mapping	write words and doodle or draw pictures or symbols inspired by the topic
journal writing	several times a week, on a regular basis, write in a separate notebook on subjects that interest you
response journal writing	once a week, write your reaction to subjects covered in each of your classes
hybrid technique	more than one prewriting technique combined
outline	a listing of main ideas

Using Discovery Online with MyWritingLab

For more practice with prewriting, go to www.mywritinglab.com.

CHAPTER 3

Composing: Creating Topic Sentences and Supporting Sentences

GETTING STARTED...

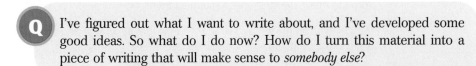

Q I've figured out what I want to write about, and I've developed some good ideas. So what do I do now? How do I turn this material into a piece of writing that will make sense to *somebody else*?

A By identifying what you want to write about and generating some solid ideas, you've already laid the groundwork for an effective piece of writing. Now you need to convert those prewriting ideas into correct, complete *sentences*—units containing subjects and verbs that communicate your meaning to your reader.

Overview: Composing

Once you have discovered a subject and generated examples and details about it, you must *transform* your ideas so that your reader can understand them. In the writing process, this step is called **composing.** When you compose, you follow up on the exploration you began in prewriting. You examine the most promising ideas and identify a main point or focus for further development. Then, to ensure that these ideas make sense to others, you express them in units that contain a subject and a verb and that convey complete thoughts. In other words, you present them in sentences. Sentences vary in length, and some contain multiple subjects and verbs. Regardless of length or complexity, however, a group of words is not a sentence if it lacks a subject or verb or fails to communicate independent meaning. (For more on what makes a sentence a sentence, see Chapters 6 and 7.) Consider these examples:

NOT A SENTENCE: The streets a dangerous mess after the ice storm. (The verb is missing.)

SENTENCE: The streets WERE a dangerous mess after the ice storm.

NOT A SENTENCE: Even though Zoe had downloaded all the songs legally. (The unit doesn't express a complete thought.)

SENTENCE: Even though Zoe had downloaded all the songs legally, she received an e-mail demanding that she delete the music.

Finally, once you've expressed your ideas in complete sentences, you then organize them into paragraphs. Your main idea appears in a topic sentence and all the ideas about the topic appear in supporting sentences.

Navigating This Chapter In this chapter, you will learn how to create two important paragraph elements:

- topic sentences
- supporting sentences

The Paragraph

ESL Note
See "Writing Paragraphs," pages 496–497, for more on paragraph structure and arrangement.

A **paragraph** is a group of sentences that relate to one main idea or topic. How many sentences you include in any one paragraph will always depend on your purpose and the needs of your reader.

Longer documents such as *essays* contain multiple paragraphs, each of which discusses a different aspect of your main idea. (For more information about essays, see Chapter 5.) In this and other academic courses, however, you will often be asked to write paragraphs that range between seven and ten sentences long (approximately 150–250 words). These paragraphs are like miniature essays, with one sentence stating the main point and the other sentences supporting it.

As the following figure illustrating how a paragraph is arranged shows, you *indent* the first sentence, moving the first word in about one-half inch on the paper. In longer documents, this visual cue tells readers that they are about to encounter a new topic.

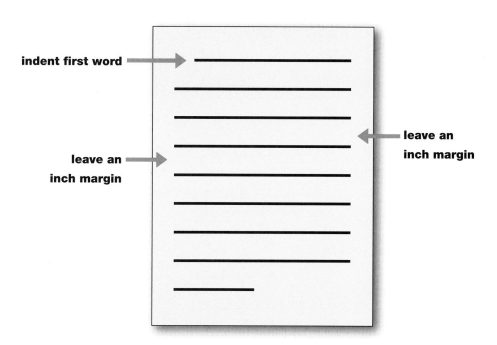

indent first word

leave an
inch margin

leave an
inch margin

The rest of the sentences in the paragraph—called the **body**—flow from the left to right margin, one following the other. After the last sentence in the paragraph, you leave the remainder of the line blank, and indent for the next new paragraph.

Consider this sample paragraph:

> **In today's world, rude and aggressive behavior seems to be all around us.** For example, many drivers treat streets and highways like they are racetracks. They speed and cut off other drivers, barely missing pedestrians. Yesterday I saw someone drive his car up onto the sidewalk to avoid a traffic jam, and he barely missed a young couple pushing a baby carriage. People waiting in line to shop are also often impolite and hostile. I have frequently heard people making rude comments to store clerks because the line wasn't moving quickly enough. A few weeks ago at the supermarket, I even saw two customers get into a shoving match because one of them had 14 items in the 12 items or fewer checkout lane. But the worst cases of offensive behavior are the ones that occur during youth sports games or matches, sometimes resulting in physical fights among spectators. In some cases, the fights have moved down onto the field, with parents attacking the coaches or officials. Whether it's on the roads, in a shop or store, or in the grandstands, polite and respectful behavior is in short supply

The paragraph opens with the **topic sentence** (shown in **bold print**), the group of words that state the main idea and answer the reader's unstated question: "What's the point?" The sentences that follow, known as the *body* of the paragraph, support or illustrate the topic sentence. When a paragraph stands as an entire document, like this sample one, it also includes a **closing sentence.** This final sentence brings the paragraph to an appropriate and logical close, reminding your reader of the significance of what you've just presented.

The Composing Process

1. In your own words, explain the steps in the composing process.

   First, you decide which ideas you want to use from your prewriting. Next, you have to

   put those ideas into sentences. Then you need to arrange the sentences into a paragraph

   that has a topic sentence and supporting sentences.

2. What is the difference between the topic sentence and the sentences in the body of the paragraph?

   The topic sentence explains the main idea of the entire paragraph. The other sentences

   explain the topic sentence, providing examples and details.

COMPREHENSION
AND PRACTICE

3.2

Topic Sentences

1. The following passage contains two paragraphs run together. After reading the passage, put a paragraph symbol (¶) at the point where the second paragraph should begin and underline the two topic sentences.

<u>Professor Chen's U.S. history course was the most demanding class I took last semester.</u> For this course, we had an enormous amount of material to cover. We studied all the major events in American history from the Civil War to the present. Every week, I had to read fifty fact-filled pages in our textbook and pass a twenty-question true/false quiz. Professor Chen also posted weekly PowerPoint presentations, videos, and podcasts on the class's Web site for us to study and then prepare a brief summary in response. In addition we had to give a five-minute speech, using props, about an important historical leader we admired. ¶ <u>Even though it was challenging, Dr. Roy's math course was far more appealing to me.</u> We covered some pretty complex math during the semester, but the workload seemed more manageable. He always assigned at least ten problems after every class meeting, but they were always directly related to the problems that Dr. Roy had covered. After every class meeting, I reviewed my notes and then carefully copied them over, which made studying for the weekly quizzes and the section exams easy. Throughout the course, I never felt rushed to learn.

2. On the following lines, briefly explain why you think the second paragraph should begin at that point.

The paragraph symbol belongs after the sixth sentence. The first six sentences focus on

the history class, but the final five deal with the math class, indicating the need to begin

a new paragraph.

Topic and Body Sentences

1. Here are two paragraphs with the topic sentences removed. Below each are three possible topic sentences. Read each paragraph, and circle the topic sentence that best fits each paragraph.

Many of our grandparents can remember a time when they dialed only four numbers to call people locally. Telephone operators had to place all long-distance calls, and they were enormously expensive. In some cases, the phones they used were *party lines,* with more than one household sharing the same telephone line. If someone in the other household was using the phone, they had to wait to make or receive a call. People paid to use public phone booths if they were away from home or couldn't afford a phone in their house. Today, cell phones are so common that many people no longer even have landlines. The latest generation of cell phones has a variety of features, including Internet connections, allowing people to talk, text-message, or e-mail anywhere in the world. Some people skip the phone entirely. They use computers with video cameras, and have real-time video conferencing through the Internet.

a. Telecommunication providers aggressively pursue customers by offering enhanced services and special rates.

b. In a relatively short period of time, the world of personal communication has changed dramatically.

c. If people change phone companies, they can still keep their phone number through a few easy steps.

The grass in the back was matted and tangled, and the ground still oozed when you stepped on it. The flowers on the rhododendron bush next to the cellar door had fallen off, and the drainpipe had broken away from the gutter. In front of the house next to the stairs, the water had formed a pool several inches deep and four feet across. The stream running alongside the driveway had spilled over its banks, and the water was running rapidly. Several of the bushes and smaller trees next to the stream had been uprooted and were leaning into the water. In another hour or so, they'd be gone.

a. The damage to our house and yard from two days of thunderstorms was unbelievable.

b. A lush lawn is an important feature when it is time to sell a home.

c. Natural disasters cost insurance companies millions of dollars each year.

2. On the following lines, explain your choices.

Paragraph one: Topic sentence b is the proper choice because the sentences in the

body all discuss ways that personal communication has changed in recent times.

Paragraph two: Topic sentence a is the proper choice because the sentences in the body all deal with the damage that occurred as a result of severe weather.

Topic Focus

When you prewrite, as the previous chapter illustrates, you examine a subject, focusing on a main idea and generating details that will support, illustrate, or explain that idea. Consider, for instance, the sample clustering that first appeared on page 22 of the last chapter. The student was asked to write about what she would keep if she had to reduce her possessions down to what would fit in a single shoebox. After spending a little time thinking about this subject, she produced the following:

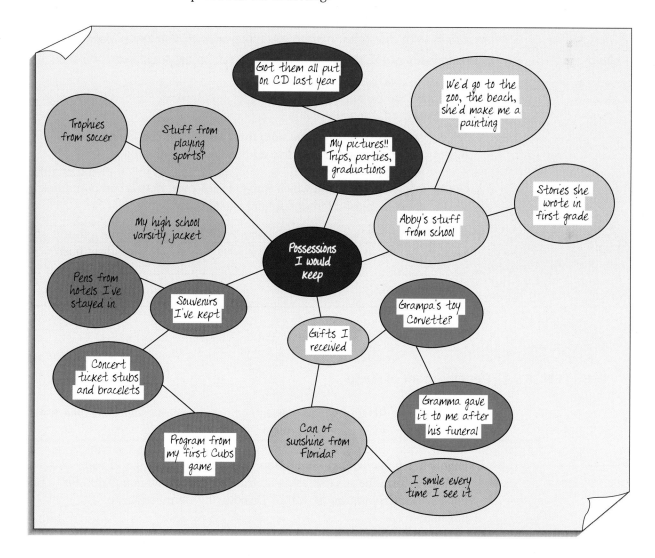

This clustering features several good ideas, but the highlighted ones represent the ideas the writer wishes to focus on. Look at these items carefully and see if you can identify a common theme among them.

Selection of Topic Focus

collaboration

1. Working with a classmate, take a look at the following prewriting on the subject *a special place.*

> A special place?-special, don't know-room? can't seem to get started-how about the beach, the best, espec. in the winter, walk for a couple of miles, no other people, just seagulls-ok, what now, stuck, stuck, stuck!! help! being alone, same as lonely? no, big difference-back to the beach, love the smell, hair thick with moisture, take shoes off sometimes even in winter, sand always feels so damp, like to go there to think, totally relaxing, like taking a nap. Now what? relaxing, not lonely, by myself, private time, what else about the beach? Yes!! the little kids in the summer at the beach, little kids there are cool, just playing, making things with the sand, running along the edge of the water, makes me remember when I was a kid, no worries, no job, no school, just going to the beach and hating to leave

   Select a section or idea that you both think holds promise. On a separate sheet of paper, develop at least five additional details about it.

2. On the following lines, note which three of these new details you both think a reader would be most interested in and explain why.

   Answers will vary depending on the details selected.

   _____

   _____

   _____

CHALLENGE 3.1   **Development of Focus**

1. On a separate sheet of paper, prewrite on the subject *managing my time*, using the prewriting technique you prefer.

2. Highlight, circle, or underline the most promising ideas. Or, if you prefer, perform these same steps on the prewriting you completed for For Further Exploration (p. 62) or Discovering Connections (p. 34) in Chapter 2.

collaboration

3. Exchange your prewriting with a classmate. On the prewriting you receive, put an * in the margin next to one idea that sparks your interest. On the same paper, write one or two questions you have about this subject. Then return the paper to the writer.

Topic Sentence Development

Once you have decided which idea or topic you want to examine, you need to express it in the form of a topic sentence. Typically, a topic sentence communicates two things: (1) the *topic* itself, and (2) the writer's *attitude or reaction* to it. When you develop a topic sentence, it's important that the sentence get right to the point, so always avoid the following:

- *Announcing* what you plan to do. Instead, concentrate on *expressing* what makes your point interesting or significant.
- Beginning with words such as "I am going to write about _____" or "This paragraph will cover _____." Instead, express your point in simple, direct terms, answering the reader's implied question, "What's your point?"

Let's look again at the topic sentence from the paragraph on page 38 about rude and aggressive behavior:

EXAMPLE   In today's world, **rude and aggressive behavior** *seems to be all around us.*

(topic / attitude or reaction)

The topic is rude and aggressive behavior; the writer's attitude concerns the apparent inability to avoid such behavior.

Your next task is to create a topic sentence that verbalizes your topic and your attitude about it. Use the clustering you completed in Chapter 2 (see Comprehension and Practice 2.6) on the personal possessions you would keep in a shoebox. Here's a topic sentence that expresses the view that personal or sentimental possessions mean the most:

EXAMPLE   If I could keep **only one shoebox full of belongings**, I would select items *with great personal or sentimental worth, not monetary value.*

(topic / attitude or reaction)

This topic sentence is effective because it answers the question, "What's the point?" concerning why certain possessions have special value. It therefore meets the needs of the reader.

COMPREHENSION AND PRACTICE 3.5

The Effectiveness of Topic Sentences

1. On the lines that follow, explain what makes the following topic sentence effective: *Answering essay questions successfully is a skill that can be learned.*

   This topic sentence is effective because it contains both a topic—answering essay questions—and a clearly expressed attitude about taking such tests—it is a skill that can be learned.

2. On the lines that follow, explain what makes the following topic sentence ineffective: *I am going to write about ways you can successfully take an essay test.*

This topic sentence is ineffective because it is an announcement. It should be revised to

eliminate the words that announce the writer's intent and to make the attitude or reaction

about the topic clearer.

Topics and Writer Attitudes

Read the possible topic sentences that follow. In each sentence, circle the topic, then underline the writer's attitude or reaction to it. Use the example as a guide.

EXAMPLE   (Children) should be (given pets) only if they are able and willing to care for them.

1. (Auto makers) still have not committed enough resources to develop affordable hybrid cars.
2. (Powerful laptop computers) have transformed today's office environment.
3. (Too much television) may actually stifle children's imaginations.
4. (Hollywood's portrayal of teenagers) reinforces negative stereotypes about them.
5. (Most of today's computer games) feature extraordinarily realistic graphics.

CHALLENGE 3.2   Topic Sentence Writing

collaboration

1. Here are ten topics. Working with a classmate, write a possible topic sentence for each on the available lines. Answers will vary. Sample responses are shown.

    a. The availability of new medications means an improved quality of life for people with asthma.

    b. Theme parks like Six Flags and Universal Studies do a great job with crowd management.

c. NASCAR racing is the most exciting sport around.

_____

_____

_____

d. Better labeling of the ingredients of prepackaged and fast food should help people trying to maintain or lose weight.

_____

_____

e. Additional exploration of Mars may give us a better idea of the development of life on earth.

_____

_____

f. The cost of going to a theater to see a movie may not be as worthwhile, given the increased sound and picture quality of home entertainment units.

_____

_____

g. Commercials during the Super Bowl sometimes attract as much attention as the game itself.

_____

_____

h. Video sites like YouTube and Hulu have already begun to affect the television-watching habits of millions of Americans.

_____

_____

i. A complete lifetime ban for the use of steroids and other performance-enhancing substances is the only way to eliminate their use among Olympic and professional athletes.

_____

_____

j. A volunteer position in your field <u>is a great chance to demonstrate your skills</u>

<u>and abilities.</u>

_____

_____

2. For Challenge 3.1 (p. 42), you identified some promising ideas using prewriting. Using the discussion and examples on developing a strong topic sentence to guide you, write a topic sentence for that material.

Clear and Specific Topic Sentences

ESL Note
See "Writing Paragraphs," pages 496–497, for more on the importance of clear, specific writing.

The secret to creating an effective topic sentence is to keep it clear and specific. For example, imagine your subject is about socializing opportunities in your city or around campus. After doing some prewriting to develop ideas, you decide that your focus will be on the nightlife in the area. With this in mind, you set out to create a topic sentence that expresses the point you want to make.

First, consider the following ineffective topic sentence:

WEAK Nightlife in my city offers the opportunity for fun.

This topic sentence is weak because it is too vague, general, and broad in scope to communicate a clear meaning to a reader. In addition, it doesn't explain what *fun* means in relation to nightlife or identify any particular fun activities.

Now look at this revised version:

STRONG Nightlife in my city offers the opportunity for fun through a wide variety of activities, such as nightclubs, theaters, restaurants, and movies.

This second version is strong because it *specifies* activities that make nightlife in your city attractive. In addition, it sets a direction for the supporting sentences that will follow.

Effective Placement of Topic Sentences

The topic sentence presents the main idea of a paragraph, so writers frequently place it first in the paragraph. That way, readers immediately find out what the paragraph will be about and in what direction it will head. Keep in mind, however, that topic sentences can appear in other spots in paragraphs, especially when the paragraphs are parts of essays or other longer writings. Sometimes the best place for the topic sentence will be in the middle of the paragraph, with a couple sentences preceding it to draw the reader into the discussion. Since you are just learning to develop good paragraph writing, starting out by placing your topic sentence first is a good way to help you develop and improve your writing skills.

In other cases, such as in an **introduction** to a longer document, the best place for the topic sentence is at the end of the paragraph. In this arrangement, the other sentences lead up to the topic sentence, building the reader's interest, and the topic sentence then serves as a lead-in for the discussion that follows. Like so many other aspects of writing, the placement of a topic sentence ultimately depends on the purpose of the document and the needs of the reader.

COMPREHENSION
AND PRACTICE
3.7

Topic Sentence Placement

1. Where is a topic sentence usually placed within a paragraph? Why?

   Generally, the topic sentence is placed at the beginning of a paragraph so that readers

   will know right away what the paragraph will cover.

2. Here is a sample paragraph with the topic sentence listed after it:

   > About two minutes after the start of the race, I developed a mild ache in my side. I figured that I could keep going and the pain would go away. Ten minutes later the pain was worse. I found it harder and harder to breathe, but I refused to give in to the pain. I had trained for two months, and I was determined to finish. Unfortunately, after another five minutes of struggling, I had to stop and walk the rest of the way.

   Topic sentence: My first 5K road race very quickly became a complete disaster.

   In your view, where would the topic sentence fit best, at the beginning, in the middle, or at the end of the paragraph? On the lines below, explain where you think the topic sentence fits best and why.

   Most students will agree that the topic sentence fits best at the beginning of the paragraph

   because it prepares the reader for the rest of the story.

COMPREHENSION
AND PRACTICE
3.8

Effective Topic Sentences

1. Here are several potential topic sentences. Label the strong topic sentences with an *S* and the weak ones with a *W*. Study the examples first.

EXAMPLES

   W   You can get a lot of free tourist information.

   S   When stress has you frazzled, relaxation techniques can help you feel in greater control.

_____S_____ a. The encouragement that my high school math teacher gave me truly changed my self-image.

_____W_____ b. Most reality TV shows are a waste of time.

_____S_____ c. We need to be more aggressive about recycling programs in order to save money and valuable resources.

_____W_____ d. Lacrosse can be really hard.

_____W_____ e. Part-time jobs are important to college students.

_____S_____ f. Membership on a parents' council is a great way to help your child get a good education.

_____W_____ g. Some online games are really complicated.

_____W_____ h. I don't enjoy dancing.

_____S_____ i. My success with weight loss has helped me feel good about myself again.

_____S_____ j. Reductions in staffing at the emergency room put the public at risk.

2. Select two of the weak topic sentences you identified above. On the lines that follow, rewrite them so that they are more effective.

Answers will vary depending on the weak topic sentences chosen. Here is a sample

response for sentence b: Because most reality TV shows are actually scripted, they

aren't what they claim to be and are not worth watching.

CHALLENGE 3.3 Practice Writing Effective Topic Sentences

collaboration

1. The following topic sentences are weak. Working with a classmate, improve and rewrite them on the lines that follow. Use the example to guide you.
Answers will vary. Sample responses are shown.

EXAMPLE Mario's is a good restaurant.

Mario's serves the best, most authentic Italian food in town.

a. Among digital music players, the latest iPod remains popular.

With great sound quality and ease of use, the latest iPod is the best MP3 player for

the money.

_____

_____

b. For me, an appointment with the dentist is not fun.

Because of one bad experience a few years ago, an appointment with the dentist is

not one of life's most pleasant experiences

c. I'm going to write about an important lesson I learned as a child.

When I cheated on a spelling test in fourth grade, I ended up learning a lesson about

living.

d. The office where I work is an interesting place.

If you want to see a diverse group of people work successfully together, come visit

my office.

e. New technology can be frustrating.

My uncle found installing his satellite radio system so complicated that he finally gave

up and paid to have it set up.

f. Museums are great places.

Museums such as the Art Institute of Chicago and the Metropolitan Museum of Art in

New York offer people the opportunity to view works by the world's greatest artists up

close.

g. Drivers face many hazards on the road.

The xenon headlights available on some new cars are so bright that other drivers

complain of being blinded.

_____

_____

h. Many states have some form of legalized gambling.

Advocates for gambling casinos fail to mention the increase in crime and personal

financial problems that often occur in surrounding areas when casinos are established.

_____

_____

collaboration

2. Exchange the topic sentence you wrote for item 2 of Challenge 3.2 (p. 50) with a classmate. Evaluate the draft topic sentence you receive to make sure it is clear and specific. If it is, mark it with a ✓. If not, circle the area that you feel needs to be adjusted, write a sentence explaining what you think it lacks, and return it to your classmate.

Supporting Ideas

ESL Note
See "The Needs of Your Reader," page 496, for more about providing the appropriate information for your reader.

Once you have developed a clear topic sentence, you need to develop strong supporting sentences. To do so, you reevaluate the ideas you highlighted in your prewriting, deciding which ones will do the best job of explaining or illustrating your point.

Here again is the topic sentence about the most significant personal possessions:

EXAMPLE

If I could keep **only one shoebox full of personal belongings**, I would select items _with great personal or sentimental worth, not monetary value._

Now let's review the highlighted ideas from the clustering (p. 41), categorized into four groups. These groups match the four spokes or threads of the clustering in which they appear:

My pictures!! Trips, parties, graduations

✓ Got them all put on CD last year

Abby's stuff from school

✓ We'd go places, she'd make me a painting

✓ Stories she wrote in first grade

Gifts I received

✓ Grampa's toy Corvette?

✓ Gramma gave it to me after his funeral

Souvenirs I've kept

✓ Concert ticket stubs and bracelets

✓ Program from my first Cubs game

All of these ideas are clearly related to and support the topic sentence. But, now you need to figure out the best way to present those ideas so that your reader can make sense of them. In particular, you must express the ideas in correct, complete sentence form.

COMPREHENSION
AND PRACTICE
3.9

Supporting Details

1. What process should you follow to identify supporting ideas for your topic sentence?

   To identify supporting ideas for your topic sentence, you should reevaluate the

   highlighted material in your initial prewriting.

2. What is the advantage of putting the potential supporting ideas you have developed into general categories or groups?

   Arranging promising prewriting details in general categories or groups makes it easier

   to decide which ideas to keep, which to combine, and which to exclude.

CHALLENGE 3.4 Practice with Developing and Grouping Details

1. Read the brainstorming about *television* that follows. Choose a category or section, and, on a separate sheet of paper, develop a draft topic sentence. Then create at least three specific supporting sentences, using details from the category you chose or from additional ideas that the subject suggests to you.

   Television—two sides, good and bad
   good shows and great reruns
        comedies—The Simpsons, 30 Rock, Everybody Loves Raymond,
         Saturday Night Live
        dramas—Law and Order, House, CSI Miami, 24, sports
        basketball, baseball, hockey, college and pros
        even classic games

> Time spent watching
>> Watch too much now
>> put off stuff I should be doing like studying.
> Innovations
>> DIRECTV-500 channels to pick from
>> TiVo system-records TV shows, skips commercials
> Public television
>> good science shows
>> weekly political interviews
>> so many fundraisers!
> TV of the future?
>> Wall-size flat-screen TVs?
>> broadcast in 3D?

collaboration

2. Exchange your draft topic sentence and supporting sentences with a class-mate. Evaluate the material you receive to see if the supporting sentences adequately illustrate or explain the topic sentence. Put a ✓ next to any detail that you think should be more specific and return the paper to the writer. After considering your classmate's suggestions about your supporting sentences, make any necessary adjustments.

3. Earlier in the chapter you did some prewriting for which you later created a topic sentence. You and a classmate then reevaluated this topic sentence for Challenge 3.3 (pp. 48–50). Now, using the material above to guide you, make a list of the information that offers the strongest support for that topic sentence.

Effective Arrangement of Details and Examples

ESL Note
See "Unity," page 496, for more on making sure you keep ideas clearly connected and presented.

After you have identified which prewriting ideas seem to offer the strongest support for your topic sentence, you need to consider the most effective way to present them. The order you choose will always depend on the needs of your reader and the subject you are writing about.

Common methods of arrangement include:

- **chronological order**—presentation based on time
- **spatial order**—presentation based on location of one item or individual relative to others
- **emphatic order**—presentation based on the relative importance of the supporting details and examples

For more complete details on these methods of arrangement, see Chapter 4 (p. 70).

To consider how to arrange your supporting details, think again about the clustering example concerning personal possessions. The topic sentence developed from this material indicates a focus on items with important personal or sentimental value. Presumably, some of these items have more significance than others. Therefore, arranging this paragraph in emphatic order (presenting ideas based on relative importance), seems ideal.

Now let us review the promising ideas that were highlighted in the clustering. The information about souvenirs is strong. Most people would understand why memorabilia like concert wristbands or ticket stubs to sport events would be important. The information about the CD filled with pictures is even stronger, as these kinds of photos are signposts for key life events. Stronger still is the information concerning special keepsakes made by a young child. Most people will appreciate the value of a simple gift made by a child. But the strongest information of all involves the toy car, a link to a beloved grandparent. Below is a list of these supporting ideas, arranged in emphatic order:

1. *Souvenirs I've kept*
    - Concert ticket stubs and bracelets
    - Program from my first Cubs game

2. *My pictures!! Trips, parties, graduations*
    - Got them all put on CD last year

3. *Abby's stuff from school*
    - We'd go places, she'd make me a painting
    - Stories she wrote in first grade

4. *Gifts I received*
    - Grampa's toy Corvette?
    - Gramma gave it to me after his funeral

With a preliminary order in place, and using what you've learned about units of thought containing subjects and verbs, you are now ready to transform your ideas into a form that will communicate their meaning fully to a reader: complete sentences.

The Importance of Order and Development

1. Once you have grouped the details in your prewriting, what kinds of adjustments should you make?

   Once you have arranged your prewriting ideas in groups, you should consider subdividing

   the groups into smaller categories, restating some of the ideas, combining related ideas,

   and considering the most logical order for the material.

2. Look again at the four groups of information about items that would be kept in a single shoebox. Which of these groups do you think would be easiest to develop? On the following lines, explain your choice.

   Answers will vary somewhat, depending on personal interests. Those who especially

   like pictures will identify the section about the photo CD. Others who have received a

   gift from a special relative will choose the section about the toy car.

3. Choose a detail from one group of information. On the lines that follow, turn this idea into a supporting sentence.

Answers will vary, depending upon the detail chosen. A representative sentence is

provided: I still have the program from my first Chicago Cubs game, during which

Sammy Sosa hit two home runs.

CHALLENGE 3.5 Organization of Supporting Details

collaboration

1. Here is a brainstorming on the subject *nature*. Working with a classmate, select one section of the brainstorming and, on a separate sheet of paper, copy it, adding at least five details or examples. Group these ideas and set a preliminary order. Then, on the same paper, explain why you both chose that order.

> camping trips every summer
> > swimming in Cosmo's Lake
> > day trips hiking
> pollution, ruining environment
> > that landfill outside of the city, ruining water
> > smell is awful
> > trash all over the city-really ugly mess
> my trip to the desert-so wide open and lonely
> > cactuses and weird rock formations
> > miles and miles of open road with no gas stations, etc.-scary!
> rain forest-check notes from environment class!!
> > destruction of one species of plant or animal a day
> > reason for destruction-economic
> > land only good for one or two years of farming
> > affects weather in the rest of the world
> > what cures are we missing out on-herbs, etc.?
> zoos
> > try to seem more natural
> > elephants and lions in Regional Zoo given room to roam
> > new plains section

2. For Challenge 3.4 (pp. 51–52) you selected details from an earlier prewriting that you had identified as promising. Now, referring to the discussion and examples on organizing selected details and examples, arrange on a separate sheet of paper your supporting ideas in an effective order.

collaboration

3. Exchange your listing with a classmate. On the sheet you receive, check the order. If you think the order is logical, put a ✓ on the page. If you have a suggestion for change, write it on the bottom of the page, explaining why your suggestion might work better. Return the list to your classmate.

Writer-Centered Words; Reader-Centered Sentences

ESL Note
See "The Needs of Your Reader," page 496, for more about providing the appropriate information for your reader.

In general, prewriting material isn't expressed in complete thoughts. This raw form of your first ideas is *writer centered* because it makes sense only to you, the writer. It doesn't necessarily make sense to anyone else until you make the ideas *reader centered*. It isn't enough to *tell* your reader something. You need to *show* what you mean by **amplifying**—adding or clarifying details and examples. At the same time, you need to express your points in a refined form, one that an independent reader can understand. That means transforming your thoughts into *complete sentences*.

Think of making out a grocery list. When you write down *peanut butter*, you probably don't include a brand name or size because you know exactly what you want to buy. Your list is *writer centered*.

However, if you were asking a friend to do your grocery shopping, you would need to provide more complete detail: *Please pick up a 16-ounce jar of Snazzle brand crunchy, reduced-fat peanut butter.* Anyone who can understand written English could fulfill your request. The material is therefore *reader centered*, making sense even to someone who doesn't share with the writer the specific background or knowledge of the subject.

Consider this writer-centered material about a child's simple gifts to a special adult:

WRITER CENTERED

Abby's stuff from school

- We'd go places, she'd make me a painting
- Stories she wrote in first grade

In this form, the material *suggests* the importance of these keepsakes. Right now, however, it doesn't offer enough detail to show what makes them special. In short, it doesn't address the needs of the reader.

Look at how much more effectively the point is made in this reader-centered version, which takes the needs of the reader into account:

READER CENTERED

I would keep my niece's many crayon drawings and a couple of stories she wrote when she first started school. These pictures and stories illustrate the two of us doing things together like going to the playground and the beach

Reader Evaluation Checklist

You can assume that your reader knows basic, general information about many subjects, but nothing in depth or specific. The following **Reader Evaluation Checklist** will help you supply the kinds of supporting details and examples that meet the needs of your reader. Simply insert your topic in the blanks, and then write your answers to the questions.

✓ **READER EVALUATION CHECKLIST**

☐ What does the average reader need to know about _____?

☐ What do I think the average reader already knows about _____?

☐ What information would help the average person better understand _____?

☐ What did I find the hardest to understand about _____ at first?

☐ What helped me to figure out _____?

☐ What's the best example or explanation I can give the average person about _____?

The answers to these questions will help you focus on what your reader needs in order to understand the point you are trying to make.

Definition of Writer Centered and Reader Centered

1. In your own words, explain the difference between writer-centered and reader-centered information.

   Writer-centered information is often brief and lacks detail. It is fully understood only by

   the writer. Reader-centered information is clear, detailed, and specific, easily

   understood by anyone.

   _____

2. Here are two details from a branching about common fears or phobias. On the lines provided, turn these writer-centered fragments into reader-centered sentences. Answers will vary. Representative answers are shown.

   a. **spiders** My sister actually shrieks out loud and runs out of the room when she

   sees even the smallest spider.

   _____

   b. **claustrophobia** Airplanes are closed spaces, so people with claustrophobia find

   flying highly stressful.

   _____

CHALLENGE 3.6 Reader-Centered Sentences

collaboration

1. Make a copy of a page of your notes from another class and exchange those notes with a classmate. On a separate sheet of paper, transform your class-mate's notes from writer-centered writing into reader-centered writing. Then return the notes and your version of them to the writer.

2. Compare the version of the notes your classmate wrote with yours. Below your partner's version of your notes, list any details that were misunderstood or not fully explained, and then rewrite them so that they accurately reflect your original meaning.

3. Using the Reader Evaluation Checklist (p. 56), evaluate the material you have been preparing for the previous question to assess whether the information will meet the needs of your reader.

The Complete First-Draft Paragraph

ESL Note
See "Writing Paragraphs," pages 496–497, for more on meeting the needs of your reader and main-taining unity and clarity.

If you have followed all the steps discussed so far, you have come a long way in your composing process. You have prewritten on a general topic and identified us-able ideas. You have developed a topic sentence, chosen supporting ideas, and built a plan for ordering them to support your topic sentence. You have also learned how to change your writer-centered prewriting into reader-centered sen-tences. Now you are ready to write a *first draft* of your paragraph.

The key here is to relax. Your first draft doesn't have to be perfect. You will have the opportunity to *revise* it, to rework the less effective parts, and to polish it overall, as Chapter 4 will demonstrate. For now, concentrate on getting a reason-able version down on paper.

In fact, think in terms of creating *two* initial versions of your document: a rough draft and a first draft. The rough draft is the first complete version, and it is for your eyes only. Once this rough draft is complete, take a brief break and then scan it for any obviously awkward or unclear spots and any noticeable errors in form. Correct those, and you will have your first draft.

To prepare these drafts, use a computer if possible. Various word-processing tools, including grammar and spell checkers, make it easier to identify problem spots as you work through the writing process. But do not rely solely on these tools; you will learn later that even computers make mistakes. Always double- or triple-space your draft. This way, you'll have extra space in the printout to make corrections by hand—a necessary step prior to preparing additional drafts.

Take a look at this first draft about reducing personal possessions to whatever would fit inside a shoebox:

A Shoebox Full of Meaning

The topic sentence expresses the main idea and the attitude about it.

If I could keep only one shoebox full of belongings, I would select items

with great personal or sentimental worth, not monetary value. I would stick

in the ticket stubs and wristbands I have saved from all the concerts and

The supporting details and examples are expressed in complete sentence form.

sporting events I have ever attended. My favorite is from the first time I saw the Chicago Cubs at Wrigley Field. In 2009, the National Hockey League actually held one of its Winter Classic outdoor hockey games at Wrigley Field. I would add a photo CD with pictures from vacation trips and other special occasions. In addition, I would keep my niece's many crayon drawings and a couple of stories she wrote when she first started school. These pictures and stories illustrate the two of us doing things together like going to the playground and the beach. Finally, I would keep a coin bank in the shape of a Chevrolet Corvette, which used to sit on my grandfather's workbench. My grandmother gave it to me after my grandfather's funeral. Every time I look at it, it reminds me of him. *The things I would keep have no monetary value, but I consider them the most valuable things I own because of the memories they hold.*

The closing sentence restates the main point.

A strong topic sentence opens the paragraph, and the supporting ideas, now in complete sentences, appear in emphatic order, as suggested on page 52. This paragraph is intended to be a complete document, so it features a closing sentence that reemphasizes the point of the paragraph.

Certainly this first draft is not perfect. There is work still to be done, but that's all right. A first draft should never be your final draft. Instead, it should be a solid beginning, as this paragraph is.

COMPREHENSION
AND PRACTICE
3.12

The Importance of the First Draft

1. What is the final step in the process of composing?

   The final step in composing is to write a first draft—to write a clear paragraph with a

   topic sentence and supporting sentences.

2. What is the difference between a rough draft and a first draft?

   A rough draft is the initial version a writer produces. It sometimes contains obvious

   errors in form and content. A first draft is the rough draft with the most noticeable

   errors eliminated.

3. What purpose does the closing sentence serve in this paragraph about special possessions?

The closing sentence underscores the significance of the points expressed in the

paragraph, that the most important keepsakes often have no monetary value.

CHALLENGE 3.7 Rough-Draft and First-Draft Paragraphs

Using the first-draft paragraph on those items that would be saved in a single shoebox to guide you, take the topic sentence and supporting ideas you have developed for the various Challenge exercises in this chapter, and write a rough-draft paragraph on your chosen topic. Scan it for any obvious errors and weaknesses and then prepare a first draft. Save this draft for later use.

THE COMPLETE FIRST-DRAFT WRITING

Here's a paragraph about facing a difficult challenge by Scott Lopes (his prewriting appeared on p. 18 of Chapter 2). Scott feels immense pride for just being in college: "No one in my immediate family finished high school, never mind college." Scott feels his writing skills "are 50 times better now than they were" before he took his first writing class. Being able to write well is important to Scott: "Since I want to go into teaching, writing will help me to write out assignments, and in my job now as an EMT, it helps me with my narratives of patient care." Read Scott's paragraph and the accompanying annotations, which show how well he supports his topic sentence. Then answer the questions that follow.

Impossible Really Is Nothing

Scott's **topic sentence** is clear and specific.

Of the challenges I've faced in my life, the death of my grandfather was the hardest one for me to deal with. It marked my transition from a 14-year-old boy to the man of the house. On August 30, 2002, two days after my birthday and just before I started high school, my grandfather Bill Mason was struck by a vehicle in front of our house and killed. That night my immediate challenge was to exercise self-control. I wanted more than anything to go after that driver who had carelessly taken the life of the person who had raised me. However, the thought of my 10-year-old brother and my grandmother, who had also seen the accident, kept me from doing it. I won't lie to you and tell you that I never broke down and cried over this terrible loss, because I did. But I also knew that my grandfather would want me to help my grandmother run the household and to become a successful high-school student. At first, it all seemed impossible, but, as the slogan from the old Adidas commercial starring the great Muhammad Ali stated, "Impossible is nothing." To this day, dealing with the death of my grandfather is still not easy. However, I am living, walking, talking proof that if you work enough at it, you can handle the challenges that life presents, no matter how difficult they might be.

This **supporting sentence** explains the tragic event, thus helping the reader understand the point expressed in the topic sentence.

These sentences offer solid support for the topic sentence because they detail what he wanted to do and why he showed restraint.

This supporting sentence clarifies how Scott addressed his grandfather's death, reiterating the meaning expressed in the topic sentence.

This **concluding sentence** builds on the idea expressed in the topic sentence, emphasizing that, no matter how difficult, challenges can be successfully addressed.

COMPREHENSION AND PRACTICE 3.13

Reading Exploration

1. Here again is Scott's topic sentence: Of the challenges I've faced in my life, the death of my grandfather was the hardest one for me to deal with.
   On the lines that follow, list the topic and then identify the attitude or reaction.

   Scott's topic is the death of his grandfather and the attitude or reaction is how hard

   this death was for him.

_____

_____

_____

_____

2. Several of Scott's supporting sentences are highlighted. In your view, which offers the strongest support for the topic sentence? What about this sentence leads you to this conclusion? On the lines that follow, explain your choice.

Answers will vary, although many students will select the first supporting sentence

because it specifies the tragic nature of Scott's grandfather's death. Others may

choose the second and third sentences because of the dramatic situation

Scott faced.

_____

_____

3. Imagine that Scott has asked you to read and evaluate his draft. On the lines that follow, first identify what you think is the strongest part of his paragraph, and then offer one suggestion that would help him turn this already good paragraph into an even better one.

Answers will vary. In terms of the strongest aspect of the paragraph, many

students will refer to the specific and emotionally powerful examples Scott

supplies. Some may note his strong concluding sentence. In terms of suggested

improvements, students will likely request more detail about the grandfather

himself or more about Scott's expanded role in the household after his

grandfather's death.

Understanding the Subject through Writing

As he comes to the end of his paragraph, Scott Lopes refers to the slogan of an Adidas advertisement featuring Muhammad Ali: "Impossible is nothing." On a separate sheet of paper, write a brief paragraph (50–100 words) explaining what this slogan means to you.

FOR FURTHER EXPLORATION

1. Consider one of the subjects that follow. Explore the topic, using your favorite prewriting technique, and make note of the purpose you might fulfill as you write about it.

   • The person who commands the most respect from you
   • Public behavior that you find unacceptable
   • Advantages of living in a big city—or in a small town

2. Evaluate your prewriting material, identify a focus, and create a draft paragraph of at least seven to ten sentences.

3. Exchange your draft with a classmate. Using the material in this chapter as a guide, evaluate the draft you receive. Note any problems with topic or supporting sentence development, and return the draft to the writer.

4. Revise your draft, eliminating any errors identified by your writing partner.

collaboration

DISCOVERING CONNECTIONS

For this assignment, concentrate on the picture and one of the following questions (or another that the picture inspires). After you prewrite, consider the purpose you might fulfill, and create a draft paragraph of at least seven to ten sentences, following the steps outlined in this chapter. Save your work for later use.

A. This picture shows a police officer on the job. What do you think is the most difficult aspect of this career? Why do you feel this way?

B. The officer appears to be performing basic traffic duty. Is there a traffic rule—or law in general—that you think should be changed? Why?

| **RECAP** | Composing: Creating Topic Sentences and Supporting Sentences |

Key Terms in This Chapter	Definitions
composing	transforming ideas into complete sentence form so the reader can understand them
paragraph	a group of sentences that relate to one main idea or topic
body	sentences in a paragraph that support or explain the topic sentence
topic sentence	the sentence in a paragraph that states the main idea and the writer's attitude or reaction to it

Key Terms in This Chapter	Definitions
closing sentence	a sentence that brings a paragraph-length document to an appropriate, logical close, reemphasizing the significance of the paragraph
amplifying	the addition of details and examples to clarify your meaning
chronological order	organization on the basis of time order
spatial order	organization on the basis of location
emphatic order	organization on the basis of importance or significance
reader evaluation checklist	series of questions designed to help writers ensure that their supporting information meets their readers' needs

Steps to Developing an Effective Paragraph

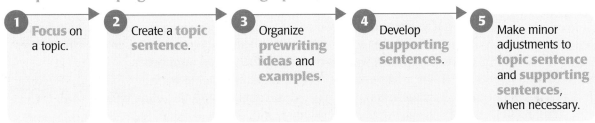

1. Focus on a topic.
2. Create a topic sentence.
3. Organize prewriting ideas and examples.
4. Develop supporting sentences.
5. Make minor adjustments to topic sentence and supporting sentences, when necessary.

Using Discovery Online with MyWritingLab
For more practice composing, go to www.mywritinglab.com.

CHAPTER 4
Revising: Refining Your Draft

GETTING STARTED...

 Q OK, now I've completed my first draft. I've made it as good as I could, so what do I gain by going back to work on it again?

 A Yes, you've worked hard, developing good ideas and an effective focus, and then you figured out the best way to express your ideas. But here's the problem: You might not think of it this way, but writing is tiring work, and when you're fatigued you tend to overlook both weaknesses and possibilities for improvement. Let some time pass, and seek the response of an objective reader. You'll then see ways to make something good even better.

Overview: Revision

Writing that's as good as it can be requires time, patience, and work. If you think that you can create a truly effective piece of writing in just one draft, here is some news: It's simply not true. Instead, you must reevaluate, reconsider, and rework that initial version. In other words, you must **revise** it.

Think of revision as *re-vision,* that is, as *seeing* your writing again. When you revise, you first **reassess** your writing, evaluating it and identifying what works and what doesn't. You check your writing for several things: (1) *unity,* or focus; (2) *coherence,* or smoothness and order; and (3) *effective language.* When you reassess, you also enlist the aid of an objective reader.

Second, you **redraft.** This step involves rewriting to eliminate any problems with unity and coherence. It also involves **amplifying**—adding or clarifying details and examples so that they communicate your meaning fully to your reader.

Finally, you **edit** your document. When you edit, you focus on eliminating any remaining errors in form. This step is vital because these kinds of weaknesses distract a reader from the good ideas—the *content*—of a piece of writing. When you follow all these steps, the result is a greatly improved version of the initial draft.

Navigating This Chapter This chapter explains how to improve, refine, and polish your first draft, making it clearer and more effective. You will learn that revising involves:

- reassessing
- redrafting
- editing

Reassessment

Before you reassess your draft, put it aside for a day or so *to create a distance.* You've worked hard, and you may sincerely believe that you have made your draft as good as it can be. A little time away from the draft will enable you to look at your work with a fresher, more objective eye. When you are able to be objective, you're in a better position to evaluate your draft in terms of *unity, coherence,* and *effective language.*

ESL Note
See "Unity," page 496, for more on the importance of ensuring that all the information you include is directly connected to your main idea.

Unity

In writing, **unity** means that all the examples and details relate directly to your subject. When your writing is unified, your reader can easily follow and understand the point you are making. To maintain unity in your writing, you need to weed out any material that doesn't contribute directly to your main idea.

Look at this paragraph about witnessing an in-line skating accident, and consider which material isn't directly connected to the topic sentence:

(1) Last week I saw an accident downtown that reminded me always to focus on what I am doing. (2) I had just walked out of a small convenience store when a young woman in-line skating passed in front of the store. (3) I stop at that store just about every day to buy a cup of coffee. (4) The coffee is inexpensive, and the man who runs the store loves to talk about sports. (5) Earlier in the day, the city's public works department had been working on the sidewalk a few doors down and had marked the site with an orange cone. (6) Just beyond the cone, a segment of the sidewalk was missing. (7) Unfortunately, the skater was looking back over her shoulder as she reached the work area and didn't notice the cone. (8) She skated past the cone, dropped into the trench, and immediately fell backward. (9) When I reached her, she was unconscious, with her right wrist bent out at a strange angle and the back of her head bleeding heavily. (10) While the man in the convenience store called the ambulance, a nurse who had been at the counter rushed out to help the skater. (11) The shortage of nurses in some areas of the United States is critical.

If you chose the third, fourth, and eleventh sentences, you are correct. These sentences have nothing to do with the accident mentioned in the topic sentence and discussed in the body. Eliminate these three sentences, and the paragraph is unified.

COMPREHENSION AND PRACTICE 4.1

Unity

1. How do you make sure your writing is unified?

   To ensure that your writing is unified, you take out any information that is not directly

   related to your topic sentence.

2. Underline the topic sentence in each of the following paragraphs. Then cross out any sentences that are not directly related to the topic.

A. (1) <u>The number of people who read a daily newspaper is declining for several reasons.</u> (2) For one thing, many people lead very busy lives. (3) Some people say they can't even spare twenty minutes in their hectic days to sit down and read a paper. (4) ~~Stress from pressure at work can have serious health effects.~~ (5) They tune into the news on their car radios as they drive to work or catch the highlights on TV as they get ready for bed at night. (6) Also, newspapers are printed only once a day, so the news in them may be a day or more old. (7) ~~By adding a lot of color, *USA Today* has influenced the way newspapers look.~~ (8) Television, however, can update the news any time during the day and can bring events as they are happening to our living rooms. (9) ~~Today's satellite TV systems are much more compact and much less expensive.~~ (10) Finally, an ever-increasing number of people prefer to get their news from various news sources on the Internet.

B. (1) <u>When I started school, I didn't always feel accepted by my classmates because of my hearing deficiencies.</u> (2) In first grade, for example, Timothy Julius, the boy who sat next to me, used to stick his fingers in his ears whenever he talked to me. (3) The teacher spoke with him about it several times, but he would still tease me whenever the teacher wasn't looking. (4) On many mornings, I ended up in tears. (5) ~~When Timothy was a sophomore in high school, he was arrested for breaking into a warehouse.~~ (6) ~~Now he is studying to be a minister.~~ (7) As a result of his teasing, I became more self-conscious and less confident. (8) <u>For instance, I began to think that all the kids in class were staring at my hearing aids.</u> (9) I finally started meeting with the school psychologist, who worked with me to improve my self-image. (10) Thanks to her help, I began to feel more confident within a few months.

CHALLENGE 4.1   Unity in Your Writing

1. Using the paragraphs on page 65 on the in-line skating accident, write a draft paragraph of at least seven to ten sentences about a time when you lost focus or failed to pay attention to something or witnessed someone else do so.

collaboration

2. Exchange your draft paragraph with a classmate. Assess the paragraph you receive for unity. Put a ✓ next to any material you think isn't directly related to the topic sentence and the supporting sentences, and return the paragraph to the writer.

3. Make any necessary adjustments to your paragraph, using your reader's comments to guide you.

Coherence

When you reassess, you also need to keep your writing **coherent**, meaning that all sentences are logically arranged and connected so that the ideas flow smoothly. The two basic components of coherence are *transition* and *organization* of sentences.

Transition   One way to make your writing coherent is through **transition**, words and expressions that emphasize the connections, or relationships, among your ideas. To provide transition for your readers,

- repeat key words and phrases;
- use **synonyms**—words with a similar meaning; and
- include transitional words or expressions

Repeating key words or replacing a key word with a synonym or pronoun helps to keep the ideas foremost in the reader's mind. These techniques, like transitional words and expressions, also tie ideas together. The italicized words in the following sentences illustrate how this transitional technique works:

EXAMPLE   *My Uncle Tom* worked as a sales representative for an *auto paint manufacturer* until *he* was almost *75 years old. He* had more energy than most people half *his age,* and *he* had more extensive knowledge of *his product* than anyone else in the *company.*

In these sentences, *he* and *his* take the place of *My Uncle Tom, age* refers back to *75 years old,* and *product* and *company* rename *auto paint manufacturer.*

   Adding transitional expressions is another proven strategy to signify connection between ideas. The following common transitional expressions are grouped according to the kind of relationships between ideas they show.

Common Transitional Expressions to Illustrate or Show Cause and Effect

accordingly	consequently	indeed	particularly
after all	for example	in fact	specifically
as a result	for instance	of course	therefore
because	for one thing	overall	thus

EXAMPLE   The special effects in that movie were outstanding. *Specifically,* the performances by the lead actors were excellent.

Common Transitional Expressions to Add, Restate, or Emphasize

again	finally	in conclusion	next
also	further	in other words	too
and	in addition	moreover	to sum up
besides			

EXAMPLE   I enjoy spending time riding my mountain bike, *and* I *also* enjoy hiking in the state forest.

Common Transitional Expressions to Show Time or Place

above	currently	once	to the right (left)
after	earlier	presently	under
as soon as	here	since	until
before	immediately	soon	when
below	lately	then	whenever
beyond	now	there	where

EXAMPLE   The crowd waiting for the bus began to cheer as it drove up to the station. *As soon as* the door opened, people began pushing their way up the stairs and into the empty seats.

Common Transitional Expressions to Compare or Contrast

although	despite	likewise	though
and	even though	nevertheless	yet
as	however	on the other hand	
at the same time	in contrast	regardless	
but	in spite of	still	

EXAMPLE   The shipment arrived late, *even though* Chris had paid extra for overnight delivery.

Take a look at the italicized and boldfaced words in the following paragraph:

My cousin Danny may be the most intense pro football fan I've ever met. *Once* football season arrives in the fall, Danny focuses on **his** favorite team, the Philadelphia Eagles. **His** fascination with **the Eagles** affects **his** life in several ways. *For example,* **he** has season tickets on the 50-yard line, and **his** **seat** costs as much as a two-week vacation at a beach resort. *Also,* Danny travels to at least one out-of-town game every year. Last year, *for instance,* **he** drove down to see **his team** play the Carolina Panthers. *Of course,* this **trip** required him to spend two nights in an overpriced hotel. *When* he can't travel to see the team play, Danny puts on his official Philly green, turns off the phone, and turns on the huge high-definition television **he** bought to watch the games.

In some sentences, the pronouns *he, his,* or *him* are used in place of *Danny.* In others, the synonyms *team* or *Philly* substitute for *Philadelphia Eagles,* and *seat* replaces *season tickets.* Also, several transitional expressions, including *once, for example, also, for instance, of course,* and *when,* are used. These transitional devices help to hold the paragraph together and make the connections between ideas clear for the reader.

COMPREHENSION
AND PRACTICE
4.2

Coherence and Transition

1. When you reassess your writing for coherence, what are you checking for?

   When you reassess your writing for coherence, you check that your sentences and

   ideas are connected and arranged in logical order.

2. What are three techniques you can use to provide transition in your paragraph?

   1. Repeat key words and phrases; 2. use synonyms or pronouns; 3. use transitional

   words or expressions.

3. Underline the transitional expressions you find in the following paragraph and circle any repeated words, synonyms, or pronouns in each paragraph. Use the paragraph above on the pro football fanatic to guide you.

   Jeri's fear of insects and spiders has affected (her) life in many ways. For one thing, (she) always shakes (her) shoes before putting (them) on because somebody once told (her) that spiders hide (their) babies there. (She) is allergic to bee stings, so whenever Jeri goes on a picnic, (she) spends (her) time watching out for bees. When she is driving, Jeri worries about insects. Every morning, (she) checks (her) car for any (bugs) buzzing around or hiding under the seats. Overall, Jeri says a world without (bugs) would be wonderful.

4. On the lines that follow, write three related sentences about one of the following subjects: *cosmetic surgery* or *computer games.* In the brief passage you write, include at least two of the common transitional expressions listed on pages 67–68:

Answers will vary.

_____

_____

_____

CHALLENGE 4.2 **Transition in Your Writing**

1. Write a draft paragraph of at least seven to ten sentences about your own or someone else's deep interest in some activity or hobby, using the paragraph on the pro football fanatic (pp. 68–69) as a model.

collaboration

2. Make a copy of your draft paragraph, and exchange it with a classmate. Assess the paragraph you receive in terms of transition. Underline any transitional expressions and circle any other uses of repeated words, synonyms, or pronouns and put a ✓ next to any spot that would be improved if transition were added. Return the paragraph to the writer.

3. Make any necessary adjustments to your paragraph, using your reader's comments to guide you.

ESL Note
See "Unity," page 496, for more on the importance of effective organization in your writing.

Effective Organization   When you reassess your writing for coherence, make sure your ideas are organized so that readers can easily follow your point. You select the order for each piece of writing according to the subject. Three common methods of organization are *chronological order, spatial order,* and *emphatic order.*

Using Chronological Order   The word *chronological* refers to the order of time. With *chronological order,* you present events in the order in which they occurred. With *linear order*—a variation of chronological order—you write about processes that must be performed in a step-by-step fashion such as instructions or recipes. The goal with both types of time order is to present the ideas so that a reader can easily follow and understand them.

Look at this paragraph about an encounter with the police:

> Yesterday I had one of those days that made me wish I'd stayed in bed. I left the house late, so I was driving over the speed limit to make up some lost time. Five minutes later, I looked in my rear-view mirror and saw flashing blue lights. The state trooper pulled me over and then asked for my license and registration. I took the registration out of the glove box and handed it to her, but when I reached in my pocket for my wallet, it was missing. After a moment of confusion, I remembered that I had left my wallet on the kitchen table. After I explained this to the trooper, she first smiled and handed me a ticket for $75 for speeding. She then told me that I had an hour to produce my license at the state police barracks the next town over or she would double the fine.

With the events in the order in which they occurred, the reader can more easily understand the entire experience. The writer was behind schedule and began driving over the speed limit. *A few minutes later,* a trooper pulled the writer over and *then* asked for his license and registration. *When* the writer realized that his license was at home, he explained what had happened. The trooper issued a ticket anyway and *then* warned the writer to produce the license or face an even higher fine.

COMPREHENSION
AND PRACTICE
4.3

Chronological Order

1. Why is the organization of your sentences important?

   The organization of your sentences is important because arrangement of information

   helps the reader easily follow the point of the writing.

2. Read the following paragraph. Underline the transitional expressions. Then, on the lines that follow, summarize the sequence of events the paragraph describes. On a separate sheet of paper, explain how the transitions help the reader follow the event.

   The morning I went for my driver's license was a disaster. First, the instructor from the driving school arrived almost half an hour late. I therefore had no time for the lesson I was scheduled to have before the actual driving test. Then when we finally arrived at the Department of Motor Vehicles, the computer system was down, so the clerk couldn't process my application. As a result, I had to wait another 45 minutes in line, and I missed my scheduled test time. After all these delays, the inspector finally joined us in the car for the test. I turned the key, but the car wouldn't start. Fortunately, the driving school had a second car, so I was finally able to take my test and get my license. Once I made it home, I took a nap, hoping to forget all the headaches I had endured just to get my license.

   The driving school failed to pick up the writer at the appointed time, causing the

   cancellation of a scheduled lesson before the driving test. The processing of the

   writer's paperwork was delayed because of a computer problem. The driving school

   car wouldn't start, but the driver was able to use another car from the driving school

   to take the test. The writer passed the test and headed home for a nap.

COMPREHENSION
AND PRACTICE
4.4

collaboration

Maintenance of Chronological Order

1. The following sentences are part of a paragraph on a holiday celebration. They are presented here out of chronological order. Working with a class-mate, put the sentences in an order that makes sense, inserting numbers (1, 2, 3, etc.) in the spaces following the sentences.

Nobody takes the games seriously, so we spend most of the time yelling and laughing at our bad play.   5

We set up two gas grills and cook marinated steak, barbecued chicken and ribs, hot dogs, and the thickest, juiciest hamburgers around.   2

We have an afternoon of coed volleyball, croquet, and wiffle ball.   4

The mouth-watering aroma fills the whole neighborhood.   3

We all walk to Washington Park and join thousands of others who are waiting for the exciting fireworks display.   6

On the Fourth of July, my family hosts a big cookout for about fifty people, including grandparents, aunts, uncles, cousins, and friends.   1

2. Now write out the paragraph on a separate sheet of paper, adding transition to improve the flow. Use the list of transitional expressions on pages 67–68 as a guide. Answers will vary. Likely choices will include *Soon* at the beginning of sentence 3; *After that* at the beginning of sentence 4; and *Finally* at the beginning of sentence 6.

CHALLENGE 4.3   Evaluation of Chronological Order

1. Write a draft paragraph in which you tell the story of a particular holiday cel-ebration you enjoyed yourself or witnessed.

2. Make a copy of your draft paragraph and exchange it with a classmate. Assess the order of the paragraph you receive. Put a ✓ next to any point at which the time order isn't easy to follow and transition would improve the flow. Return the paragraph to the writer.

collaboration

3. Make any necessary adjustments to your paragraph, using your reader's com-ments to guide you.

Using Spatial Order   To explain the location of one object, person, or place in relation to another, use *spatial order*. Through this method of arrangement, you present information in a logical, easy-to-follow method—bottom to top, front to back, left to right, and so on—to make it easy for your reader to visualize a scene. Consider the use of spatial order in this paragraph about a campground:

When I was five, my family stayed in a campground so beautiful that I can still remember it clearly today. At the entrance, a one-room store where the owner sold food and camping supplies stood. Behind the shack was a playground area with a slide that seemed fifty feet high. To the left of the playground, a big grove of pine trees gave the whole area its wonderful pine scent. Picnic tables and stone fireplaces were spread throughout the grove. To the right along a curving road the campsites stood, each with water and electrical hookups in the front. My favorite spot was at the end of that road: the pond with the paddleboat that all the campers could use. For a child my age, no better place existed.

In this paragraph, spatial order makes it easy for the reader to visualize the entire campground. The store was *at the entrance.* The playground was *behind* the store, and a pine tree grove was to its *left.* Picnic tables and fireplaces were *throughout the grove,* and the campsites were on a curving road *to the right.* The pond was *at the end of that road.* Thanks to spatial order, the reader can take an imaginary stroll through the special place that the writer remembers so well.

COMPREHENSION
AND PRACTICE
4.5

Spatial Order

1. In your own words, explain spatial order.

   Spatial order is a method of arrangement through which you describe elements in

   terms of their location to each other.

2. With spatial order, in what ways can you present details so that they are logical and easy to follow?

   Answers will include bottom to top, left to right, and front to back.

COMPREHENSION
AND PRACTICE
4.6

Spatial Order Transition in a Paragraph

1. Read the following paragraph, look closely at the image on page 74, and answer the questions that follow it.

   Vincent Van Gogh's *The Starry Night* is one of the most recognizable and most beautiful paintings in the world. A greenish gray form dominates the left side of the painting. The image resembles a bush, shattered tree trunk, or castle turret. The brush strokes make the form appear to be flowing upward toward the sky. To the right below this shape, a small village appears, set against a hillside. The violet and purple of the hillside seem to spill down onto the buildings, with small squares of yellow indicating the life within the little cottages. A sky of swirling blue, violet, yellow, and white brush strokes hovers above the scene. Glowing yellow stars surrounded by circles of light hang in the sky. In the upper right corner, a yellow orange crescent moon casts its light on the world below. The scene is alive with color, so it's no wonder that the painting remains widely recognizable and popular.

Vincent van Gogh, Starry Night. 1889. Oil on canvas, 29 x 36 1/4". Acquired through the Lillie P. Bliss Bequest. (472.1941) Digital Image © The Museum of Modern Art/Licensed by SCALA/Art Resource, NY

a. Where is the crescent moon in relation to the village?

The crescent moon is to the right above the village.

b. Where is the hillside in relation to the greenish gray shape?

The hillside is to the right of the greenish gray shape, rising up from the village.

2. Circle transitional words that help to maintain spatial order. Select one of them and then, on the lines below, briefly explain how this expression helps you visualize the painting.

Answers will vary, but students will generally note that the transitional expression

specifies a particular area of the canvas.

CHALLENGE 4.4 Evaluation of Spatial Order Cues

collaboration

1. Take a classmate on a brief tour of a room in your home by using spatial order to describe it. As you speak, have your partner make a diagram or sketch of the room on a separate sheet of paper. Then switch roles and repeat the activity.

2. Is the sketch or diagram that your classmate made accurate? On the lines that follow, explain.

Answers will vary.

3. What transitional expressions that your classmate used helped you visualize the room? On the following lines, list them and then briefly explain how they helped you get a sense of the layout.

Answers will vary.

CHALLENGE 4.5 Spatial Order in Your Writing

1. Write a draft paragraph in which you explain a particular location that you remember from your childhood. Use the paragraph from pages 72–73 on the campground as a model.

collaboration

2. Make a copy of your draft paragraph and exchange it with a classmate. Assess the order of the paragraph you receive. Put a ✓ next to any point at which the spatial order isn't easy to follow and a transition would help bring the scene into clearer focus. Return the paragraph to the writer.

3. Make any necessary adjustments to your paragraph, using your reader's comments to guide you.

Ordering for Emphasis   In some paragraphs, especially those in which the primary purpose is to persuade, you want to present your supporting ideas in a way that provides the most impact. In other words, you will want to use *emphatic order*. With emphatic order, writers often begin with the least important details and end with the most significant information. This organization builds and holds the reader's interest in much the same way a play or story customarily does—by building to a climax. Consider the order of the supporting ideas in this paragraph advocating mandatory public service for all eighteen-year-olds:

> All 18-year-old citizens should have to register for a minimum of 500 hours of service to the government over a two-year period. For one thing, many other countries around the world already require service of young people, in many cases with a one- or two-year stint in the military. Government service for the equivalent of about seven weeks a year for two years is minor in comparison. Furthermore, various volunteer organizations, non-profit groups, environmental associations, schools, and so on desperately need help but can't afford to pay additional workers. Young people fulfilling this requirement can fill that need. In addition to the good feeling that comes with helping others, these young people would receive valuable, on-the-job training and experience. As with educational internships, a successful stint as a volunteer with an organization or agency could even lead to a paid position later on. Most important of all, we all have an obligation to support our country. Regardless of its flaws, the United States offers extraordinary freedoms and opportunities for success. To donate a little time in return is a small price to pay. The United States is a great country, and mandatory national service will ensure that it stays great for generations to come.

The supporting details and examples in this paragraph are arranged in emphatic order. A strong reason to require mandatory service at age eighteen is that, by comparison with other countries, the mandated sacrifice is small. More important, the need among volunteer or government organizations and institutions for additional help far outstrips their ability to pay. Even more significant, such service will greatly benefit the service workers, both in terms of personal satisfaction and experience and training. The strongest reason of all, however, is that the time commitment is small payment for all that the United States provides for its citizens. Arranged this way, these supporting details and examples draw and feed the reader's interest.

COMPREHENSION
AND PRACTICE
4.7

Aspects of Emphatic Order

1. On the following lines, briefly explain emphatic order.

Emphatic order involves presenting supporting details and examples in a way that

stresses their relative significance or importance.

2. Why is emphatic order a good choice for writings whose primary purpose is to persuade?

   Emphatic order is a good choice for persuasive writing because this arrangement

   draws and feeds the reader's interest.

3. Read the following paragraph concerning physician-assisted suicide. Circle the transitional expressions, consulting the lists on pages 67–68. Then, on the lines that follow, explain how these words help to maintain emphatic order.

   Physician-assisted suicide for terminally ill patients should be legalized. First of all, these patients know they are dying, and they should be able to exercise some control over their situations. If they choose not to prolong their suffering when they have no hope for survival, that's their business. More important, these patients have serious concern for their family members. The around-the-clock care for people suffering from the advanced stages of cancer or degenerative muscular diseases is unbelievably expensive. The emotional toll from watching a loved one die by inches is even more costly. Most important of all is the patients' loss of dignity. The terminally ill face absolute dependence on others as well as tremendous pain, with no hope of recovery. Why should they be forced to linger in life when a humane alternative is available?

   Students will likely agree that the transitional expressions indicate an increasing level

   of significance.

CHALLENGE 4.6 Emphatic Order in Your Writing

1. Write a draft paragraph in which you support or reject one of the following statements:
   a. The government should be able to block or censor objectionable material circulating on the Internet.
   b. Professional athletes should be allowed to use steroids if they want—the only people they are hurting are themselves.

c. An additional tax of at least ten cents a gallon should be added to the price of gasoline to convince consumers to purchase smaller cars with better gas mileage.

Use the paragraph about mandatory public service on page 76 as a model.

collaboration

2. Make a copy of your draft paragraph and exchange it with a classmate. Assess the order of the paragraph you receive. If you think the order should be adjusted to add particular emphasis to one of the supporting points, write a brief note explaining your reasoning. Also, put a + at any point where you think added transition will help the paragraph persuade, and then return the paragraph to the writer.

3. Make any necessary adjustments to your paragraph, using your reader's comments to guide you.

Effective Language

Your choice of words has a great impact on how well you communicate your ideas to your reader. When you reassess, you need to check your writing for **effective use of language.** Think of the words you choose as a window into your thoughts. A fogged-up window doesn't give anyone much of a view. Wipe that haze away, however, and the view is clear. To eliminate any fog in your writing, you need to use *specific* and *concise language.*

ESL Note
See "Confusing Words," pages 493–494, for a discussion of words that may present particular problems for you, and "Clarity," page 497, for more on the importance of keeping your language clear and specific.

Make Your Writing Specific When you think of *dog,* what image comes into your mind? Chances are that when you close your eyes, you see a particular dog, perhaps one you've owned or one familiar to you. Regardless of what kind of dog you picture, chances are that nobody else thinking of *dog* will have exactly the same picture in mind. That's because the word *dog* is a *general* word.

If you want your reader to visualize the same picture as you have in your mind, you need to replace general terms with *specific language.* To do this, you need to use words that are detailed and to the point. Instead of *dog,* write *the one-year-old, purebred pug with light brown fur named Mugwump.* Then your reader will be able to share your specific image.

Which details in the following paragraph about a terrible work experience help you better understand what the writer went through?

The dirtiest property I ever saw was a small cottage that I had to clean out last summer. The real estate agent who gave me the job had just purchased the one-acre plot on which the house was set. Her plan was to build another house on the property and convert the tiny 10-foot by 15-foot house into a garage. My job was to remove everything from the house and put it in a trash dumpster that was almost as big as the house. The place had been locked up for ten years, so when I opened the door, dust began swirling around, filling the air. Two of the three tiny rooms contained broken-down furniture covered with a thick layer of dust. A love seat and recliner with torn and stained cushions filled one room. The second room contained a heavily scratched mahogany bed with matching bureau. The remaining room was filled with just odds and ends and junk. This collection included a broken table lamp, empty paint cans, several foot-long pieces of aluminum siding, and two truck tires.

> Bundles of old newspapers filled one wall from floor to ceiling. The whole cleaning job took me almost ten hours and left me with aching muscles, grime-covered clothes, and dust-filled lungs.

You probably identified several details, including the size of the house—ten-foot by fifteen-foot—and the similarly sized dumpster. You also probably noted how long the house had been locked up—ten years—and the conditions that resulted from having the windows and door closed—dust-filled air. You also no doubt noted the stained, torn, scratched, and dust-covered furniture in two of the rooms and the listing of junk filling the third. Combined, these details make it easy to see what the writer faced on that long day of work.

Keep Your Writing Concise   As you reassess your draft, you also need to ensure that your writing is *concise*—brief but to the point. To streamline what you have written, you need to eliminate any *deadwood,* vague or general words that add no real meaning to your writing. Words such as *definitely, quite, extremely, somewhat,* and *a lot* are examples of deadwood. General words such as *very* and *really* are also examples of deadwood, especially when they are coupled with weak or imprecise terms such as *nice* or *warm.* Concentrate on selecting the best word or words for a particular situation, and always avoid phrasing that is unnecessarily wordy. Here is a list of common wordy expressions, with alternatives that say the same thing but more concisely:

Deadwood	Concise Version	Deadwood	Concise Version
due to the fact that	because	in order that	so
a large number	many	at the present time	now
in the near future	soon	take action	act
prior to	before	the month of October	October
completely eliminate	eliminate	give a summary of	summarize
come to the realization of	realize	mutual cooperation	cooperation
with the exception of	except for	make an assumption	assume

Now take a look at the following paragraph. Which words could be changed to make it more concise?

> The biggest challenge for today's high school students is always dealing with the constant peer pressure. As they are growing up, a large number of adolescents are unsure of themselves, and they really lack self-esteem. Some of these teenagers make poor decisions, especially relative to alcohol and drug use, due to the fact that they feel pressured to conform. They take chances to create an impression on others but often end up feeling even less confident as a result.

Several of the sentences are unnecessarily wordy. In the first sentence, for example, *always* is not needed because *constant* indicates the same thing. In the second sentence, *a large number of* can be replaced with the more concise version, *many.* In addition, *unsure of themselves* can be replaced with *insecure,* and *really* doesn't add any meaning to the sentence and should be eliminated. In the third sentence, *due to the fact that* can be changed to *because,* and *to create an impression* in the fourth sentence can be shortened to simply *impress.* Make these changes, and you have a more concise paragraph.

Specific and Concise Language

1. What can you do to make your writing more specific?

    Replace general words with words that are clear and precise and that offer enough detail.

2. What are two strategies you can use to make your writing more concise?

    You can eliminate words or phrases that aren't necessary. You can avoid using two or

    more words when one word will do.

3. Refer to the list of wordy phrases and concise alternatives on page 79. Then read the following paragraph, and on the lines that follow it, list all deadwood that appears in the paragraph. Next to each phrase, list a suitable alternative.

    People with food allergies have to be careful when it comes to eating out. Due to the fact that food at a restaurant is prepared fresh each time, it doesn't come with a full list of ingredients. Restaurant patrons aren't always aware of what has been used to prepare the food. Many people are especially sensitive to certain things, but they don't come to the realization about what's in their food until they start to eat. In some cases, this situation can turn deadly. Last year, for example, a woman on vacation in the Southwest died after eating at a small restaurant known for its award-winning chili. Her only food allergy was to peanut butter, so she made an assumption that the chili was safe to eat. Unfortunately, one of the secret ingredients in the chili was peanut butter. She died before the ambulance arrived.

    due to the fact that—because

    come to the realization about—realize

    made an assumption—assumed

Practice with Writing Specific, Concise Language

1. Revise these general words to make them concrete and specific.
    Answers will vary. Representative answers are given.

    a. a house

        a five-story brick apartment building

b. a computer

a seventeen-inch MacBook Pro

_____

_____

_____

2. Here is a paragraph explaining the effects that a fear of swimming can produce. Cross out any deadwood, and then, on a separate sheet of paper, write a more concise version of the entire passage. Rephrase portions if you believe that the new phrasing will improve the paragraph.
Representative deletions and changes are shown.

Every time I would ~~go to~~ try swimming ~~in the water~~, the same things

would happen. My heart would begin to pound ~~really, really hard in my chest~~,

and I would start to feel a _∧choke ~~feel a choking in my throat~~. Then my fingers ~~on my hands~~

would become numb. I would start to ~~kind of~~ shake, and my feet would feel as

if they were covered ~~over~~ with cement. Whenever I would walk toward the

deeper water ~~where the water was over my head~~, I would begin to feel as if I

was going to pass out ~~or something~~.

CHALLENGE 4.7 The Language in Your Writing

1. Write a draft paragraph in which you discuss a difficult work experience. Use the paragraph from pages 78–79 on cleaning out a filthy cottage as a model.

collaboration

2. Make a copy of your draft paragraph and exchange it with a classmate. Assess the language of the paper you receive. Circle any word or expression you think should be more specific or concise, and then return the paragraph to the writer.

3. Make any necessary adjustments to your paragraph, using your reader's comments to guide you.

Feedback from an Objective Reader

In addition to reassessing your draft yourself, you should also ask another reader for a reaction. This kind of analysis can help you gauge how well your words communicate your ideas. A classmate, friend, relative—anyone you can count on to read your work with an unbiased eye and respond honestly—can serve as your sounding board. Have your reader use the following **Reader Assessment Checklist,** which focuses on concerns you have already considered, to make this task easier. Answers to the same questions from an objective reader will tell you how effectively you have made your point.

✔ READER ASSESSMENT CHECKLIST

- ☐ Do you understand the point I am making?

- ☐ Do I stick to that point all the way through?

- ☐ Are all my ideas and examples clearly connected and easy to follow?

- ☐ Are the words I've used specific and concise?

- ☐ What changes do you think I should make?

Sample: Peer Response

Here again is the first-draft paragraph on things that would be preserved in a single shoebox, featured at the end of the previous chapter:

A Shoebox Full of Meaning

If I could keep only one shoebox full of belongings, I would select items with great personal or sentimental worth, not monetary value. I would stick in the ticket stubs and wristbands I have saved from all the concerts and sporting events I have ever attended. My favorite is from the first time I saw the Chicago Cubs at Wrigley Field. In 2009, the National Hockey League actually held one of its Winter Classic outdoor hockey games at Wrigley Field. I would add a photo CD with pictures from vacation trips and other special occasions. In addition, I would keep my niece's many crayon drawings and a couple of stories she wrote when she first started school. These pictures and stories illustrate the two of us doing things together like going to the playground and the beach. Finally, I would keep a coin bank in the shape of a Chevrolet Corvette, which used to sit on my grandfather's workbench. My grandmother gave it to me after my grandfather's funeral. Every time I look at it, it reminds me of him. The things I would keep have no monetary value, but I consider them the most valuable things I own because of the memories they hold.

Now consider this peer response to the draft:

> I like your paragraph. I think I would probably keep the same kinds of things myself. Your topic sentence definitely let me know where you were planning to go with this paragraph, and your language is pretty much clear and easy to understand. I think a couple of things would make the paragraph better. For one thing, the fourth sentence, the one about the hockey game the NHL held at Wrigley Field is about a different subject, so do you think it makes sense to eliminate it? Maybe you could add some details about the pictures on the CD, too—I'm really curious about that—and about the toy truck from your grandfather. I've put a ✔ where an additional transition would make your sentences flow better, too. I hope my comments help you.

The insights of an objective reader can be valuable. Such comments help identify what is already effective in a piece of writing and what still needs work.

COMPREHENSION
AND PRACTICE
4.10

The Usefulness of Feedback

1. Who is a suitable candidate to serve as your objective reader?

Anyone who will read and react to your writing with an unbiased eye, including a

classmate, friend, or family member, would make a good objective reader.

2. How can getting feedback from an objective reader improve your writing?

The reaction of an objective reader gives you a sense of how clearly and effectively

you have expressed your ideas, thus guiding you in improving your draft.

COMPREHENSION
AND PRACTICE
4.11

Difficulties in Giving and Receiving Feedback

1. Of the questions in the Reader Assessment Checklist on page 82, which one do you think is the most difficult to answer? On the following lines, identify this category and explain your reasoning.

Answers will vary. Many students will focus on the last question, noting that they don't

always know exactly how to improve the writing.

2. Suppose your reader finds an area of your writing that still needs work. On the lines that follow, explain how getting this feedback about your work would make you feel.

Answers will vary. Some students may feel unhappy or angry when faced with the

feedback, while others will say that they look forward to a reaction that will help them

improve their writing.

CHALLENGE 4.8 Objective Feedback

collaboration

1. In Challenge 3.7 on page 59, you completed a first-draft paragraph. Now make a copy of that draft or another draft paragraph you have created, and exchange it with a classmate.

2. Read through the draft you receive. Complete the following steps, using the Reader Assessment Checklist on page 82 as a guide.

   a. Put a + next to the topic sentence if it provides a clear direction. Put a ✓ if this main idea still isn't clear.

   b. Underline any section or sentence that disrupts the unity because it is not relevant to the main idea of the paragraph.

   c. Put an * at any point where additional transition would make the writing more coherent. If sentences should be reordered, number them to show the change you would make.

   d. Circle all vague words and deadwood, and write any suggested substitutes above the words.

3. Return the copy to the writer.

Redrafting

ESL Note
See "Clarity," page 497, for more on the importance of explaining your ideas more fully, in other words, of amplifying.

Once you have reassessed your draft paragraph, had someone else assess it, and identified any problems, you need to *redraft* it. In other words, you need to write a new version that addresses the issues you and your reader have noted.

Redrafting will be different for each paper you write. Sometimes you'll have to make adjustments in only one category of the Reader Assessment Checklist. Other times, you will need to make changes in several categories.

With many paragraphs, your task will be to *amplify*—to include information that effectively answers questions a reader might have. This might mean adding additional specific examples or details to support your point. It could also mean changing the wording of a detail or example so your reader can better visualize or understand it. Clarifying your ideas in this way will be worth the extra work because the paragraph will better express what you want to say.

Here again is the first draft on items that would be saved in a single shoebox. This time, however, the sentences are numbered and annotations are included. The annotations indicate the problem spots that need to be addressed before the paper fulfills its promise.

Some transition in sentence 2 would help.

Sentence 3 lacks specific detail. Amplify.

Sentence 4 isn't directly related to the topic— eliminate it.

A Shoebox Full of Meaning

(1) If I could keep only one shoebox full of belongings, I would select items with great personal or sentimental worth, not monetary value. (2) I would stick in the ticket stubs and wristbands I have saved from all the concerts and sporting events I have ever attended. (3) My favorite is from the first time I saw the Chicago Cubs at Wrigley Field. (4) In 2009, the National Hockey League actually held one of its Winter Classic

outdoor hockey game at Wrigley Field. (5) I would add a photo CD with pictures from vacation trips and other special occasions. (6) In addition, I would keep my niece's many crayon drawings and a couple of stories she wrote when she first started school. (7) These pictures and stories illustrate the two of us doing things together like going to the playground and the beach. (8) I would keep a coin bank in the shape of a Chevrolet Corvette. (9) My grandmother gave it to me after my grandfather's funeral. (10) The things I would keep have no monetary value, but I consider them the most valuable things I own because of the memories they hold.

This information in sentence 5 is vague and general. Amplify.

Some transition in sentence 8 would help.

Additional specific details in sentence 9 would help. Amplify.

As the annotations indicate, additional transition in several spots would improve the flow of the paragraph. In some cases, as with the second sentence, a single transitional expression can improve the coherence:

IMPROVED TRANSITION

For example, I would stick in the ticket stubs and wristbands I have saved from all the concerts and sporting events I have ever attended, especially from the first time I saw the Chicago Cubs play.

The notes also point out that the fourth sentence, the one about the outdoor hockey game, disrupts the unity of the paragraph. It should be eliminated.

Furthermore, the comments make clear that a couple of areas should be amplified—additional specific examples and details are needed. For instance, the eighth and ninth sentences provide little specific information about the special keepsake from a grandparent:

NONSPECIFIC

I would keep a coin bank in the shape of a Chevrolet Corvette. My grandmother gave it to me after my grandfather's funeral.

Now consider how much more effective the same material is once it has been amplified (and the transitional word **finally** has been included).

AMPLIFIED AND IMPROVED

Finally, I would keep a coin bank in the shape of a Chevrolet Corvette, **which used to sit on my grandfather's workbench.** My grandmother gave it to me after my grandfather's funeral. **That bank would take up almost a quarter of the box, but how could I not keep it?** Every time I look at it, it reminds me of him.

As these samples show, when you redraft, you fill in gaps and refine the points made in your initial draft. Redrafting takes time, but it is time well spent. The result will be a greatly improved piece of writing, one that more accurately expresses your message.

COMPREHENSION
AND PRACTICE
4.12

The Significance of Redrafting

1. What do you do when you redraft a paragraph?

   When you redraft a paragraph, you write a clearer, stronger version of it, including the

   corrections and improvements gathered through reassessment.

   _____

2. Why is this step of revising important?

   It helps the writer turn something good into something better.

   _____

   _____

COMPREHENSION
AND PRACTICE
4.13

Paragraph Assessment

1. Read the following paragraph and act as an objective reader. Using the Reader Assessment Checklist on page 82 and the sample peer response on page 82 to guide you, suggest changes to improve this paragraph. Write your suggestions on a separate piece of paper.

   Insomnia is a very frustrating experience. I can't sleep. I worry about how I will feel the next day. I know I will feel terrible. I worry so I can't relax. I can't go to sleep. Counting sheep doesn't help and drinking warm milk doesn't help. The most frustrating thing about insomnia is that I can't do anything about it except listen to the clock tick and wait for the alarm to go off.

2. Now, on a separate sheet of paper, use your own assessment to redraft this paragraph.

CHALLENGE 4.9 Redrafting Practice

1. For Challenge 4.8 (pp. 83–84), a classmate reassessed one of your drafts. Discuss the comments and suggestions with your classmate, asking for clarification and making sure you understand why your reader believes you should make the proposed changes.

2. Redraft your paragraph, addressing any weaknesses that you and your reader have identified. Use the redrafted examples from the paragraph on special possessions as a guide.

Avoid Plagiarism

As you redraft your writing, you may find that you'll need to amplify some of your supporting details with other people's ideas and words. This is acceptable as long as *you acknowledge that the additional material is not your own.* When you fail to tell your reader that the information actually came from somewhere else (for example, a print, video, or electronic source), you are guilty of **plagiarism.** When you plagiarize, you are passing off someone else's work as your own—this includes using someone else's actual words (called a **direct quotation)** or ideas. It also does not matter if you express the ideas in your own words or condense the basic thoughts and ideas of another (called a **paraphrase** and **summary**), either. If you fail to mention the material's *origin* in your paper, you have essentially committed a crime. Plagiarism is serious business—it is literary theft, and the penalty can range anywhere from failure on an assignment to failure in a course to dismissal from school. It makes no difference if the plagiarism is accidental. You are just as guilty of the crime.

Avoiding plagiarism is easy. First, if you plan to include information that is not your own, you simply have to record all the sources you are consulting (for example, books, Web sites, blogs, newspaper articles, DVDs, personal interviews, and so forth). In most cases, you will need to format this record of sources according to a particular style. Many styles exist, but throughout your college career, you will likely encounter these three: the Modern Language Association (MLA) style, the American Psychological Association (APA) style, and the Chicago Manual (CM) style. The style you use will depend on the subject, the course, and your instructor's preference; so, your second step is to consult your professor about which style to use.

Say you're writing a paper for your English class. Your professor will probably ask that you use the MLA style for **citing sources,** which is the standard style used in most English and writing courses. So, if you're citing (or referring to) an article in *Newsweek* magazine, record the name of the author and the page on which the article appears, and place these details in parentheses immediately after the information in the body of your paragraph (Ulrich 54). Note that only a last name is required. A full citation for the article will then appear in a section at the end of your paragraph or paper called Work Cited (or Work*s* Cited, if you've referred to more than one source):

Work Cited

Ulrich, Lars. "It's Our Property." *Newsweek* 5 June 2000: 54. Print.

If you've referred to an article online, or other electronic source, place the name of the author in parentheses (Boehlert) after the information in the body of your paragraph. Under Work(s) Cited, list the author, title of article in quotation marks, and name of Web site in italics. Conclude with a period, followed by the publisher, publication date, the medium, and access date. End with a period.

Work Cited

Boehlert, Eric. "Artists to Napster: Drop Dead!" *Salon.com.* Salon Media Group,

24 Mar. 2000. Web. 17 Oct. 2009.

If your list contains more than one source, make sure to cite each in alphabetical order (by author's last name, generally).

For additional guidance on how to properly cite a multitude of sources in various styles, consult your college library, your university writing or tutoring center, and your instructor. You can also visit the MLA, APA, and CMS Web sites for help online. Remember: Always acknowledge your sources. Plagiarism is never acceptable—never!

Editing

Up to this point, your primary area of concentration has been the message of your paper: the content. Your goal has been to generate a main point—a topic sentence—and plenty of good supporting examples and details. In addition, you've focused on making sure that the material is unified, coherent, and effectively phrased.

But good content isn't enough to make a piece of writing effective. To be wholly successful, it must be free from errors. In other words, the language you use must follow the rules of standard English. This step in revising is especially important because errors in form can negatively affect how people respond to your writing. Sentence errors or mistakes in agreement or spelling distract your reader. Instead of focusing on your good ideas, your reader is interrupted by the weaknesses in form. As a result, the quality of your content is overshadowed by the errors.

A Personal Proofreading System

It's simple: Good writing is the sum of solid content and correct form. Reassessing and redrafting ensure that your ideas are clear and complete. *Editing* enables you to express them correctly. Therefore, once you've identified and corrected content problems, you are ready to *proofread* your writing for errors in grammar, usage, spelling, punctuation, and capitalization.

The secret to effective proofreading is timing. Fatigue and familiarity with your own material increase the chances that you will overlook errors. You will see what *you meant to write* rather than what you have *actually written*. For instance, you may see *quite* even though what's really there is *quiet*. In some cases, you may see a word that isn't even on the page. You *intended* to write the word, so you mentally insert it when you read the sentence. It's important, then, to proofread when you are rested.

As you do more writing, you will discover which mistakes you are prone to make. For now, though, rely on the following Proofreading Checklist, which covers the most common mistakes writers make in form. Included with each listing is the abbreviation commonly used to identify the error when it appears in a piece of writing.

ESL Note
See "Sentence Basics,"
pages 483–485;
"Agreement," pages
487–489; "Spelling,"
pages 492–494;
"Confusing Verb Forms,"
pages 489–491;
"Clarity," page 497; and
"Revise to Correct
Errors," page 497, for
more on dealing with
these problem spots.

✓ PROOFREADING CHECKLIST

☐ Have I eliminated all sentence fragments? *(frag)*

☐ Have I eliminated all comma splices? *(cs)*

☐ Have I eliminated all run-on sentences? *(rs)*

☐ Is the spelling *(sp)* correct throughout?

☐ Is the verb tense *(t)* correct throughout?

☐ Do all subjects agree with their verbs? *(subj/verb agr)*

☐ Do all pronouns agree with their antecedents? *(pro/ant agr)*

Although this list covers many common concerns, it doesn't cover all possible sources of errors. For instance, you may have trouble with double negatives or punctuation. Don't worry if you do not yet understand these problems or how to solve them. Parts 2 through 5 of this book provide practice in identifying and eliminating various errors in form. In addition, the Sentence Skill Locator on the inside back cover shows you where to look for help with particular problems.

As you discover which of the categories you handle well and which ones still give you trouble, you can adapt the Proofreading Checklist so that it reflects your individual needs. That way, you'll establish a personal proofreading system you can use to check all your final drafts before handing them in for evaluation.

A Proofreading Partner

When it comes to checking your writing for errors, two sets of eyes are better than one. No matter how carefully you screen your own work, you sometimes overlook errors. A reader who hasn't invested the time and energy you have may be better able to find these errors. Although you might not notice that you wrote *beleive* instead of *believe,* your proofreading partner probably will.

In short, working with a proofreading partner will benefit you in two ways: First, it will help make your paper error-free. Second, it will help you develop your own proofreading skills.

Computer Tools

A computer can help you find and correct errors, especially spelling mistakes. If you use a computer, take advantage of the spelling and grammar checkers. These functions highlight misspelled words and detect serious sentence and agreement errors. They will then offer alternatives or solutions to correct the errors.

But keep in mind: Even computers make mistakes. You need to consider the suggested changes carefully. Remember—replacing a misspelled word with the wrong word is no improvement. Also, computers don't reason the way that humans do—at least not yet. They don't know, for example, that you meant *calm* when you wrote, "The ocean had been especially *clam* before the sudden storm struck." It also doesn't necessarily comprehend when one homophone is used in place of another, for example, "The woman running the courtesy booth went on her *brake* early, leaving the front of the store unattended." The correct word is *break,* but the computer may not catch the error.

Furthermore, these programs are not consistently reliable with issues like subject-verb agreement and sentence fragments. Sometimes, they seem to misread the subject, choosing a noun or pronoun closest to the verb rather than the word that is actually serving as the subject. In addition, some sentences, especially imperative or *command* sentences, are incorrectly labeled as sentence fragments.

The point of all this is simple: When it comes to proofreading, take advantage of all the tools available. Just make sure that you do one final proofreading, slowly and carefully, to catch any errors the computer may have missed.

COMPREHENSION
AND PRACTICE
4.14

The Importance of Editing

1. What effect do errors in form have on the overall effect of a piece of writing?

   Errors in form make a piece of writing less effective because they distract the reader

   from the content.

2. How does editing differ from reassessing and redrafting?

   In reassessing and redrafting, you concentrate primarily on content. In editing, your

   focus is on matters of form.

COMPREHENSION
AND PRACTICE
4.15

The Significance of Proofreading

1. Why is it important to proofread when you are rested?

   You shouldn't proofread when you are tired because fatigue increases the chance that

   you will overlook some mistake in form.

2. How can you develop a personal proofreading system?

   To develop a personal proofreading system, add the particular problem spots that

   appear in your own writing to the Proofreading Checklist.

3. How will working with a proofreading partner benefit you?

   Working with a proofreading partner will benefit you in two ways: (1) A proofreading

   partner will catch errors you miss. (2) You will become a better proofreader of your

   own work as you practice on a partner's work.

COMPREHENSION
AND PRACTICE
4.16

Personal Proofreading Strengths and Weaknesses

1. Which of the errors on the Proofreading Checklist on page 89 is a major problem spot in your writing? Why do you think you find this area difficult? Explain on the lines that follow.

Answers will vary.

2. Which of the problem spots on the Proofreading Checklist isn't a problem for you? Why do you think you find this aspect easy to deal with? Explain on the lines that follow.

Answers will vary.

CHALLENGE 4.10

Paragraph Improvement

1. Read the following paragraph. Put a ✓ above any errors.

> Getting contact lenses has made a tremendous difference in my life. First of all, contacts are far more convenent than glasses. Now I don't have to contend with wet or fogged up glasses. I also don't have to keep pushing it up my nose when my face gets sweaty, in addition, contact lenses have improved my vision. For the first time that I can remember. I can now look out of the sides of my eyes and see something this feature have been particularly useful when I am involved in sports and other outdoor activities. Most of all, I love the change they have make in my appearance. I never liked the way I looked in glasses, so wearing contact lenses has also boosted my self-confidence.

collaboration

2. Compare your findings with a classmate's. Then check your answers against the corrected version that appears on page 96. Make a note of any errors you had originally missed.

3. For Challenge 4.9 (pp. 86–87), you redrafted a paragraph. Using the Proofreading Checklist, proofread your own paragraph to identify any remaining errors, and then exchange it with a classmate.

4. Proofread your classmate's paper, using the Proofreading Checklist. Circle any errors, and then return the paper to the writer.

5. Correct any errors that you and your proofreading partner have noted on your work, and then submit the paper to your instructor.

A Final Draft

ESL Note
See "Writing Paragraphs," pages 496–497, for more on revising a paragraph.

So what happens when you follow all these steps? After you have successfully completed the three stages of the revision process, you have proven that you are ready to write a final draft. In preparing this draft, make sure that you have not only addressed any weaknesses identified during the reassessing and editing stages, but that you also present your paragraph in the proper format.

Formatting Your Paper   **Format** refers to the arrangement of the words on the page. In accordance with MLA guidelines, you should *double-space* your entire document. In addition, you need to indicate your last name and the page number in the upper-right corner (an element called a **running head**) in the *header* (or top) of the page. This running head must appear on each page of your document. In a word-processing program such as Microsoft Word, select and click on "View" from the toolbar. The drop-down menu will open and present you with a "Header and Footer" option. Click on that. The header of the document will open, allowing you to type in your last name and the page number. The program will then automatically include your last name and the appropriate page number in the header of each page that follows.

In addition to the running head, you will also need to include a four-line heading in the upper-left corner of the first page. This includes your full name on the first line, the name of the course on the second line, the instructor's name on the third line, and the date you submit the paper on the fourth line. Hit the return/enter key at least once, center the title, and hit return/enter again at least once. Then begin the paragraph, making sure to indent.

Now let's consider this final-draft version of "A Shoebox Full of Meaning."

Manchebo 1

Jamie Manchebo
English 010.40—Basic College Writing
Dr. Kelly
October 15, 2010

A Shoebox Full of Meaning

If I could keep only one shoebox full of belongings, I would select items

with great personal or sentimental worth, not monetary value. For example,

I would stick in the ticket stubs and wristbands I have saved from all the concerts and sporting events I have ever attended, especially from the first time I saw the Chicago Cubs play. I still remember the clutch two-run homer Sammy Sosa hit in the ninth inning to win the game. I would fill the rest of the box up with several other things. One would be a CD with about 100 photos from my childhood showing everything from vacations at Disneyworld and Yellowstone National Park to birthday parties to graduations. In addition, I would keep my niece's many crayon drawings and a couple of stories she wrote when she first started school. These pictures and stories illustrate the two of us doing things together like going to the playground and the beach. If I folded them up carefully, I'd still have almost half the box available. Finally, I would keep a coin bank in the shape of a Chevrolet Corvette, which used to sit on my grandfather's workbench. My grandmother gave it to me after my grandfather's funeral. That bank would take up almost a quarter of the box, but how could I not keep it? Every time I look at it, it reminds me of him. The things I would keep have no monetary value, but I consider them the most valuable things I own because of the memories they hold.

The weaknesses identified during reassessing have been addressed during redrafting (see the highlights). The paragraph also has been carefully edited to eliminate any errors in form. Thanks to this hard work, the final-draft version is clearly better than the first draft, as these instructor's comments indicate:

This version shows much improvement—and your first draft was already good. Congratulations. The added details about your visit to Wrigley Field and about the pictures on your CD make your reasons for including those items in your shoebox clearer for your reader. I especially like the new material about the keepsake your grandmother gave you. Through your added description, you are showing its importance, not just telling your reader that it's important to you. Also, the additional transition makes the ideas flow far more smoothly. Overall, this paragraph is an excellent first paper.

Journal Writing

Revising means carefully reconsidering a piece of writing with the goal of making it as good as it can be. Can you think of another situation in school, in your personal life, or at work when you reconsidered something and as a result ended up with a better solution? Consider this subject and then spend twenty to thirty minutes exploring the subject in your journal.

SPOTLIGHT PIECE

A SAMPLE FINAL DRAFT

Here's a revised paragraph about a peaceful place by Grace Trecarichi. (Grace's prewriting appeared on p. 25 of Chapter 2.) Grace, who plans to become a fourth-grade teacher, claims that college is "not as scary as it seemed at first. As long as you do all your work, you are bound to do well." As Grace sees it, being able to write well is central to academic and professional success: "Writing is more than just passing English class—it is something you will take with you throughout college. As for the job force, for me, it is something I need to really know extremely well. I can't teach children if I do not know what I am teaching." Read Grace's essay and the accompanying annotations, which focus on the unity, coherence, and effective language featured in her writing. Then answer the questions that follow.

Grace's **topic sentence** makes her focus clear for her reader.

The Beach on a Fall Evening: My Place of Peace

No other place puts me at ease the way the beach does. There is something so invigorating yet so comforting about it at the same time.

All the **supporting examples and details** are directly related to the main idea, maintaining unity.

Transitional words like these help to maintain **coherence**.

Grace employs **emphatic order**—the beach at dark appeals to her even more than the beach at sunset—to capture and sustain her reader's interest.

Uses of **specific language** like these help the reader visualize the scene.

Grace's **concluding sentence** effectively restates the significance of her main and supporting ideas.

I especially love to go to the beach on cool fall evenings to sit and relax. The experience is totally different from what it's like during the middle of the day in the summer. If I get there before the sun sets, I hear the occasional sound of seagulls crying back and forth. Personally, I love the sound of seagulls; something about it puts me in a calming trance. When it gets dark, the beach is even more beautiful to me. As I sit there in my sweatshirt and jeans, I kick off my shoes to feel the soft, cold sand between my toes. The waves sound like thunder crashing into the shore, a rhythm never to miss a beat. It feels so mysterious. I can hear the sound of the waves, but when I look all I can see is the empty darkness surrounding me. I can't tell what is out in the ocean or where it stops. All I see is the black starry sky and the black ocean. Relaxed, I can think clearly, and time seems to slip away. In these moments, I know that the beach will always be my place of comfort, no matter what time of year it is.

Exploration of the Reading

1. Grace expresses her paragraph's main idea in a topic sentence: *No other place puts me at ease the way the beach does.* On the lines that follow, explain how the supporting sentences explain her main idea.

   Most students will note that the sentences in the body of the paragraph all discuss

   aspects of the beach in the evening that Grace finds appealing.

   _____

   _____

   _____

   _____

collaboration

2. Working with a classmate, decide which area or example in Grace's paragraph is the most effective. Then on the lines that follow, explain what

about this particular detail or sentence makes it stand out more than the others.

Answers will vary. Some teams will identify Grace's discussion of the sound of the

seagulls at sunset because of the emotion it evokes. Most teams, however, will more

likely focus on one of more of the sentences in which Grace describes the beach at

darkness because of how beautifully she captures the scene.

3. Imagine that Grace is your classmate and she has asked you to assess her paragraph before she completes one more draft. Using the Reader Assessment Checklist on page 82, evaluate her essay. Then, on a separate sheet of paper, write a peer response to the paragraph, using the sample on page 82 as a model.

Understanding the Subject through Writing

In her paragraph, Grace says that a trip to the beach at night leaves her relaxed and able to think clearly. On a separate sheet, write a brief passage (50 to 100 words) that details what you do or where you go when you need to think clearly and why you think this strategy works for you.

Corrected Version of Challenge 4.10

Getting contact lenses has made a tremendous difference in my life. First of all, contacts are far more convenient *✓sp* than glasses. Now I don't have to contend with wet or fogged up glasses. I also don't have to keep pushing them *✓pro/ant agr* up my nose when my face gets sweaty. In *✓cs* addition, contact lenses have improved my vision. For the first time that I *✓frag* can remember, I can now look out of the sides of my eyes and see something. This *✓rs* feature has been *✓sub/verb agr* particularly useful when I am involved in sports and other outdoor activities. Most of all, I love the change they make *✓t* (or have made) in my appearance. I never liked the way I looked in glasses, so wearing contact lenses has also boosted my self-confidence.

FOR FURTHER EXPLORATION

1. Examine one of the following topics carefully through the prewriting technique you prefer.

   - The way you hope others will describe you twenty or thirty years from now
   - The potential problems involved in keeping a secret
   - The best bit of advice anyone ever shared with you

2. Identify a specific focus for discussion as well as the purpose you might fulfill in writing about the topic. Complete a draft of at least seven to ten sentences and then, following the guidelines outlined in this chapter, revise it.

collaboration

3. Exchange your draft with a classmate. Using the material in this chapter as a guide, evaluate the revised draft you receive. Note any problems that your partner may not have detected, and return the draft to the writer.

4. Edit your own draft again, eliminating any errors identified by your writing partner.

DISCOVERING CONNECTIONS

For this assignment, examine the picture and one of the following questions (or another that the picture suggests). After you prewrite and compose a draft paragraph of at least seven to ten sentences, use the steps you practiced in this chapter to reassess, redraft, and edit the paragraph.

A. How would you describe the teacher-student relationship depicted in the image? Can you think of an instructor, past or present, who made a lasting impression upon you? Was it positive or negative? Why?

B. Organizations such as Big Sister or Big Brother exist to provide children and teenagers with positive adult influences. Have you ever volunteered to work with such an organization or dedicated your free time to helping others? What was the experience like?

RECAP Revising: Refining Your Draft

Key Terms in This Chapter	Definitions
revise	to refine and polish a draft
reassess	to evaluate writing to see what works and what doesn't
redraft	to create a new version of a piece of writing by correcting problems and incorporating new material into the original draft
amplify	to add details or examples to make your meaning clearer
edit	to check language in a piece of writing to eliminate errors in grammar, usage, spelling, punctuation, and capitalization
unified	focused on one subject

Key Terms in This Chapter	Definitions
coherent	clearly connected and effectively arranged or organized
transitions	words or expressions that connect ideas and show relationships between them
synonyms	words that are different from one another but have a similar meaning
effective language	language that is specific (detailed and to the point) and concise (brief but clear)
reader assessment checklist	series of questions to help an objective reader evaluate a draft
plagiarism	to include material without acknowledging the author
direct quotation	to use someone's exact words within quotation marks
paraphrase	to express another's ideas in your own words.
summary	to reduce greatly an original passage
citing sources	to let your reader know the origin of included material in accordance with an accepted system of documentation such as the Modern Language Association (MLA) method
format	the way a document is arranged on a page
running head	the writer's last name and page number, positioned in the upper-right corner of each page of a document

The Process of Revising

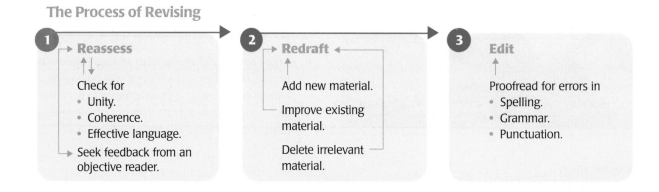

1 → Reassess ↑↓

Check for
• Unity.
• Coherence.
• Effective language.
→ Seek feedback from an objective reader.

2 → Redraft ←

Add new material.

Improve existing material.

Delete irrelevant material.

3 Edit ↑

Proofread for errors in
• Spelling.
• Grammar.
• Punctuation.

Using Discovery Online with MyWritingLab

For more practice revising, go to www.mywritinglab.com.

CHAPTER 5

Moving from Paragraph to Essay

GETTING STARTED...

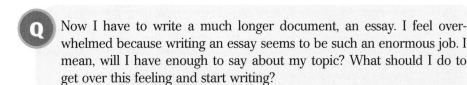

Q Now I have to write a much longer document, an essay. I feel over-whelmed because writing an essay seems to be such an enormous job. I mean, will I have enough to say about my topic? What should I do to get over this feeling and start writing?

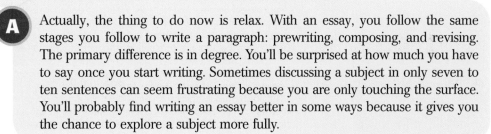

A Actually, the thing to do now is relax. With an essay, you follow the same stages you follow to write a paragraph: prewriting, composing, and revising. The primary difference is in degree. You'll be surprised at how much you have to say once you start writing. Sometimes discussing a subject in only seven to ten sentences can seem frustrating because you are only touching the surface. You'll probably find writing an essay better in some ways because it gives you the chance to explore a subject more fully.

Overview: The Difference between a Paragraph and an Essay

As a student and as a working professional, you will often have to write longer pieces of writing. Among the most common college writing assignments you will face are **essays**, multiparagraph writings that deal with a subject in greater detail than is possible in a single paragraph.

The most significant difference between a paragraph and an essay is *scope*. An essay covers a subject more thoroughly, exploring multiple facets and angles in fuller detail. But the writing process is the same for an essay as for a paragraph. You'll be able to apply what you have already learned about paragraph writing to essay writing.

Navigating This Chapter In this chapter you will learn what you need to know about writing an essay, including:

- the structure of an essay
- the stages of essay writing: prewriting, composing, and revising
- the importance of the thesis
- the importance of meeting your reader's needs
- the role of the introduction and conclusion

Essay Structure

An essay is a multiparagraph document consisting of three parts: an *introduction*, a *body,* and a *conclusion.*

The Structure of an Essay

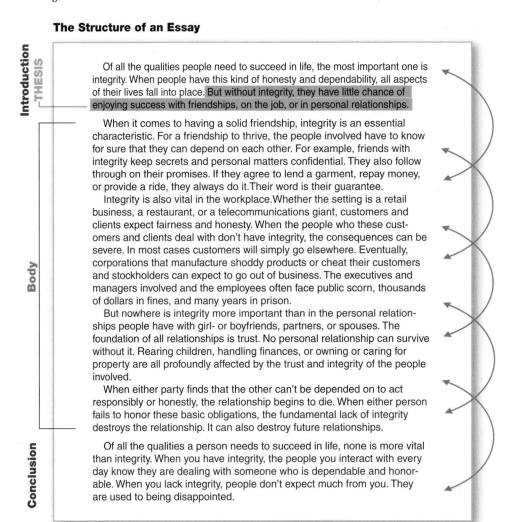

Introduction — THESIS

Of all the qualities people need to succeed in life, the most important one is integrity. When people have this kind of honesty and dependability, all aspects of their lives fall into place. But without integrity, they have little chance of enjoying success with friendships, on the job, or in personal relationships.

Body

When it comes to having a solid friendship, integrity is an essential characteristic. For a friendship to thrive, the people involved have to know for sure that they can depend on each other. For example, friends with integrity keep secrets and personal matters confidential. They also follow through on their promises. If they agree to lend a garment, repay money, or provide a ride, they always do it. Their word is their guarantee.

Integrity is also vital in the workplace. Whether the setting is a retail business, a restaurant, or a telecommunications giant, customers and clients expect fairness and honesty. When the people who these customers and clients deal with don't have integrity, the consequences can be severe. In most cases customers will simply go elsewhere. Eventually, corporations that manufacture shoddy products or cheat their customers and stockholders can expect to go out of business. The executives and managers involved and the employees often face public scorn, thousands of dollars in fines, and many years in prison.

But nowhere is integrity more important than in the personal relationships people have with girl- or boyfriends, partners, or spouses. The foundation of all relationships is trust. No personal relationship can survive without it. Rearing children, handling finances, or owning or caring for property are all profoundly affected by the trust and integrity of the people involved.

When either party finds that the other can't be depended on to act responsibly or honestly, the relationship begins to die. When either person fails to honor these basic obligations, the fundamental lack of integrity destroys the relationship. It can also destroy future relationships.

Conclusion

Of all the qualities a person needs to succeed in life, none is more vital than integrity. When you have integrity, the people you interact with every day know they are dealing with someone who is dependable and honorable. When you lack integrity, people don't expect much from you. They are used to being disappointed.

The Introduction

The **introduction** of an essay is usually a single paragraph that indicates the subject and direction of the paper. This paragraph sparks interest, compelling your reader to continue reading. In one document that you may prepare, called the **five-paragraph essay,** the introduction raises three specific points about a topic that the body then discusses in detail. The key part of the introduction is the **thesis,** the element that specifies the subject and focus of the entire essay. Just as a topic sentence serves as the main idea for a paragraph, the thesis serves as the main idea for an entire essay.

The Body

The **body** of an essay is the series of paragraphs that follow the introduction and support and illustrate the thesis. The number of paragraphs that comprise the body depends on the specific focus and direction of the writing. In a five-paragraph essay, the body consists of three paragraphs. Each paragraph discusses in detail one of the three points identified in the introduction. This type of essay can be used to effectively complete timed assignments such as essay examinations or writing assessments.

Of course, in many essays, the body may be longer, in some cases totaling ten or more paragraphs, depending on the focus and direction of the writing. Regardless of the number, however, each paragraph must contain a clear topic sentence and supporting details, all relating to the thesis.

The Conclusion

The **conclusion** of an essay, which comes after the body, is a paragraph that strengthens the overall message of the thesis and the supporting examples and details. This paragraph brings the essay to a logical and appropriate end, restating or summing up the *significance* of the essay. The figure on the preceding page shows the structure of an essay.

Notice that the introduction contains the *thesis*—the main point in sentence form—and the conclusion restates or reemphasizes it. Notice also that the arrows between paragraphs point in both directions, signifying that the paragraphs relate to each other as well as to the thesis expressed in the introduction and reemphasized in the conclusion.

COMPREHENSION AND PRACTICE 5.1

Essay Structure

1. In your own words, explain the structure of the essay.

   An essay includes three sections: the introduction, which features the thesis; the body,

   which consists of paragraphs that support the thesis; and the conclusion, which

   restates the significance of the essay.

2. What role does the introduction play in an essay?

   The introduction presents the main idea and prepares the reader for the material to

   follow in the body.

3. What is the purpose of the conclusion?

   The conclusion serves to emphasize the significance of the points presented in the

   essay.

CHALLENGE 5.1 **Development of Essay Awareness**

1. What do you think you will find most difficult about writing an essay rather than a paragraph? Why? On the lines below, briefly explain your reasoning.

   Answers will vary. Most students, however, will admit to feeling intimidated about

   producing a paper that is considerably longer than the paragraphs they have

   developed so far.

collaboration

2. Working with a classmate, choose an essay from Part 6, "Discovering Connections through Reading." After you both read the piece, write the title of the essay on a separate sheet of paper, and then below it, explain how the paragraphs in the body support the main idea expressed in the reading's introduction.

The Essay Writing Process

When you write an essay, you explore a subject far more thoroughly than you do with a paragraph, but you still employ the same process: *prewriting, composing,* and *revising.* Writing an essay, like writing a paragraph, is *recursive,* which means that you often need to repeat steps.

Prewriting

The first stage of essay writing is prewriting, during which you generate the ideas you'll need to complete your essay. In Chapter 2, you discovered which prewriting technique—or combination of techniques—you prefer. You prewrite to generate supporting ideas and develop a well-focused topic for your essay, just as you do when you write a paragraph.

ESL Note
See "Unity," page 496, for more on the importance of keeping your writing on target; "Clarity," page 497, for more on the importance of keeping your writing clear; and "The Needs of Your Reader," page 496, for the importance of providing details that your reader needs to understand your point.

Composing

Once you know what you are going to write about and have developed examples and details to support your point, you move to the second stage of writing, *composing.* When you compose, you transform your prewriting material into sentences and arrange your sentences into paragraphs while also

- developing an effective thesis
- recognizing the needs of your reader
- creating an effective introduction and conclusion

Developing an Effective Thesis   During the composing stage, you draft the **thesis**, a signpost in sentence form that lets the reader know what is to come. A topic sentence states the main idea of a paragraph, but a thesis states the main idea of the *entire* essay. Like a topic sentence, an effective thesis generally has two parts: a *subject* and the *writer's attitude or opinion about* or *reaction to* that subject.

Imagine that you have been asked to write about the issues associated with driving. Having encountered some ridiculously aggressive driving in your life, you settle on the subject of *road rage*. After prewriting with this focus in mind, you develop the following thesis:

EFFECTIVE THESIS

——————————— Subject ———————————
This kind of behavior, known as road rage,
——————— Attitude or Opinion ———————
is a *growing problem on today's roads and highways.*

This thesis is effective because it features both a subject and an attitude or opinion about the subject.

Keep in mind that an effective thesis is *not*

- an **announcement** of your intent, featuring words such as *I plan, I intend,* or *This paper concerns*:

INEFFECTIVE THESIS   I want to talk about the problem of road rage.

- a **simple statement of fact:**

INEFFECTIVE THESIS   Road rage is a violent overreaction to problems encountered while driving.

- a **title:**

INEFFECTIVE THESIS   Road Rage: The Newest Highway Threat

ESL Note
See "The Needs of Your Reader," page 496, for the importance of providing details that your reader needs to understand your point.

Recognizing Your Reader's Needs   To create an effective draft essay, you need to select the most promising prewriting ideas, group any related points, and fully develop them. How you arrange the material is also important. The goal is to present your ideas in the way that best expresses or supports the thesis.

The secret here is to keep your reader's needs in mind so that your writing will be *reader centered.* As Chapter 3, "Composing," explained, you often know a great deal about your subject. When you conclude that your reader automatically shares your specific background and frame of reference, you may fail to provide enough information. The result is *writer-centered writing*—it makes sense to you, but it isn't sufficiently clear or complete to make sense to someone else.

The trick to meeting the needs of your reader is to consider what you knew about the subject *before* you learned about it. For example, how much specific information did you need to understand the issue of road rage fully? What specific examples and details best illustrate the issue of road rage for you? Provide this kind material, expressed in complete sentences, and your writing will be reader centered.

The Thesis and the Needs of the Reader

1. What are the two parts of the thesis?

   The two parts of the thesis are the subject and the writer's attitude or reaction to that

   subject.

2. Briefly explain the difference between writer-centered and reader-centered writing.

   Writer-centered writing makes sense to the writer only. It lacks the kinds of information

   that someone without the writer's background and experience needs to understand

   the point. Reader-centered writing contains sufficient information to allow someone

   without the writer's background to understand it.

An Effective Thesis

1. Turn each of the following into an effective thesis: Answers will vary. Representative answers are shown.

   a. The discharge of heated water from the Commonwealth Power Plant has been linked to a decline of two types of fish in the Taunton River.

      The owners of the Commonwealth Power Plant should be forced to pay a fine and

      restore the stocks of two types of fish that discharge waters have reduced.

   b. I plan to show that reading to toddlers will help them develop a love of books.

      Reading to toddlers can go a long way in helping them develop into lifetime readers.

  c. Most newspapers now publish a complete electronic version of their paper, available before the paper copy.

> The move by a number of major U.S. newspapers to publish a complete electronic
>
> version may mean the beginning of the end for traditional paper newspapers.

_____

  d. Cooperative Education: Gaining Academic Credit and Valuable Work Experience

> Cooperative education courses represent a great way to learn and to develop job
>
> skills.

_____

  e. I want to talk about the increasing popularity of Twittering—brief online updates of activities in real time.

> Twittering has opened a window for the public into a number of fields, with
>
> professionals, for example, surgeons, sharing tweets as they do their jobs.

_____

2. On a separate sheet of paper, prewrite to develop at least three supporting ideas for one of these theses.

CHALLENGE 5.2   Support for a Thesis

collaboration

1. Consider the following thesis: *One of the best ways for the average person to live a greener life is also one of the simplest: basic energy conservation.* Working with a classmate or writing group, make a list on a separate sheet of paper of several details and examples that could be used to support this thesis.

2. In your view, what is the most important personal quality? Prewrite, and then, on a separate sheet of paper, isolate the most promising ideas. Develop a thesis, similar to the sample thesis on road rage, and at least three supporting ideas that address your issue.

ESL Note
See "The Needs of Your Reader," page 496, for more on the role of an effective introduction and conclusion.

An Effective Introduction and Conclusion An essay contains two paragraphs that perform specialized functions: the *introduction* and the *conclusion.* The introduction contains the thesis, engages the reader, and previews the structure of the essay. Where you place the thesis depends on your intent and your reader's needs. In some cases, the thesis works best as the first or second sentence of the introduction. This arrangement lets your reader know the point of the essay from the start. Other times, however, the thesis is most effective at the end of the introduction, serving as a bridge to the body, as this introduction for the essay about road rage illustrates:

You've probably witnessed the behavior yourself. You are in a car someplace, stalled in traffic. After a minute or two, someone behind you begins honking the horn, revving the engine, and yelling and swearing out the window. In some cases, the driver even gets out of the car and walks up to where the traffic is stalled and begins yelling and gesturing. The actions may even escalate until the driver is pounding or kicking the other car and perhaps physically fighting with other drivers. *This kind of behavior, known as road rage, is a growing problem on today's roads and highways.*

Several techniques can help you develop an effective introduction. For example, along with the thesis, you can include

- an **anecdote**—a brief, entertaining story that emphasizes the thesis
- pertinent facts or statistics
- a relevant saying or quotation
- a **rhetorical question**—a type of question not to be answered, but to provoke thought or discussion

The conclusion summarizes the point of the essay and brings it to a logical and appropriate end. It is the writer's last word on the subject, a final thought or a question for the reader to consider. In general, conclusions don't present new information in detail. New thoughts and ideas should be developed in the body, not the conclusion.

As with an introduction, sometimes an anecdote that embodies the point of the paper can conclude an essay. Other times, a relevant question or quotation will be the best alternative. The technique that helps you bring the essay to an effective close is the correct choice for that essay.

Here, for instance, is the conclusion for the essay on road rage:

Life is full of annoyances, and people need to learn how to deal with them, especially when it comes to driving. But for some people, irritation on the road quickly grows to enormous proportion. When it does, simple annoyance becomes road rage, and the results are bound to be unpleasant and, sometimes, deadly.

Introductions and Conclusions

1. How can you ensure that your reader knows the point of your essay from the start?

   You can ensure that your reader knows right from the start what your essay is about

   by making the thesis the first or second sentence in the introduction.

2. What techniques do writers often use in combination with a thesis to create an effective introduction?

   Writers often use one or more of the following techniques: an anecdote, pertinent

   facts or statistics, a relevant saying or quotation, or a rhetorical question.

3. Why should you generally not include new information in the conclusion of an essay?

You generally don't include new ideas in the conclusion because they can't be

developed fully. The place for such development is in the body.

Revising

The final stage in the writing process is *revising*. When you revise, you refine and polish your draft essay, turning something good into something better. Before you revise, however, take a break from your draft for a day or so. This time away creates a distance and enables you to bring a rested and refreshed eye to this vital part of the writing process.

You revise an essay the same way you revise a paragraph: you *reassess*, *redraft*, and *edit*.

ESL Note
See "Unity," page 496, for more on the importance of keeping your writing on target; "Clarity," page 497, for more on the importance of keeping your writing clear; and "The Needs of Your Reader," page 496, for the importance of providing details that your reader needs to understand your point.

Reassessing   As with a paragraph, when you reassess an essay, you make sure it is
- *unified*—all examples and details must be directly connected
- *coherent*—all the material must have clear transitions, be expressed in standard English, and be arranged in a logical order
- *effectively worded*—all ideas must be specific and concise

Asking an objective reader for a reaction to your paper is also a great idea. This person is not involved in writing the paper and so can offer a fresh view. Choose someone who will respond honestly and intelligently to your work, and then suggest that your reader use the following Essay Assessment Checklist to evaluate your draft.

✓ESSAY ASSESSMENT CHECKLIST

☐ Do you understand the point I am making? Does my thesis clearly state the subject along with my opinion or attitude about it?

☐ Do I stick to that point all the way through?

☐ Are all my ideas and examples clearly connected and easy to follow?

☐ Are the words I've used specific and concise?

☐ What changes do you think I should make?

Take a look at this first-draft version of a paragraph from the essay on road rage:

Occasional annoyance while driving is normal. What makes road rage different from normal annoyance is the degree of emotion involved. When road rage hits, it's like the unexpected eruption of a volcano. At one moment, things are normal. Then there is an incident of some kind. Suddenly, a formerly

calm driver is completely transformed.

It's not that the paragraph doesn't hold potential. For one thing, the paragraph is related to the thesis, so it doesn't disrupt the unity of the essay. At this point, however, it is too limited to be wholly effective.

ESL Note
See "Clarity," page 497, for more on the importance of keeping your writing clear.

For instance, this draft paragraph doesn't define or explain what *normal* means relative to anger. It also doesn't adequately detail what may instigate such behavior or what actions affected drivers may take. Comments from an objective reader, highlighted here, point out the same concern:

I know what you mean about road rage—a lot of people out there driving just seem out of control! I think your main point is clear, and both your introduction and your conclusion are good. I found a couple of spots that you might want to go back over, though. I think the second paragraph would be even stronger if you explained what these crazy drivers do when they get upset. Also, the example about the guy with the crossbow is great. I remember hearing that story. What kind of lunatic shoots somebody else with an arrow because of bad driving!! Maybe you could explain it in greater detail to make it stand out even more. That's about it from me. I hope my comments help.

Adding specific details—**amplifying**—will address this problem.

Redrafting With the weaknesses in your essay identified, you can begin *redrafting*. When you redraft, you address any problems that you and your objective reader identified in terms of unity, coherence, logical order, and specific language. In many cases, you also amplify, providing additional examples and details to bring a scene or situation into better focus for your reader.

Consider this redrafted version of the second paragraph from the essay on road rage:

Occasional annoyance while driving is normal. What makes road rage different from normal annoyance is the degree of emotion involved. When road rage hits, it's like the unexpected eruption of a volcano. At one moment, traffic on a street or highway is moving along smoothly enough. Then there is an incident of some kind. Maybe it's a driver on a phone, drifting across lanes, or a car moves to the passing lane but begins to travel at or below the speed limit. Suddenly, a formerly calm driver is completely transformed, screaming, leaning on the horn, gesturing wildly, and driving

dangerously, sometimes even cutting off whoever caused the problem in the

first place.

A number of changes that improve the paragraph have been made, as the highlighted sections show. This new material explains what *normal* means in this context, as well as specifies what triggers road rage and illustrates how enraged drivers often behave. The result is a much clearer, more complete view for the reader.

Editing   The final step in revising an essay, as in revising a paragraph, is *editing,* during which you eliminate any remaining grammatical errors. The Proofreading Checklist that appears on page 89 of Chapter 4 lists several of the most common writing problems, along with the abbreviations commonly used to call out these errors in a piece of writing. Use that list to identify specific weaknesses in your essay.

If this list doesn't fully reflect the errors that most trouble you, adapt the list so that it includes your own particular problem areas. Use the resulting personal proofreading list every time you write, whether it's an essay, a term paper, a blog, a posting on a message board, a letter, and so on.

Another excellent technique is to work with a proofreading partner, someone who will look for errors with a fresh perspective. If you are using a computer, take full advantage of any spell checking or style checking features. Keep in mind, however, that these tools are far from foolproof. For example, if you use the wrong homonym—*waist* instead of *waste* or *here* instead of *hear*—the error may go undetected. Also, sometimes a perfectly correct imperative or command sentence is incorrectly identified as a fragment. Therefore, after using these functions, always carefully proofread your paper one more time.

COMPREHENSION AND PRACTICE 5.5

The Value of Editing

1. Why should you give yourself a break between the composing and revising stages of writing?

   You should take some time between composing and revising in order to bring a rested eye to the process.

2. What does it mean to *amplify?*

   To amplify means adding or specifying details and examples.

3. How can having an objective reader help you improve your draft?

   An objective reader has not been involved in writing the essay and so can offer

   a fresh perspective.

4. Briefly explain the purpose of editing.

   The purpose of editing is to eliminate any remaining errors in form.

The Essay Writing Process: A Sample

The following figure summarizes the process you follow when you write an essay. The arrows in the figure indicate the recursive nature of the process. In other words, if you discover a gap or weakness during reassessing, you return to prewriting to generate material to address this problem. Then you move again to composing to turn those ideas into complete sentences.

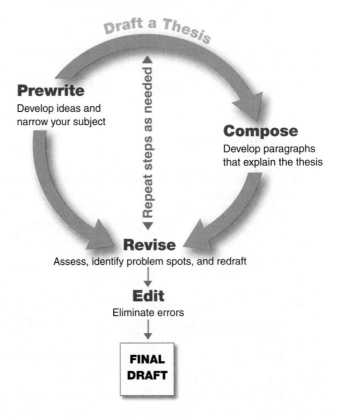

The Process of Writing an Essay

The final-draft essay about road rage is an example of the product that results from this process. Note the annotations, which emphasize the key points in the essay.

Road Rage: The Anger That Can Kill

Notice how the introduction prepares the reader for the paragraphs to follow.

You've probably witnessed the behavior yourself. You are in a car someplace, stalled in traffic. After a minute or two, someone behind you begins honking the horn, revving the engine, and yelling and swearing out the window. In some cases, the driver even gets out of the car and walks up to where the traffic is stalled and begins yelling and gesturing. The actions may even escalate until the driver is pounding or kicking the other car and perhaps physically fighting with other drivers. This kind of behavior know as road rage, is a growing problem on today's roads and highways.

Placed here, the thesis serves as a bridge to the supporting paragraphs.

This first paragraph of the body offers support for the thesis by explaining how road rage differs from ordinary annoyance.

Occasional annoyance while driving is normal. What makes road rage different from normal annoyance is the degree of emotion involved. When road rage hits, it's like the unexpected eruption of a volcano. At one moment, traffic on a street or highway is moving along smoothly enough. Then there is an incident of some kind. Maybe it's a driver on a phone, drifting across lanes, or a car moves to the passing lane but begins to travel at or below the speed limit. Suddenly, a formerly calm driver is completely transformed, screaming, leaning on the horn, gesturing wildly, and driving dangerously, sometimes even cutting off whoever caused the problem in the first place.

This second paragraph of the body supports the thesis by discussing a key factor of road rage: the inability to recognize the random elements involved in most traffic problems.

When people suffer from road rage, they seem to have no sense of perspective or intent. A traffic delay because of rush hour traffic is no one's fault. Even a jackknifed 18-wheeler that shuts down a highway for hours is not intentional. It is simply an unfortunate accident. But when road rage takes over, the affected drivers seem to think that the delay is deliberate, directed specifically at them, and they respond as if they have been personally attacked. The reaction is the same intense, unreasonable anger.

Unfortunately, road rage sometimes extends beyond simply honking a horn repeatedly or driving aggressively. In fact, road rage can lead to serious violence, escalating until someone has been killed. A few years ago in New England, for example, a driver became convinced that another driver had deliberately cut him off. He chased the other car at high speed for several miles. Eventually, he forced the other car off the road. Then he took a hunting bow out of his trunk and shot the other driver to death.

Life is full of annoyances, and people need to learn how to deal with them, especially when it comes to driving. But for some people, irritation on the road quickly grows to enormous proportion. When it does, simple annoyance becomes road rage, and the results are bound to be unpleasant and, sometimes, deadly.

This third paragraph of the body supports the thesis by providing an example of the severe consequences that can occur as a result of road rage.

The conclusion brings the essay to a logical close by restating the significance of the thesis about road rage and the supporting examples constituting the body.

Clearly, this essay is a successful piece of writing, as these instructor's comments indicate:

Congratulations-you have done a fine job revising your paper. From the time when I saw the first draft a week ago in conference, you made a number of great changes. I especially like how you have amplified. The new details about intent and perspective in the third paragraph and about that terrible incident involving the hunting bow bring your subject into even greater focus. If you want to develop the paper further, you might consider adding another category or two about road rage, perhaps dealing with the way drivers sometimes behave in mall parking lots or when leaving concerts or sporting events. Remember – an essay doesn't have to be only five paragraphs long. In any case, what you have here is already good – you should consider submitting it for our class anthology.

The Essay Writing Process

1. On the lines below, briefly explain the recursive nature of essay writing.

   The recursive nature of writing means that writers generally need to return to earlier

   stages in the writing process to eliminate weaknesses identified during reassessing.

2. Assume that a classmate has written the essay on road rage. On a separate sheet of paper, review it, briefly giving your reaction to the essay and listing any suggestions for change.

CHALLENGE 5.3 ## The Complete Essay

1. Now it's your turn. For Challenge 5.2 (page 105), you prewrote on what you considered the most important personal quality, isolated the key ideas, and developed a thesis. Now, with this material as your foundation, create an essay of at least five paragraphs. Use the essay on road rage as a model.

collaboration

2. Exchange your draft essay with a classmate. Evaluate the draft you receive, using the Essay Assessment Checklist on page 107, and return the draft to the writer.

3. Redraft your essay, considering the assessment your objective reader has supplied.

collaboration

4. Exchange your redrafted essay with a classmate who has not previously seen it. Check the essay you receive for any remaining errors in form, using the Proofreading Checklist on page 89. Return the draft with your comments to the writer.

5. Correct any errors in form identified by your reader, and hand your paper in for grading.

Journal Writing

The move from paragraph writing to essay writing involves covering a subject more thoroughly. Consider some other situation that involves a movement from something limited to something more extensive. For example, was there a time when you moved from working part time to full time? Or did you go from playing a sport or music as a hobby and then become part of an organized team, league, band, or organization? Maybe it was a personal relationship that went from being casual to serious and exclusive. What did the change from one stage to the other feel like? Consider this subject and then spend 20 to 30 minutes exploring it in your journal.

CONSIDERING A FINAL DRAFT

SPOTLIGHT PIECE

Here's a short essay by Vanessa Pareja about an important decision that she made—and that she has since questioned. For Vanessa, the adjustment to life and school in the United States has meant a great deal of hard work, especially since she had limited experience with English before her family moved here from Bolivia. But she is quick to add that the work is definitely worth it, that developing strong skills in spoken and written English will be the key to her success as a student and a professional. Read Vanessa's essay and the accompanying annotations, which focus on the elements that make up the essay. Then answer the questions that follow.

Vanessa's **introduction** prepares her reader for the discussion to follow in the body of her essay.

Her **thesis** specifies her main point.

A Time I Wondered If I Made the Correct Decision

Have you ever made a decision under the influence of someone you respected and in the end realized that it might not have been the best thing for you? A few years ago, I had the chance to study at the University of Argentina. However, I eventually turned it down because of my mother's disapproval, and I ended up wondering if I made the right decision.

When I finished high school in Bolivia, I had the opportunity to pursue higher education in Argentina for free. I was so happy with this chance that, when I finished my high school, I started to prepare all my application papers. However, my mother was not too happy when she saw that I had everything prepared and was determined to head out to Argentina.

To try to convince me not to go, my mother came up with a list of all the inconveniences that I would face during my journey. She said that in Argentina, I would have to live with my aunt and to deal with different rules, economic limitations, and my three cousins. She made me think back upon my previous trip to Argentina, especially on my three very loving and friendly but very disorganized cousins. On one hand, they were always thinking of others and looking after them. If their mother or someone else needed any help, they would always be there. On the other hand, I recalled that although my aunt would send my cousins to clean their room and do the dishes, they would not do it. Their room could be falling apart, their clothes piled up from not doing the laundry, the kitchen filled with dirty plates, but they still would not straighten things out.

Most important, she reminded me that my family was moving to the United States. Even though I did not speak any English at that time, my mother made a lot of sense when she said that in the U.S., I would have better opportunities for my future. She pointed out to me that most of the schools are better in the U.S., and degrees from these schools would also be recognized in most parts of the world.

She also pointed out that if I did not adjust to life with my cousins in Argentina, I would not be able to return back home

---

The **first paragraph** in the **body** outlines the opportunity Vanessa had to leave her home country and study for free in a neighboring country. It therefore supports her thesis.

The **second paragraph** in the body also supports her thesis. It details her mother's response to Vanessa's plans.

The **third paragraph** in the body also supports the thesis by offering a more compelling reason presented by her mother— that her family was moving to the United States, a land that held great educational opportunities for Vanessa.

The **fourth paragraph** of the body provides additional support for the thesis by offering her mother's most compelling reason for Vanessa to move with her family to the U.S.: If things in Argentina did not work out, she would not have a local support system.

Vanessa's **conclusion** restates the significance of what she has expressed in the **introduction** and the **body**. Her final sentence acts as an echo of her **thesis**.

because they would have already fled to the U.S. Thus, I would have to go through the long process of obtaining my travel documents all by myself, and figure out how to support myself while awaiting for approval to reunite with my parents. My mother's reasoning was convincing, so I gave up the idea of studying in Argentina and came to the United States with my family.

Now that I am in the U.S., I am still pursuing my dreams. I go to college every day and I study very hard because taking classes in a different language is very challenging. Every day I am a step closer to reaching my goal, but I know that moving to the U.S. delayed my dreams a bit. Sometimes I can't help wondering what things would be like today if I had ignored my mother's advice and followed my original plans to attend college in Argentina.

COMPREHENSION AND PRACTICE 5.7

Exploration of the Reading

1. Vanessa began her introduction with a rhetorical question rather than a stated thesis. On the lines that follow, briefly explain why you think she made this choice and whether you agree with her strategy.

   Most students will agree with Vanessa's decision, arguing that the rhetorical question

   prepares the reader for the point raised more explicitly in the thesis.

2. Which paragraph in the body of Vanessa's essay did you find strongest and most effective? Why? On the following lines, explain your choice.

   Answers will vary, although some students will focus on paragraph 3, the second body

   paragraph, because of the description of her cousins and their habits. Others will likely discuss paragraph 5, the fourth body paragraph, which makes it clear that she

would largely be on her own if things did not work out in Argentina.

3. Imagine that Vanessa is your classmate. Your instructor has recommended that Vanessa submit this essay to the first-year-student writing contest. Before she does so, Vanessa plans to create one more draft and has asked you to evaluate the essay. Working with a classmate, use the Essay Assessment Checklist on page 107 to evaluate the essay. Then, on a separate sheet of paper, write a brief paragraph in which you offer comments and any suggestions to improve the essay.

Understanding the Subject through Writing

In her essay, Vanessa recounts a time that she followed someone else's advice rather than her own intuition and now questions whether she made the correct choice. Have you ever had the same kind of experience, following advice that was contrary to your own desires and then questioning your decision? Or have you had the opposite experience, rejecting someone's advice that you now wonder if you should have followed? On a separate sheet of paper, write a brief passage (50 to 100 words) in which you discuss the advice you took—or rejected—and the concerns you had as a result of your decision.

FOR FURTHER EXPLORATION

1. Choose one of the following subjects and use the prewriting technique you prefer to give it careful consideration.

   - Why some people believe in stereotypes—common conceptions held about an entire group—and the consequences that can result when they believe them
   - A misconception that some people hold about a group that you understand or are part of, for example, college students, teenagers, senior citizens, an ethnic or cultural population, athletes, musicians, and so on
   - How you learned to disregard stereotypes and judge a person as a unique individual rather than as someone who is just like the others in some group

2. Identify a specific focus, and using what you've learned in this chapter, write an essay of at least 500 words.

collaboration

3. Exchange your draft with a writing partner. Evaluate the essay you receive, using the material in this chapter as a guide. Identify the introduction, body paragraphs, and conclusion, and assess their effectiveness. Locate the thesis, making sure it provides a clear direction. Use the Proofreading Checklist (Chapter 4, p. 89) to identify any remaining problems in form, and return the essay to your partner.

4. Revise your own essay, eliminating any errors identified by your writing partner.

DISCOVERING CONNECTIONS

Look closely at the image and consider one of the following questions (or another that the photo inspires). Refer to the material in this chapter, especially the sample essay on road rage, to see how to turn your prewriting ideas into an essay of at least 500 words.

A. What kind of spirit do you think it takes to do something as high risk as a parachute jump? Could you see yourself involved in such an activity? Why or why not?

B. What outdoor activity do you most prefer to do? What special qualities or experiences continue to draw you to it? What would you say about it to convince people who are hesitant to try this activity?

RECAP | Moving from Paragraph to Essay

Key Terms in This Chapter	Definitions
essay	a multiparagraph writing that deals more extensively with a subject than a paragraph does
introduction	a paragraph that opens an essay, providing a clear thesis and engaging the reader
five-paragraph essay	an essay that introduces three points in the opening paragraph that are discussed one at a time in the body, with the conclusion reiterating them
thesis	the sentence in the introduction that specifies the main subject of the essay and the writer's attitude or position on it
body	the series of paragraphs that provide support and illustration for a thesis
conclusion	a paragraph that closes the essay, summarizing the essay's point and bringing it to a logical and appropriate end
anecdote	a brief, entertaining story often used to make a point; an anecdote can be effective in an introduction or a conclusion
rhetorical question	a question designed not to be answered, but to provoke thought or discussion; a rhetorical question can be effective in an introduction to engage readers
amplifying	the process of providing additional, specific details and examples

The Process of Writing an Essay

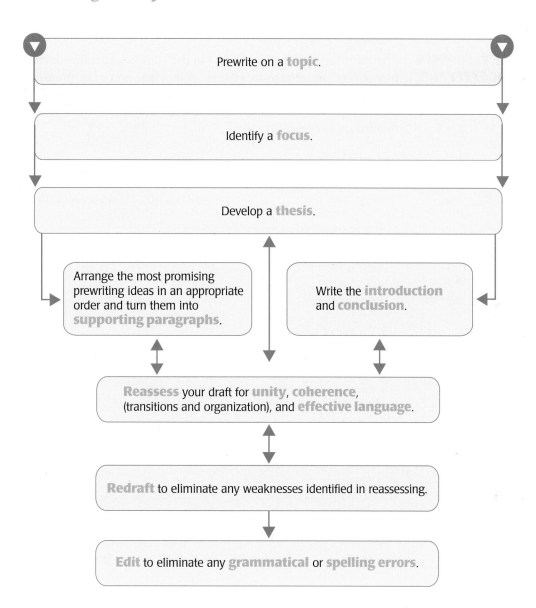

Prewrite on a **topic**.

Identify a **focus**.

Develop a **thesis**.

Arrange the most promising prewriting ideas in an appropriate order and turn them into **supporting paragraphs**.

Write the **introduction** and **conclusion**.

Reassess your draft for **unity**, **coherence**, (transitions and organization), and **effective language**.

Redraft to eliminate any weaknesses identified in reassessing.

Edit to eliminate any **grammatical** or **spelling errors**.

Using Discovery Online with MyWritingLab

For more practice with moving from paragraph to essay, go to www.mywritinglab.com.

Assessment: a process of evaluation designed to identify your level of mastery and help improve your performance

THE ELEMENTS OF EFFECTIVE WRITING

The material you have completed in Part 1 focuses on **the writing process**. To assess your understanding of this information and your progress as a **Writer, Reader, Editor,** and **Student,** complete the following charts. First check off your level of confidence for each item, and then take the recommended action to improve your performance.

- As a **Writer,** I understand

	Confident	Moderately Confident	Not Confident
1. the stages of the writing process (Chapter 1)			
2. prewriting techniques (Chapter 2)			
3. the role of topic sentences and supporting sentences (Chapter 3)			
4. the goal of reassessment, redrafting, and editing (Chapter 4)			
5. the differences between paragraphs and essays (Chapter 5)			

- If you are **confident,** you are all set. Move on.

- If you are **moderately confident,** review the Recaps for the appropriate chapters.

- If you are **not confident,** go through the appropriate chapters, perhaps completing exercises and activities again.

- As a **Reader,** I understand

	Confident	Moderately Confident	Not Confident
1. the level of language used to discuss the writing process			
2. the intent and significance of each of the **Spotlight** pieces			

- If you are **confident,** you are all set. Move on.

- If you are **moderately confident,** scan the chapters for unfamiliar words and briefly review the Spotlight pieces.

- If you are **not confident,** list and write definitions for all unfamiliar words. Reread the Spotlight pieces, underlining or highlighting all key ideas, and write a 100-word summary of each.

- As an **Editor,** I understand

	Confident	Moderately Confident	Not Confident
1. the process and importance of amplifying for successful writing (Chapters 3, 4, 5)			
2. the steps to eliminate errors in a piece of writing (Chapters 4 and 5)			

- If you are **confident,** you are all set. Move on.

- If you are **moderately confident,** compare a draft of one of your pieces of writing to a second or later draft, noting where you improved it by amplifying and proofreading.

- If you are **not confident,** reexamine examples of **amplifying** and **proofreading** in Chapters 3, 4, and 5, perhaps completing appropriate exercises and activities again.

- As a **Student,** I understand

	Confident	Moderately Confident	Not Confident
1. how to use the course syllabus			
2. the importance of effective time management to success in class			
3. the need to complete all out-of-class assignments and activities			

- If you are **confident,** you are all set. Move on.

- If you are **moderately confident,** check your class notes to review your instructor's comments about following the syllabus and meeting all deadlines.

- If you are **not confident,** reread the syllabus, and set up a weekly schedule that lists all assignments and due dates.

PART **2**

Effective Sentences: Constructing Meaning

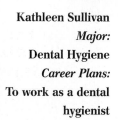

The level of language in speech is generally less formal than it is in writing. Do you think this difference is really necessary in order to communicate your ideas fully?

Both writing and talking come naturally to me. One kind of feeds the other—talking helps my writing and writing helps my talking. In writing, you have to explain yourself in detail to get your point across, so writing needs to be more formal. I can talk to someone and they will clearly understand me. In writing, I have to go into more depth.

Nicholas Coleman
Major:
Communications
Career Plans:
To run his own entertainment company

A native of Mississippi, Nick credits his grandmother, with whom he lived for the first twelve years of his life, for teaching him to read and convincing him of the importance of education. "What was great about my grandmother is when she was teaching me things, she would use her life experience to explain and emphasize the point. She used to tell me of times when opportunity for education wasn't available to everyone." Before he started college, Nick gave little thought to his writing. Now he feels that his writing skills have improved and he claims, "I learn something new with every paper I write."

Most people are more comfortable speaking than writing. Has taking a writing course made you more comfortable with this means of communication?

I have always been more comfortable talking to someone rather than writing. I think it's easier to talk to people because you can see their reactions. When you talk, you can answer questions in what you've said and clear up any confusion they might have. It's not as easy when you write. I think by writing more, I started to lose some of the slang I used regularly because I can't use these words in writing. I am starting to feel more comfortable with writing, and I know that it will get better the more I write.

Kathleen Sullivan
Major:
Dental Hygiene
Career Plans:
To work as a dental hygienist

The biggest surprise for Kathy Sullivan, who graduated from high school more than fifteen years ago, is that "I'm not the only one who didn't come straight here from high school. Not many of my relatives went to college, but most of my friends went right out of high school. I was definitely a little nervous coming back after all these years." Since beginning her college studies, Kathy has seen enormous improvements in her writing. "I catch my own mistakes now and would not have even realized I had made them before." Says Kathy, "I want to be a role model for my younger cousins because the 'family tradition' of not needing to go to college needs to change. Coming back to school is the best decision I've ever made, and I know I'll always be glad I did it."

How do you think writing influences other aspects of communication, such as conversing with people in school and on the job?

Being able to write well also means being able to speak well. I feel that when I talk, I have more time to explain myself. And, people can tell by the pitch and tone of my voice how I feel. When I write, I need to describe my feelings. By writing papers, I learn more words that can make me sound smart and sophisticated. Learning to write in proper English also helps me speak proper English, especially at work, where street talk is inappropriate.

Nina Coulombe
Major:
General Studies
Career Plans:
To become an accountant

For Nina, college is welcome relief from the restrictions of high school: "College makes me feel more independent, and I enjoy going because no one is telling me I have to." Since beginning her college studies, Nina feels, "I am more confident writing papers and expressing myself with words. I feel like I have learned more in my first semester of college than I ever learned in high school. I realize that writing is more than punctuation and grammar."

When you write, whom do you envision as your reader, and what do you do to adjust your writing to make sure it suits the needs of this reasder?

Envisioning myself having a conversation with only one person—no matter who it is—helps me focus better on what I am trying to get through to the reader. At the end of whatever I write, I put myself in this reader's position and start to correct whatever is not clear. I always wait until the end because I want to write everything down first. If I stop and correct things as I am going along, I will forget what I want to say. It is also less stressful for me to write this way because I am able to focus on one thing at a time.

Robert Giron
Major:
Criminal Justice
Career Plans:
To become an attorney

Rober Robert Giron represents the first generation in his family to attend college, and he is determined to succeed. "Neither of my parents went to college, but they worked hard to give us a comfortable life. Most of my cousins who are around my age went straight to work after high school because they felt college was a waste of time and money." Rob has been pleasantly surprised at how well he has done in his classes. "I thought since I didn't do well in high school that I would never do well in school again. I just got used to the negative feedback my teachers gave me in high school." He is particularly excited about his progress in writing. "Practice has helped me tremendously. Now I feel a lot better about my writing skills."

CHAPTER 6

Subjects and Verbs

GETTING STARTED ...

 Q I'm set to begin writing, so what do I do now to make sure that I express my ideas in complete sentence form?

 A You've already done the hard work—prewriting to generate ideas, identifying a focus, and selecting and shaping the strongest supporting points. Now, to ensure that your ideas come across clearly for your reader, you need to make sure that each verb you write has an appropriate subject so that each unit expresses a complete thought.

Overview: Elements of a Complete Sentence

"Always write in complete sentences."

You have probably heard this directive many times, but you may have found it hard to follow. To follow this instruction, you need to understand what makes a sentence complete. By definition, a **sentence** is a series of words that contains a subject and a verb and expresses a complete thought. The **subject** is the doer of the action or the focus of the verb. The **verb** shows action or otherwise completes the statement. To express your ideas so that your reader understands them, you must understand the role of these two parts of a sentence.

Navigating This Chapter This chapter helps you learn the proper use of subjects and verbs. To help you express your thoughts in complete sentences, you will learn to identify and use:

- action verbs, linking verbs, verb phrases, and compound verbs
- simple subjects, complete subjects, and compound subjects

Action Verbs

In most sentences, subjects come before verbs. However, it's more helpful to go to the heart of the sentence and consider verbs first. Most verbs indicate some action on the part of the subject. They are called **action verbs.** To identify the action verb in a sentence, ask yourself *what word shows action?*

Look at these sentences:

EXAMPLE My friend *spends* about three hours a day on Facebook.
Suddenly, the dishes *crashed* to the floor.

In the first sentence, the verb is *spends,* and in the second, it is *crashed.* These words show action in the sentences.

Verbs can show different kinds of action. Verbs such as *spends* and *crashed* show action that can be witnessed, while other verbs such as *think, judge, desire,* or *wonder* show thought or implied action.

COMPREHENSION AND PRACTICE   **Action Verb Identification**

6.1   Underline all the action verbs in the paragraph below. Use the example as a guide.

EXAMPLE   Maria's fingers <u>tapped</u> the keyboard quickly during the word processing exam.

(1) My friend Mike <u>exercises</u> six days a week. (2) He <u>lifts</u> weights, with emphasis on his upper body, on Mondays, Wednesdays, and Fridays. (3) His training sessions <u>last</u> almost three hours. (4) He <u>focuses</u> on toning and definition rather than on strength. (5) On Tuesdays, Thursdays, and Fridays, Mike <u>concentrates</u> on another important aspect of fitness, his aerobic conditioning. (6) In good weather, he <u>runs</u> anywhere from three to five miles around the city reservoir. (7) In bad weather, he <u>uses</u> either the treadmill or elliptical machine at the gym for at least a half an hour. (8) On Sundays, Mike just <u>rests</u> in preparation for another week's activity.

COMPREHENSION AND PRACTICE   **Action Verb Use**

6.2   Choose ten action verbs from the following list. On a separate sheet of paper, write ten sentences using those verbs. Use the example to guide you.

EXAMPLE   That electrician installs alarm systems in buildings.

talk	run	think	write	drive
wonder	laugh	imagine	paint	read
ask	consider	call	visit	cook

CHALLENGE 6.1   **Levels of Significance in Action Verbs**

1. On a separate sheet of paper, list three action verbs. Using a *thesaurus*—a compilation of synonyms—choose three alternative verbs for each.

collaboration

2. Exchange your paper with a classmate. For each of the listings on the paper you receive, identify which alternative best captures the sense of action the original verb expresses and briefly explain why.

Linking Verbs

ESL Note
See "Sentence Basics,"
pages 483–485, for
more on the use of
forms of the verbs
to be.

A second type of verb, the **linking verb,** does not show action. Most linking verbs are forms of the verb *to be* (*is, are, were, will be, might have been,* and so on). They link or connect the subject to some other word that restates or describes the subject. Notice how the verbs in the following sentences provide links.

EXAMPLES

My cousin *was* the winner of one of the regional tryouts for *American Idol* two years ago.

Alice Walker's novel *The Color Purple is* truly powerful.

In the first sentence, the linking verb *was* connects the subject, *My cousin,* with the words that rename it: *the winner.* In the second sentence, the linking verb *is* connects the subject, *Alice Walker's novel The Color Purple,* with the words that describe it: *truly powerful.*

The following verbs usually serve as action verbs, but they can also be used as linking verbs:

appear	feel	look	taste
become	grow	smell	sound

Look at these sentences.

EXAMPLES

action verb

Before every game, enthusiastic fans looking for autographs *appear* outside the players' parking area.

linking verb

From this angle, the lines *appear* fuzzy.

In the first sentence, the action verb *appear* tells what the fans do. In the second, however, *appear* performs the same function as the linking verb *are,* connecting the subject *lines* with the adjective *fuzzy.*

COMPREHENSION AND PRACTICE

6.3

Linking Verb Identification

Underline the linking verbs in the paragraph. Remember that linking verbs connect the subject with a word that restates or describes it. Use the example to guide you.

EXAMPLE

The effects of positive reinforcement are immediately noticeable.

(1) Fetal alcohol syndrome is a serious problem for some children. (2) This preventable syndrome is a result of a mother's alcohol intake during pregnancy. (3) The effects of the syndrome are devastating. (4) From the moment of their birth, babies with fetal alcohol syndrome are behind their peers in every mark of development. (5) For example, children with fetal alcohol

syndrome <u>are</u> smaller and thinner than most kids their age. (6) As a result of physical weaknesses, they <u>are</u> frequent victims of viruses and other communicable diseases. (7) In school, children with fetal alcohol syndrome <u>are</u> almost always far behind their peers. (8) Learning, especially with higher level skills like reading and mathematical computation, <u>is</u> extremely difficult for them.

COMPREHENSION AND PRACTICE

Linking Verb Use

6.4 Complete the paragraph below. Fill in the blanks with the appropriate linking verbs. In some cases, more than one verb will fit the sentence. You may use each verb more than once. Use the example as a guide. Answers may vary slightly in some cases. Representative answers are shown.

EXAMPLE Scorpions __are__ relatives of spiders.

(1) Professional sports leagues for women __are__ a relatively new phenomenon in North America. (2) Since 1996, however, the WNBA __has been__ a part of the sports scene in major cities across the United States. (3) With only eight teams in the beginning, the WNBA __was__ small compared to the NBA. (4) Today, thirteen teams __are__ part of the WNBA, with successful franchises in Atlanta, New York, Seattle, and Los Angeles. (5) With games on both ABC and ESPN2, the WNBA __is__ likely to become even more popular.

COMPREHENSION AND PRACTICE

Appropriate Action and Linking Verbs

6.5 Fill in the blanks in the following paragraph with appropriate action or linking verbs. Label action verbs with an *A* and linking verbs with an *L*. Answers may vary in some cases. Representative answers are given.

EXAMPLE Wolves __travel__ in packs.

(1) Award-winning author Gabriel García Márquez __spent__^A his childhood in the northern Colombian town of Aracataca. (2) As a young man, García Márquez __attended__^A the University of Bogotá, where he studied journalism. (3) After he graduated from college, he __took__^A a job as a reporter

for a Columbian newspaper. (4) Later in his life, García Márquez $\overset{\text{A}}{\underline{\text{moved}}}$ to Mexico City, where he began to write novels and short stories. (5) *One Hundred Years of Solitude, Love in the Time of Cholera,* and *Of Love and Other Demons* $\overset{\text{L}}{\underline{\text{are}}}$ some of his most famous works of fiction. (6) Readers of his work $\overset{\text{A}}{\underline{\text{admire}}}$ him for the way he weaves realism and fantasy into his stories and novels, using a technique called magical realism. (7) This approach $\overset{\text{A}}{\underline{\text{plays}}}$ a prominent part in his short story "A Very Old Man with Enormous Wings," in which an angel falls to earth. (8) In 1982, he $\overset{\text{A}}{\underline{\text{won}}}$ the Nobel Prize for literature. (9) Now in his 80s, García Márquez, in remission from cancer, $\overset{\text{A}}{\underline{\text{continues}}}$ to write.

CHALLENGE 6.2 Your Own Verb Use

collaboration

1. Choose a paragraph you created for an earlier assignment or create a new paragraph of at least seven to ten sentences that supports the following topic sentence: *The continuing popularity of performance-based reality shows like American Idol says a great deal about Americans and their love of fame and celebrity.*

2. Make a copy of your writing and exchange it with a classmate. On the copy you receive, underline the linking verbs and circle the action verbs.

Identifying Subjects

ESL Note
See "Word Order,"
pages 485–486, for
more on the placement
of subjects.

In a sentence, the *subject* is the doer of the action or the focus of the verb. Often the subject is a **noun**, a word that names a person, place, or thing. But it may be a **pronoun**, a word that substitutes for a noun, such as *he, she,* or *it.* Ask yourself *who or what is doing the action or being discussed?* The answer to this question is the subject. Look at these sentences:

EXAMPLES   The running back spiked the football in the end zone.

Friday nights are always the busiest times at the store.

To discover the subject in these sentences, follow these simple steps.

1. Identify the verb.

2. Ask *who or what did this?* Or *who or what is being described?*

In the first sentence, the verb is *spiked.* Who or what spiked the football? The answer to the question, and therefore the subject of the sentence, is *The running back.*

In the second sentence, the verb is *are*. Who or what are always the busiest times at the store? The answer, and therefore the subject of the sentence, is *Friday nights*.

Subject Identification

6.6   Underline the verbs in the following sentences. Then find the subjects by asking who or what is doing the action or being described. Circle each subject. (It may be more than one word.) Use the example as a guide.

EXAMPLE   My (Uncle Milt) tripped over the cat in front of the couch.

(1) In the last few years, (meditation) has become increasingly popular in the United States. (2) (People) from many walks of life now meditate on a daily basis. (3) Regular (meditation) offers a number of benefits. (4) This ancient (practice) improves overall health, including circulation and respiration. (5) As a result, (meditators) enjoy a higher overall level of energy. (6) Also (meditation) is a safe stress reliever. (7) According to some research findings, blood (pressure) goes down after only fifteen minutes of meditation a day. (8) This relaxation (technique) offers people an inexpensive alternative to medication.

CHALLENGE 6.3   Focus on Subjects

collaboration

1. The subjects are missing from the sentences in the following paragraph. Fill in the blanks in each sentence with appropriate nouns or pronouns. Use the example to guide you. Answers may vary. Representative answers are given.

EXAMPLE   On weekdays, *the bakery* closes at 8 P.M.

(1) Last Sunday, everyone came out to the park to enjoy the beautiful fall day. (2) The parking lot was filled with cars. (3) The lawn was covered with blankets, radios, and coolers. (4) Teenagers threw frisbees and footballs along the lakefront. (5) Children played on the swings and see-saw in the playground. (6) Meanwhile, families ate at the picnic tables nearby. (7) In a small grove of pine trees, my parents sat and quietly talked. (8) A little girl flew a kite in the little league field.

collaboration

2. Choose a paragraph you created for an earlier assignment or create a new paragraph of at least seven to ten sentences that supports the following topic sentence: *To make sure that the right person is convicted, police investigators need to pay more attention to DNA evidence.* Make a copy of your writing and exchange it with a classmate. On the copy you receive, underline the subjects. Put an *X* in front of any sentence in which you think a subject is missing.

3. Check any sentences your reader has identified as missing a subject and make necessary adjustments.

The Simple Subject versus the Complete Subject

Every sentence has a **simple subject.** It is the one noun or pronoun that answers the who or what question. The **complete subject** includes the simple subject plus any words or phrases that describe or modify it. Identifying the simple subject is important because the verb must agree with, or match, the simple subject. (For more on subject-verb agreement, see Chapter 11.)

Take a look at the verbs and complete subjects in the following example sentences:

EXAMPLES

┌──────────complete subject──────────┐ ┌ verb

The faded, blurry photos on the bookcase **are** family heirlooms.

┌──────────────────complete subject──────────────────┐ ┌ verb

The most powerful and versatile phone with the latest features and applications **costs** *under $200.*

What single word in each complete subject answers the question *who or what is doing the action or being discussed?*

In the first sentence, the simple subject is *photos,* and in the second it is *phone.* The rest of the italicized words in the two examples are **modifiers,** words that tell you *which* photos or *what kind* of phone.

Sometimes modifiers in the complete subject can make the simple subject difficult to identify. For example, a **prepositional phrase**—a preposition plus a noun or pronoun following it, called the *object of the preposition*—can trick you.

Take another look at the sentences, this time with the prepositional phrase in italics and the object of the preposition underlined:

EXAMPLES

prepositional
┌ phrase ┐

The faded, blurry photos *on the* <u>bookcase</u> are family heirlooms.

prepositional
┌ phrase ┐

The most powerful and versatile phone *with the latest* <u>features and applications</u> costs under $200.

When the object of the preposition comes right before the verb, as it does in these examples, it's easy to mistake it for the subject. You can avoid this mistake if you remember a simple rule: The noun or pronoun following a preposition *cannot* be the subject of a verb. In other words, an *object* can't be a *subject*.

Learning to recognize the following common prepositions will give you an advantage.

ESL Note
See "Agreement,"
pages 487–489, for
more about matching
subjects and verbs cor-
rectly, and
"Prepositions,"
page 494, for more on
prepositional phrases.

about	behind	during	on	to
above	below	except	onto	toward
across	beneath	for	out	under
after	beside	from	outside	underneath
against	besides	in	over	unlike
along	between	inside	past	until
among	beyond	into	since	up
around	but (except)	like	than	upon
as	by	near	through	with
at	despite	of	throughout	within
before	down	off	till	without

Once you can recognize prepositional phrases, you can mentally cross them out and find the subject more easily.

COMPREHENSION
AND PRACTICE

Simple Subject Use

6.7   Underline the complete subject in each sentence below. Then find and circle the simple subject. Remember that the complete subject includes the simple subject plus any words that describe it. Use the example as a guide.

EXAMPLE   In the store, the video (monitor) behind the counter shows any movement in the aisles.

(1) A violent (storm) on a summer night can really get your attention. (2) Two weeks ago, a fierce (thunderstorm) with accompanying hail hit my town, shaking everyone up. (3) (People) in my area suffered property losses during the storm. (4) For example, the picnic (table) next to my neighbor's driveway flipped and broke into pieces. (5) The shattered (pieces) of the table flew over the fence and into our yard. (6) A (branch) of a maple tree above my neighbor's car crashed through the windshield. (7) The (damage) to the glass led to water damage inside the car. (8) In addition, a huge (section) of shingles on the building across the street blew off the roof.

COMPREHENSION
AND PRACTICE

Simple Subject Identification

6.8   Circle the complete subject in each sentence in the following paragraph. Then underline all prepositional phrases in each complete subject. Last, cross out all other modifiers. Refer to the list of prepositions to help you identify prepositional phrases. Use the example to guide you.

EXAMPLE   The large package <u>in the hallway</u> was filled with discarded toys.

(1) The small bookstore in the Student Union is always crowded.
(2) The overworked staff of the bookstore tries to keep the lines of people moving. (3) Unfortunately, the one narrow doorway from the Student Union slows the flow of traffic. (4) Yesterday, several students with big armloads of books were blocking the entrance. (5) The huge piles of new books next to the registers also got in everyone's way.

CHALLENGE 6.4   Simple and Complete Subjects

1. On a separate sheet of paper, write five sentences with subjects with no modifiers except for the *articles* (*a, an,* or *the*).

2. Exchange your sentences with a classmate. Underline the subjects in the sentences you receive. Then, above the subjects you have identified, add suitable modifiers—words or phrases or both—and return the sentences to the writer.

3. Rewrite your sentences, including the modifiers your classmate has suggested and other modifiers of your own choice.

collaboration

Verb Phrases and Compound Verbs

Not all verbs are single words. Many sentences contain verb phrases or compound verbs. A **verb phrase** is a *main* verb plus one or more *helping verbs.* Various forms of *be, have,* and *do* serve as helping verbs. A list of common helping verbs follows.

am	can	had	might	were
are	could	has	must	will
be	did	have	shall	would
been	do	is	should	
being	does	may	was	

Consider the verbs in these two sentences:

EXAMPLES   We are discussing the Vietnam War in my American History class.

Michelle *can study* for six hours on Mondays.

In the first sentence, *discussing* is the main verb, but *discussing* cannot by itself fully communicate the action. It needs the helping verb *are* to do that. Therefore, *are discussing* is the verb phrase. In the second sentence, the main verb *study* needs the helping verb *can* to communicate the full meaning of the action. The two words together, *can study,* constitute the verb phrase.

Some sentences express more than one action or state of being. These sentences have **compound verbs,** two or more action verbs connected by the conjunctions *and* or *or.* (For more on conjunctions, see Chapter 8, "Subordination," and Chapter 9, "Coordination.")

Consider the compound verbs in the following sentences:

EXAMPLES

Tyrone draws, paints, and plays the piano.

All participants register prior to the deadline or pay a late fee.

In the first sentence, the compound verb consists of three verbs—*draws, paints,* and *plays*—connected by *and,* and in the second, two verbs—*register* and *pay*—connected by *or.*

COMPREHENSION AND PRACTICE

6.9

Verb Phrases and Compound Verbs

Find and underline the verb phrases and compound verbs in the following passage. With the compound verbs you identify, circle the conjunctions *and* and *or.* Use the example as a guide.

EXAMPLE

The instructor guided the young student through the first steps of the dance (and) then sat down to watch.

(1) I have been coaching a softball team of 9- to 12-year-old girls for the past two years. (2) This season, the kids played hard (and) won all but two regular season games. (3) Katrina, the youngest girl on the team, pitched (and) hit better than anybody else. (4) She also showed great leadership (and) demonstrated good sportsmanship throughout the season. (5) She always cheered (or) encouraged her teammates, even following occasional bad plays. (6) During the playoffs, Katrina and the other girls concentrated (and) played even better. (7) For the championship game, they were determined to play at the same level. (8) By the end of the second inning in this game, they had already scored seven runs, ultimately celebrating a 7 to 0 championship victory.

COMPREHENSION AND PRACTICE

6.10

Identification of Verb Phrases and Compound Verbs

Complete the sentences below by writing a verb phrase or a compound verb in each blank. Refer to the list of common helping verbs on page 134. Use the example to guide you. Answers may vary. Representative answers are shown.

EXAMPLE Without considering what the people around us would think, Greg
yelled at me and stomped angrily away .

(1) Extremely bad economic conditions in my community have hurt (verb phrase) my family directly. (2) Because the employees at my brother's plant didn't get a raise this year, they protested and struck (compound verb). (3) The manager has filled (verb phrase) their positions with workers who will work for lower wages. (4) Because of declining sales, one of the small independent grocery stores in my neighborhood lost money and closed (compound verb). (5) My mother can shop (verb phrase) at another store, but it is not convenient. (6) Many other companies have moved (verb phrase) to other parts of the state where business is better. (7) In these conditions, how will my father, who is unemployed, find and keep work (compound verb)? (8) My family has felt (verb phrase) the effects of tough times in other ways, too.

CHALLENGE 6.5 **Verb Phrase and Compound Verb Use**

collaboration

1. Below is a list of verb phrases and a list of compound verbs. Working with a classmate, select five verb phrases and five compound verbs from the lists. Then on a separate sheet of paper, write ten sentences, each with one of your chosen word groups.

Verb Phrases	_Compound Verbs_
have thought	smile or laugh
can speak	washed, dried, and ironed
am trying	memorize and study
must return	screamed and jumped
can understand	call or write
might arrive	push, pull, or lift
is crying	sat and rested

2. Select one of the sentences and on a separate sheet of paper, write at least three sentences related to the same idea. Underline all the verbs and circle their subjects.

3. Choose an essay from Part 6, "Discovering Connections through Reading." After reading the essay, select a four-paragraph passage, and on a separate sheet of paper, list all verbs, verb phrases, and compound verbs.

Compound Subjects

A **compound subject** is two or more nouns or pronouns connected by *and* or *or.* Take a look at the compound subjects in these sentences:

EXAMPLES

Alex, Ava, or Austin had broken the antique plate.

The DVDs and CDs in that cabinet were still in the original packaging.

In the first sentence, the verb is *had broken,* and the answer to the question who or what *had broken?* is the compound subjects *Alex, Ava, or Austin.* In the second sentence, the verb is *were,* and the answer to the question *who or what were still in the original packaging?* is the compound subject *DVDs and CDs.*

COMPREHENSION
AND PRACTICE

Compound Subjects

6.11   Underline the compound subjects in the following paragraph. Use the example as a guide.

EXAMPLE

In many cases, fruit juice or water is more refreshing than carbonated drinks.

(1) Shelley and Shannon are identical twins with totally different personalities. (2) At first glance, their eyes, the shape of their faces, and their lips look almost identical. (3) In addition, their speaking voices and their laughs seem exactly the same. (4) But their smiles and some facial expressions are quite different. (5) Also, their interests and attitudes are completely different. (6) Sports, dancing, and music fascinate Shelley. (7) She and her friends regularly go out to sporting events and dance clubs, especially on karaoke nights. (8) For Shannon, however, books, movies, and politics are her main interests.

COMPREHENSION
AND PRACTICE

Focus on Compound Subjects

6.12   Some of the sentences below have compound subjects and some do not. Before you begin, review the differences between simple and complete subjects. Then underline each compound subject and circle each simple subject, using the examples below to guide you.

EXAMPLES

Most action movies have little character development.

Pollen, mold, and dust can cause breathing difficulties for people with allergies.

(1) Golf and auto racing are among the most popular spectator sports in the United States today. (2) Over the past few years, both sports have built large fan bases. (3) Despite golf's reputation as a sport of the rich, fans from all economic backgrounds now follow golf. (4) Tiger Woods, Phil Mickleson, and other stars of the golf world are household names for millions. (5) NASCAR has also enjoyed a phenomenal growth in popularity over the past decade. (6) UPS, Visa, McDonald's, and America Online are among the thousands of companies involved in auto racing through sponsorship. (7) For people from all walks of life, Dale Earnhardt Jr., Tony Stewart, and Jeff Gordon are immediately recognizable names. (8) Year after year, spectators pack stadiums to see premier racing events like the Daytona 500.

COMPREHENSION AND PRACTICE

Use of Compound Subjects

6.13 Below is a list of compound subjects. Choose ten of these subjects, and on a separate sheet of paper, write a sentence using each.

basketball and football	satellite radio and cable television
apartments and condominiums	ice and snow
bottles or cans	cars, buses, or trains
books and magazines	tables, chairs, and desks
fruit and vegetables	glasses or contact lenses
braids and hair extensions	family and friends

CHALLENGE 6.6 **Practice with Simple and Compound Subjects**

1. On a separate sheet of paper, write four sentences with simple subjects: one subject a person, one a place, one a thing, and one an idea or concept.

collaboration

2. Exchange your sentences with a classmate. On a separate sheet of paper, rewrite the sentences, turning each of the simple subjects into appropriate compound subjects.

✓ SUBJECTS AND VERBS CHECKLIST

☐ Have you made sure that every group of words you intend as a sentence contains either an action or linking verb?

☐ Have you asked, "Who or what is doing this or who or what is being described?" to make sure that each verb has a subject?

☐ Have you used an appropriate helping verb to form any verb phrases?

☐ Have you connected compound verbs by using an appropriate conjunction such as *and* or *or?*

☐ Have you connected compound subjects by using an appropriate conjunction such as *and* or *or?*

Journal Writing

As this chapter shows, the way to communicate your ideas effectively is to express them in complete sentences. When things are complete, they are easier to understand. Can you think of something that you have witnessed or thought of that didn't make sense until you had the full picture? What is or was the missing element? Why was there such a difference without it? For example, was there a time that you saw a friend react in an uncharacteristic fashion to a phone message? Her reaction didn't make sense until you discovered the significance of the message she had received over the phone. Consider a topic like this and then spend 20 to 30 minutes exploring it in your journal.

CHAPTER QUICK CHECK   Subjects and Verbs

Find all the subjects and verbs in the following paragraph. Circle each simple and compound subject, and underline each verb, including helping verbs in verb phrases and the conjunctions in compound subjects and verbs.

(1) Through the efforts of some horse lovers, an extinct breed of horse has been re-created. (2) This breed is the Tarpan, a short, stocky horse with a round belly and a distinctive mane. (3) Many prehistoric artifacts and cave paintings contained images of the Tarpan's earliest ancestors. (4) These horses lived and thrived throughout the Middle East and Europe after the last Ice Age. (5) The number of wild Tarpans dwindled over many centuries and then died out in the 1890s, according to the American Tarpan Studbook Association. (6) Within a couple of decades, some breeders and horse lovers took steps to develop a modern-day Tarpan. (7) They struggled but eventually accomplished their aim by mating horses with physical characteristics like a Tarpan. (8) Other contemporary Tarpan breeders have focused on wild mustangs in the U.S. West. (9) The ancestry of these mustangs apparently extends

to horses of Spanish explorers. (10) These horse(lovers)have bred mustangs with strong Tarpan features and created a horse with the Tarpan's round belly and bushy mane.

SUMMARY EXERCISE   Subjects and Verbs

Find all the subjects and verbs in the following essay. Circle each simple and compound subject, and underline each verb, including helping verbs in verb phrases and the conjunctions in compound subjects and verbs.

(1) My next-door (neighbor) is running for the city council. (2) Over the past two years, (Madeleine) has been involved in several political campaigns. (3) After working for other people,(she)has become a candidate herself. (4)(She) truly believes in the power of the vote to create change and wants others to feel the same way. (5)(Bumper stickers and signs)for Madeleine are posted all over the city. (6) Every day,(she)visits another neighborhood and introduces herself to the people. (7) Fortunately,(Madeleine) is very personable. (8)(She) looks right at the people, smiles, and explains her positions on various issues. (9) Newly registered(voters)and older(citizens)have been the most receptive to her message.

(10) Of course, a serious political(campaign) takes time and costs money. (11) To defray her expenses, (Madeleine) has held several fund-raisers. (12) Neighborhood pancake(breakfasts)or block(parties)draw the biggest crowds. (13) For these fund-raisers, Madeleine's campaign(volunteers)make and sell a variety of food. (14)(Madeleine)goes from table to table and introduces herself to the voters. (15) So far(she)has held five of these events. (16)(They) have raised money for her campaign signs as well as for several newspaper advertisements. (17) With the election a month away,(Madeleine and her volunteers)are hoping for the best. (18)(Madeleine) has knocked on doors and shaken hands in every part of the city. (19)(She)has worked hard and explained her positions on various important issues. (20) Now her(goals and plans)are in the hands of the voters.

FOR FURTHER EXPLORATION

1. Focus on one of the following subjects and examine it closely, using the prewriting technique you prefer.

   - What you consider to be signs of true intelligence
   - A currently popular device, activity, innovation, or fad that holds no interest for you and why
   - The most creative individual you know

2. Evaluate your prewriting material, identify a focus, and create a draft paragraph of at least seven to ten sentences.

collaboration

3. Exchange your draft with a writing partner. Using the material in this chapter as a guide, evaluate the draft you receive. Note any problems with subjects and verbs as well as any other weaknesses, and return the draft to the writer.

4. Revise your draft, eliminating any errors that your reader identified.

DISCOVERING CONNECTIONS

For this assignment, concentrate on the photo and consider one of the following questions (or some other that the picture inspires). Explore your ideas and then create a draft paragraph of a least seven to ten sentences. When you have completed this exercise, highlight the subject and verb in each of your sentences.

A. To what part of this photo is your focus drawn? Why? The photo captures quite a moment in this biker's life; how would you describe what the biker is feeling? What do you think he has achieved?

B. Have you ever been involved in a special event of some kind, large or small? What was your role? What did you find most satisfying about participating in this event?

RECAP Subjects and Verbs

Key Terms in This Chapter	Definitions
sentence	a series of words containing a subject and verb and expressing a complete thought
subject	doer of the action or focus of the verb answer to the question *who or what is doing the action or being discussed?* EXAMPLE *Petra* asked a question.
verb	a word that shows action or completes a statement
action verb	a word expressing action EXAMPLE Mike accidentally *broke* the window.

Key Terms in This Chapter   Definitions

linking verb	a word connecting the subject with other words that restate or describe it
	EXAMPLE Sally *is* a volunteer in the tutoring center.
noun	a word that names a person, place, or thing
	EXAMPLE The *mountain* was covered with heather.
pronoun	a word that substitutes for a noun
	EXAMPLE *She* was concerned about the cast on Lauren's arm.
simple subject	main word or group of words that answers the question *who or what is doing the action or being discussed?*
complete subject	simple subject plus any words or phrases that describe or modify it
	EXAMPLE *The streets around the campus* are crowded.
modifier	a word or group of words that tells you which or what kind when used with a noun or pronoun
	EXAMPLE The *rusty* nail lay on the ground.
prepositional phrase	a group of words beginning with a preposition and ending with a noun or pronoun called the object of the preposition Prepositional phrases often come between the simple subject and verb.
	EXAMPLE The pancake mix *in the cupboard* is two months old.
verb phrase	a main verb plus a helping verb
	EXAMPLE Teresa *is learning* her Spanish vocabulary.
compound verb	two or more verbs connected by a conjunction
	EXAMPLE Steve *slipped and fell* on the ice.
compound subject	a subject consisting of two or more nouns or pronouns connected by a conjunction
	EXAMPLE *Dogs and cats* remain America's favorite pets.

The Basic Elements of a Sentence

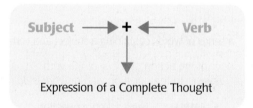

 **Using Discovery Online with MyWritingLab**
For more practice with subjects and verbs, go to www.mywritinglab.com.

Sentence Fragments

GETTING STARTED ...

 I understand what sentences are supposed to be. I'm just not always confident that I know how to write them. How can I make sure that I don't end up with sentence fragments?

A Focus on each unit that you have set off as a sentence. Check the unit—if it contains a subject and verb and expresses a complete thought, then you have a sentence.

Overview: Complete Sentences

A *fragment* is a piece of something. It's not complete or whole. A **sentence fragment** is part of a sentence. It doesn't express a complete idea and cannot stand alone. As a writer, you must transform sentence fragments into complete thoughts, or sentences, that communicate your ideas fully and clearly to readers.

Several types of sentence fragments appear in writing. Writers may accidentally omit a subject or verb, or they might mistake a phrase or a subordinate clause for a complete sentence. (Subordinate clauses are discussed in detail in Chapter 8, "Subordination.") Whatever the reason for the fragment, the result is a failure to communicate the intended meaning of the information.

Navigating This Chapter This chapter helps you to discover ways to recognize and correct sentence fragments by making sure that each sentence you write includes:

- an action or linking verb that communicates a complete action or meaning
- a subject that answers the question, *"Who or what is doing the action or being discussed?"*
- a complete thought that can stand on its own

Fragments with Missing Verbs

In order to be a sentence, a group of words must contain a verb and a subject. You must check that each unit you intend to be a sentence contains a verb and a subject.

Start with the verb. As you have seen, it can be either an action or a linking verb. Without a verb, the group of words is a fragment, not a sentence. Look at the two groups of words below:

FRAGMENT

Those expensive disposable contact lenses.

The runaway car with ten other cars on the highway.

Both groups of words lack verbs. You correct each sentence fragment by adding a verb and completing the thought, as these corrected examples show:

SENTENCE

Those expensive disposable contact lenses *are* not good for the environment.

The runaway car *collided* with ten other cars on the highway.

ESL Note
See "Word Order," pages 485–486, for more on the use of verbs (words ending in *-ing* or *-ed*).

Sometimes a group of words contains a verb form that doesn't communicate a complete action or meaning. For example, some verb forms are not complete unless they have helping verbs. (See Chapter 6, p. 134, for a discussion about helping verbs.) Look at the following examples:

FRAGMENT

The professor always *trying* to make us comfortable.

On the day of the concert, the afternoon *grown* especially warm.

Trying and *grown* do not communicate the action fully, so these word groups are sentence fragments. To correct the fragments, add a helping verb to create a verb phrase, or use the present or past form of the verb, as these corrected examples show.

SENTENCE

The professor *is* always *trying* to make us comfortable.

or

The professor always *tries* to make us comfortable.

SENTENCE

On the day of the concert, the afternoon *had grown* especially warm.

or

On the day of the concert, the afternoon *grew* especially warm.

Part 3, "Verbs: Conveying Action and Time," provides more practice in using verbs correctly.

Sometimes words that normally act as verbs take another role in a sentence. **Verbals** are forms of verbs, but they function as nouns, adjectives, or adverbs. Look at these examples:

EXAMPLES

To err is human; *to forgive* is divine.

We could hear the *howling* wind.

In the first sentence, the verbals *to err* and *to forgive* are used as nouns. (They are subjects.) In the second, the verbal *howling* is used as an adjective describing the wind. These forms may cause confusion because at first glance, you may think that a fragment contains a verb, when it in fact contains a verbal.

FRAGMENT

My best friend *to meet* Stephen Colbert of *The Colbert Report* someday.

The thought is incomplete, because *to meet* does not function as a verb here, but as a noun. Add a verb, and consider the words again.

SENTENCE   ⌐S.⌐ ⌐V.⌐⌐D.O.⌐
My best friend *hopes* to meet Stephen Colbert of *The Colbert Report* someday.

The thought is now a complete sentence. *Friend* is the subject, *hopes* is the verb, and *to meet* is a verbal acting as a direct object—a noun telling *what* the friend hopes to do. (Refer to Chapter 16, p. 145, for a discussion of direct objects.)

When you look for the verb in a sentence, don't be fooled by verbals. Instead, look for the word or words that completely express the action or state of being of the subject.

COMPREHENSION AND PRACTICE

Fragments with Missing Verbs

7.1 The following passage contains several fragments with missing verbs. Put an * in front of each fragment and write an appropriate verb above the line where one is needed. Use the example as a guide.

EXAMPLE   had
* The Denim Center a sale on jeans.

(1) My aunt and uncle truly *love* the warm weather of spring and summer.

(2) They both enjoy biking, sometimes riding 50 miles or more in an afternoon.

(3) They *drive* to the state reservation to park their truck in the lot next to the water filtration plant. (4) Then they pedal off along one of the many roads running for miles through the forest. (5) Sometimes they *ride* side by side at a comfortable pace, enjoying the scenery. (6) Other times, they *increase* their speed for miles at a time.

(7) They take turns leading, with the other taking advantage of the draft to coast behind. (8) After their ride, my aunt and uncle *return* to their truck, tired but happy.

COMPREHENSION AND PRACTICE

Use of Verbs to Eliminate Fragments

7.2 The following groups of words are all fragments because they lack verbs. Write an appropriate verb in each space provided. Use the example as a guide. Answers may vary. Representative answers are given.

EXAMPLE   The dog in that yard _barks_ all day long.

1. Weeds _fill_ the front yard of the abandoned house.

2. The artist _paints_ portraits in the center of the mall.

3. A security camera _surveys_ the entire area.

4. Every afternoon, the cat __takes__ a nap on the windowsill.

5. Lenny __plays__ tennis three afternoons a week.

6. My new backpack __has__ a special compartment for pens and pencils.

7. Her leg __is__ in a cast.

8. The new convenience store __opens__ next week.

Identification and Revision of Fragments with Missing Verbs

Some groups of words in the passage below are fragments because they lack an appropriate verb. Identify each of these fragments by underlining them. Then, on a separate sheet of paper, turn each fragment into a sentence by supplying a verb. Use the example to guide you. Some fragments may be corrected in several ways.

EXAMPLE

Meals from fast food restaurants still often containing high degrees of fat.

Meals from fast food restaurants still often contain high degrees of fat.

(1) Every year, some areas of the United States to face serious water prob-
— can expect —
lems as a result of drought. (2) In fact, in many recent years, more than half the nation has experienced moderate to severe drought conditions. (3) Ruined crops and forest fires being just a couple of the more serious effects of prolonged
— are —
drought. (4) In terms of severity, experts point to the summer of 1934 as the worst in modern times. (5) In that summer, moderate to severe drought 80
— affected —
percent of the United States. (6) But other historical indicators pointing to even
— point —
worse drought conditions than in the summer of 1934. (7) At one point during
— afflicted —
the 1800s, drought afflicting the country for seven years straight. (8) Today's climate change experts are of course concerned about the destruction that a repeat of this weather pattern could cause.

CHALLENGE 7.1   Practice Avoiding Fragments with Missing Verbs

1. Choose one of the topic sentences below, and draft a paragraph of at least seven to ten sentences to support it.
   a. Advanced computer skills are essential for anyone looking for a good job.
   b. Responsible pet owners must provide daily care to have a healthy animal.

collaboration

2. Exchange your paragraph with a classmate. Check the paragraph you receive to make sure each sentence includes a verb, underlining any verbal incorrectly used as a verb. Return the paragraph to the writer.

3. Consider your reader's comments, and make any necessary changes in your paragraph.

Fragments with Missing Subjects

Once you determine that a group of words has a verb, the next step is to check whether it has a subject. As Chapter 6 showed, you can find the subject by asking, "*Who or what is doing the action or being discussed?*" The word or group of words that answers that question is the subject. Look at the two groups of words below:

FRAGMENT

Mailed the package yesterday.

In the middle of the mall, sat on a bench alone.

Neither group of words is a sentence. The first group has a verb—*mailed*—but it has no word that answers the question, "*Who or what mailed the package yesterday?*" The second group also has a verb—*sat*—but there is no word that answers, "*Who or what sat alone on a bench in the middle of the mall?*" Neither group of words has a subject, so both are fragments.

You can correct both fragments the same way, by adding subjects, as these versions show:

SENTENCE

Dji mailed the package yesterday.

In the middle of the mall, *a frail old man* sat on a bench alone.

COMPREHENSION
AND PRACTICE
7.4

Fragments with Missing Subjects

The following passage contains several fragments that lack subjects. Put an * in front of each fragment. Where a subject is called for, write an appropriate subject above the fragment. Make changes in capitalization as needed. Use the example as a guide. Answers may vary somewhat.

EXAMPLE

The used car salesman lied
* L̶i̶e̶d̶ about the number of miles the car had been driven.

(1) Of all my classes in middle school, my favorite course was art. (2) My teacher, Mrs. Joseph, loved her job and her students. (3) *Her lessons taught* T̶a̶u̶g̶h̶t̶ my classmates and me much more than just colors and perspective. (4) *She inspired* I̶n̶s̶p̶i̶r̶e̶d̶ us all, even the most troubled kids, to learn. (5) Of all our class projects, my favorite one was a family collage. (6) We had to collect pictures of different events in our

family histories and other family keepsakes. (7) Then for almost two weeks, *we* cut and glued the material to big sheets of white cardboard. (8) Somewhere at home *I* still have it in a closet or in the basement. (9) Mrs. Joseph taught her classes more than just art, however. (10) *We learned* ~~Learned~~ to take our work and ourselves seriously.

COMPREHENSION
AND PRACTICE
7.5
Appropriate Subjects to Eliminate Fragments

The following groups of words are fragments because they lack subjects. Write an appropriate noun or pronoun in each space provided. Use the example as a guide. Answers may vary.

EXAMPLE   *The minister* conducted the special memorial service.

1. Every summer _____workers_____ clean(s) the streets throughout the city.

2. _____The Gap_____ is having a big sale.

3. _____Television_____ is a very popular form of entertainment.

4. _____Babies_____ demand a lot of attention.

5. _____My best friends_____ have now become vegetarians.

6. _____A North Face jacket_____ costs $100 less than the competing brand.

7. _____Everyone_____ should have access to quality health care.

8. _____A window_____ was broken during the demonstration at City Hall.

COMPREHENSION
AND PRACTICE
7.6
Identification and Revision of Fragments with Missing Subjects

Find and underline the sentence fragments in the paragraph below. Then, on a separate piece of paper, write their numbers and beside their numbers, rewrite the fragments by adding a subject. Use the example to guide you.
Answers may vary.

EXAMPLE   After her workout at the gym, rewarded herself with a sundae.

After her workout at the gym, Marlene rewarded herself with a sundae.

(1) $\overset{\text{The iPod is}}{\underset{\wedge}{\text{Is}}}$ Apple's version of an MP3 player for downloading and listening to recorded music. (2) It ranks as one of the most successful computer devices ever created. (3) The public immediately fell in love with the iPod in 2001, even at the original price of around $400. (4) Since then, hundreds of millions of iPods have been sold. (5) In 2003, $\overset{\text{Apple}}{\underset{\wedge}{}}$ launched its iTunes Music Store, an on-line service for downloading music at $.99 a song. (6) Also, iTunes will import and store music from CDs that users already own. (7) As a result, the iTunes application has made it easier for iPod users to manage their music. (8) Today $\overset{\text{users}}{\underset{\wedge}{}}$ can purchase seversal different types of iPods, all at prices under $250. (9) The list includes the iPod Touch and iPod Nano, both featuring video screens and huge storage capacity. (10) For under $50, $\overset{\text{the truly budget conscious}}{\underset{\wedge}{}}$ can purchase an iPod Shuffle, a tiny clip-on device that can store over 200 songs.

CHALLENGE 7.2   Practice Eliminating Fragments with Missing Subjects

1. On a separate sheet of paper, turn each of the following into complete topic sentences by adding subjects.
   a. Needs to establish a higher minimum wage.
   b. Increased people's interest in politics and willingness to be involved in the entire political process.
   c. To reduce waste, should replace all plastic packaging with biodegradable material.

2. Choose one of the sentences and on the same paper, write three sentences that support or explain it.

collaboration

3. Exchange your sentences with a classmate. Check the sentences you receive to make sure each has a subject. Put an * next to any point where you think a subject is needed, and return the paper to the writer.

4. Consider your reader's comments, and make any necessary changes in your sentences.

Phrase Fragments

Another kind of fragment involves **phrases** mistakenly used as sentences. By defin-ition, a phrase is two or more words acting as a single unit but lacking a subject–verb combination. The phrase *under the maple tree,* for example, consists of a preposition plus its object and modifiers. It contains no subject or verb. The phrase *was answered* has a helping verb plus a main verb, but it lacks a subject. (See Chapter 6, pp. 132–133, for a discussion of prepositional phrases and a list of common prepositions, and pp. 135 for more on verb phrases.)

Look at the following examples:

FRAGMENT

At the finish line.

Has agreed.

The first example is a prepositional phrase, which lacks both a subject and a verb. The second example is a verb phrase, which lacks a subject. To create sentences from these fragments, you need to supply the missing elements.

SENTENCE

The *Nigerian sprinter passed* the U.S. runner *at the finish line.*

Jackie has agreed to serve as club president.

COMPREHENSION AND PRACTICE

Phrases Incorrectly Used as Sentences

7.7 The following passage contains several phrase fragments. Put an * in front of each fragment. Then, on a separate sheet of paper, add the missing sentence elements, turning the fragments into sentences. Make changes in capitalization as needed. Use the example to guide you. Answers may vary.

EXAMPLE

The nurse was   the doctor's instruction to the patient.

*Was repeating,

(1) Like anything else, the lives of professional athletes have good points and bad points. (2) Certainly these athletes will earn millions in salaries and bonuses. (3) In addition, many of these athletes make additional money from endorsements, and (4) For personal appearances at sports memorabilia shows. (5) Of course, behind the scenes, these stars must work hard. (6) They keep themselves in superb shape. (7) In some cases, they have no guarantee of being on the team for the next season. (8) Even a star could Could be traded for younger players with less lucrative contracts.

COMPREHENSION AND PRACTICE

Correct Use of Phrases

7.8 The following groups of words are all fragments because they are phrases. On a separate sheet of paper, turn these phrases into sentences. Some need only a subject and some need both a subject and a verb. Use the example as a guide. Answers will vary.

EXAMPLE ⎡ was watching

⎣ *My grandmother was watching a game show.*

1. behind the building

2. should be studying

3. through the entire store

4. between two huge trees

5. are cleaning

6. will be speaking

7. over the bridge

8. have bought

CHALLENGE 7.3 Practice Correcting Phrase Fragments

collaboration

1. Make a copy of a piece of writing that you are working on and exchange it with a classmate. On the paper you receive, identify and underline any prepositional phrases and verb phrases. Then make sure each sentence that includes a prepositional phrase also includes a subject and a verb. Also check that each sentence with a verb phrase contains a subject. Return the writing to your classmate.

2. Consider your reader's comments and then correct any fragments in your document.

Appositive Phrase Fragments

Another group of words that is sometimes used incorrectly as a sentence is an **appositive phrase.** This type of phrase is a group of words placed next to a noun or pronoun in order to identify or explain it, as this example shows:

                              ⎣———— appositive phrase ————⎦
EXAMPLE ⎡ Clarice was glad to see Shari, *her best friend from the old neighborhood.*

Some appositive phrases are long, so writers sometimes incorrectly set them off as sentences. However, these phrases cannot stand alone and should never be separated from the word that they identify. They are a part of the sentence in which that word appears. Consider these examples:

                              ⎣———— appositive fragment ————⎦
SENTENCE AND ⎡ The local hangout was Mugsy's. *A neighborhood diner with blaring music and*
FRAGMENT   ⎣ ⎣————⎦
           great fries.

The appositive phrase *a neighborhood diner with blaring music and great fries* identifies the noun *Mugsy's*. This phrase can't express a complete thought on its own, however. Therefore it should be placed next to *Mugsy's*, set off by a comma.

CORRECTED SENTENCE

The local hangout was Mugsy's, a neighborhood diner with blaring music and great fries.

COMPREHENSION AND PRACTICE

7.9

Identification and Revision of Appositive Fragments

The following passage contains several fragments resulting from appositive phrases incorrectly used as sentences. Put an * in front of each fragment. Then correct the errors by joining the fragments to the sentences of which they are a part. Remember to use capitals and punctuation correctly. Use the example as a guide.

EXAMPLE

, the
I never go to school in the summer, ~~The~~ prime time for earning tuition money.

---

(1) Two years ago, I worked as a driver's assistant for Express Wishes,
a
~~(2) A~~ delivery service specializing in overnight delivery. (3) My main activity was to bring the packages to the door, *a* ~~(4) A~~ fairly simple task, even for a beginner. (5) I would ring the doorbell for the customer to sign for the package,
the
~~(6) The~~ most important part of the transaction. (7) Heavy packages were a problem in multilevel office buildings and warehouses. (8) Of course, these places always received the most deliveries. (9) After four hours, the driver and I would take a break at Dot's, *a* ~~(10) A~~ small coffee shop on the route.

COMPREHENSION AND PRACTICE

7.10

Sentences with Appositive Phrases

The following groups of words are appositive phrases. On a separate sheet of paper, write a sentence to include each appositive. Check each sentence to be sure that it expresses a complete thought and that a comma precedes the appositive phrase. If the appositive phrase appears in the middle of a sentence, place a comma before and after it. Use the example as a guide. Answers will vary.

EXAMPLE

my counselor and mentor

On my first day back on campus, I met with Jenny, my counselor and mentor, to get advice and support.

1. the most civilized form of transportation

2. the best spot in the stadium

3. a big hit with the crowd

4. the smallest child in the school

5. a secluded spot in the city

6. the most popular sports figure of the past decade

7. a rusty, broken-down bus

8. a priceless piece of art

CHALLENGE 7.4 Evaluation of Appositive Phrases

1. Read a selection in Part 6, "Discovering Connections through Reading," a one- or two-page section in one of your other textbooks, or an article in an online or print magazine or newspaper. Identify three sentences that contain appositive phrases and write them on a separate sheet of paper.

2. Exchange your sentences with a classmate. On the paper you receive, underline the appositive phrases and below each sentence, briefly explain how the appositive phrase contributes to the meaning of the sentence.

collaboration

Subordinate Clause Fragments

ESL Note
See" Agreement,"
pages 487–489, for
more about clauses.

It's important to remember that a subject and a verb are not enough to make a group of words a sentence. To be a sentence, a group of words must also express a complete thought.

Consider the following example.

FRAGMENT Because the lighting was poor.

This example has a verb (*was*) and a subject (*lighting*). However, it isn't a sentence because it doesn't express a complete thought. Instead, it is a **subordinate clause.** A subordinate clause is a group of words that contains a subject and a verb but doesn't make sense on its own. Alone, a subordinate clause fails to communicate the whole idea. It leaves the reader waiting for more information. *What happened* because the lighting was poor?

It is called *subordinate* because its meaning is *dependent* on another group of words—a *main clause*—to express a complete thought. Unlike a subordinate clause, a main clause does express a complete thought on its own. When a subordinate clause is correctly joined to a main clause, however, the resulting sentence presents more information than the main clause alone could.

Many subordinate clauses are introduced by *subordinating conjunctions,* words that provide connections or links between parts of a sentence and show how those parts are related. Here is a list of common subordinating conjunctions.

Common Subordinating Conjunctions

after	before	since	whenever
although	even though	so that	where
as	if	though	wherever
as if	in order that	unless	whether
as soon as	once	until	while
because	rather than	when	

Another type of subordinate clause, called a **relative clause**, is introduced by one of the following *relative pronouns:*

Relative Pronouns

what	whom
which	whose
who	that

There are options for correcting subordinate clause fragments. One is to re-state the clause or to add or delete words. For instance, dropping the subordinating conjunction *because* from the lighting example turns it into a sentence, as this version shows:

SENTENCE The lighting was poor.

With the subordinating conjunction deleted, the statement expresses a complete thought.

Now consider the next example:

FRAGMENT Which caused the delay.

Replacing *Which* with the actual cause of the delay turns this fragment into a complete sentence, as this version shows.

SENTENCE The misplaced change-of-address form caused the delay.

Another way to correct a subordinate clause fragment is to join the subordinate clause to a main clause. Your ability to make this type of correction means that you are capable of more complex thinking in your writing. You are showing how ideas are related to each other, as in the following examples:

SENTENCE *The dust in the room was hardly noticeable* because the lighting was poor.

The change-of-address form was misplaced, which caused the delay.

Marquez was the person who asked the first question.

Sometimes a simple punctuation error can cause a subordinate clause fragment. You might place a period after a subordinate clause rather then the appropriate comma. One way to catch this kind of error in a paragraph is to read it from last sentence to first sentence. That way, it may be easier to find subordinate clauses incorrectly set off by themselves.

To correct this kind of subordinate clause fragment, link the two part:

EXAMPLES

$\overline{\qquad\text{fragment}\qquad}$

My daughter learned to be more responsible. *After she lost her backpack filled with personal possessions.*

$\overline{\qquad\text{main clause}\qquad}$ $\overline{\qquad\text{subordinate clause}\qquad}$

My daughter learned to be more responsible *after she lost her backpack filled with personal possessions.*

$\overline{\qquad\text{fragment}\qquad}$

Once I pay all my bills. The cash I have left is very limited.

$\overline{\qquad\text{subordinate clause}\qquad}$ $\overline{\qquad\text{main clause}\qquad}$

Once I pay all my bills, the cash I have left is very limited.

Be sure to make any necessary changes in punctuation and capitalization when you join a subordinate clause fragment to a main clause. When a subordinate clause introduced by a subordinating conjunction comes *before* the main clause, put a comma between the clauses, as the sentence above shows. When the subordinate clause follows the main clause, a comma isn't necessarily needed, as this example shows:

EXAMPLE

$\overline{\qquad\text{main clause}\qquad}$ $\overline{\qquad\text{subordinate clause}\qquad}$

The cash I have left is very limited *once I pay all my bills.*

COMPREHENSION AND PRACTICE 7.11

Subordinate Clause Fragments

The following passage contains several subordinate clauses incorrectly used as sentences. Put an * in front of each of the fragments. Then correct the fragments by deleting subordinating conjunctions or combining subordinate clauses with an appropriate main clause. When you combine clauses, make sure you use punctuation and capitals correctly. Use the example as a guide.

EXAMPLE

*Although most people enjoy going to the movies, Nobody wants to pay a huge amount of money for a ticket.

(1) All sun-worshippers need to protect themselves against skin cancer. (2) For their own health, people must keep themselves safe. (3) When they

lie out in the sun. (4) The hours between 10 A.M. and 3 P.M. represent the

biggest danger, (5) ~~Because~~ ultraviolet rays from the sun are strongest dur-
*   because

ing this period. (6) Whenever people go out into the sun for a prolonged
*

period, (7) ~~They~~ should apply a good sunscreen to exposed skin. (8) If
, * they

their skin is fair, they need sunscreen with a sun protection factor (SPF) of

15 or higher. (9) Finally, if a mole or skin spot begins to darken, itch, or
*

change in appearance, (10) ~~People~~ need to see a doctor right away for a
,   people

skin-cancer screening.

**COMPREHENSION
AND PRACTICE**

7.12

Conversion of Subordinate Clause Fragments into Sentences

The following groups of words are fragments because they are subordinate
clauses. On a separate sheet of paper, turn these subordinate clauses into sentences. Remember that you may restate the clause, add or subtract words, or join
it to a main clause. Use the example to guide you. Answers will vary.

EXAMPLE

whenever Karen feels a tightness in her chest

Whenever Karen feels a tightness in her chest, she uses her asthma inhaler.

1. after the class was over

2. that has scratched several children in the neighborhood

3. whenever the alarm goes off

4. if the hurricane causes severe high tides

5. who wants to major in early childhood education

6. that decorate the health office

7. until the semester ends

8. which indicate permission to park in a restricted area

CHALLENGE 7.5   **Practice Correcting Subordinate Clause Fragments**

collaboration

1. Take a paragraph that you have already completed and exchange it with a
classmate. Or, if you prefer, turn one of the following topic sentences into

a full paragraph by supplying at least five additional supporting sentences, and then exchange it.

a. A trip to an unfamiliar place can be both exciting and stressful.

b. The funniest person I know is _____.

On the paper you receive, underline any subordinate clauses. If any of these clauses is incorrectly set off as a sentence, put an * above it and then return the paragraph to the writer.

2. Check the suggestions your reader has made and then make any necessary corrections.

✓ SENTENCE FRAGMENTS CHECKLIST

Have you made sure

☐ each unit you have set off as a sentence contains a verb?

☐ none of the words you have chosen as verbs is actually a verbal?

☐ you have supplied a subject for each verb?

☐ you haven't incorrectly set off a phrase as a sentence?

☐ you haven't incorrectly set off an appositive as a sentence?

☐ you haven't incorrectly set off a subordinate clause as a sentence?

Journal Writing

A sentence fragment is a *piece* of a sentence. It doesn't tell the entire story. You need to add something to it—or add it to something—before it will do that. Think of a small part of something else, for instance, an item of clothing, a ticket stub, or a cash register receipt, that represents a fragment of a story. Consider this subject, and then spend 20 to 30 minutes with your journal, exploring the role this fragment of a story played in the entire incident.

CHAPTER QUICK CHECK   Sentence Fragments

The following passage contains several fragments. Put an * in front of any fragment. Then, in the space above each fragment, make the corrections, choosing an appropriate technique from the different methods discussed in the chapter. Remember that fragments can be corrected in more than one way.

Representative answers are shown.

(1) Today, folks with a taste for adventure with a twist can enjoy a unique

experience, (2) *If* ~~If~~ they are willing to crawl inside a Zorb. (3) This strangely

named device is a 12-foot-tall, clear plastic sphere, (4) *that* ~~That~~ closes with a huge rubber plug. (5) Zorbing attendants then push the Zorb and its passenger, affectionately known as a zorbonaut, down a long incline. (6) Inside the Zorb, the rider tumbles around, ~~(7) Like~~ *like* clothes in a dryer. (8) A flat area at the bottom of the slope hundreds of feet away slows the Zorb to a gradual stop. (9)* ^*Zorbing has* ~~Has~~ attracted thousands of riders following its invention in New Zealand more than a decade ago. (10) With Zorbing now available at Zorb Smoky Mountains in Tennessee and plans for attractions in other areas of North America, prospective zorbonauts can enjoy this unique experience in United States.

SUMMARY EXERCISE   Sentence Fragments

The following passage contains a number of fragments. Put an * in front of any fragment. Then, in the space above each fragment, make the corrections, choosing an appropriate technique from the different methods discussed in the chapter. Remember that fragments can be corrected in more than one way. Answers may vary.

(1) I still remember the most exciting day in my fifth-grade class. (2) A bookcase fell on my friend Laura's foot, smashing her toe. (3)* Within a few minutes, the entire school ^*was* in an uproar.

(4) Laura's accident occurred during lunchtime, (5)* ^*when* ~~When~~ our teacher was out of the classroom. (6) At the back of the room, one of the boys pinched Laura. (7) She bumped into the big bookcase full of textbooks, (8)* ^*the* ~~The~~ big heavy ones for geography and reading. (9) At that point, the bookcase started to fall on Laura, (10)* ^*who* ~~Who~~ was desperately trying to avoid it.

(11) Unfortunately, the bookcase landed on her foot. (12) Immediately, a couple of the boys ^*lifted* the bookcase so that Laura could free her foot. (13) Blood was already soaking her sock, (14)* ^*because* ~~Because~~ the impact had crushed and cut her big toe.

(15)* Once everyone saw the blood, (16)* ^*the* ~~The~~ scene became even more chaotic. (17) Laura started to scream in reaction to the pain and the blood. (18) The noise drew Mrs. Leio back into the classroom, (19)* ^*from* ~~From~~ the

teachers' lounge down the hall. (20) Mrs. Leio immediately $\wedge$ for the nurse,
called
and she contacted Laura's father. (21) Within half an hour, her father $\wedge$ to
came
take her to the hospital. (22) Meanwhile, the rest of us cleaned up the room.

(23) At the hospital, Laura was treated for a deep cut and a broken big
toe. (24) For the next week, she $\wedge$ out of school. (25) The accident was all the
was
rest of the students wanted to talk about for months.

FOR FURTHER EXPLORATION

1. Choose one of the following topics and consider it carefully, relying on the prewriting technique you prefer.

   - Who—or what—has the greatest influence on children
   - The career or profession that in your view holds the greatest possibility for personal happiness and satisfaction
   - The place where you go whenever you need to be alone

2. Evaluate your prewriting material, identify a focus, and create a draft paragraph of at least seven to ten sentences.

collaboration

3. Exchange your draft with a writing partner. Using the material in this chapter as a guide, evaluate the draft you receive. Note any problems with fragments as well as any other weaknesses, and return the draft to the writer.

4. Revise your draft, eliminating any errors that your reader identified.

DISCOVERING CONNECTIONS

For this assignment, concentrate on the photo and respond to one of the following questions (or some other that the picture inspires). Explore your ideas and then create a draft paragraph of at least seven to ten sentences. Remember what you learned about subjects and verbs and make sure that all your sentences contain one of each so that you avoid sentence fragments.

A. Have you or someone you know ever considered a career as a musician? Was there a particular event or person that inspired such a choice? What was it? What about the event made it so significant?

B. What does the demeanor of these performers, as captured in the photo, suggest to you about their approach to entertainment? Have you ever performed before a live audience? What was the occasion and what was the experience like?

RECAP Sentence Fragments

Key Terms in This Chapter	Definitions
sentence fragment	a group of words that is incomplete as a sentence because it does not express a complete thought and cannot stand alone EXAMPLE *After the class was over.*
verbal	a verb form that functions as a noun, adjective, or adverb in a sentence Verbals *cannot* act as verbs in sentences. EXAMPLES The driver stopped *to ask* directions. adjective A *worried* face is not a happy face.
phrase	two or more words acting as a single unit but lacking a subject–verb combination Correct by adding the missing subject or verb or inserting the phrase in a sentence. ⌐v. phrase⌐ ⌐prep. phrase⌐ EXAMPLE The children *were looking for the crayons*.
appositive phrase	a group of words identifying or explaining a noun or pronoun next to it Correct an appositive fragment by including it in the sentence with the noun or pronoun it identifies. Set the appositive phrase off with commas. EXAMPLE The crossing guard, *a retired police officer,* escorted the children across the street.
subordinate clause	a group of words containing a subject, verb, and subordinating conjunction, but not expressing a complete thought
relative clause	a type of subordinate clause introduced by one of the relative pronouns: *which, what, who, whom, whose,* and *that* Correct a subordinate clause fragment by (a) joining it to a main clause to complete its thought, or (b) adding or subtracting words to make a complete thought in itself. EXAMPLE *The child who had screamed* suddenly laughed.

Eliminating Fragments

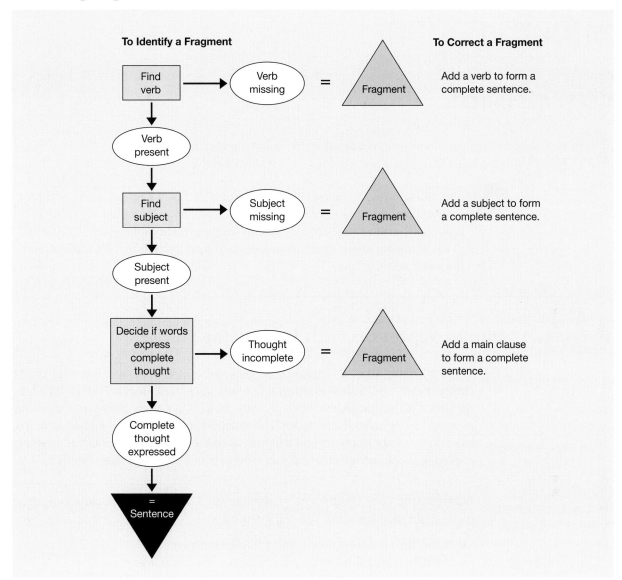

Using Discovery Online with MyWritingLab

For more practice with sentence fragments, go to www.mywritinglab.com.

CHAPTER 8
Subordination

GETTING STARTED ...

Q I'd like to make my sentences more interesting by extending the ideas in them. How can I do this and not lose the focus of the main idea?

A Subordination is the answer you are looking for. With subordination, you use a subordinating conjunction or relative pronoun to combine subject–verb units. This arrangment enables you to suggest relationships—time, causation, place, condition—between units of ideas and thus to focus greater attention on the other unit.

Overview: Complex Sentences with Supporting Clauses

There are many ways to compose sentences so that your ideas will stand out and be clearly understood. **Subordination** is one way to connect ideas and show their relationship. This technique involves combining an idea in a main clause with an idea in a dependent or *subordinate* clause. The main clause conveys a complete idea. The subordinate clause supports and depends upon the main clause for its full meaning. Exploring subordination can help you express your good ideas more clearly.

Navigating This Chapter This chapter gives you the opportunity to discover more about subordination. You will learn to

- distinguish between simple and complex sentences
- identify, use, and correctly punctuate complex sentences
- use subordinating conjunctions that connect and show relationships
- identify relative pronouns used to introduce subordinate clauses that describe or specify a noun or pronoun

Simple and Complex Sentences

A sentence must contain a subject and a verb and express a complete thought. A **simple sentence** consists of only *one* subject–verb unit, although its subject or verb may be compound. Here are some examples of simple sentences:

SIMPLE

subject   ┌ verb ┐
Tia often *visits* the art museum.

┌ subject ┐┌ verb ┐   ┌ verb ┐
The *landlord changed* the lock on my apartment and *installed* dead-bolt locks.

[The verb is compound, but there is still only one subject–verb unit.]

A simple sentence conveys a main idea. When it is combined with a **subordinate clause,** which contains supporting information, then the simple sentence becomes the **main clause** of the new sentence. (See Chapter 7, pp. 153–155, for more on subordinate clauses.) A subordinate clause combined with a main clause is called a **complex sentence.** Here are examples of two complex sentences:

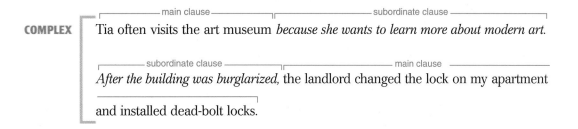

COMPLEX

main clause | subordinate clause

Tia often visits the art museum *because she wants to learn more about modern art.*

subordinate clause | main clause

After the building was burglarized, the landlord changed the lock on my apartment and installed dead-bolt locks.

By themselves, the subordinate clauses would be fragments. But when they are added to main clauses, the subordinate clauses become part of a larger, complete sentence. Notice that the subordinate clause in the preceding example comes *before* the main clause. It is equally correct for the subordinate clause to come *after* the main clause:

EXAMPLE

main clause | subordinate clause

The landlord changed the lock on my apartment *after the building was burglarized.*

No matter which clause comes first in a complex sentence, the ideas in each are related or linked by the subordinating conjunction. When the subordinate clause comes before the main clause, you need a comma to separate them. When the main clause comes first, as in this last version, no comma is necessarily needed.

COMPREHENSION AND PRACTICE

8.1

Subordinate Clauses

The following sentences are complex, meaning that they contain both a main clause and a subordinate clause. Underline the subordinate clause in each complex sentence, using the example as a guide.

EXAMPLE

Even though we were prepared, the hurricane did extensive damage to our home.

(1) Gambling in one form or another is a pastime that has existed since civilization itself began. (2) As widespread exposure to gambling advertising increases, more people than ever are gambling for recreation. (3) Most people who buy lottery tickets or visit a casino are able to gamble for fun. (4) Before some

people know it, they are suddenly facing addiction, however. (5) Unfortunately for them, scientists have found this kind of addiction difficult to overcome unless the victims are highly motivated.

CHALLENGE 8.1 The Use of Simple and Complex Sentences

1. Think about your own eating habits. Then write a paragraph of at least seven to ten sentences in which you address this subject.

collaboration

2. Make a copy of your draft and exchange the copy with a classmate. On the paper you receive, circle any simple sentences and underline any complex sentences. Remember that a complex sentence contains a main clause and a subordinate clause.

Subordinating Conjunctions

ESL Note
See "Agreement," pages 487–489, for more on the use of subordinate clauses.

Subordinate clauses are often introduced by **subordinating conjunctions.** *Conjunctions* are words that provide connections or links. As Chapter 7 (pp. 153–155) demonstrated, a subordinating conjunction links the subordinate clause it introduces to a main clause. Here again is a list of subordinating conjunctions:

Common Subordinating Conjunctions

after	before	since	whenever
although	even though	so that	where
as	if	though	wherever
as if	in order that	unless	whether
as soon as	once	until	while
because	rather than	when	

In addition to connecting clauses, subordinating conjunctions indicate a relationship between the main clause and the subordinate clause. Look at the following examples, with the subordinating conjunctions underlined, and consider the relationship the subordinating conjunction suggests in each:

EXAMPLES

We will have to cancel the party unless we can raise some money.

Although the temperature had grown cold, the children remained in the pool.

In the first sentence, *unless* indicates a contingency relationship. The party won't occur *without* additional funds. In the second, *although* suggests a contrasting or contradictory relationship. The children's swimming continued *despite* the cold.

In a complex sentence construction, the main clause has the most emphasis. Notice how the emphasis changes depending on the placement of the subordinate clause:

EXAMPLES

Damon bought his plane ticket before the prices increased.

After Damon bought his plane ticket, the prices increased.

The first sentence emphasizes buying the ticket. The second emphasizes the increase in prices. When you write a complex sentence, be sure the idea you want to emphasize is in the main clause.

COMPREHENSION AND PRACTICE

8.2

Sentences with Subordinating Conjunctions

On a separate sheet of paper, write each subordinate clause listed below. Then add a main clause to make each a complex sentence. Use appropriate capitalization and punctuation. Use the example as a guide. Answers will vary.

EXAMPLE

because the other restaurants had closed

We finally settled on a small diner because the other restaurants had closed.

1. whenever I have the chance

2. after gold was discovered in California

3. because Nick was late

4. if the building is condemned

5. unless the city enforces the ban on outside water use

6. before I go to bed

7. although the movie had some funny parts

8. since Jacqueline started playing the piano

COMPREHENSION AND PRACTICE

8.3

Changes in Meaning with Subordinating Conjunctions

Following are three simple sentences, each followed by two subordinating conjunctions. On a separate sheet of paper, write two versions of each sentence, adding a subordinate clause beginning with the conjunctions supplied. Use the example as a guide. Answers will vary.

EXAMPLE

One of my coworkers won't be in for a week *because/after*

One of my coworkers won't be in for a week because she has jury duty.

1. The worst thing about moving to a new apartment is packing *unless/if*

2. Computer literacy is important *before/whenever*

3. The federal government should offer new businesses tax breaks *until/so that*

CHALLENGE 8.2 **Complex Sentences Featuring Subordinating Conjunctions**

1. Choose five of the following ten subordinating conjunctions and use each to write a complex sentence:

because	whenever	unless	if	before
as	until	although	where	after

collaboration

2. Exchange these sentences with a classmate. On a separate sheet of paper, copy three of the sentences you receive, reversing the order of the clauses. Below the sentences, indicate which order, the original one or the new one you have created, is better in your view and why.

Relative Pronouns

Not all subordinate clauses are introduced by subordinating conjunctions. Some are introduced by one of the following *relative pronouns:*

Relative Pronouns

that	who
what	whom
which	whose

A subordinate clause that begins with a relative pronoun (sometimes called a **relative clause**) describes or specifies a noun or pronoun in the main clause.
Look at the following examples:

EXAMPLE

subordinate clause

Any high school or college athletic coach *who hits one of his or her players* should be fired immediately.

subordinate clause

Merchandise *that is marked with a red tag* is half price.

In the first sentence, the relative pronoun *who* introduces the subordinate clause. This clause specifies which athletic coaches should be fired. In the second sentence, the relative pronoun *that* introduces the subordinate clause. This clause describes which items are half price.

COMPREHENSION AND PRACTICE

8.4

Relative Pronouns in Subordinate Clauses

Each sentence in the following paragraph contains a subordinate clause introduced by a relative pronoun. Underline each subordinate clause and circle the relative pronoun. Use the example to guide you.

EXAMPLE

Professor Malone, (who) is my adviser, will be retiring at the end of the semester.

(1) My sister Dawn, (who) is in her ninth month of pregnancy, is preparing for her baby's arrival. (2) She has furnished a nursery with a rocking chair, a dresser, and a crib (that) she bought at a flea market and repaired. (3) The crib, (which) she washed and painted, now looks almost new. (4) Dawn also made curtains (that) will keep the bright morning sun out of the nursery. (5) Any baby (whose) mother prepares for her with so much love will be a lucky child.

COMPREHENSION AND PRACTICE

8.5

Subordinate Conjunctions and Relative Pronouns

Most paragraphs contain a variety of simple and complex sentences. The following paragraph, however, is composed of only simple sentences. On a separate piece of paper, revise it, joining ideas that you think go well together to create complex sentences. Use subordinating conjunctions and relative pronouns to introduce subordinate clauses. Be sure that the ideas you want to emphasize are in the main clauses of your new sentences. You may decide to leave some simple sentences just as they are. Answers will vary.

(1) In 2004, a long-awaited event in the world of sports occurred. (2) The Red Sox won the World Series by beating the St. Louis Cardinals in four games. (3) The Sox had battled the New York Yankees in the American League playoffs. (4) The Red Sox had last won the World Series in 1918. (5) Babe Ruth was a star pitcher and hitter for the Sox. (6) In 1920, Harry Frazee, the owner of the Red Sox, sold Ruth's contract to the rival New York Yankees for $100,000 and a loan. (7) Frazee wanted to finance a Broadway musical starring his girlfriend. (8) The Red Sox won the American League pennant four times following Ruth's trade, in 1946, 1967, 1975, and 1986. (9) They couldn't win the World's Series. (10) Following Boston's victory over the Cardinals in fall 2004, Red Sox fans everywhere felt a huge sense of relief.

CHALLENGE 8.3

Subordinate Conjunctions and Relative Pronouns

collaboration

1. Make a copy of the paragraph that you revised in Comprehension and Practice 8.5, and exchange the copy with a classmate. Compare your classmate's revision with your own. Put a + in front of sentences that you both combined in the same way.

2. Put an * in front of any remaining sentences on your classmate's paper that you think would be more effective if they were combined through subordination. Underneath the essay or on the back of the paper, briefly

explain why you feel subordination would help. Then return the paper to your classmate.

3. Consider what your classmate has suggested. If you agree, make the changes in your own paper.

Punctuation of Subordinate Clauses

Some subordinate clauses beginning with a relative pronoun are set off by commas while others are not. How can you decide when commas are needed? As a general rule, if the clause is used to describe or add extra information about a noun or pronoun, it is set off by commas. Sometimes these clauses are called *nonrestrictive* because they don't *restrict* or change the basic or *essential* meaning of the sentence.

EXAMPLE

_____ subordinate clause _____

Vincent van Gogh, *whose paintings now sell for millions of dollars,* was penniless during his lifetime.

Ask yourself if the sentence would have the same general meaning if the subordinate clause were left out. Would it express the same idea? If the subordinate clause were removed from the example about van Gogh, it would read *Vincent van Gogh was penniless during his lifetime.* The meaning would remain the same, so the clause should be set off by commas.

However, if the clause is essential to the meaning of the sentence, then it is classified as *restrictive* because it specifies or *restricts* the noun or pronoun. In this case, *do not* use commas. Take a look at these complex sentences:

EXAMPLES

subordinate
_____ clause _____

Elected officials *who commit perjury* should be impeached and removed from office.

_____ subordinate clause _____

Perishable food *that has been left out in the heat for more than an hour* cannot be saved.

What happens if you leave out the subordinate clauses in these sentences?

EXAMPLES

Elected officials should be impeached and removed from office.

Perishable food cannot be saved.

Without the subordinate clauses, these sentences have very different meanings. The first sentence now suggests that everyone elected to office should face legal sanctions and lose their positions. The second now indicates that no perishable food can be stored. Clearly, these versions don't reflect the writer's meaning. The subordinate clauses are essential to meaning; they should not be set off with commas.

COMPREHENSION
AND PRACTICE
8.6 **Punctuation of Subordinate Clauses**

As you read the following paragraph, consider the underlined clauses. Add commas before and after the underlined clauses that need them. Remember: Set off a clause if it describes a noun but does not change the meaning of the sentence. Use the examples to guide you.

EXAMPLES

The mall's senior discount day, which falls on the first Tuesday of every month, has boosted sales dramatically. *[Subordinate clause gives extra, describing information; add commas.]*

A lizard that is poisonous makes a dangerous pet. *[Subordinate clause gives essential meaning to sentence; no commas needed.]*

(1) According to my high school business teacher, all students who study regularly will succeed. (2) Study skills that are practiced often are the only ones to become life-long habits, she stressed. (3) This teacher, whose advice I ignored, was right. (4) I learned by experience, which can be a hard teacher, to review each day's lessons every night. (5) Students learn what is important by practice.

COMPREHENSION
AND PRACTICE
8.7 **Subordinate Clauses Introduced by Relative Pronouns**

In the space provided, add a subordinate clause beginning with a relative pronoun to each of the following sentences. If the clauses you supply are nonrestrictive, add commas. Answers will vary. Representative answers are shown.

EXAMPLE

The part of the movie *that scared me most* was the closing scene. *[Subordinate clause gives essential meaning to sentence; no commas are needed.]*

1. My friend Barry , who never seemed to care about his weight, has lost more than 60 pounds in the past year.

2. The critical care center , which didn't exist two years ago, recently received a citation for high-quality service.

3. The movie that I thought was very funny received bad reviews.

4. Two cars that had skidded on the ice were blocking the exit.

5. The newest museum exhibit is an ancient mummy <u>that was discovered</u>
   <u>last year</u>.

6. Their last concert <u>, which drew a huge audience,</u> was more than a year ago.

7. The books <u>that did not sell well</u> are on sale.

8. Last year's drought <u>, which was completely unexpected,</u> has affected the price
   of fresh fruit and vegetables.

CHALLENGE 8.4 Punctuation of Subordinate Clauses

1. Choose one of the sentences from Comprehension and Practice 8.7 and, on
   a separate sheet of paper, turn it into a paragraph by adding five to seven related sentences.

2. Exchange your paragraph with a classmate. Identify any sentences that have
   subordinate clauses introduced by relative pronouns. Make sure that any
   clauses that *are not* essential to the meaning of the sentence are set off by
   commas. Put an * to indicate where you think a comma is needed. Also, circle any commas setting off clauses that you believe are essential to meaning.
   Use the discussion about comma use with restrictive and nonrestrictive
   clauses (p. 168) to guide you. Return the paragraph to the writer.

collaboration

3. Consider your classmate's suggestions, and make any necessary changes.

✔ SUBORDINATION CHECKLIST

☐ Are you clear on the differences between a simple and a complex
   sentence?

☐ With any subordinating conjunctions you have used, have you carefully
   considered the relationship they suggest between the main clause and
   the subordinate clause?

☐ Have you carefully considered the order of clauses in complex sentences
   featuring subordinating conjunctions so that you provide the emphasis
   you want?

☐ Are you clear on the differences between a restrictive and a nonrestrictive clause in complex sentences featuring relative pronouns?

☐ Have you distinguished between restrictive and nonrestrictive clauses
   and used commas to enclose only the nonrestrictive ones?

Journal Writing

This chapter illustrates that subordination involves combining ideas to make one part or section dependent to some degree on the other. Now consider other relationships in life that involve dependence, for example, a parent and child, a new employee and an experienced worker, an owner and a pet, or a teacher and nursery school or kindergarten students. Focus on one of these subjects and then spend 20 to 30 minutes in your journal exploring what can be good and what can be troubling or problematic about such a subordinate relationship.

CHAPTER QUICK CHECK   Subordination

The following passage contains both simple sentences and complex sentences. Put an * in front of each simple sentence and circle each complex sentence, underlining the subordinate clauses.

(1) Archeologists still don't have the definitive answer to one mystery about Egypt's Great Pyramid that has long been a puzzle. *(2) This pyramid was built some 4,500 years ago by the Pharaoh Khufu. (3) While nineteenth-century explorers were examining the inner chambers of the Great Pyramid, they discovered several eight-inch square shafts rising at angles from the pyramid's chamber area. *(4) The purpose of these unusual shafts has mystified Egyptologists for many years. (5) Researchers pursued the mystery because they were particularly interested in a small limestone door with brass handles at the top of one of the shafts. *(6) The door is at the end of the shaft about 200 feet above the floor of an inner chamber. *(7) To gain access to the door, engineers designed a tiny robot with special treads to grip the walls of the shaft. *(8) The research team then used the robot to drill a hole in the door and insert a tiny light and camera. (9) When they got their first glance inside, they found a space leading to another door, not a chamber or artifacts of some kind. (10) Although the mystery remains, researchers hope to continue the exploration of this unique feature of the Great Pyramid.

SUMMARY EXERCISE   Subordination

The following essay contains both simple sentences and complex sentences. Put an * in front of each simple sentence and circle each complex sentence, underlining the subordinate clauses.

*(1) Spanish painter, sculptor, and graphic artist Pablo Picasso was one of the most famous artists in the history of painting. (2) He was a central figure in the artistic movement that was known as Cubism.

*(3) Picasso was born on October 25, 1881, in Malaga, Spain. (4) When he was 15, he attended the School of Fine Arts in Barcelona. (5) Because he was impatient and did not enjoy this formal training, the young Picasso went to Paris in 1900. (6) Picasso became interested in the city's street life when he had lived in Paris for a few months.

*(7) Between 1900 and 1906, Picasso tried out many styles of contemporary painting. (8) After he discovered the work of the Spanish painter El Greco, twenty-year-old Picasso began to sink into a depression. *(9) His work at the time reflected his feelings of misery and despair. (10) This is known as Picasso's Blue Period since most of these paintings are dominated by various shades of blue and gray.

*(11) Picasso's Blue Period of deep depression began to change to a mild sadness in 1904. (12) The colors that he chose for this group of paintings were more natural, with many red and pink tones. *(13) This period is called Picasso's Pink Period.

(14) By 1907, Picasso began to paint in a style that deviated from his earlier styles. *(15) The faces of the people in some of these paintings can be seen from the front and side at the same time.

*(16) Picasso's most celebrated painting is called *Guernica*. (17) Guernica is a Spanish city that was destroyed by bombs in the Spanish Civil War.

(18) Picasso, who felt great pain and anger about the bombing of Guernica, used only black, white, and gray paints in this creation. (19) Once World War II had concluded, Picasso moved to the south of France. (20) Long after his death in 1973, he is universally recognized as an artistic genius and visionary.

FOR FURTHER EXPLORATION

1. Take a look at the following subjects. Choose one and use the prewriting technique you prefer to study it more closely.

   - The process you follow when you need to solve a complex problem
   - The importance of daydreaming
   - A decision that you now wish you hadn't made and why

2. Evaluate your prewriting material, identify a focus, and create a draft paragraph of at least seven to ten sentences.

collaboration

3. Exchange your draft with a writing partner. Using the material in this chapter as a guide, evaluate the draft you receive. Note any problems with subordination as well as any other weaknesses, and return the draft to the writer.

4. Revise your draft, eliminating any errors that your reader identified.

DISCOVERING CONNECTIONS

For this assignment, think about this picture and respond to one of the following questions (or another the photo suggests). Then, after exploring your ideas on this topic, create a draft paragraph of at least seven to ten sentences, with at least two to three being complex sentences.

A. Featured in this photo are a group of citizens practicing peaceful protest. Have you ever been in a situation where you disagreed with a local, state, or federal law and felt the need to express your disagreement in an act of civil disobedience? What was the situation and what did you do? If not, would you?

B. Think about the inalienable rights afforded you as an American citizen. Some countries, for example, could have a citizen arrested for practicing civil disobedience. What civil rights do you feel should be given to every human being—no matter where he or she may live? Why?

RECAP Subordination

Key Terms in This Chapter	Definitions
subordination	a way to combine ideas, show their relationship, and add emphasis in a sentence
simple sentence	one complete thought containing one subject–verb unit, set apart by a beginning capital letter and an ending punctuation mark **EXAMPLE** The skunk wandered across the busy highway.
subordinate clause	a subject–verb unit that doesn't express a complete thought by itself Subordinate clauses are often introduced by *subordinating conjunctions.* **EXAMPLE** *Before that volcano erupted last week,* it had been dormant for fifty years. Subordinate clauses may also be introduced by *relative pronouns: that, who, what, which, whom, whose* **EXAMPLE** The chili *that caused her allergic reaction* has peanut butter in it.
main clause	a subject–verb unit that expresses a complete idea and that has been combined with a subordinate clause
complex sentence	a unit consisting of a main clause and one or more subordinate clauses **EXAMPLE** The protesters plan to remain outside city hall *until the mayor agrees to meet with them.*
subordinating conjunction	a word that connects and shows a relationship between clauses: *after, although, as, as if, because, before, even though, if, in order that, rather than, since, so that, than, though, unless, until, when, whenever, wherever, whether, while*
relative clause	a subordinate clause that begins with a relative pronoun

Structure of a Complex Sentence

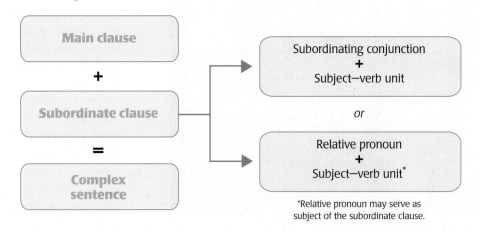

*Relative pronoun may serve as subject of the subordinate clause.

Using Discovery Online with MyWritingLab

For more practice with subordination, go to www.mywritinglab.com.

CHAPTER 9
Coordination

GETTING STARTED ...

 Q When I write, my sentences sometimes seem choppy. Is there something I can do to eliminate this choppiness and make my writing flow better?

 A One way to make your writing smoother is to use coordination. Using *coordinating conjunctions* to combine sentences is the dominant method of coordination, but a *semicolon* is a great choice when you want to signal a particularly close relationship between sentences. You can also use a *conjunctive adverb* such as *however* or *therefore* along with the *semicolon*. When you connect ideas in these ways, you reduce choppiness and give both subject-verb units equal importance.

Overview: Compound Sentences

Writing with short, choppy sentences inhibits the smooth flow of ideas. **Coordination** is one way to keep your sentences flowing. This approach involves using a *coordinating conjunction* or a *semicolon* to join simple sentences that express equally important, related ideas. This sentence-combining technique is vital because it can help you better communicate your ideas to your reader.

Navigating This Chapter This chapter shows how coordination can make your writing more effective. You will learn to join two simple sentences and create one compound sentence by using:

- a coordinating conjunction and a comma
- a semicolon
- a semicolon and a conjunctive adverb

Coordinating Conjunctions

A simple sentence consists of one subject–verb unit that stands on its own. Sometimes, two or more simple sentences are linked by a **coordinating conjunction,** which is a word used to join words, phrases, or clauses of equal importance. The result is a **compound sentence.** Here are the coordinating conjunctions:

Coordinating Conjunctions

and	nor	so
but	or	yet
for		

With a compound sentence, the two subject–verb units are equally important, or balanced. Writers show the relationship between these equally important ideas by choosing an appropriate coordinating conjunction:

- *And* suggests that one idea is added to another.
- *But* and *yet* suggest a difference between the two ideas.
- *So* suggests that one idea happens as a result of another.
- *For* suggests that one idea is a reason for the other happening.
- *Or* and *nor* suggest that the two ideas offer a choice.

Take a look at how the coordinating conjunctions connect the units in the following compound sentences.

EXAMPLES

Jason had to find a way to get help, *or* he would be stranded on the darkened highway.

No one answered the knock at the door, *so* the delivery person left.

In the first example, the coordinating conjunction is *or,* and in the second, the coordinating conjunction is *so.* As these examples show, a comma is always placed before a coordinating conjunction connecting two subject–verb units.

What is the advantage of using coordination? Consider how abrupt the following sets of simple sentences seem.

SIMPLE

The breeze at the beach was chilly. The water was warm.

Carlos runs three miles each morning. He runs another three miles each evening.

Now read these compound sentence versions in which each set of sentences has been connected:

COMPOUND

The breeze at the beach was chilly, *but* the water was warm.

Carlos runs three miles each morning, *and* he runs another three miles each evening.

The compound sentences flow much better than the simple sentences alone. They are also easier to understand. When using a compound sentence, a writer balances two equally important ideas and shows how they are related.

COMPREHENSION AND PRACTICE

9.1

Coordinating Conjunctions and Compound Sentences

On the lines provided, complete each of the following sentences. One clause and a conjunction are already provided. Add another independent clause—a subject–verb unit that could stand as a simple sentence itself—to create a compound sentence. Use the example to guide you. Answers will vary. Representative answers are shown.

EXAMPLE The man's shoes were wet, *and* _his pants were muddy_ .

1. The movie was good, *but* _my friend Ellie talked through the whole thing_ _____ .

2. _We were too tired to hike anymore_ , *so* we walked back to the car.

3. The small dog must have run away from its owner, *or* _it must have_ _become lost somehow_ .

4. _Nobody had taken in the mail_ , *nor* had anyone picked up the trash outside the house for weeks.

5. An accident had blocked the main street, *so* _traffic was at a standstill_ _____ .

6. My cousin Terry is a nurse, *and* _her children want to work in the_ _medical field, too_ .

7. _Everybody else in my family is a hockey fan_ , *but* I am more interested in soccer.

8. _The city better fix these potholes soon_ , *or* they will have to repave the entire street.

CHALLENGE 9.1 **Revision for Appropriate Coordination**

1. The following paragraph suffers from too much coordination. Some of the sentences would be more effective if the clauses were separated so that they stand alone. Decide which compound sentences should be revised. On a separate sheet of paper, rewrite the paragraph so that the writer's ideas are expressed through a variety of compound and simple sentences. Answers will vary.

(1) Obtaining health insurance can be difficult for many reasons, and many people have to take their chances without it. (2) Some insurance plans are very expensive, but these policies may be the only options available for people without employee health benefits, so they have to pay high premiums. (3) People with certain health problems, such as high blood pressure, can't even find insurance, or the price is too expensive, so they couldn't buy it anyway. (4) A deductible is the amount of a bill an insured person will

pay, and the higher the deductible is, the lower the cost of a policy, so many people will promise to pay a high deductible, yet they can't afford to pay that either. (5) Some insurance policies limit the amount of coverage for some conditions, and that hurts people with chronic illnesses, or they won't pay for certain procedures.

collaboration

2. Exchange your revised paragraph with a classmate. If you have made changes that your classmate hasn't, justify why your version better communicates the writer's meaning.

Semicolons

ESL Note
See "Punctuation and Capitalization," pages 494–496, for more on the correct use of semicolons.

Another way to create a compound sentence is to use a *semicolon* (;) as a connector. A semicolon has the same power to connect as a coordinating conjunction, but the semicolon calls attention to the connection in a different way.

Look at the two versions of the same sentence below.

EXAMPLE

The food at Billy J's Sports Bar is bad, *but* the service is even worse.

The food at Billy J's Sports Bar is bad; the service is even worse.

In the first version, the coordinating conjunction *but* points out the contrast between the linked thoughts: The service is worse than the food. In the second example, the use of the semicolon makes the connection between the simple sentences more dramatic. It emphasizes the writer's annoyance.

It's important to remember that both of the examples above are correct. They represent differences in *style.* You can experiment with both coordinating conjunctions and semicolons to add variety to your writing.

COMPREHENSION
AND PRACTICE
9.2

Compound Sentences Connected with Semicolons

The following compound sentences are composed of independent clauses connected by coordinating conjunctions. On a separate sheet of paper, rewrite each sentence, substituting a semicolon for the coordinating conjunction. Beneath each of these new sentences, explain which version—the original with the coordinating conjunction or the new version with the semicolon—you believe is better and why. Use the example as a guide. Answers will vary.

EXAMPLE

Her badly aligned teeth had always made Jasmine too self-conscious to socialize with others, but braces changed her outlook completely.

Her badly aligned teeth had always made Jasmine too self-conscious to socialize with others; braces changed her outlook completely.

I think the version with the semicolon is better than the version with the coordinating conjunction because the semicolon helps to emphasize the change that braces made.

1. Exercise at any age improves health, but it is especially good for people over the age of 55.

2. According to current research, exercise slows down aging, and people live longer and feel better because of exercise.

3. In addition, physically fit elderly people recover from illness quickly, yet family and friends often fail to see the importance of physical activity in maintaining that health.

4. Older people are encouraged to monitor their health, but they are also urged to abandon healthful physical activities like weightlifting and jogging.

5. Exercise keeps muscles working well, and participation in an exercise program can truly transform lives.

CHALLENGE 9.2   **Evaluation of Different Methods of Coordination**

1. For Comprehension and Practice 9.2, you evaluated the use of coordinating conjunctions versus semicolons to connect pairs of sentences. Choose one combined sentence in which you feel a semicolon is a more effective connector than a coordinating conjunction. Then choose a sentence in which you feel the coordinating conjunction is the superior connector. Write these sentences on a separate sheet of paper. Underneath each sentence, justify your choice of connector.

2. Exchange your paper with a classmate and evaluate the sentences and explanations you receive. If you disagree with your classmate's decision, briefly explain your own reasoning in a sentence or two.

collaboration

Conjunctive Adverbs

Another way to combine ideas of equal importance is by using a semicolon plus a **conjunctive adverb,** a word that points out a relationship between sentences. Take a look at this list of common conjunctive adverbs:

Common Conjunctive Adverbs

also	however	similarly
besides	instead	still
consequently	meanwhile	then
finally	moreover	therefore
furthermore	nevertheless	thus

It's important to remember that these words are *adverbs*, NOT conjunctions. Adverbs can't connect—instead, they merely modify or describe verbs, adjectives, or other adverbs. (See Chapter 18, "Working with Adjectives and Adverbs," for more on the function of adverbs.) When you want to include a conjunctive adverb between subject–verb units, you must place a semicolon before the conjunctive adverb and a comma after it, as these examples show:

EXAMPLE

> *The Fat-Free Cookbook* is expensive; *however,* it contains hundreds of great recipes for people concerned about their health.
>
> On vacation, we didn't visit the White House; *instead,* we spent the time visiting various museums and monuments.

In each case, the semicolon connects the two ideas, and the conjunctive adverb *emphasizes* the difference between them.

COMPREHENSION AND PRACTICE

9.3

Conjunctive Adverbs in Compound Sentences

For each compound sentence below, add the conjunctive adverb that best suggests a relationship between the ideas. (See the list of conjunctive adverbs on p. 179.) Remember to add a comma after the conjunctive adverb. Use the example to guide you. Answers may vary.

EXAMPLE

My math assignment was very confusing; *nevertheless,* I managed to finish it.

1. A movie makes money when people buy a ticket to see it; *however,* that is not the only way movies make money.

2. People rent or buy DVDs or videocassettes even after the movie leaves the theaters; *therefore,* producers keep earning money.

3. Premium cable TV stations pay producers to air the movies; *consequently,* this is another way movies make money.

4. Advertisers also pay to have their products appear in movies; *moreover,* some companies buy the right to produce products based on movie characters.

5. For example, toy companies don't have to think of new ideas for best-selling toys and games; *instead,* they just pay producers for the rights to make and sell action figures and other merchandise.

COMPREHENSION AND PRACTICE

9.4

Coordination to Improve a Paragraph with Coordination

The paragraph below is composed of simple sentences. Decide where it would be improved through coordination. Use a coordinating conjunction with a comma, or a semicolon with a conjunctive adverb and a comma, to create compound sentences. Rewrite the revised version of the paragraph on a separate piece of paper. You may decide not to change some sentences. Answers will vary.

(1) Rude behavior is becoming more and more common. (2) I can't stand this trend. (3) Just yesterday on the bus, a woman was having an animated argument on her cell phone. (4) She didn't seem to mind all the people staring at her. (5) Another very rude person works at my bank. (6) This man, a supervisor, doesn't even make an effort to treat the tellers respectfully. (7) He simply has no tact. (8) Maybe our schools should teach manners. (9) Businesses could offer refresher courses. (10) Ongoing education might cut down on rude behavior.

CHALLENGE 9.3 Evaluation of Your Use of Coordination

1. Choose a paragraph that you are currently working on or develop a paragraph of at least seven to ten sentences to support the topic sentence: *The hardest words for most people to say are, "I'm sorry."* Underline any compound sentences and circle the coordinating conjunction or semicolon providing the connection.

collaboration

2. Exchange your paragraph with a classmate. The different methods of coordination provide writers with distinct stylistic approaches to combining sentences. Take one of the sentences that your classmate has identified and rewrite it, using another method of coordination. Then identify which method of coordination works best with this sentence and explain why.

✓ COORDINATION CHECKLIST

☐ Are you clear on how coordinating conjunctions allow you to indicate relationships between subject–verb units while also keeping them equal in importance?

☐ Do you understand how semicolons function?

☐ Can you see how the connection a semicolon provides differs from the connection a coordinating conjunction provides?

☐ Are you clear on the different roles played by coordinating conjunctions and conjunctive adverbs?

☐ Do you understand the additional link you can suggest between subject–verb units by using a semicolon to connect them and adding a conjunctive adverb?

Journal Writing

Coordination is a kind of balancing act, one that involves combining subject–verb units so that each unit has the same general level of importance. What else in your life depends on maintaining balance? Is it a personal relationship? Is it school or work—or both? What about your own physical health or well-being? Focus on some aspect of balance and then spend 20 to 30 minutes in your journal exploring its importance or effects.

CHAPTER QUICK CHECK   Coordination

The following passage contains a series of simple sentences presented in sets of two within brackets. Turn each pair of simple sentences into a compound sentence, using one of the techniques illustrated in this chapter. Write the revised sentences on a separate sheet of paper. Representative answers are shown.

(1) [Thomas Edison probably never envisioned it, ~~The~~ sheer amount of
                              , but the

electric light in our modern world can be a real problem.] (2) [In big cities, the

problem is particularly bad, ~~Residents~~ never experience a natural level
                   ; residents

of evening darkness except during a power blackout.] (3) [The sun goes

down, ~~Lights~~ all over these cities go on.] (4) [Portions of large office buildings
     , and lights

remain lit long after closing, ~~Many~~ also have extensive exterior lighting.]
                   ; furthermore, many

(5) [Few stores and fast food restaurants ever shut off their lights, ~~They~~ keep
                                    , or they

them on until 1 or 2 A.M. even during the week.] (6) [On the clearest nights,

the excess light makes it nearly impossible to see most stars, ~~Any~~ clouds com-
                                    , and any

pletely obscure the sky.] (7) [The amount of illumination in the sky has also

increased in other areas, ~~Even~~ tiny cities and towns have far more external
           ; even

lighting than at any time in the past.] (8) [Amateur astronomers find the ex-

cess light a genuine problem, ~~They~~ have to travel far from home to view stars
             , so they

and planets through their telescopes.] (9) [Bright lights illuminating some

Florida beachfront hotels have also created problems, ~~This~~ situation under-
                              , and this

scores the seriousness of light pollution.] (10) [Turtle hatchlings instinctively

follow the light of the full moon to the safety of the water, ~~Some~~ have been
                                  ; however, some

known to head toward the bright lights of the hotels to their deaths.]

SUMMARY EXERCISE   Coordination

The following essay contains a series of simple sentences presented in sets of two within brackets. Turn each pair of simple sentences into a compound sentence, using one of the techniques illustrated in this chapter. Write the revised sentences on a separate sheet of paper. Representative answers are shown.

(1) [I have a number of personal faults, *, but the* The worst habit I have by far is lateness.] (2) [Time after time, I agree to show up at a particular time, *, and no* No matter what, I just don't make it on time.] (3) [This bad habit is a major source of embarrassment, *; however, I* I don't seem to have the willpower to change.]

(4) [One time, my aunt teased me about being late for my own birthday party, *; she* She turned out to be right.] (5) [On the way to the party, I got a flat tire, *, and it* It took me a half hour to change it.] (6) [I had left my house 15 minutes early to allow for any problems, *, yet I* I still didn't make it on time.] (7) [I walked in all full of grease, *, and all* All the guests started laughing.]

(8) [Last year, my best friend was curious about my frequent tardiness. She *, so she* kept a record of my lateness.] (9) [We live only two blocks apart, *, yet I* I was late picking her up for classes four out of every five days.] (10) [At first I wouldn't believe her, *; however she* She had the proof.]

(11) [I have a good excuse for some of my lateness, *; I* I work until 11 P.M. many weeknights.] (12) [Most nights I don't fall asleep until 1 or 2 A.M. *; therefore it's* It's hard for me to wake up before 7:30 A.M.] (13) [I am simply too tired to answer the alarm clock, *, but this* This excuse doesn't change the facts.]

(14) [At work, I really have to avoid being late, *; my* My supervisor pays close attention to employees' time cards.] (15) [Sometimes, Pete, one of my friends at work, punches in for me, *; however, he* He is taking a chance of losing his own job by doing this.] (16) [On two occasions in the last month, my supervisor called me into her office to discuss my work habits, *, and she* She docked my pay for being late.] (17) [I'm worried about losing my job, *, yet I* I still can't seem to change this bad habit.]

(18) [Last week, I read an article about chronic tardiness, I am now committed to becoming more punctual.] (19) [To try to break this habit, I am setting my watch ten minutes ahead, I am going to bed earlier on weeknights.] (20) [With a little luck, these changes will help, My reputation will begin to change.]

(handwritten insertions above the lines: "‚ and I" at sentence 18; "; moreover, I" at sentence 19; "‚ and my" at sentence 20)

FOR FURTHER EXPLORATION

1. Choose one of the following subjects and use the prewriting technique you prefer to develop focus and supporting ideas.

   - A change you believe would make the college experience less intimidating
   - The importance of music in your life
   - A story, book, or performance of some kind (film, play, video) that affected the way you view an issue or situation

2. Examine your prewriting material, identify a focus, and create a draft paragraph of at least seven to ten sentences.

collaboration

3. Exchange your draft with a writing partner. Using the material in this chapter as a guide, evaluate the draft you receive. Note any problems with coordination as well as any other weaknesses, and return the draft to the writer.

4. Revise your draft, eliminating any errors that your reader identified.

DISCOVERING CONNECTIONS

For this assignment, focus on the photo and one of the following questions (or some other that it inspires). Explore your ideas and then create a draft paragraph of at least seven to ten sentences. Try to include a mix of both compound and simple sentences.

A. What do you imagine life is like for a professional artist? How do you think an artist balances the desire to create meaningful art with the need to make the money necessary to survive—and thrive?

B. Take a look at the various objects in the background—do you think this artist relies on these things to develop a piece of art? In what ways can behind-the-scenes elements actually play a significant role in the production of a piece of artwork or any other kind of creative piece?

RECAP Coordination

Key Terms in This Chapter	Definitions
coordination	the combining of simple sentences into compound sentences to eliminate choppiness and repetition
coordinating conjunction	one of a set of words used to join other words or groups of words: *and, but, for, nor, or, so, yet*
	A coordinating conjunction can be used to join simple sentences to make a compound sentence. Place a comma before the coordinating conjunction in a compound sentence. **EXAMPLE** Joe always eats hot dogs, *but* Mary Beth prefers Polish sausage.
compound sentence	a sentence created by joining simple sentences with a connector:
	a coordinating conjunction and comma a semicolon a semicolon, conjunctive adverb, and comma
conjunctive adverb	one of a set of words used with a semicolon to join simple sentences: *also, besides, consequently, finally, furthermore, however, meanwhile, instead, moreover, nevertheless, similarly, still, then, therefore, thus*
	A conjunctive adverb cannot connect simple sentences by itself, but it does emphasize the connection provided by a semicolon. Place a comma after the conjunctive adverb used with a semicolon to join simple sentences. **EXAMPLE** Cheetahs are an endangered species; *however,* many cheetahs were born at zoos last year.

Structure of a Compound Sentence

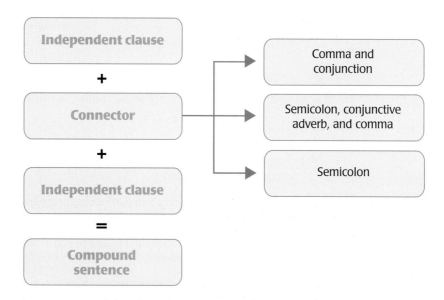

 **Using Discovery Online with MyWritingLab**
For more practice with coordination, go to www.mywritinglab.com.

CHAPTER 10
Comma Splices and Run-On Sentences

GETTING STARTED ...

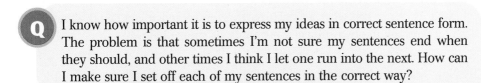

Q I know how important it is to express my ideas in correct sentence form. The problem is that sometimes I'm not sure my sentences end when they should, and other times I think I let one run into the next. How can I make sure I set off each of my sentences in the correct way?

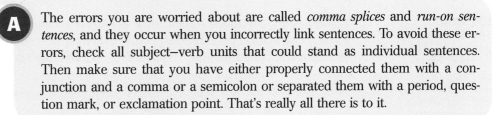

A The errors you are worried about are called *comma splices* and *run-on sentences*, and they occur when you incorrectly link sentences. To avoid these errors, check all subject–verb units that could stand as individual sentences. Then make sure that you have either properly connected them with a conjunction and a comma or a semicolon or separated them with a period, question mark, or exclamation point. That's really all there is to it.

Overview: Sentence-Combining Errors

As Chapters 8 and 9 have shown, *subordination* and *coordination* are important techniques in writing. These techniques can be tricky, however, and even very experienced writers may make errors when they combine sentences. Two of the most common sentence-combining errors are the comma splice and the run-on sentence. A **comma splice** occurs when a comma is used to connect two sentences. But commas can't connect—they merely indicate a pause. A **run-on sentence** occurs when two sentences are put together with no punctuation or conjunction. Discovering how to recognize and eliminate these problems is crucial if you want to make your ideas clear to your reader.

Navigating This Chapter This chapter explores ways to avoid both comma splices and run-on sentences. You will learn options to correct these sentence errors by using:

- a coordinating conjunction and a comma
- a semicolon
- a subordinating conjunction
- a period

Comma Splices and Run-On Sentences

Before you can eliminate comma splices and run-on sentences, you have to find them. When you write what you think is a correct compound sentence—two sentences properly connected, each with its own subject and verb—make sure you have correctly combined the sentences.

Look at the example below:

EXAMPLE

subject verb   subject verb

My New Year's *party was* a flop, *I couldn't wait* for my friends to leave.

As you can see, the sentence contains two separate sets of subjects and verbs.

Next, check to see whether each part of the sentence can stand alone. Put a slash (/) between the two subject–verb units, as shown below.

EXAMPLE

My New Year's party was a flop, / I couldn't wait for my friends to leave.

ESL Note
See "Sentence Basics," pages 483–485, for more on the structure of a sentence and "Punctuation and Capitalization," pages 494–496, for more on the use of commas.

Both units can stand on their own, so each is a simple sentence. The problem is that a comma has been used to connect them, and *commas alone can't connect.* As Chapter 9, "Coordination," explained, a coordinating conjunction is needed in addition to a comma to connect two simple sentences. When a comma is used alone, as it is in this first sentence, the error is called a *comma splice.*

The example below shows a similar kind of problem. There are two subject–verb units, each of which can stand as an independent sentence, as the / between them indicates:

EXAMPLE

subject verb   subject verb

Her *clothes were* torn and dirty / *she was* obviously disoriented.

As you can see, nothing—not even an incorrect comma—appears between the sentences. The first sentence just runs right into the second, which is why this kind of error is called a *run-on sentence.* In the rest of this chapter, four options to correct both comma splices and run-ons are discussed.

COMPREHENSION
AND PRACTICE

10.1

Comma Splices and Run-Ons

The following paragraph is composed of comma splices and run-ons. First, underline and label the subject and verb in each clause. Then put a / between clauses that can make sense on their own. Use the example to guide you.

EXAMPLE

S   V
The equipment in the schoolyard needs replacing, / for example, the swing's
S   V
plastic seat is cracked.

S   V
(1) The movie *Jaws* greatly misinformed the public about sharks,/these
S   V
predators aren't actually a big threat to humans. (2) Over 350 known species
V   S   V
of sharks exist/only a few represent a danger to people. (3) For example, the

whale shark, the largest species, can grow up to 60 feet,/it feeds on plankton, not people. (4) Reports about shark attacks always catch the public's attention/attacks are actually quite rare. (5) The number of unprovoked shark attacks annually ranks under 100 worldwide,/only seven deaths were attributed to shark attacks in 2004. (6) Many attacks on humans are actually cases of mistaken identity/sharks apparently mistake humans for sea lions or seals. (7) Sharks prefer these creatures to humans,/seals and sea lions have higher fat content. (8) More important, sharks help to maintain the balance of the ocean/they feed on dead and dying creatures. (9) Right now, sharks are under attack,/ironically, we represent the threat to their well-being. (10) Shark fin soup has become a popular delicacy in some countries,/millions of sharks are killed annually to feed this appetite.

COMPREHENSION AND PRACTICE 10.2

More Comma Splices and Run-Ons

The following paragraph contains several run-on sentences. Put an * in front of each run-on. Then put a / where one sentence should end and the next should begin. Use the example as a guide.

EXAMPLE

*My first babysitting job was terrible/six-year-old Michelle cried for her mother all night.

(1) Regardless of any stereotype to the contrary, the life of a lifeguard isn't easy or glamorous. (2) First of all, the heat often gets to be unbearable/you can't just jump in the water to cool down while on duty. (3) Instead, you spend the day sweating and roasting,/everyone else looks cool and comfortable. (4) You also have to be on duty on bad weather days. (5) On cold days, you have to stand there freezing in your bathing suit/you still have to be ready for any emergency. (6) On weekdays sometimes only a few people are in your as-signed area/the job can be boring. (7) Then on weekends the job is almost too much to handle. (8) On sunny Saturdays and Sundays, people start arriving early in the morning/they keep pouring in until noon.

CHALLENGE 10.1   Identification of Comma Splices and Run-Ons

1. Select one of the journal entries or paragraphs you have already completed and make a copy of it. Or write a paragraph of at least seven to ten sentences to support the following topic sentence:

    If I could change one thing about my earlier years of schooling, it would

    be _____ .

collaboration

2. Exchange the copy of your paragraph with a classmate. Identify the subjects and verbs in each sentence of the entry you receive. Check for any subject–verb units that are incorrectly connected or run together. Put an * in front of any sentence that you suspect is a comma splice or run-on, and then return the paragraph to the writer.

3. Check the sentences your classmate has identified. Make necessary corrections.

Correcting Comma Splices and Run-Ons with Coordinating Conjunctions

One way to correct a comma splice or run-on is to use a coordinating conjunction to connect the two simple sentences. As Chapter 9 explained, a coordinating conjunction links independent thoughts to eliminate choppiness. This result is called a *compound sentence.* Here again are the coordinating conjunctions:

Coordinating Conjunctions

and	nor	so
but	or	yet
for		

Look at these examples, which have a / between the clauses:

RUN-ON   Lines for the concert tickets ran all around the block / some people had even set up tents.

COMMA SPLICE   Walter usually plays practical jokes on others,/ he was the victim this time.

In the first example, the first simple sentence ends with *block,* and the second begins with *some.* Because nothing connects or separates them, it is a run-on sentence. The second sentence contains two independent clauses separated by a comma. *Commas cannot connect,* however, so this example is a comma splice.

Now consider the versions below, with coordinating conjunctions linking the clauses.

COMPOUND SENTENCE   Lines for the concert tickets ran all around the block, *and* some people had even set up tents.

Walter usually plays practical jokes on others, *but* he was the victim this time.

The clauses are now joined by coordinating conjunctions: *and* and *but.* The sentences flow better, and they are correct. Remember—when you use a coordinating conjunction to link simple sentences, place a comma before the conjunction.

COMPREHENSION
AND PRACTICE
10.3

Use of Coordinating Conjunctions to Connect Clauses

The paragraph below contains some run-ons and comma splices. Find these errors, and put a / between clauses that are not correctly connected. Then, between these clauses, add the coordinating conjunction (*and, or, but, for, nor, so,* or *yet*) that best connects the thoughts. Check each sentence to be sure commas are used correctly. Use the example as a guide.

Representative answers are shown.

EXAMPLE

My computer is now four years old , so / most new software will not run on it.

(1) The 1964 murder of Kitty Genovese in Queens, New York, shocked the public at large , and /the event still sparks people's interest. (2) Early in the morning on March 13, Kitty Genovese returned from work , and /she noticed a man following her. (3) The man grabbed and stabbed her several times , but /he was scared away by a cry from a neighbor in Genovese's apartment. (4) She was still alive , so /her assailant returned twice to stab and sexually assault her. (5) The assault and murder of Kitty Genovese took more than 30 minutes. (6) Thirty-eight people observed the event from their apartments , yet /no one called the police. (7) At first glance, this situation seems to indicate complete apathy on the part of her neighbors. (8) This interpretation is logical , but /some psychologists see it as an example of the Diffusion of Responsibility Theory. (9) According to this theory, most bystanders want to help , yet /each bystander waits for or anticipates the response of someone else in the group. (10) In Kitty Genovese's case, this hesitation led to her death.

COMPREHENSION
AND PRACTICE
10.4

Identification and Correction of Comma Splices and Run-Ons

The following paragraph contains several comma splices and run-ons. Put an * in front of each comma splice or run-on sentence and insert a / between the clauses that are not correctly connected. Then choose an appropriate coordinating conjunction (*and, but, for, or, nor, so,* or *yet*), and write it above the place where the correction is needed. Add a comma if one is needed. Use the example to guide you.

EXAMPLE

, but
*Rose wanted to start school with me / she had to find a full-time job.

(1) Just about every region of the United States was affected by last year's severe drought. (2) In the Midwest, farmers had trouble irrigating their
, and
fields / they also had to plow some crops under. (3) In the Far West, ranchers had to deal with wildfires. (4) In some cases, firefighters from neighboring
, but
states were called in to help fight the fires / they couldn't do much to stop them. (5) All along the East Coast, cities had to impose some strict
, and
rules / citizens had no choice but to follow them. (6) In some places, resi-
, or
dents had to cut back their outdoor water use / they would face stiff fines and possible termination of water service. (7) People were allowed to water
, but
their vegetable gardens / they could do so only three times a week for a half hour at a time. (8) For some reason, however, the South wasn't as severely affected by the drought this time.

CHALLENGE 10.2 Evaluation of the Use of Coordinating Conjunctions

1. Underline each independent clause in the following passage.

   The lake was the heart of the resort, and the design took full advantage of its beauty. Rustic old cottages were nestled among the trees along its shore, and hills rose in tiers around it. Long porches with big picture windows behind them had been placed on the water side, for everyone wanted to make the most of the view. The big lodge sat on a hill rather than on the water's edge, but it also gazed out on the shining water. From first light to starlight, the sight of water offered tranquility, and the sound offered comfort.

collaboration

2. Working with a classmate, evaluate each compound sentence, discussing which would be better: leaving the sentence as it is or turning it into two simple sentences. Then, on a separate sheet of paper, write the version of the paragraph you are both comfortable with as well as a brief explanation of your decisions.

Semicolons

A second way to eliminate a comma splice or run-on is to use a semicolon (;) to connect the two simple sentences. As Chapter 9 discussed, semicolons emphasize a very close connection between simple sentences.

Look at these examples, which have a / between the simple sentences:

COMMA SPLICE
> The old woman in the wheelchair was sleeping,/ her husband stood sadly at her side.

RUN-ON
> I just wanted a fast cup of coffee / things didn't work out that way, though.

Correcting these errors is a simple matter of inserting semicolons between the simple sentences, as these versions show:

COMPOUND SENTENCE
> The old woman in the wheelchair was sleeping; her husband stood sadly at her side.
>
> I just wanted a fast cup of coffee; things didn't work out that way, though.

To heighten or emphasize the relationship between sentences, you can include a conjunctive adverb after the semicolon, as Chapter 9 showed. Here again is the list of common conjunctive adverbs:

Common Conjunctive Adverbs

also	however	similarly
besides	instead	still
consequently	meanwhile	then
finally	moreover	therefore
furthermore	nevertheless	thus

Remember that conjunctive adverbs aren't conjunctions. They are *adverbs,* and adverbs DON'T connect. Adverbs modify or describe, so a semicolon is necessary to make the connection. Look at these examples:

EXAMPLES
> The movie was entertaining; *however,* it was very violent.
>
> Shirley went inside to look for a wrench; *meanwhile,* Chuck crawled under the car.

The semicolons provide the connection in both examples while the conjunctive adverbs offer an additional dimension to the connection. As the examples show, always include a comma after the conjunctive adverb.

COMPREHENSION AND PRACTICE

10.5

Semicolon Use to Connect Clauses

Identify the independent clauses in the paragraph below, and put a / between them. If commas are used incorrectly, cross them out. Then insert a semicolon alone or with a conjunctive adverb and comma to connect the clauses and show their relationship. Use the example as a guide.

EXAMPLE

Many manufacturers and retailers no longer waste valuable natural resources or

[;] or [;instead,] [they]

unnecessary packaging /~~They~~ rely on such innovations as reusable cases for

small, easily lost or stolen items.

(1) Many animal lovers criticize the use of animals for medical

[;] or [; however,]

research,/there is another side to the controversy. (2) Some studies involv-

ing animals are necessary for the good of humanity. (3) For instance, research

[;] or [; meanwhile,]

may help find a cure to a serious illness such as AIDS,/other studies investigate

[;] or [; furthermore,]

genetic problems. (4) In addition, most laboratory animals are well fed,/the labs

themselves are generally clean and comfortable. (5) Not all experiments are cruel

[;] or [; also,]

either,/animals receive necessary painkillers and medical care.

COMPREHENSION AND PRACTICE 10.6

Identification and Correction of Comma Splices and Run-Ons with Semicolons

The following paragraph contains several comma splices and run-on sentences. Put an * in front of each comma splice or run-on. Correct each error by inserting a semicolon, or a semicolon and a conjunctive adverb, above the place where a correction is needed. If commas are incorrectly used between sentences, cross them out. Use the example to guide you.

EXAMPLE

[;] or [; however,]

*Management presented their last, best offer, the workers rejected it and
returned to the picket line.

(1) The massive tsunami in South Asia in December 2004 killed more

than 150,000 people in several countries, including Sumatra, Indonesia, Sri

*

Lanka, and India. (2) Before this disaster, the public in general knew little

[;] or [; however,]

about tsunamis media discussions following the disaster have changed all this.

*   [;]

(3) The name tsunami comes from Japanese, it means *harbor wave*. (4) People

*

sometimes refer to tsunamis as tidal waves, but no tides are involved. (5) The

[;] or [; also,]

most common cause of a tsunami is an underwater earthquake undersea

volcanoes, landslides along coastal areas, and meteor strikes can create

*

tsunamis. (6) The South Asia tsunami was caused by two plates of the earth

[;] or [; consequently,]

shifting deep beneath the sea near Sumatra, the ocean rose dramatically.

(7) Water moved upward and then outward in waves as long as 100 miles from end to end, heading for landfall. (8) On shore, the telltale sign of a coming tsunami is an unexpected and severe draining of beaches and
[;]
harbors ˄scientists call this a *washout.* (9) Sometimes residents, unaware of the
[;] or [; meanwhile,]
tragedy about to strike, head out across the now dry area,/˄the water is heading back to shore in the form of higher, more powerful waves. (10) In the South East Asia disaster, a series of waves roared inland up to 1,000 feet in some areas before receding.

CHALLENGE 10.3   Evaluation of Coordinating Conjunctions and Semicolons as Options to Correct Comma Splices and Run-Ons

1. Evaluate the following paragraph. Put an * in front of each comma splice or run-on sentence that you identify and decide how to correct the errors. Then, on a separate piece of paper, rewrite the paragraph, correcting the errors by using a coordinating conjunction, a semicolon, or a semicolon with a conjunctive adverb. Be sure you use commas where they are needed. Representative answers are shown.

(1) Jamie Foxx is among today's biggest stars,/˄; he has enjoyed success as a standup comic, a television comedian, and a serious actor. (2) He was
and
born Eric Morlon Bishop in Terrell, Texas,˄ he was adopted and raised
, but
there by his grandparents. (3) He was a talented high school athlete˄he was an even more talented musician. (4) Foxx studied classical piano at Julliard,
and
˄he attended United States International University in San Diego on a music scholarship. (5) He changed his name to Jamie Foxx at the beginning of
;
his standup career˄the extra *x* in Foxx is a tribute to comedian Red Foxx. (6) He made his mark in television as a cast member of *In Living Color,*
and
˄his performances led to a role on *Roc* and his own sitcom, *The Jamie Foxx Show.* (7) By the end of the 1990s, Foxx was already a legitimate television
, but
star˄he had Hollywood on his mind. (8) Foxx's breakthrough role came in
, and
1999's *Any Given Sunday* alongside Al Pacino and Cameron Diaz˄he also

costarred with Tom Cruise in *Collateral.* (9) In 2005 he won the Oscar for
Best Actor in *Ray,* critics called his portrayal of musical superstar Ray
Charles masterful. (10) Foxx had made it to the top of his field, yet he
made sure to use his acceptance speech to thank the person most responsible for his success: his late grandmother.

collaboration

2. Share your revised paragraph with a classmate, and discuss the changes that
each of you made. Together, revise the paragraph one more time. Use the
versions of the sentences that you both agree are most effective.

Subordinating Conjunctions

Another way to correct a comma splice or run-on sentence is to use a
subordinating conjunction, a connector that indicates a particular relationship between the subject–verb units it connects. As Chapter 8 explained, when you
use subordinating conjunctions to connect sentences, the result is a *complex sentence*—a main clause plus a subordinate clause. Here again is a list of common
subordinating conjunctions:

Common Subordinating Conjunctions

after	if	until
although	in order that	when
as	once	whenever
as if	rather than	where
as soon as	since	wherever
because	so that	whether
before	though	while
even though	unless	

Consider these examples, which include a / between the two subject–verb units.

COMMA SPLICE Darrell volunteered to coach the Pop Warner 12-and-under football team, / no
one else wanted to do it.

RUN-ON Only one cell phone provider offered unlimited texting / other companies
provided more overall minutes per month.

These sets of simple sentences have been joined but not properly connected.
Remember: *Commas cannot connect.* These sentences require connectors that
show their relationship if they are to be left together.

Look at these versions, with subordinating conjunctions added.

COMPLEX SENTENCE

Darrell volunteered to coach the Pop Warner 12-and-under football team *because* no one else wanted to do it.

Although only one cell phone provider offered unlimited texting, other companies provided more overall minutes per month.

In each case, the subordinating conjunction links the simple sentences and also indicates the relationship between them. Darrell will coach *because* no one else volunteered. Only one phone pact gives unlimited texting, *although* other programs offer more total time. Note that you must use a comma between subject-verb units when the subordinate clause appears before the main clause, as the second corrected sentence shows.

COMPREHENSION AND PRACTICE 10.7

Use of Subordinating Conjunctions to Correct Comma Splices and Run-Ons

Use subordinating conjunctions to correct the comma splices and run-ons in the following paragraph. First, identify the incorrectly joined clauses and put a / between them. Then add a subordinating conjunction that shows the relationship between the clauses and corrects the error. Remember that you can place a subordinating conjunction *before* the first clause or *between* the clauses. See page 196 for a list of subordinating conjunctions. Add a comma wherever one is needed, and cross out any unneeded commas. Use the example as a guide.

EXAMPLE

because
Satellite radio continues to grow in popularity listeners would rather pay a monthly fee than listen to annoying commercials. Representative answers are shown.

(1) Phishing is among the most serious problems facing Internet
because
users/innocent people can lose their money and their identities. (2) A phisher sends out huge numbers of e-mails about problems with financial accounts
even though
from well-known firms like PayPal or BankAmerica,/the phisher has no
While the
connection to these companies. (3) The links on the e-mail lead to genuine-looking Web sites,/the sites aren't legitimate. (4) The phisher can gain access
once
to financial accounts and steal identities,/people supply the requested personal or financial information. (5) Unfortunately, phishing schemes are serious
because
concerns/these scams have led to more than $1 billion a year in losses.

COMPREHENSION
AND PRACTICE

Subordinating Conjunction Use to Connect Clauses

10.8   The following paragraph contains several comma splices and run-ons. Put an * in front of each comma splice and run-on sentence. Then choose an appropriate subordinating conjunction from the list on page 196, and write it above where one sentence should end and the next should begin. Change punctuation as necessary. Use the example to guide you.

EXAMPLE

*Our politicians often complicate our lives, *because* they work so slowly.

(1) My friend Danielle has trouble getting around school *because* she is in an electric wheelchair. (2) Many of the doorways inside the buildings are very narrow *even though* federal regulations call for wide doors and corridors. (3) Danielle faces other obstacles on campus. (4) For example, the crushed stone walkways cause her difficulty. (5) She sometimes becomes stuck *when* the wheels of her chair sink in the loose stone. (6) Also, in some of the buildings, the desks are bolted to the floor. (7) Danielle can't enter or leave these rooms, *until* all the other students leave. (8) Most of the desks on campus are the wrong height for her to use. (9) She has to use a big textbook on her lap as a desktop, *unless* the instructor requests a special desk for her. (10) Without her determination, Danielle would have dropped out long ago.

CHALLENGE 10.4   Practice with Subordinating Conjunctions

1. The following paragraph is composed of complex sentences, each of which features the subordinate clause before the main clause. Evaluate each sentence, deciding whether you should leave it as it is or reverse the order of the clauses. Then, on a separate sheet of paper, rewrite the paragraph and briefly write down your reasons for any changes.

    (1) Because my car is unreliable, I have been late for work on several occasions. (2) Even though my supervisor has been supportive in the past, she has begun to lose patience with me. (3) After I arrived 15 minutes late last Wednesday, she wrote me up and put the complaint in my personnel file. (4) When I found out about the complaint, I was both angry and worried about my job. (5) Although I understand her reasoning, she could have given me a break by issuing an oral warning.

collaboration

2. Exchange your version of the paragraph with a classmate and compare the sentences. Discuss any differences, deciding together which order is better.

Periods

Perhaps the simplest way to eliminate comma splices and run-ons is to put a period between the subject–verb units to create two separate sentences. Look at these examples, which have a / between the simple sentences.

COMMA SPLICE

> The trip from Chicago to Miami, with a stop in Atlanta, was the longest part of my trip, / the flight to Grand Bahama, the second most popular destination in the Bahamas, took less than an hour.

RUN-ON

> Ali's new job is much easier than her old job at the self-service gas station near the busiest avenue in town / now she works in the florist department at a supermarket, making various floral arrangements.

As you can see, the subject–verb units in each example are incorrectly connected. If you corrected the errors by using a conjunction or a semicolon, the resulting sentences would be long—each over thirty-five words—which would make them difficult to follow.

A better choice is to use a period and create separate sentences, as these versions show:

REVISED

> The trip from Chicago to Miami, with a stop in Atlanta, was the longest part of my trip. The flight to Grand Bahama, the second most popular destination in the Bahamas, took less than an hour.
>
> Ali's new job is much easier than her old job at the self-service gas station near the busiest avenue in town. Now she works in the florist department at a supermarket, making various floral arrangements.

When the sentences involved are short, however, using a period to separate the units may be a bad strategy because the result might not flow smoothly:

CHOPPY

> The trip from Chicago to Miami took five hours. The flight to Grand Bahama took less than an hour.
>
> Ali's new job is much easier than her old job. Now she works in the florist department at a supermarket.

A better stylistic choice would be to use a conjunction or a semicolon to connect sentences, as these versions show:

IMPROVED

> The trip from Chicago to Miami took five hours, **but** the flight to Grand Bahama took less than an hour.
>
> Ali's new job is much easier than her old job; **now** she work in the florist department at a supermarket.

Period Use to Separate Independent Thoughts

The paragraph below contains run-on sentences and comma splices. Put a /
between the incorrectly joined clauses. Then insert a period and a capital letter
where each is needed. Use the example to guide you.

EXAMPLE

A planet is a large, fairly cool body traveling in a path around a star, /extend [. often]

smaller bodies called satellites or moons orbit planets.

(1) An Israeli company has developed a revolutionary vehicle, the X-Hawk,

with the same ability as a helicopter to take off and land vertically/the advan- [. The]

tage of the X-Hawk is its ability to maneuver in tight quarters. (2) Instead of a

helicopter's typical exposed top-mounted rotors, the X-Hawk's rotors are within

the body of the vehicle,/the X-Hawk can therefore easily avoid power lines and [. The]

hover closer to structures like skyscrapers or cliffs. (3) The unique design of the

X-Hawk makes it possible for the pilot to move forward and backward with

ease/it is also significantly quieter than a typical helicopter. (4) The X-Hawk is [. It]

expected to be able to reach a speed of 125 mph and to fly for up to an hour

and a half without refueling. (5) The price tag will be somewhere between

$1.5 and $3.5 million per vehicle,/safety and aeronautic agencies in several [. Safety]

countries have already expressed interest in purchasing an X-Hawk, expected

to be available within the next few years.

**Identification and Correction of Comma Splices
and Run-Ons with a Period**

The following paragraph contains several comma splices and run-on sentences. Put
an * in front of each comma splice or run-on sentence. Insert a period where the
first sentence should end. Then capitalize the first letter of the word that begins the
second sentence. Cross out any incorrect commas. Use the example as a guide.

EXAMPLE

*People without an adequate income may lead uncertain, disrupted lives, the [. The]

most ordinary events may be an ordeal.

(1) Panic attacks are unbelievably frightening events, they can make peo- [* . They]

ple's lives a nightmare. (2) For no apparent reason, the affected individuals

begin to feel an overwhelming sense of fear. (3) Then their hearts seem to
be racing out of control_{.For} for many people, the incident feels like a heart attack.
(4) At this point, their fear accelerates the attack_{,.They} they begin to feel completely
out of control, struggling to breathe and remain calm. (5) Sometimes, victims
even end up in an emergency room. (6) Doctors often prescribe medications
to control panic attacks_{,.Overall} overall, though, counseling and relaxation techniques
have better results. (7) With these kinds of treatment, most people can return
to their regular lifestyle. (8) They don't have to live in fear anymore_{,.These} these
proven strategies help them deal with these disturbing episodes.

<table>
<tr><td>COMPREHENSION
AND PRACTICE
10.11</td></tr>
</table>

Subordinating Conjunctions or Periods to Correct Comma Splices and Run-Ons

Identify the comma splices and run-ons in the paragraph below. Mark each with
an *. On a separate sheet of paper, rewrite the paragraph, revising the incorrectly connected sentences by inserting a period or a subordinating conjunction
where you think is best. Check your work for correct use of punctuation and
capitals.

(1) With an optimistic outlook, a person will likely live a much happier
life. (2) Some people see a partially filled glass and call it half empty, the
people I admire see it half full. (3) Pessimistic people never seem satisfied
they often have all they need and more. (4) One woman with whom I work
is always complaining. (5) On Monday she dreads the start of a new work
week, she should be grateful she has her job and good health to enjoy the
weekend. (6) By Wednesday, she begins to whine about the work piled on
her desk. (7) A new project comes her way, she moans about being overworked. (8) Optimists would see the added responsibility as a sign of the
boss's confidence this type of upbeat attitude helps to make people happier
in the long run. (9) Most of the things pessimists complain about cannot be
changed. (10) They should be more like optimists they should look for
opportunities in what comes their way.

CHALLENGE 10.5   Evaluating Different Ways of Correcting Comma Splices and Run-Ons

1. For Comprehension and Practice 10.1 on pages 188–189, you identified several comma splices and run-on sentences. Decide which would be the best way to correct the errors: connecting them with a coordinating conjunction or semicolon (with or without a conjunctive adverb) or separating them with a period. On a separate sheet of paper, rewrite the paragraph with your corrections.

2. Exchange your corrected paragraph with a classmate and compare your corrections. If you have made different choices, discuss your reasoning and then decide together which methods of correcting the sentences are best and why.

collaboration

✓ COMMA SPLICES AND RUN-ON SENTENCES CHECKLIST

☐ Have you remembered that commas cannot serve as connectors?

☐ Have you checked all subject–verb units to determine which ones can stand as simple sentences?

☐ Are you clear on how the connection supplied by a semicolon differs from the connection supplied by a coordinating conjunction?

☐ Have you considered the dependent relationship created when you use a subordinating conjunction to connect subject–verb units?

☐ Have you considered situations for which using a period to separate sentences would be a better choice than connecting them?

Journal Writing

Comma splices and run-on sentences occur when sentences are incorrectly joined. Eliminating these errors involves correctly linking or correctly separating subject–verb units. In other words, it's a matter of connection or separation. Now consider connection and separation as they exist in the world. What is the most difficult part of either of these experiences? Think of an incident you've seen or experienced in which connection or separation played an important role. In what ways can either have a positive or a negative effect on a person's life? Select some aspect of separation or connection and explore it for 20 to 30 minutes in your journal.

CHAPTER QUICK CHECK   Comma Splices and Run-On Sentences

The following passage contains a number of commas splices and run-on sentences. First, identify any errors by putting an * in front of each faulty sentence. Then, using the techniques discussed in this chapter, correct the comma splices and run-ons. Check your work to be sure you have used punctuation and capitals correctly. Representative answers are shown

(1) For many years, astronomers focused their attention far away from Earth ; they had largely ignored regions closer to home. (2) More recently, however, they have been focusing attention on our own neighborhood, relative to the entire universe. (3) Not long ago, the International Astronomical Union (IAU) agreed on a new definition of the term *planet* on the basis of size and type of orbit ; Pluto is now classified as a dwarf planet as a result. (4) Over the last several years, astronomers have also discovered a number of large objects a billion miles beyond Pluto. (5) In 2002, California Institute of Technology's Michael Brown and a team of astronomers discovered Quaoar (pronounced KWA-wahr) . Its its name is drawn from the mythology of the ancient inhabitants of the Los Angeles area. (6) Quaoar is about half the size of Pluto, . This this huge object was found in the Kuiper Belt, a cold, dark region extending from Neptune to the edges of the solar system. (7) At the time of its discovery, Quaoar ranked as the largest body found in the solar system in over 70 years. (8) In 2004, two additional objects, Orcus and Sedna, were discovered ; both are larger than Quaoar. (9) Then in 2006 Michael Brown discovered an object larger than Pluto at the edge of the solar system. (10) The IAU has named this new object Eris, and it has been classified as a dwarf planet like Pluto.

SUMMARY EXERCISE   Comma Splices and Run-On Sentences

The following essay contains a number of comma splices and run-on sentences. First, identify any errors by putting an * in front of each faulty sentence. Then, using the techniques discussed in this chapter, correct the comma splices and run-ons. Check your work to be sure you have used punctuation and capitals correctly. Representative answers are shown.

(1) Last year, I had the chance to go downhill skiing for the first time. (2) Skiing sounded easy enough to me, ; however, I discovered the truth before too long.

(3) Early in the morning, my friend Pat drove us for about four hours to reach the mountains. (4) Unlike me, Pat had been skiing several times,[so] he kept telling me not to worry about not knowing how to ski. (5) He even talked me out of taking a professional lesson[;] instead, he promised to teach me himself.

(6) At the resort, I rented skis, poles, and boots[, and] I also bought a full-day lift pass. (7) Pat took me to the beginner's slope first to show me the basics of skiing. (8) Before going to the top of the slope, he demonstrated "snow-plowing," a technique for slowing by turning the ski tips inward. (9) The beginner's area had an old-fashioned rope tow to pull skiers up the small slope. (10) Unfortunately, Pat forgot to warn me about letting the rope slide through my hands,[so] I ended up flat on my face and completely embarrassed.

(11) Meanwhile, Pat impatiently was waiting for me at the top of the beginner's slope. (12) I followed him down the hill and tried to snowplow to keep my speed down[, but] I just seemed to pick up speed. (13) Finally, I fell down on purpose to stop myself. (14) Meanwhile, one of my skis fell off and went down the slope by itself[.] I had to take off the other ski and walk the rest of the way to the bottom.

(15) Pat finally went off to the intermediate slope, and I spent the remainder of the morning mastering the beginner's slope. (16) [Although] I had made a few runs down the hill without falling before lunch, I still didn't know how to stop very well. (17) I did feel a little more confident[;] the thought of skiing down the beginner's slope no longer terrified me.

(18) Then, during lunch, I made a big mistake,[when I let] Pat convinced me to try the intermediate slope. (19) As I rode the chair lift to the top of the mountain and looked down, the slope seemed more like a cliff than a hill. (20) At the top of the run, Pat smiled and told me to ski from side to side down the mountain[. He] then sped off down the slope. (21) I fell at least seven times on my trip down, and even little kids were passing me. (22) By

the time I reached the lodge at the bottom, I was wet and sore, ^and^ I just wanted to go home.

(23) I've been on several skiing trips since that first time, ^and^ I have improved as a skier with each trip. (24) I finally figured out how to slow down and stop effectively, so I regularly ski on intermediate slopes. (25) Still, I'll never forget my first ski trip; I couldn't sit down for three days afterward.

FOR FURTHER EXPLORATION

1. Select one of the following topics and examine it more closely, using the prewriting technique you prefer.

   - The biggest motivation in your life
   - Something about you or your life that most people would be surprised to learn
   - Which time period is superior, the current one or the time when your grandparents were your age

2. Evaluate your prewriting material, identify a focus, and create a draft paragraph of at least seven to ten sentences.

collaboration

3. Exchange your draft with a writing partner. Using the material in this chapter as a guide, evaluate the draft you receive. Note any comma splices and run-on sentences as well as any other weaknesses, and return the draft to the writer.

4. Revise your draft, eliminating any errors that your reader identified.

DISCOVERING CONNECTIONS

For this assignment, focus on the photo and consider one of the following questions (or some other the picture inspires). Explore your ideas and then create a draft paragraph of at

least seven to ten sentences. Be mindful of misplaced commas or missing conjunctions that could result in a comma splice or a run-on sentence.

A. If you had the time, what activities would you engage in to improve your own physical condition? Why?

B. Some individuals like to engage in physically challenging sports, such as mountain biking, kayaking, climbing, and so forth. Have you ever participated in such an activity? What did you do to prepare? How did you get involved in it? If not, which would you choose and why?

RECAP | Comma Splices and Run-On Sentences

Key Terms in This Chapter   **Definitions**

comma splice	a sentence-combining error in which two sentences are joined by only a comma
	EXAMPLE The wall was covered with graffiti, the ground was covered with litter.
run-on sentence	a sentence-combining error in which two sentences run together without any punctuation to separate or conjunction to connect them
	EXAMPLE The nurse took the patient's blood pressure the doctor stitched the wound.

Four Ways to Correct Comma Splices and Run-on Sentences

1   **Subject–verb unit + Connector + Subject–verb unit**

Comma and coordinating conjunction

2   **Subject–verb unit + Connector + Subject–verb unit**

Subordinating conjunction

or

Connector + Subject–verb unit and comma + Subject–verb unit

Subordinating conjunction

3   **Subject–verb unit + Connector + Subject–verb unit**

Semicolon

or

Subject–verb unit + Connector + Subject–verb unit

Semicolon and conjunctive adverb and comma

4   **Subject–verb unit + Separator + Subject–verb unit, beginning with a capital letter**

Period or other appropriate end punctuation

Using Discovery Online with MyWritingLab

PEARSON **mywritinglab**

For more practice with comma splices and run-on sentences, go to www.mywritinglab.com.

> **assessment:** a process of evaluation designed to identify your level of mastery and help improve your performance

EFFECTIVE SENTENCES: CONSTRUCTING MEANING

The material you have completed in Part 2 focuses on **recognizing and writing correct sentences**. To assess your understanding of this information and your progress as a **Writer**, **Reader**, **Editor**, and **Student**, complete the following charts. First check off your level of confidence for each item, and then take the recommended action to improve your performance.

- As a **Writer**, I understand

	Confident	Moderately Confident	Not Confident
1. the roles of subjects and verbs (Chapter 6)			
2. how to identify and correct sentence fragments (Chapter 7)			
3. the purpose and function of subordination (Chapter 8)			
4. the purpose and function of coordination (Chapter 9)			
5. how to identify and correct comma splices and run-on sentences (Chapter 10)			

- If you are **confident**, you are all set. Move on.

- If you are **moderately confident**, review the Recaps for the appropriate chapters.

- If you are **not confident**, go through the appropriate chapters, perhaps completing exercises and activities again.

- As a **Reader**, I understand

	Confident	Moderately Confident	Not Confident
1. the level of language used to discuss the parts and construction of correct sentences			
2. the purpose and usefulness of each **Chapter Checklist**, **Summary Exercise**, and **Journal Writing** feature			

- If you are **confident**, you are all set. Move on.

- If you are **moderately confident**, review again the **Chapter Checklists**, **Summary Exercises**, and **Journal Writing** features to ensure that you see the connection between these features and the material in the chapter.

- If you are **not confident**, return to the **Chapter Checklists** and identify the pages on which the various points are explained; then, underline or highlight key words in the **Journal Writing** feature that will help you make the connection between the assignment and the chapter focus.

- As an **Editor**, I understand

	Confident	Moderately Confident	Not Confident
1. how to express all my ideas in complete, correct sentences containing subjects and verbs (Chapters 6 and 7)			
2. how to use subordination and coordination to improve the meaning and flow of my writing (Chapters 8 and 9)			
3. how to identify and correct sentence errors (Chapter 10)			

- If you are **confident**, you are all set. Move on.

- If you are **mildly confident**, reevaluate a paragraph you are currently working on. Identify all subjects and verbs, ensure that all units express complete thoughts, and consider whether combining sentences using subordination or coordination will improve the meaning and flow of your ideas.

- If you are **not confident**, review some of the examples provided in each of the chapters. Consider completing the activities and exercises again, or find a passage of 200 words or so in one of your textbooks or some other piece of writing—a blog, a newspaper article—and highlight or underline all subjects and verbs as well as simple, complex, and compound sentences.

- As a **Student**, I understand

	Confident	Moderately Confident	Not Confident
1. the role that writing plays in my other classes			
2. the importance of being an active participant in all my classes			
3. the importance of taking advantage of campus services available to help me succeed			

- If you are **confident**, you are all set. Move on.

- If you are **moderately confident,** review the Faces of Discovery feature highlighting past and current students who have come to recognize the importance of good writing skills, participating in class, and taking advantage of campus services. Read why they feel these things are important and reevaluate your own thoughts. Reconsider the type of work you do for all your classes, your typical classroom behavior, and the types of services (writing center, study groups, tutoring center, etc.) provided on campus.

- If you are **not confident**, list all the writing tasks you face in your classes (note taking, summarizing, minute papers, analytical or research papers, etc.), the number of times you actively participate in class each week, and the location and operating hours of the campus program or center that would provide the most help for you.

PART 3

Verbs: Conveying Action and Time

In your view, what are the advantages to completing your writing on a computer? Are there situations when you feel that writing a paper by hand is superior to creating it on a computer?

I think that a computer is a great tool, and it allows a very easy cleanup process while working on a piece of writing. However, there are many times—especially when I am prewriting—when I still feel more comfortable writing something down on a piece of paper and staring at it for a while to brainstorm for ideas.

Joshua Fay
Major:
Human Services
Career Plans:
To become a social worker or case manager

For Josh Fay, succeeding in college is important for several reasons, not the least of which is demonstrating he can meet a challenge head on. "I never gave high school a 100 percent effort, so college is a test for me to prove that I can be successful." He also recognizes the importance of education in reaching other goals in his life, including having a family and being able to provide for their needs, both emotional and physical. "Being successful will allow me to provide opportunity for my family." Before he started college, Josh felt he had "somewhat poor" writing skills, but now "I consider myself a good writer. I am able to structure my information in an effective way to reach my reader as well as to avoid making the mistakes I used to make—I'm more aware of them now." Any concerns about facing up to a challenge have dissipated, too. "College hasn't been as hard as I thought it was going to be. I have given it a great effort, and I am doing fairly well thus far."

What techniques have you found most helpful in managing, developing, and improving the vocabulary you use as a writer?

Dictionary.com—I am always on the site, whether it is looking up a definition or using its thesaurus. I don't like using the same word over and over again. With the thesaurus I am able to find different words, yet they all mean about the same.

Sara M. Penuel
Major:
Baking and Pastry Arts
Career Plans:
To open her own café/bakery

As Sara Penuel sees it, "College is about finding who you are, what you want to do in life, what you want to become." In terms of her own future, she has settled on a plan: "I will be the second to graduate from college in my family. I will be the first in my whole family to do Baking and Pastry." And Sara is making the most of her time as a college student. "College has opened so many doors for me. When I want something, I work hard for it. I want to be the best I can be. I am already on the Dean's list and in the Honors Program." Although she occasionally found English classes difficult in high school, she has adjusted well to writing for college. "I feel more confident now. I can write about almost anything if I set myself to it. I just need time to think about the subject or topic. I feel as if I can write more and know how to fix problems I might have, if it's adding detail or simply using a different verb."

What is your favorite time of day and favorite place to write? Why? Are there other elements you prefer, for example, playing music, snacking on food, working in silence, or working completely alone?

When I need to write, I like it to be very quiet. I usually write on a table in my house when nobody is around, so I can have complete peace and quiet. That way, I'm able to think with no distractions. That's what works best for me.

High school was not the best of times for Erin Turcotte. Things got so bad that she had to attend summer school after her senior year in order to earn her high school diploma. "I wasn't allowed to go to my graduation and stand up with my class. That's a once-in-a-lifetime thing, and I blew it." College, however, has been a different story for Erin. "I love college. Now I'm trying the best I can because I know I can do it. That's such a good feeling to have when you know you are going somewhere in life." She also feels much better about her ability to write. "After my first semester in college, I already could tell my writing was a lot better. I had horrible writing skills before college. When I would write something, forget it—I didn't know how to properly write sentences. Now I know how to write paragraphs and develop essays."

Erin Turcotte
Major:
Medical Secretarial
Career Plans:
To work as a secretary in a physician's office and continue on in school for massage therapy.

When you are working on longer pieces of writing, how do you make the decision to begin a new paragraph?

I decide to begin a new paragraph by paying attention to when I am coming to the end of an idea. When my discussion of an idea is coming to a close, I give an ending statement for that paragraph, and I start a new paragraph with a new idea and new supporting statements.

"I hated high school," David Wilkerson readily admits. "I didn't 'grow up' with my classmates. I started attending school with them in the sixth grade. Usually you have made your friends by then, and I was too late. So feeling that I still didn't fit in was probably the biggest difficulty for me in high school." After barely graduating, David took a year off. "I learned that I had to do something besides just work, so I decided to go to college and make something of my life." His college studies have given him greater confidence and improved writing skills. "Before I started college, I wasn't a very good writer, and I am still learning every day. But in one short year, I feel I have learned more about writing than I learned in all my past years." To David, there is no question about the importance of writing well in school and beyond it. "Being able to write well helps you communicate with your colleagues and other people that you cross paths with at your job or in life in general."

David Wilkerson
Major:
Liberal Arts
Career Plans:
To become a nurse

CHAPTER 11
Maintaining Subject–Verb Agreement

GETTING STARTED ...

Q Sometimes after I write a sentence and read it back, I notice that the subjects and verbs don't sound right. What am I doing wrong?

A You are running into trouble maintaining subject–verb agreement. For a number of reasons, you are choosing a form of a verb that doesn't match the subject in *number*—either singular or plural. When you match the wrong words—a singular verb form with a plural subject or a plural verb form with a singular subject—you make an error that distracts your reader from your message.

Overview: Subject–Verb Agreement

To make your sentences clear and understandable, your subjects and verbs must agree, meaning singular subjects need singular verb forms, and plural subjects need plural verb forms. Correct **subject–verb agreement** can be difficult to establish in sentences in which the verb precedes the subject or several words come between the subject and the verb. Constructions involving certain indefinite pronouns, collective nouns, and singular words that appear to be plural can also complicate agreement.

Navigating This Chapter In this chapter, you will discover how to avoid agreement problems with:

- subjects following verbs
- sentences beginning with *There* or *Here*
- subjects and verbs separated by other words
- compound subjects
- indefinite pronouns, collective nouns, and singular nouns ending in *-s* used as subjects

Agreement When the Subject Follows the Verb

In the majority of the sentences you write, the subject comes before the verb. But in many direct questions, part of the verb comes before the subject:

EXAMPLES

verb subject verb

What *did Kenny ask?*

verb subject   verb

Did Ava really *oversleep* yesterday?

ESL Note
See "Sentence Basics,"
pages 483–485, for
more on subjects and
verbs and "Agreement,"
pages 487–489, for
more on issues of
agreement.

Although maintaining subject–verb agreement with questions is generally not too difficult, the contraction *don't* can sometimes trip you up. For example, look at the use of *don't* in the following questions.

FAULTY

Don't Jacqueline *know* how to deal with such a delicate matter?

Don't Jeremy *understand* how to turn a person down?

Both sentences are incorrect because *don't* is a *contraction,* a shortened form of two words: *do not.* But *do* is the verb that agrees with plural subjects, not singular subjects such as *Jacqueline* and *Jeremy.*

CORRECTED

Doesn't Jacqueline *know* how to deal with such a delicate matter?

Doesn't Jeremy *understand* how to turn a person down?

COMPREHENSION
AND PRACTICE

11.1

The Subject Following the Verb

Fill in the blanks in the questions below with the correct verb taken from the following list, and underline the subject of that verb. Use the example as a guide.

Hasn't *or* Haven't   Does *or* Do   Has *or* Have
Was *or* Were   Doesn't *or* Don't

EXAMPLE

<u>*Were*</u> many good <u>seats</u> still available for the concert on Sunday?

1. <u>Have or Haven't</u> you enjoyed yourself tonight?

2. <u>Does or Doesn't</u> that old <u>refrigerator</u> need to be replaced?

3. <u>Has or Hasn't</u> the <u>leader</u> of our study group called you yet?

4. <u>Was or Wasn't</u> <u>Karrie</u> the winner of the scholarship?

5. <u>Do or Don't</u> those in-line <u>skates</u> cost $200?

COMPREHENSION AND PRACTICE
Identification of Subjects and Verbs When Subjects Follow Verbs

11.2   All the sentences in the following passage are questions. First circle the proper verb for each sentence from the pair in parentheses, and then underline the subject of that verb, as the example shows.

EXAMPLE   (Doesn't, Don't) Terry and Lucy want to go with us tonight to see if we can find the comet?

(1) (Doesn't, Don't) people know how easy it is to shop online? (2) (Is, Are) anyone still unaware that this kind of shopping is among the fastest-growing areas of the U.S. economy? (3) (Hasn't, Haven't) everyone received a gift purchased through the Internet by now or heard of someone who has? (4) (Isn't, Aren't) the many stories of satisfied customers enough to make the public at least curious about this type of e-commerce? (5) (Is, Are) a concern about releasing a credit card number stopping some people from investigating some of the fine companies doing business over the Internet? (6) Or (has, have) they had a negative experience in the past with some mail-order business? (7) (Isn't, Aren't) they aware that major companies are working hard to make online shopping simple, easy, and fun? (8) (Isn't, Aren't) the average person truly interested in using computers for more than just word processing?

COMPREHENSION AND PRACTICE
Subject–Verb Agreement in Questions

11.3   Write ten questions on a separate sheet of paper, including five questions that contain the contraction *don't* or *doesn't*. Make sure that you maintain agreement between the subject and verb in each question. Answers will vary.

CHALLENGE 11.1   Review for Errors with Subjects That Follow Verbs

collaboration

1. Exchange the questions you wrote in Comprehension and Practice 11.3 with a classmate. Rewrite each of the questions you receive as a statement to verify that the subjects agree with the verbs in each sentence. Suggest any revisions that are necessary to maintain agreement, and return the paper to the writer.

2. Check the comments your classmate has made, and then make any necessary changes to your questions. Answers will vary.

Sentences Beginning with *There* and *Here*

Only a noun or pronoun can be the subject of a sentence. Sentences beginning with *There* or *Here* often present problems with subject–verb agreement. In sentences beginning with *There* or *Here*, the subject always comes *after* the verb.

A common error in this type of sentence construction is to use the singular form of the verb with a plural subject, as these examples show:

FAULTY

There is several factors leading to network failure.

Here comes the largest suitcases.

In the first sentence, *is* is a singular verb. *There* can't act as the subject, so you must look for a noun or pronoun that answers the question, *There is who or what?* In this case, the answer is *factors,* which is plural. In the second sentence, the verb is also singular: *comes*. *Here* can't act as a subject, so the subject follows the verb. Ask *Here comes who or what?* and you'll find that the subject is *largest suitcases,* which is plural.

Once you discover an error in subject–verb agreement, you'll find it easy to correct. Simply make both subject and verb plural or singular, as these versions show:

CORRECTED

There *are* several *factors* leading to network failure.

or

There *is* a primary *reason* leading to network failure.

CORRECTED

Here *come* the largest suitcases.

or

Here *comes* the largest suitcase.

You might also restate the sentence and eliminate *there* or *here* completely:

CORRECTED

Several *factors* contribute to network failure.

The largest *suitcases* are coming.

COMPREHENSION
AND PRACTICE

11.4

Sentences Beginning with *There* or *Here*

Each of the following sentences calls for either *is* or *are.* Underline the subject, and then write the appropriate verb in the space provided, as the example shows.

EXAMPLE There _____are_____ elaborate costumes to make for LaWanda's performance next week.

(1) There _____are_____ many ways a person can improve study skills. (2) Here _____is_____ one of the best methods to increase reading comprehension: preparing a brief summary of a passage. (3) There _____is_____ something to be gained through restating the ideas of an author in your own words. (4) For one thing, there _____is_____ the value of the work involved in reducing the original passage, which forces you to identify the most important material. (5) Also, there _____is_____ the additional advantage in terms of extra writing practice.

COMPREHENSION AND PRACTICE

Subjects and Verbs in *Here/There* Sentences

11.5 A pair of verbs in parentheses appears in each sentence in the following passage. Circle the correct verb and underline its subject, using the example as a guide.

EXAMPLE There (is, (are)) several <u>reasons</u> why a person might drop out of school.

(1) For anyone seeking a vacation that combines sun and fun, there ((is,) are) no <u>shortage</u> of possible destinations. (2) First, there (is, (are)) numerous theme <u>parks</u> throughout the United States. (3) (Is, (Are)) there <u>people</u> in this world who wouldn't want to spend warm-weather time in a place like Universal Studios, Six Flags, or Disney World? (4) Then there ((is,) are) the <u>Caribbean</u>, with so many different, beautiful island destinations. (5) Whether it's Aruba, Jamaica, or the Virgin Islands, there (is, (are)) many <u>things</u> for tourists to do. (6) There (is, (are)) <u>swimming, snorkeling, deep sea fishing, windsurfing, and kiteboarding,</u> to name only a few. (7) However, there ((is,) are) a vacation <u>destination</u> that ranks at the top of the list for millions each year: Hawaii. (8) There ((is,) are) <u>everything</u> a tourist could ever want to do on this island paradise.

CHALLENGE 11.2 Elimination of *There* or *Here* Sentence Openings

1. Restating a sentence to eliminate *there* or *here* can help you maintain agreement as well as write concise, direct sentences. Choose five of the sentences from Comprehension and Practice 11.5 and on a separate sheet of paper, revise them to eliminate *there* or *here.*

collaboration

2. Exchange your sentences with a classmate. Compare your classmate's revised sentences to the original versions. Then, on the same page, explain which sentences are most effective and why.

Words That Separate Subjects and Verbs

Words that appear between the subject and verb can also cause errors in subject–verb agreement. Consider the following sentence. Which of the two verbs is correct?

EXAMPLE   The old scrapbook in the closet under the storage boxes (belongs, belong) to my grandmother.

What is confusing about sentences like this one is that a plural word, *boxes,* comes right before the verb. As a result, it's easy to make the mistake of choosing *belong* because it agrees with *boxes.* But the subject of the sentence is *scrapbook,* not *boxes.* Therefore, the proper verb choice is *belongs.*

In this sentence, the words that come between the subject and verb are **prepositional phrases:** *in the closet* and *under the storage boxes.* As Chapter 6, "Subjects and Verbs," explains, a prepositional phrase consists of a preposition and the *object of the preposition,* the noun or pronoun following it. The word *boxes* is the object of the preposition *under,* so it can't be the subject in this sentence. Remember—an *object* cannot be the *subject.*

Here again is the list of *common prepositions,* as well as a list of *common compound prepositions:*

Prepositions

about	before	by	into	over	under
above	behind	despite	like	past	underneath
across	below	down	near	since	unlike
after	beneath	during	of	than	until
against	beside	except	off	through	up
along	besides	for	on	throughout	upon
among	between	from	onto	till	with
around	beyond	in	out	to	within
as	but (except)	inside	outside	toward	without
at					

Compound Prepositions

according to	because of	instead of
along with	in addition to	in the place of
aside from	in front of	next to
as to	in spite of	out of

To ensure that you don't mistake the object of a preposition for the subject of a sentence, always identify any preposition you've used. Once you find a preposition, look for the noun or pronoun following it, and you'll have the complete prepositional phrase. If you envision parentheses around the phrases, you may find it easier to identify the real subject, as this version of the sentence shows:

EXAMPLE

┌─ subject ─┐┌──── prepositional phrases ────┐┌─verb─┐

The old *scrapbook* (in the closet) (under the storage boxes) *belongs* to my grand-

mother.

Another construction that might confuse you is when compound prepositions such as *along with* and *in addition to* introduce prepositional phrases that come between the subject and verb. In the following sentence, which is the correct verb?

EXAMPLE

Dr. Fiscus, along with Dr. Howard and Dr. Fine, (owns, own) that new office building.

If you look at the sentence quickly, you might conclude that because three people are mentioned, the verb should be *own.* But the compound preposition *along with* introduces a prepositional phrase. *Dr. Howard* and *Dr. Fine* are the objects of that preposition, so these doctors can't also be part of the subject. Envision parentheses around the prepositional phrase, and ask the question, *Who or what owns/own that new building?* The answer is *Dr. Fiscus,* so the correct verb in the sentence above is *owns.*

Sometimes, subordinate clauses may come between subjects and verbs, too. A subordinate clause is a group of words that contains a subject and verb but cannot stand on its own. (For more on subordinate clauses, see Chapter 7, pp. 153–155.) Take a look at the following sentence. Which verb in parentheses is the proper choice?

EXAMPLE

The security guards who had been hired at the beginning of the week (was, were) asleep in the back room of the unfinished building.

To check subject–verb agreement in sentences like this, find the verb in the main clause, envision parentheses around the subordinate clauses, and then ask the question *who* or *what?*

Here again is the sentence, this time with the subordinate clause in parentheses:

EXAMPLE

┌──── subject ────┐

The *security guards (who had been hired at the beginning of the week) were* asleep

in the back room of the unfinished building.

Once the subordinate clause is isolated, you can more easily see the essence of the sentence. Now ask the question *Who or what was/were asleep?* The answer is *security guards,* which is plural. Therefore, the proper verb choice is *were.*

COMPREHENSION
AND PRACTICE
11.6

Correct Verb Choice

A pair of verbs in parentheses appears in each sentence in the following passage. Circle the correct verb and underline its subject, using the example to guide you.

EXAMPLE

My relatives from Virginia, who haven't seen my parents in years, (is, (are)) planning to visit my family this year.

(1) Electronic books, which a few years ago were just part of science fiction, (is, (are)) now widely available. (2) Technology in development for many years now ((makes,) make) it possible for a consumer to use one device to read and store hundreds of books. (3) Over the past few years, retail giants like Amazon.com and Sony (has, (have)) introduced e-book readers. (4) These devices, retailing for under $300, (relies, (rely)) on an innovation that replicates ink on a page, eliminating glare from a backlit screen. (5) Consumers who purchase Amazon.com's Kindle, with its wireless capability, (is, (are)) able to shop and then download titles from the Internet retailer's entire listing of books in a matter of minutes.

COMPREHENSION
AND PRACTICE
11.7

Words That Separate Subjects and Verbs

On a separate sheet of paper, write ten sentences, placing the prepositional phrases or subordinate clauses listed below between the subject and verb. Be sure that your subjects and verbs agree, as the example shows. Answers will vary.

EXAMPLE

next to me on the bus

The boy next to me on the bus was asleep.

1. according to educators

2. who worked overtime every day

3. in spite of the discounted price

4. aside from the small fines

5. at the end of each month

6. except for his cell phone bill

7. after ten great years had passed

8. next to the chairs in the back of the room

CHALLENGE 11.3   Sentences with Separated Subjects and Verbs

1. Underline the subjects and circle the verbs in the sentences you created for Comprehension and Practice 11.7.

collaboration

2. Exchange your sentences with a classmate. Evaluate the sentences you receive, looking closely at all words, phrases, and clauses that come between subject and verb to make sure that all subjects and verbs agree. Put an * next to any subject or verb that you believe is incorrect and return the sentences to the writer.

3. Check the potential problems your classmate has identified and then make any changes necessary to maintain correct subject–verb agreement.
Answers will vary.

Problems with Compound Subjects

As Chapter 6 (p. 137) explained and illustrated, many sentences have *compound subjects,* more than one noun or pronoun connected by a conjunction. The words making up the compound subjects are connected by *coordinating conjunctions (and, or, but,* and so on) or *correlative conjunctions (either/or, neither/nor, not only/but also,* and so on). Like single-word subjects, some compound subjects are singular and some are plural. The difference depends on what conjunction connects them. Consider this example:

EXAMPLE   A campaign sign and small crowd of supporters (signifies, signify) the candidate's visit.

Ask the question, *Who or what signifies/signify the candidate's visit?* The answer: *A campaign sign and a small crowd of supporters.* The two parts of this compound subject are connected by *and,* the conjunction that indicates more than one. Therefore, the proper verb choice for this sentence is *signify.* Compound subjects connected by *and* are almost always plural. The exceptions are subjects that are commonly thought of as one, such as *pork and beans, peanut butter and jelly, peace and quiet, ham and eggs,* and *rock and roll.* Now look at this sentence:

EXAMPLE   Either Marc or Shelly (know, knows) the address.

Here, the situation is different. Connecting the subjects with *either/or* indicates that only one of the individuals mentioned knows the address. Both parts of the compound subject are singular, so for this sentence, the proper verb choice is *knows.* If these two subjects were connected by *neither/nor*, it would be the same as saying *no one* or *nobody*, so the correct verb would still be *knows.*

But if the two parts of a compound subject connected by *or, either/or,* or *neither/nor* are plural, then the proper verb choice would also be plural:

EXAMPLE   *Books or magazines make* a visit to a doctor's office easier to bear.

In this sentence, the subject indicates that either of the items helps pass the time, but not both of them. Both words of the compound subject are plural, however, so *make* is the correct verb.

When the compound subject consists of one singular word and one plural word connected by *or, either/or,* or *neither/nor,* the verb agrees with the word closest to it. What's the correct verb in the following example?

EXAMPLE   Neither the captain nor the firefighters (is, are) meeting with the television crew.

Because *firefighters* is closer to the verb, the correct choice is the form that agrees with *firefighters: are.* But if the parts of the subject were reversed, then the proper choice would be *is:*

EXAMPLE   Neither the firefighters nor the captain *is* meeting with the television crew.

COMPREHENSION
AND PRACTICE
11.8

Proper Verbs for Compound Subjects

A pair of verbs in parentheses appears in each sentence in the following passage. Circle the correct verb and underline its subject, using the example as a guide.

EXAMPLE   Either the college president or the union chief (is,) are) to blame for the current impasse in contract negotiations.

(1) My brother Sammy and my sister Carla (seems, seem)) completely unconcerned about keeping the house or their own clothes clean. (2) For instance, unless somebody else in the house irons for them, their shirts and pants (is, are)) always wrinkled. (3) In addition, Sammy's car magazines or homework (is,) are) always in a disorganized pile in his room. (4) Carla's iPod or earrings (is, are)) always spread out across her bureau. (5) Unfortunately for the rest of the family, neither Sammy nor Carla (worries,) worry) much about the mess that results.

Sentences with Compound Subjects

On a separate piece of paper, write a sentence for each of the compound subjects below. Make sure you maintain agreement between the subject and verb in each sentence. Answers will vary.

1. Love and marriage

2. The Super Bowl and the World Series

3. Playing computer games or sending text messages to her friends

4. Math, science, and foreign language

5. The individual music files and the actual CDs

6. Neither diet nor exercise

7. Facebook, MySpace, Flickr, and Twitter

8. Either my parents or my brother

CHALLENGE 11.4   **Subject–Verb Agreement with Compound Subjects**

1. Underline the subjects and circle the verbs in the sentences you created for Comprehension and Practice 11.9.

2. Exchange your sentences with a classmate. Evaluate the sentences you receive, looking closely at all compound subjects to make sure that all subjects and verbs agree. Put an * next to any subject or verb that you believe is incorrect and return the sentences to the writer.

collaboration

3. Check the potential problems your classmate has identified and then make any changes necessary to maintain correct subject–verb agreement. Answers will vary.

Agreement with Indefinite Pronouns

Errors in subject–verb agreement can also occur when a subject is an **indefinite pronoun,** which refers to a general rather than a specific person or thing. Some indefinite pronouns are singular, some are plural, and some are either singular or plural depending on the words to which they refer.

Singular Indefinite Pronouns

another	each	everything	no one	somebody
anybody	either	neither	nothing	someone
anyone	everybody	nobody	one	something
anything	everyone			

Because they are singular, these indefinite pronouns need a singular verb. Words such as *each, everybody,* and *everyone* may confuse you because they seem to suggest more than one. But they are singular, so they require singular verbs:

EXAMPLES

Everyone around the accident scene *was* silent.

Each is tricky, but the tenth hole is probably the worst.

These indefinite pronouns are always plural:

Plural Indefinite Pronouns

both	many
few	several

Whenever you use one of these plural indefinite pronouns, use a plural verb:

EXAMPLES

Of the musicians who start groups, *few* ever really *make* any money.

Several of the smaller cars *have received* good ratings from safety agencies.

The following indefinite pronouns are either singular or plural, depending on the word they refer to in the sentence:

Indefinite Pronouns Affected by the Words That Follow Them

all	more	none
any	most	some

Consider these examples:

SINGULAR

All of his strength *disappears* after only ten minutes on a treadmill.

PLURAL

All of those windows *need* to be cleaned once a month.

SINGULAR

Some of her frustration *results* from the lack of cooperation from her mother.

PLURAL

Some of these regulations *create* more difficulty than they eliminate.

In the first example, *All* refers to *strength,* a singular word, so the proper verb choice is *disappears.* In the second, though, *All* refers to *windows,* a plural word, so the proper verb choice is *need.* In the third sentence, *Some* refers to *frustration,* a singular word, so the proper verb choice is *results.* But in the final sentence, *Some* refers to *regulations,* a plural word, so *create* is the proper verb choice.

COMPREHENSION AND PRACTICE

Correct Verbs for Indefinite Pronoun Subjects

11.10 A pair of verbs in parentheses appears in each sentence in the following passage. Circle the correct verb and underline its subject, using the example to guide you.

EXAMPLE

Nobody at the station (appears, appear) concerned that the train hasn't arrived on time.

(1) Many of the social problems that plague our country (is, are) connected in some way to the economy. (2) Some of the issues, like inadequate health care, (is, are) fairly apparent. (3) Not all of the concerns (is, are) that obvious, however. (4) For example, everyone (knows, know) that K–12 public education is guaranteed for all children in the United States. (5) Yet not everybody (recognizes, recognize) the economic issues at play in terms of support for schools, and that insufficient funding often leads to poor classroom performance.

COMPREHENSION
AND PRACTICE

Indefinite Pronouns as Subjects

11.11

A pair of verbs in parentheses appears in each sentence in the following passage. Circle the correct verb and underline its subject, using the example to guide you.

EXAMPLE

When each of the customers (is, are) more considerate, there won't be so much trash on the floor of the movie theater.

(1) Each of NASA's missions to explore the outer reaches of our universe (provides, provide) scientists with valuable information. (2) Everyone (seems, seem) to support initiatives such as the Hubble Space Telescope, which has provided views of the universe that would otherwise not be possible. (3) Still, for a number of years, some of the people holding the congressional purse strings (was, were) unwilling to fund NASA at reasonable levels. (4) With so many other worthy programs, too few of the voices NASA counted on (was, were) ready to step forward and offer support. (5) Recently, however, some of the support that NASA once enjoyed (has, have) returned. (6) Apparently, more of the people in the position to help NASA now (recognizes, recognize) how space exploration has changed our world. (7) For instance, many of today's innovations in communication (is, are) the direct result of NASA's

work. (8) <u>Anyone</u> watching a television program broadcast from distant nations, for instance, or using a GPS device (is, are) relying on satellite signals, one small benefit of space exploration.

CHALLENGE 11.5 Indefinite Pronouns

1. Indefinite pronouns appear frequently in writing of all types, including slogans, proverbs, and advertisements. Think of sayings such as, "Anything is possible" and "Many are called, but few are chosen." On a separate sheet of paper, write down three common statements that include indefinite pronouns.

collaboration

2. Exchange your statements with a classmate. Check the subject–verb agreement in the sentences you receive, paying close attention to the indefinite pronouns to make sure that the correct verb is used. Remember that some indefinite pronouns are always singular, some are always plural, and some are either singular or plural depending on what they refer to. Put an * next to any incorrect verb and return the sentences to the writer.

3. Check any potential problems your classmate has identified, and then make any necessary changes. Answers will vary.

Agreement with Collective Nouns, Singular Nouns Ending in -s, and Words Indicating Amounts

If a word refers to a group of items or individuals, you might naturally assume that the word would require a plural verb. But for a group of words called *collective nouns,* this is not the case. Collective nouns such as *audience, class, committee, faculty, flock, herd, jury, swarm,* and *team* take singular verbs.

EXAMPLES

This season's basketball *team has* already won more games than last year's team.

The entire *flock was sitting* on the power line.

Certain animal names can also be confusing because the name for one of these animals in the group is the same as the name for the entire group. For example, *antelope, deer, fish, moose, sheep,* and *trout* might all refer to either one animal or a group of animals. Whether you use a singular or plural form of the verb depends on whether you mean one or more than one, as these examples show:

EXAMPLES

That *moose* at the edge of the nature preserve *visits* the public garden area every spring.

Those *moose* at the edge of the nature preserve *look* peaceful.

The first sentence deals with *one* moose, so the proper verb choice is a singular verb form, *visits.* The second sentence deals with several moose, so the proper verb choice is the plural verb *look.*

Another potential stumbling block with subject–verb agreement involves singular nouns ending in *-s.* Most nouns ending in *-s* are plural. However, some words ending in *-s,* including *economics, ethics, mumps, measles, mathematics, news, physics,* and *politics,* are actually singular and require a singular verb:

EXAMPLES   *Economics is* a difficult subject for the beginner.

Measles is no longer a serious threat to children because of improved vaccines.

Nouns that writers use to refer to *measurements, money, time,* and *weight* are also singular and call for singular verbs:

EXAMPLES   *Ninety dollars is* much more than any concert ticket is worth.

Ten minutes was as long as I could stand the complete quiet.

Forty points was too big a lead to overcome.

In each of the examples, the subject refers to a unit, so the verb is singular.

COMPREHENSION AND PRACTICE 11.12

Collective Nouns, Singular Nouns Ending in *-s,* and Words Indicating Amounts as Subjects

A pair of verbs in parentheses appears in each sentence in the following passage. Circle the correct verb and underline its subject, using the example as a guide.

EXAMPLE   I don't understand what all the fuss is about, because I think physics (is, are) the easiest course around.

(1) Mumps (was, were) the cause of a two-week shutdown of Nehi Regional High School last year. (2) When the mumps epidemic first started, the school committee (was, were) unsure what to do. (3) During the open committee meeting, the audience (was, were) adamant about closing the school for two weeks. (4) The faculty in attendance (was, were) very quiet during the presentations. (5) "Ten days (is, are) a long time, but I guess we don't have a choice," said the committee head after the two-hour meeting.

COMPREHENSION AND PRACTICE 11.13

The Correct Verb Choice

A pair of verbs in parentheses appears in each sentence in the following passage. Circle the correct verb and underline its subject, using the example to guide you.

EXAMPLE   After seeing the marks on the mid-term, the class (was̲, were) convinced that the instructor was grading unfairly.

(1) Athletics (plays̲, play) a big part in the life of many Americans, even after their high school and college years. (2) According to several national surveys, 45 minutes of some kind of athletic activity three times a week (is̲, are) the amount of time reported by a large percentage of adults. (3) Across the United States, organized basketball, hockey, softball, or volleyball leagues operate every night, and the typical team (is̲, are) composed of men and women with ages ranging from late twenties to sixties. (4) During an ESPN podcast on this subject, the scheduling committee of one of these leagues (acknowledges̲, acknowledge) how many adults want to take part. (5) The podcast also highlighted how politics (is̲, are) involved in team selection and scheduling of games in this league. (6) Apparently, an audience (motivates̲, motivate) many of the middle-aged athletes on the teams, with some bringing along spouses and children to watch. (7) During the playoffs, 100 spectators (is̲, are) not uncommon. (8) After a big game, the winning team traditionally (heads̲, head) to Phil's, a little diner not far from the health club where the games are played.

CHALLENGE 11.6 Collective Nouns, Singular Nouns Ending in *-s*, and Words Indicating Amounts as Subjects

1. On a separate sheet of paper, write sentences in which you use five of the following words as subjects of present tense verbs.

fifty dollars	news
audience	committee
mathematics	ethics
jury	audience
flock	politics

collaboration

2. Exchange the sentences you have written with a classmate. In the sentences you receive, check to make sure that singular forms of verbs have been used. Put an * next to any verbs you believe are incorrect, and return the sentences to the writer.

3. Evaluate any potential problems your classmate has identified, and correct any errors in subject–verb agreement in your sentences.

✓ MAINTAINING SUBJECT–VERB AGREEMENT CHECKLIST

☐ Have you double-checked any questions, especially those beginning with *Don't,* to ensure that subjects and verbs agree?

☐ Have you checked after the verb in any sentences beginning with *There* or *Here* to make sure you have identified the actual subject?

☐ Have you made sure you have selected the actual subject of a verb and not a word from a phrase or clause coming between subject and verb?

☐ Have you checked to ensure that you have chosen the correct verb for any compound subjects?

☐ Have you used an appropriate verb with any indefinite pronoun used as a subject?

☐ Have you double-checked your choice of verb with any collective noun, singular noun ending in *-s,* or noun indicating amount used as a subject to make sure that the subject and verb agree?

Journal Writing

Written communication fails when subjects and verbs don't match up. It's clear, then, that subject–verb agreement is vital if you want to achieve your goal in writing. How about in life in general? Is it necessary for people on a team, at work, in a relationship, or in a family to agree all the time in order for the individuals to succeed? Is it possible to achieve your goal by holding to your position even if others involved don't agree with you? Explore some aspect of this subject for 20 to 30 minutes in your journal.

CHAPTER QUICK CHECK Maintaining Subject–Verb Agreement

The following passage contains various errors in subject–verb agreement. Using the examples throughout the chapter to guide you, identify any errors in agreement. Then eliminate the errors by writing the correct form over the incorrect one. Some sentences are correct as they are.

(1) My current car, which is the main means of transportation for my friends, certainly ~~turn~~ heads. ^{turns} (2) Some of my friends ~~refers~~ to it as the Beast ^{refer} because of its terrible physical appearance. (3) Dents and rust ~~covers~~ most of ^{cover}

the body. (4) In addition, the stuffing in all the seats ~~stick~~ *sticks* through large tears in

the fabric. (5) The back door on the passenger side, which is painted a differ-

ent color from the rest of the doors, no longer ~~open~~ *opens* because of a recent acci-

dent. (6) I received a settlement from the insurance company to repair the

damage, but I used the money to pay bills instead. (7) ~~Do~~ *Does* this sound like a lux-

ury car to you? (8) All of my neighbors ~~seems~~ *seem* a little embarrassed when I park

my car in front of my house. (9) At least the Beast, unlike some of their cars,

~~start~~ *starts* up every morning. (10) I should probably look for another car, but there

~~is~~ *are* still some miles left in this ugly bucket of bolts.

SUMMARY EXERCISE Maintaining Subject–Verb Agreement

The following essay contains various kinds of errors in subject–verb agreement. Using the examples throughout the chapter to guide you, identify any errors in agreement. Then eliminate the errors by writing the correct form over
the incorrect one. Some sentences are correct as they are.

(1) The study of structures and natural processes ~~represent~~ *represents* a primary av-

enue to learn about the world. (2) In one emerging area of science, however,

the structures and processes under examination ~~becomes~~ *become* blueprints for new

approaches and products. (3) This new field is called biomimicry, and the ex-

perts doing this kind of close analysis of nature sometimes ~~goes~~ *go* by the title of

biomimics or bioneers.

(4) Actually, there ~~are~~ *is* a long history of developing products or procedures

based on nature. (5) For example, Velcro, among today's most popular fasten-

ers, ~~owe~~ *owes* its existence to the common cocklebur. (6) In the 1940s, a Swiss en-

gineer noticed how cockleburs stick to clothing and hair, studied the process,

and developed a system that mimics it.

(7) In other cases, the abilities or behavior of a particular creature ~~serve~~ as [serves] the source for inspiration. (8) For instance, anybody who has observed geckos ~~know~~ [knows] that these little reptiles can cling effortlessly to a variety of surfaces. (9) Their secret, according to scientists who have studied these creatures, ~~are~~ [is] the network of microfilaments on their feet that hold and release with no stickiness left behind. (10) Now researchers studying this natural phenomenon ~~hopes~~ [hope] to imitate the process in order to manufacture reusable adhesive tape and other temporary fasteners.

(11) In 2002, researchers looked to genetic engineering to harness the strength of a substance produced by one of nature's best engineers, the spider. (12) Orb spider silk, the threads used to create elaborate and durable webs, ~~rank~~ [ranks] as one of the strongest and most flexible substances in all of nature. (13) But there ~~were~~ [was] difficulty obtaining sufficient quantities of this spider silk, so researchers combined biomimicry with genetic engineering. (14) The gene responsible for producing silk in these spiders ~~were~~ [was] inserted in the fertilized eggs of goats. (15) The theory behind these efforts ~~hold~~ [holds] that the milk produced by these goats will contain the makings of spider silk, to be extracted and used to make lightweight but incredibly strong fabrics.

(16) In recent years, researchers, inspired by the shell of a mollusk, ~~has~~ [have] created a super strong ceramic material. (17) Other innovations from the field of biomimicry ~~includes~~ [include] improved designs for impellors based on the way water naturally flows and pools. (18) In addition, both stain-proof garments and fabrics with a self-cleaning coating, inspired by the lotus leaf, ~~is~~ [are] already on the market. (19) Other recent examples of biomimicry include a Japanese bullet train shaped like a sea bird for greater efficiency and an

African office complex constructed to remain naturally cool like termite mounds. (20) Biomimicry is proof that there ~~is~~ ^{are} still many things nature can teach us.

FOR FURTHER EXPLORATION

1. Choose one of the following subjects and use your preferred prewriting method to develop a specific focus and ideas to support it.

   - A time when you stood up to authority—or wish you had
   - Why people—including yourself—are sometimes unwilling to seek out help
   - The best way to earn the respect of other people

2. Evaluate your prewriting material, identify a focus, and create a draft paragraph of at least seven to ten sentences. Use the material you have developed to examine your topic in full detail.

collaboration

3. Exchange your draft with a writing partner. Using the material in this chapter as a guide, evaluate the draft you receive. Note any problems with subject–verb agreement as well as any other weaknesses, and return the draft to the writer.

4. Revise your draft, eliminating any errors that your reader identified.

DISCOVERING CONNECTIONS

For this assignment, study this picture and respond to one of the following questions (or some other question it inspires). After exploring your ideas, create a draft paragraph of at least seven to ten sentences. Be sure to check for correct subject–verb agreement in all cases, but especially if you include any complex or compound sentences.

A. As in many fields, food preparation depends on teamwork. When you are part of a team, what do you do to ensure that your actions contribute to the group's goal? Has there been a time when you saw or experienced teamwork disrupted by someone more interested in individual attention?

B. Some researchers believe that smells provide us with the strongest memories. Can you connect certain smells to certain memories? Describe the aroma and the experience it evokes.

RECAP Maintaining Subject–Verb Agreement

Key Terms in This Chapter	Definitions
subject–verb agreement	a state in which the subject and verb agree in number Use the singular form of a verb with a singular subject. Use the plural form of a verb with a plural subject.
prepositional phrase	a unit consisting of a preposition and a noun or pronoun following it, serving as the object of the preposition
indefinite pronoun	a pronoun that refers to general rather than specific people and things

Ways to Maintain Agreement

1. When the subject follows the verb:

in a question	*Does* Roy *know* the words to that song?
in a sentence beginning with *There* or *Here*	There *are* four days left until vacation.

Identify the verb and ask, *Who or what?* to find the subject.

2. When the subject and verb are separated by other words:

prepositional phrases	The *kitten* (across the hall) *cries* all night.
subordinate clauses	The *director* (who treats a cast well) *earns* respect.

Identify the verb and ask, *Who or what?* to find the subject.

3. When the subject is compound:

with *and* the subject is usually plural	*Morris and Shirley are* friends.
unless the compound is considered one	*Bacon and eggs is* his favorite meal.
with *or* the subject can be singular	*Running or swimming is* my usual daily activity.
with *or* the subject can be plural	*Muffins or bagels are* good for breakfast.

Find the conjunction and determine what is being connected.

4. When the subject is an indefinite pronoun:

singular	*Everybody is* well-rested now.
plural	*Both* of my cousins *are* quite tall.

Use singular verbs with singular pronouns and plural verbs with plural pronouns.

5. When the subject is a collective noun or singular noun ending in *-s:*

collective noun	The *audience chooses* the contestants.
singular noun ending in *-s*	*Economics is* known as the dismal science.

If the subject is a unit, use a singular verb.

Singular Indefinite Pronouns

another	each	everything	no one	somebody
anybody	either	neither	nothing	someone
anyone	everybody	nobody	one	something
anything	everyone			

Plural Indefinite Pronouns

both	many
few	several

Indefinite Pronouns Affected by the Words That Follow Them

all	more	none
any	most	some

Using Discovery Online with MyWritingLab

For more practice maintaining subject–verb agreement, go to
www.mywritinglab.com.

CHAPTER 12
Forming Basic Tenses for Regular Verbs

GETTING STARTED ...

 Q I sometimes find figuring out the right endings for verbs frustrating. In some cases, I add a *-d* or an *-ed* where one isn't needed, and other times I don't add an ending where one is needed. Plus, I'm not always sure when I should put *will* in front of a verb form. Why are there so many forms anyway?

 A English verbs are *inflected,* meaning they change form to signify different times. So while your frustration is understandable, this versatility enables you to explain what has already happened, what is happening, and what will happen. To avoid tense confusion, try to remember to do two things. First, identify what general time period you are discussing. Second, check back as you write to make sure that you consistently use the verb ending that signifies that time period.

Overview: The Basic Tenses

ESL Note
See "Agreement," pages 487–489, for more on the use of correct verb forms.

Verbs are words that either convey action or indicate a relationship between the subject and other words in a sentence. As a writer, no words are more important to you than verbs. Without verbs, you wouldn't be able to communicate anything.

Verbs also express time, which is referred to as **tense**, indicating when an action or situation occurs: in the present, future, or past. As verbs change tenses to signify different times, they also change their form. Most verbs are *regular,* meaning that their tenses change in consistent ways. Learning to use verb tenses correctly is vital to ensuring that your writing clearly conveys your ideas.

Navigating This Chapter In this chapter, you'll discover the correct ways to form six basic tenses for regular verbs. You will learn how to use:

- present tense to describe an action or situation that is happening now
- future tense to describe an action or situation that has not occurred yet
- past tense to describe an action or situation that has already occurred
- past perfect, present perfect, and future perfect tenses

The Present Tense

ESL Note
See "Agreement," pages 487–489, and "Confusing Verb Forms," pages 489–491, for more on the correct use of present tense regular verbs.

The **present tense** describes a fact, an action that is happening at the moment, or a situation that happens habitually. For regular verbs, the present tense is the same as the basic form, or the word you would use to complete the simplest sentence beginning with *I: I ask. I climb. I talk.* Look at the following sentences shown in the present tense.

EXAMPLES

My friend *laughs* at all the instructor's bad jokes.

Most children *watch* too much television.

For regular verbs, the form of the present tense varies according to the subject. If the subject is singular, it refers to one person or thing. For present tense singular, add -*s* to the end of the basic verb—as the first example (*laughs*) shows you—or -*es* if the verb ends in -*sh, -ch,* or -*x.*

Plural subjects refer to more than one person or thing. For present tense plural, add nothing to the verb. In the second example, the subject—*children*—is plural, meaning that the basic verb form—*watch*—doesn't change: *watch.*

If these subjects were to change, however, so would the verbs:

EXAMPLES

My friends *laugh* at all the instructor's bad jokes.

The average child *watches* too much television.

In the first example, the plural subject *friends* calls for the basic form *laugh.* In the second example, the singular subject *child* now needs a verb with the -*es* ending: *watches.*

Sometimes the subject of a sentence is a *pronoun,* a word that replaces a noun that has been used earlier. In that case, the form of the present tense will vary depending upon which pronoun is used. Look at the table below.

Present Tense Verbs with Pronoun Subjects

	Singular	**Plural**
First person	I climb.	We climb.
Second person	You climb.	You climb.
Third person	He, She, It climbs.	They climb.

As you can see, you add an -*s* or -*es* to the end of the basic verb with the third person singular pronouns *he, she,* or *it* but not with the others. The first person pronoun *I* and the second person singular pronoun *you* are singular, but you don't add an -*s* to the basic verb form. See Chapter 11, "Maintaining Subject–Verb Agreement," for more information about making sure subjects and verbs *agree* or match up.

Subjects and Present Tense Verbs

12.1   Each sentence in the following passage contains a pair of verbs in parentheses. Circle the correct verb and then underline its subject. Remember that most singular subjects take a verb ending in *-s* or *-es*. Use the example as a guide.

EXAMPLE   The <u>birds</u> (eat), eats) at my backyard feeder every morning.

(1) My <u>father</u> (try, (tries)) to record every event possible involving our family and friends using his new Flip Video camcorder. (2) <u>He</u> (love, (loves)) to get our embarrassing moments on video. (3) When he gets lucky, our resident <u>humorist</u> (manage, (manages)) to film things like someone napping in the middle of a conversation or laughing uncontrollably. (4) <u>Guests</u> at birthday parties or other social events at our house always ((hide), hides) from Dad and his ever-present Flip. (5) Even though the joke is usually on us, <u>we</u> ((enjoy), enjoys) watching the videos. And, so that our friends and family can enjoy being Internet stars, <u>Dad</u> always (post, (posts)) the videos on YouTube.

Subject–Verb Tense Agreement

12.2   In the following paragraph, subjects and verbs are italicized. Rewrite the paragraph on a separate piece of paper. Make singular subjects plural, change the verbs to match them, and adjust any other language to ensure that the sentences make sense. Use the example to guide you.

EXAMPLE   My *roommate shares* household and grocery expenses with me.

My roommates share household and grocery expenses with me.

(1) A *person* starting a small business *faces* many challenges to succeed. (2) For one thing, this *kind* of initiative *requires* enormous energy and dedication. (3) *Anyone* opening a coffee or sandwich shop soon *discovers* that long hours are the norm, not the exception. (4) A *person* starting up a childcare center quickly *recognizes* how hard it can be to care for several preschoolers. (5) A *business* like contracting or landscaping *involves* hours and hours of hard physical labor. (6) A prospective small business *owner* also *needs* to be ready to deal with serious financial issues. (7) In many cases, the *expense* involved in opening a business *adds* up to more than it will earn in a year. (8) For those who qualify, a small-business *loan addresses* this need. (9) Sometimes, though, an *entrepreneur knocks* on doors of family and friends to raise the money. (10) But the *individual* whose business succeeds *finds* all the sacrifice involved worthwhile.

CHALLENGE 12.1 **Present Tense Verbs in Directions**

1. On a separate sheet of paper, write five sentences in which you use present tense verbs to discuss challenges that college students face on a day-to-day basis.

collaboration

2. Exchange your sentences with a classmate. Check the sentences you receive to make sure that the verbs are in the present tense and that the proper endings (-s or -es) have been used. Put a ✓ next to any verb that needs to be changed and return the sentences to the writer.

3. Check your reader's comments, and make any necessary changes in verb tense.

The Future Tense

Writers use the **future tense** to describe an action that has not occurred yet or a situation that is to come. You can change regular verbs to future tense by adding *will* to the basic verb.

Note the present tense verb in the following sentence.

PRESENT | The hamsters *enjoy* their new, spacious cage.

Now here is the same sentence, with the verb in the future tense.

FUTURE | The hamsters *will enjoy* their new, spacious cage.

The sentence now conveys a new meaning. The hamsters do not have a new home yet, but when they get one, they will like it.

In the future tense, the verb endings -s and -es are not needed. Singular and plural forms are the same. For example, if we give the sentence above a singular subject, the verb ending will stay the same.

FUTURE | The hamster *will enjoy* its new, spacious cage.

This means that if you change a sentence written in the present tense with a singular subject to future tense, you need to drop the -s or -es ending from the verb.

PRESENT | Ben *commutes* to work.

FUTURE | Ben *will commute* to work.

COMPREHENSION AND PRACTICE 12.3

Future Tense Verbs

Change the underlined present tense verbs in the paragraph below to future tense. When you make the change, remember to drop any -s or -es endings. Write your answers above the underlined verbs, as the example shows.

EXAMPLE ⎡ Rosemary buys [*will buy*] groceries for her elderly neighbors.

     (1) Because of new developments in technology, communication and media always improve [*will improve*]. (2) High-definition television transmits [*will transmit*] clear, sharp video images, including, in some cases, 3-D productions. (3) Music lovers hear [*will hear*] uninterrupted music on satellite radio and commercial broadcasting with better quality sound on HD radio. (4) They also store [*will store*] hundreds of their favorite tunes on the wide variety of iPods and other MP3 players. (5) A subscriber reads [*will read*] newspapers that exist online, with some newspaper publishers eliminating print versions altogether.

CHALLENGE 12.2 Analysis of the Future Tense

1. On a separate sheet of paper, write one of the sentences you completed for Challenge 12.1 (p. 239), changing the verb from present tense to future tense. Then create three supporting sentences for it.

collaboration

2. Exchange your sentences with a classmate. On the sentences you receive, circle all future tense verbs and underline their subjects. Put a ✓ next to any incorrectly formed future tense verb or any other verb that you think should be in the future tense. Return the sentences to the writer.

3. Evaluate your classmate's comments, and then make any necessary changes in verb tense on your paper.

The Past Tense

Writers use the **past tense** to describe an action or situation that has already occurred. For regular verbs, you can form the past tense by adding -*ed* to the basic verb form. If the basic form ends in -*e*, add -*d*. The endings for singular and plural forms are the same. Take a look at the following sentences featuring past tense verbs.

EXAMPLES ⎡ After midnight, the waitress *cleaned* all the sticky tables.

    ⎣ The mayoral candidates *promised* to end all corruption at city hall.

In the first sentence, the basic form of the verb is *clean*. If the sentence were focusing on something in the present tense, the verb would be *cleans*. But this sentence discusses something in the past tense, which doesn't require an -*s*. Just adding -*ed* creates the past tense: *cleaned*. In the second sentence, the verb *promise* in its basic form already ends in -*e*. Simply adding a -*d* changes it to past tense: *promised*.

The present, future, and past tenses discussed above are called *simple tenses.* Use the following table to review ways to form them.

How to Form Simple Tenses for Regular Verbs (Example verb: *walk*)

Tenses	Basic or "I" Form	Form for Plural Subjects	Form for Singular Subjects
For the **simple present tense**, use the basic verb form. Add -*s* or -*es* for singular subjects.	I *walk* a mile every day.	Nicole and Tim *walk* a mile every day.	Norton *walks* a mile every day.
For the **simple future tense**, use the basic verb form plus *will*. Use the same verb form for both singular and plural subjects.	I *will walk* a mile every day.	Nicole and Tim *will walk* a mile every day.	Norton *will walk* a mile every day.
For the **simple past tense**, use the basic verb form plus -*d* or -*ed*. Use the same verb form for both singular and plural subjects.	I *walked* a mile every day.	Nicole and Tim *walked* a mile every day.	Norton *walked* a mile every day.

COMPREHENSION AND PRACTICE

Past Tense Verbs

12.4   The verbs in the paragraph below are in the present tense. Underline them and then change them to the past tense by adding -*d* or -*ed*. You may first have to drop the -*s* or -*es* ending if the verb is singular. Write the past tense verbs in the space above each present tense verb. Use the example as a guide.

EXAMPLE

    hesitated
I hesitate too long at that busy intersection, and the light *changes.*   *changed*

    created
(1) A top culinary arts student, my cousin Gwenetta creates a masterpiece when she bakes a cake. *baked* (2) Her specialty cake includes both *included* vanilla and chocolate layers. (3) She frosts each layer with a rich chocolate *frosted* cream. (4) Smooth fondant with fresh raspberries decorate the top. *decorated* (5) The final result looks delicious and tastes even better. *looked* *tasted*

COMPREHENSION AND PRACTICE

Effective Use of Past Tense

12.5   Use the following list of verbs to complete the paragraph below. Put all verbs into the past tense by adding -*d* or -*ed*. Write the past tense verb in the appropriate blank.

arrive	disagree	happen	post	repair
ask	fill	install	print	

(1) Recently the state highway department <u>repaired</u> a very dangerous road a mile from my apartment. (2) Road crews <u>filled</u> the potholes that developed as a result of bad weather during the winter. (3) They also <u>installed</u> new guardrails along the sides of the road to replace those damaged during the previous year. (4) All of this reconstruction <u>happened</u> only after thirty-four people had been killed or injured over a period of seventeen years. (5) The situation continued so long because state officials and county officials <u>disagreed</u> about who was responsible for maintaining the road. (6) Local citizens finally <u>asked</u> the federal transportation officials to get involved. (7) The citizens also formed a committee that <u>printed</u> flyers and <u>posted</u> them on bulletin boards all over the county. (8) Their efforts paid off when the federal officials ruled that the state was responsible, and a state highway department crew <u>arrived</u> to make Route 6 safe for motorists.

CHALLENGE 12.3   Analysis of Past Tense

1. The paragraph in Comprehension and Practice 12.5 discusses a dangerous stretch of highway. What's the most dangerous road, street, or intersection in your city, town, or neighborhood? Write a paragraph of at least seven to ten sentences in which you identify the dangerous spot and relate a specific experience you had or witnessed there.

collaboration

2. Exchange your paragraph with a classmate. Circle all the past tense verbs in the paragraph you receive. Put a ✓ next to any incorrectly formed past tense verb or any other verb that you think should be in the past tense. Return the sentences to the writer.

3. Evaluate your classmate's comments, and then make any necessary changes in verb tense on your paper.

The Perfect Tenses

ESL Note
See "Confusing Verb Forms," pages 489–491, for more on using *has* and "Agreement," pages 487–489, for more on the proper use of perfect tenses.

In addition to the simple tenses, writers can turn to other tenses to capture and present different aspects of time. For example, the *perfect tenses—past perfect, present perfect,* and *future perfect*—communicate actions that occurred earlier, that are happening now, or that will happen later. For regular verbs, the perfect tenses are formed by adding one of the helping verbs shown below to the **past participle** of the verb. For regular verbs, the past participle is the same as the simple past tense: the basic verb form plus *-d* or *-ed.*

Helping Verbs That Form Perfect Tenses

Helping Verb	+	*Past Participle*	=	*Perfect Tense*
had		walked		had walked
has		walked		has walked
have		walked		have walked

(Chapter 15, "Additional Elements of Verb Use," discusses two other groups of tenses, the *progressive tenses* and the *perfect progressive tenses.* These tenses use forms of the verb *to be* as helping verbs in combination with the present participle, the *-ing* form of a verb.)

Past Perfect Tense

As the time line below shows, the **past perfect tense** indicates actions or situations that happened a little further back in time than actions in the simple past tense. For regular verbs, form the past perfect tense by adding *had* to the past participle.

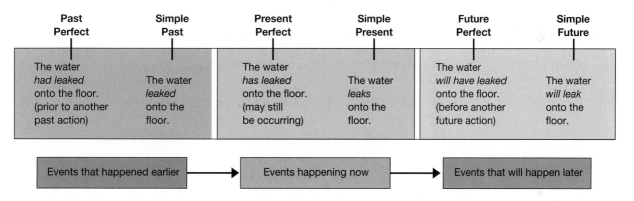

Look at the following pairs of sentences.

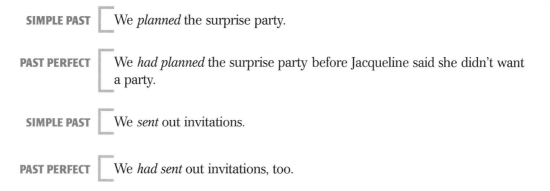

SIMPLE PAST — We *planned* the surprise party.

PAST PERFECT — We *had planned* the surprise party before Jacqueline said she didn't want a party.

SIMPLE PAST — We *sent* out invitations.

PAST PERFECT — We *had sent* out invitations, too.

The simple past and the past perfect forms of these verbs express slightly different meanings. In each instance, the past perfect tense expresses an action that was completed in the past, *before* some other past action. Jacqueline said she wanted no party. Before that, the party planners had already planned the party and sent out invitations.

Present Perfect Tense

The **present perfect tense** indicates an action that occurred at some indefinite time in the past or one that occurred in the past and is still going on. You form the present perfect by adding *has* or *have* to a past participle.

Take a look at these sentences, which feature present perfect tense verbs.

PRESENT PERFECT

The park workers *have cleaned* up the playground.

My friend Maya *has studied* dance for ten years.

The present perfect verb in the first sentence shows that the workers have completed their task, although the time of completion is indefinite. In the second sentence, the present perfect verb states that Maya's dance lessons began in the past and still continue.

Future Perfect Tense

As the time line on page 243 shows, the **future perfect tense** refers to actions or events that you expect to be completed in the future before some other future event or action. For regular verbs, this tense is easy to form. Just add the word *will* to the *have* form of the present perfect tense.

Look at the examples below.

PRESENT PERFECT

A lot of eerie events *have happened* on Halloween night.

FUTURE PERFECT

A lot of eerie events *will have happened* by the end of Halloween night.

In the first sentence, the present perfect tense *have happened* discusses incidents that have taken place during some unspecified time on Halloween. In the second sentence, the future perfect tense verb *will have happened* describes events that will occur in the future. However, they will occur *before* the end of Halloween night, which is even further in the future.

COMPREHENSION
AND PRACTICE
12.6

Perfect Tenses

Change the present tense verb in parentheses in each sentence below to a perfect tense verb. Add a helping verb (*has, had,* or *have,* plus *will* for future perfect tense) to the past participle of the verb. Use the examples as a guide.

EXAMPLES

Tre (works) <u>has worked</u> on his journal every week for the past year.

Marcy (fills) <u>will have filled</u> two journals by the end of the year.

(1) Intense headaches (plague) <u>have plagued</u> my life for the past year. (2) Even though the doctor (administers) <u>has administered</u> several tests, including a CT scan, she cannot diagnose the source of my pain. (3) Since last Thursday, I (suffer) <u>have suffered</u> from a pounding headache that just won't let

up. (4) Thank goodness I (call) <u>had called</u> the doctor to ask for a new prescription just before this headache began. (5) If the medication doesn't block the pain and I have to spend the day in bed again, I (stay) <u>will have stayed</u> home from work a total of six days this month alone.

COMPREHENSION AND PRACTICE 12.7

Errors in the Perfect Tense

The following paragraph contains some errors in verb tense. In some cases, the participle form of the verb is incorrect. In others, the participle form is correct, but the helping verb (*have, has,* or *had*) is either incorrect or missing. Put a line through any incorrect verb form, and write the correct form above it. Use the example to guide you.

EXAMPLE

Throughout history, the president of the United States ~~have~~ *has* always been a man.

(1) Over the last decade, proposed gun control legislation ~~have~~ *has* become a highly controversial topic. (2) Many people ~~has~~ *have* suggested laws that would restrict the types and number of guns one person can purchase. (3) Other people *have* ∧ said that guns, particularly handguns and automatic weapons, should be banned altogether. (4) Congress ~~have~~ *has* proposed a number of gun control measures, but not one of the measures has been approved yet. (5) Despite the heated debate, several studies ~~has~~ *have* shown that both gun owners and non–gun owners in the United States favor gun control measures.

CHALLENGE 12.4   Verb Tense Use in a Classmate's Writing

1. Select one of the following topic sentences and create a paragraph of at least seven to ten sentences. As you write, be sure you use verbs in the appropriate tense to signify when the action or situation occurs.

   The last place I would want to spend a long weekend is _____.

   The public needs to pay more attention to the way government spends money.

   When a crisis occurs, people invariably go out of their way to help those in need.

2. Exchange your paragraph with a classmate. On the paragraph you receive, underline each verb, and identify its tense. Put a ✓ next to any changes you think need to be made in verb tense and return the paragraph to the writer.

3. Evaluate your classmate's comments and then make any necessary changes in verb tense.

collaboration

✓ FORMING BASIC TENSES FOR REGULAR VERBS CHECKLIST

☐ Have you used an appropriate present tense verb when discussing a situation or relationship that is happening now or that happens regularly?

☐ Have you chosen the appropriate ending—an *-s* for singular subjects—for all present tense verbs?

☐ Have you used an appropriate future tense verb, including *will,* when discussing a situation or relationship that has not yet occurred?

☐ Have you used an appropriate past tense verb—with the correct *-d* or *-ed* ending—when discussing a situation or relationship that has already occurred?

☐ Have you used an appropriate perfect tense—with the correct form of *to have* and the past participle or *-ed* form of the verb—when discussing a situation or relationship that (1) has happened and may still be happening, or (2) will happen before some other situations or relationships in the future?

Journal Writing

When it comes to writing, *tense* refers to *time.* By shifting tense, writers can take control of time. In life in general, it's not so easy. Time is a commanding force, one that no one can challenge or control. Clocks tick; time passes. There is no stopping it, and there is no getting it back. In what aspect of your life does time play the greatest role? What do you do to help manage time? Does time pass more quickly for a child? For someone who is elderly? For someone like yourself? Consider one of these questions or some other aspect of time, and then explore it in your journal for 20 to 30 minutes.

CHAPTER QUICK CHECK   Forming Basic Tenses for Regular Verbs

Underline the verbs in the following passage. Then write the name of the verb tense above the verb.

(1) Of all the senses, smell <u>possesses</u> [present] the greatest power to re-create sensations. (2) Until recently, business and industry <u>have failed</u> [present perfect] to take advantage of these characteristics. (3) Today, however, a number of companies <u>have begun</u> [present perfect] to experiment with odor in their day-to-day operations. (4) For example, one international airline <u>pumps</u> [present] the aroma of cut grass into their lounges. (5) This pleasant fragrance <u>gives</u> [present] passengers waiting for a flight the sensation of a world far

beyond the concrete and asphalt runways. (6) Drivers often <u>used</u> [*past*] to talk about

new car odor as one of the highlights of the process of buying a car. (7) Soon, in

addition to new car smell, some cars <u>will have</u> [*future*] aroma systems to calm the driver

in the face of traffic jams or other irritating situations. (8) The technology capable

of delivering a variety of aromas on demand already <u>exists</u> [*present*]. (9) The scenting de-

vice, with more than 100 odors available, <u>links</u> [*present*] up to a computer. (10) At the

push of a button, the aroma system <u>enhances</u> [*present*] the user's work environment.

SUMMARY EXERCISE   Forming Basic Tenses for Regular Verbs

Underline the verbs in the following essay. Then write the name of the verb tense
above the verb.

   (1) Undisturbed, most teenagers <u>will sleep</u> [*future*] late in the morning. (2) They also
<u>like</u> [*present*] nightlife, often staying up well past midnight. (3) Parents generally <u>prefer</u> [*present*] an

early teen bedtime, usually with little success. (4) Scientists <u>have discovered</u> [*present perfect*],

though, that teens' biological clocks <u>contribute</u> [*present*] to this pattern. (5) This new the-

ory <u>provides</u> [*present*] support for the information that researchers <u>have accumulated</u> [*present perfect*]

about sleep.

   (6) Thanks to the efforts of this research, we <u>know</u> [*present*] a lot about sleep now.
(7) For example, without sleep we <u>find</u> [*present*] it nearly impossible to think clearly.
(8) Also, sleep requirements <u>depend</u> [*present*] on age. (9) Babies <u>sleep</u> [*present*] the most, and as
adults age, they <u>will need</u> [*future*] less. (10) Nobody <u>stays</u> [*present*] still during sleep, either.
(11) This movement <u>helps</u> [*present*] our circulation, vital to overall comfort. (12) If a muscle
<u>cramps</u> [*present*], we usually <u>will wake</u> [*future*] up to change position.

   (13) In addition to studying sleep, scientists <u>have studied</u> [*present perfect*] dreams.
(14) According to this research, we all <u>dream</u> [*present*] every night. (15) Researchers
<u>have watched</u> [*present perfect*] rapid eye movements beneath a sleeper's eyelids. (16) These
movements <u>occur</u> [*present*] only during dreams. (17) Furthermore, scientists <u>have</u> [*present perfect*]
<u>determined</u> that women and children <u>dream</u> [*present*] more than men, and dreams
<u>get</u> [*present*] longer as the night <u>goes</u> [*present*] on.

future   present
(18) Often, to feel wider awake, people will yawn. (19) A yawn increases
                                    present
oxygen supply. (20) Still, no one really understands the contagious nature of

yawns.

FOR FURTHER EXPLORATION

1. Select one of the following topics and, using the prewriting technique you prefer, examine it closely.

   - A formula or plan you depend on when you face a difficult situation
   - How your life and relationships online differ from your actual life and relationships
   - One mistake you made that you would urge your own children to avoid

2. Evaluate your prewriting material, identify a focus, and create a draft paragraph of at least seven to ten sentences.

collaboration

3. Exchange your draft with a writing partner. Using the material in this chapter as a guide, evaluate the draft you receive. Note any problems with simple and perfect tenses as well as any other weaknesses, and return the draft to the writer.

4. Revise your draft, eliminating any errors that your reader identified.

DISCOVERING CONNECTIONS

For this assignment, think about this picture and respond to one of the following questions (or another the photo inspires). Then, after exploring your ideas on this topic, create a draft paragraph of at least seven to ten sentences. To avoid confusion with verb tense, remember to identify what period of time you're writing in and consistently use the verb ending that signifies that time.

A. Anthropology is the study of the orgin, culture, and development of humans. What aspect of the beginnings, development, and behavior of humans would you like to know more about? Why?

B. Think about one of the cultural groups or communities to which you belong, for example, your ethnicity or age group. What are some of the customs or beliefs that this group or community holds?

RECAP Forming Basic Tenses for Regular Verbs

Key Terms in This Chapter	Definitions
verb tense	the form of a verb that indicates when the action or situation occurs: in the past, present, or future
present tense	the basic form of the verb plus *-s* or *-es* if the subject is singular used to show a fact, an action, or a situation now going on or occurring habitually Change the form of the verb to match the subject. EXAMPLE The cat *cries* all night outside my window. The cats *cry* all night outside my window.
future tense	the basic form of a verb plus *will* used to show action or state of being that will occur later EXAMPLE The cat *will* stay inside tonight.
past tense	the basic form of a verb plus *-ed* or *-d* used to show action or state of being that has already occurred EXAMPLE The cat *stayed* outside and *cried.*
past participle	for regular verbs, a form created by adding *-d* or *-ed* to the basic form used with a helping verb to form the perfect tenses EXAMPLE Martha had *ended* the relationship months ago.
past perfect tense	the past participle plus the helping verb *had* used to express action completed in the past, before some other past action EXAMPLE The cat *had eaten* all its food and cried for more.
present perfect tense	the past participle plus the helping verb *has* or *have* used to express action completed at some indefinite time in the past or occurring in the past and still continuing EXAMPLE The cat *has eaten* all its food.
future perfect tense	the present perfect tense plus *will* used to express action to be completed in the future before some other future action or event EXAMPLE The cat *will have eaten* all its food by Monday.

Forming the Basic Tenses for Regular Verbs

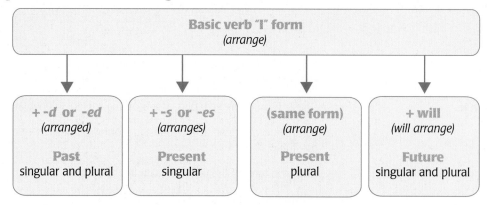

Forming the Perfect Tenses for Regular Verbs

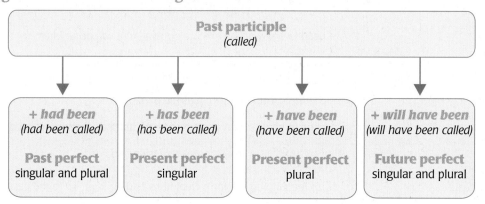

Using Discovery Online with MyWritingLab

For more practice forming basic tenses for regular verbs, go to www.mywritingLab.com.

CHAPTER 13
Using Irregular Verbs Correctly

GETTING STARTED ...

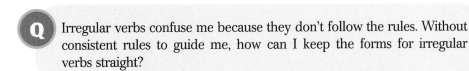

Q Irregular verbs confuse me because they don't follow the rules. Without consistent rules to guide me, how can I keep the forms for irregular verbs straight?

A Many writers have trouble keeping irregular verb forms straight. And, true, there are no rules to guide you in using them, as there are for regular verbs. To master the verbs you have difficulty with, review the list of common irregulars in this chapter and highlight only the ones that trouble you. Create a list and keep it in your notebook or next to your computer. When you use one of these verbs in your writing, stop immediately and check your list. Do this consistently and you'll find that you are making far fewer errors.

Overview: Verbs That Do Not Follow the Rules

ESL Note
See "Confusing Verb Forms," pages 489–491, for more on the correct use of irregular verbs.

Many of the verbs you will use most often in your writing—the forms of the verb *to be*, for example—are **irregular verbs.** These verbs don't conform to the rule that regular verbs follow. Fortunately, you do not have to memorize all the irregular verb tenses in order to use them effectively in your writing. In fact, you already know the basic tenses of many irregular verbs. As you learn more about these verbs, you'll discover which are particularly troublesome for you and how to master them.

Navigating This Chapter To help with your writing, this chapter provides a list you can use to look up unfamiliar irregular verbs. You will learn:

- the present, past, and past participle forms of irregular verbs
- some helpful strategies for grouping and remembering irregular verbs

A List of Irregular Verbs

Here is a list of the different forms of common irregular verbs. Keep it handy whenever you write so that you can check how to form the past tense or past participle forms. If the verb you are searching for is not on the list, it is probably regular. In that case, you can use the rules you learned in Chapter 12. If you are still unsure about whether your verb is regular or irregular, however, you can look it up in the dictionary. The past tense will appear in brackets right after the listing for the word.

As you read through the following list, remember that you must use a helping verb with the past participle form of all irregular verbs to create the perfect tense shown in the third column.

Irregular Verb Forms

Present Tense	Past Tense	Past Participle (+ *had, has, have*)
am/is/are	was, were	been
arise	arose	arisen
awaken	awoke, awaked	awoke, awaked
become	became	become
begin	began	begun
bend	bent	bent
bind	bound	bound
bite	bit	bitten, bit
bleed	bled	bled
blow	blew	blown
break	broke	broken
bring	brought	brought
build	built	built
burn	burned, burnt	burned, burnt
burst	burst	burst
buy	bought	bought
catch	caught	caught
choose	chose	chosen
cling	clung	clung
come	came	come
cost	cost	cost
creep	crept	crept
cut	cut	cut
deal	dealt	dealt
dig	dug	dug
dive	dived, dove	dived
do/does	did	done
draw	drew	drawn
dream	dreamed, dreamt	dreamed, dreamt
drink	drank	drunk
drive	drove	driven
eat	ate	eaten
fall	fell	fallen
feed	fed	fed
feel	felt	felt
fight	fought	fought
find	found	found
flee	fled	fled
fling	flung	flung
fly	flew	flown
forbid	forbade, forbad	forbidden
forget	forgot	forgotten, forgot
freeze	froze	frozen

Irregular Verb Forms *(continued)*

Present Tense	Past Tense	Past Participle (+ *had, has, have*)
get	got	got, gotten
give	gave	given
go/goes	went	gone
grind	ground	ground
hang	hung	hung
hang (execute)	hanged	hanged
have/has	had	had
hear	heard	heard
hide	hid	hidden, hid
hold	held	held
hurt	hurt	hurt
keep	kept	kept
kneel	knelt, kneeled	knelt, kneeled
knit	knit, knitted	knit, knitted
know	knew	known
lay	laid	laid
lead	led	led
leap	leaped, leapt	leaped, leapt
leave	left	left
let	let	let
lie	lay	lain
light	lighted, lit	lighted, lit
lose	lost	lost
make	made	made
mean	meant	meant
meet	met	met
mistake	mistook	mistaken
pay	paid	paid
plead	pleaded, pled	pleaded, pled
prove	proved	proved, proven
put	put	put
quit	quit	quit
raise	raised	raised
read	read	read
ride	rode	ridden
ring	rang	rung
rise	rose	risen
run	ran	run
say	said	said
see	saw	seen
seek	sought	sought

(continued)

Irregular Verb Forms *(continued)*

Present Tense	Past Tense	Past Participle (+ *had, has, have*)
sell	sold	sold
send	sent	sent
set	set	set
sew	sewed	sewn, sewed
shake	shook	shaken
shine	shone, shined	shone, shined
shine (polish)	shined	shined
shoot	shot	shot
show	showed	shown, showed
shrink	shrank, shrunk	shrunk, shrunken
shut	shut	shut
sing	sang, sung	sung
sit	sat	sat
sleep	slept	slept
slide	slid	slid
sling	slung	slung
slink	slunk, slinked	slunk, slinked
sow	sowed	sown, sowed
speak	spoke	spoken
speed	sped, speeded	sped, speeded
spell	spelled	spelled
spend	spent	spent
spit	spit, spat	spit, spat
spring	sprang, sprung	sprung
stand	stood	stood
steal	stole	stolen
stick	stuck	stuck
sting	stung	stung
stink	stank, stunk	stunk
stride	strode	stridden
strike	struck	struck, stricken
string	strung	strung
strive	strived, strove	striven, strived
swear	swore	sworn
sweat	sweat, sweated	sweat, sweated
swell	swelled	swelled, swollen
swim	swam	swum
swing	swung	swung
take	took	taken
teach	taught	taught
tear	tore	torn
tell	told	told
throw	threw	thrown
understand	understood	understood

Irregular Verb Forms *(continued)*

Present Tense	Past Tense	Past Participle (+ *had, has, have*)
wake	woke, waked	woken, waked, woke
wear	wore	worn
weave (make cloth)	wove, weaved	woven, weaved
weave (sway)	weaved	weaved
weep	wept	wept
win	won	won
wind	wound	wound
wring	wrung	wrung
write	wrote	written

Strategies for Mastering Irregular Verbs

Admittedly, you might find it hard to memorize the entire list of irregular verbs, and you may already use many of them properly. A few strategies, however, can help you remember certain words. One technique is to identify and group irregular verbs that follow the same pattern. Some keep the same form for present tense, past tense, and past participle.

Irregular Verbs That Have the Same Form

Present	*Past*	*Past Participle*
burst	burst	burst
cut	cut	cut
let	let	let
read	read	read

A number of other irregular verbs have the same form for both past tense and past participle:

Irregular Verbs That Have the Same Past Tense and Past Participle Forms

Present	*Past*	*Past Participle*
bring	brought	brought
feel	felt	felt
mean	meant	meant
teach	taught	taught

Other irregular verbs change the same way as they move from present to past tense. In the list below, note that all the present tense forms have an *i*, all the past tense forms have an *a*, and all the past participles have a *u:*

Irregular Verbs That Change Tenses the Same Way

Present	Past	Past Participle
begin	began	begun
drink	drank	drunk
ring	rang	rung
sing	sang	sung

Still other irregular verbs have past participles that are formed by adding an -*n* to the end of the present tense:

Irregular Verbs Whose Past Participles Are Formed by Adding -*n*

Present	Past	Past Participle
blow	blew	blown
grow	grew	grown
know	knew	known
throw	threw	thrown

If these lists seem confusing, keep in mind that you probably use most of the irregular verbs properly when you speak. Therefore, a good strategy is to go through the list to identify and highlight those verbs that *do* give you trouble. Then, rather than wasting time on words you already know, you can focus on your smaller list of troublesome verbs.

Another effective way to learn irregular verbs is to write a series of related practice sentences using the three forms of the verb. For the verbs *feel* and *sell*, for instance, you could write sentences like these:

EXAMPLES

I *feel* happy today. Yesterday, I *felt* sad. On many occasions, I *have felt* even sadder.

My aunt *sells* cars. Yesterday, she *sold* a Jeep. On many occasions, she *has sold* luxury cars.

COMPREHENSION
AND PRACTICE

Tenses of Irregular Verbs

13.1   Each of the sentences in the following paragraph contains a verb in parentheses, followed by a blank line. In this blank line, write the correct present perfect tense of the verb (the past participle form of the verb, plus an appropriate helping verb—*has, had,* or *have*). Refer to the list on pages 252–255 if you need help. Use the example as a guide.

EXAMPLE

When you have learned to manage time, you (lay) _have laid_ the foundations for success.

(1) Now that I (take) __have taken__ a study skills course, I am no longer scared by the thought of a history test. (2) Before, even though I knew I (read) __had read__ the chapter in a textbook, I did not feel prepared. (3) I (spend) __had spent__ time studying, but I had studied the wrong way. (4) I learned in study skills how to connect information in the new chapter with material I (understand) __had understood__ in the previous chapter. (5) This course (teach) __has taught__ me how to analyze ideas.

COMPREHENSION
AND PRACTICE
13.2

Effective Use of Irregular Verb Tenses

Practice using the forms of the irregular verbs listed below. On a separate sheet of paper, write three related sentences using the present tense, past tense, and the past participle with *have, has,* or *had* to create a perfect tense verb. Use the example to guide you. Sentences will vary.

EXAMPLE

send

I <u>send</u> an e-mail to my younger sister every day.

I <u>sent</u> e-mail messages to my younger sister during her trip to Central America.

I <u>had sent</u> e-mails to my younger sister before she left for Argentina.

1. grow	3. keep	5. shut	7. dream	9. rise
2. go	4. stand	6. begin	8. win	10. leave

COMPREHENSION
AND PRACTICE
13.3

Mastery of the Tenses of Irregular Verbs

Help yourself learn the forms of irregular verbs by grouping them into "families" that follow the same pattern. Find and write verbs from the list on pages 252–255 that fit under each of the following headings:

1. Verbs with the Same Form for Present Tense, Past Tense, and Past Participle

2. Verbs with the Same Form for Past Tense and Past Participle

3. Verbs with an *i* in the Present Tense, an *a* in the Past Tense, and a *u* in the Past Participle

Now, study these lists and decide which irregular verbs cause you the most trouble. Compile your own list of problem verbs, and keep it within easy reach for reference.

CHALLENGE 13.1   Irregular Verbs by Pattern

1. Write a paragraph of at least seven to ten sentences about your favorite outdoor activity that uses at least five of the following verbs in the present tense form.

to do	to feel	to speak
to have	to understand	to see

collaboration

2. Exchange your paragraph with a partner. On a separate sheet of paper, rewrite your partner's paragraph, substituting a past participle form and helping verb for each present tense verb. For help with the irregular verbs, consult the list on pages 252–255.

✓ **FORMING BASIC TENSES FOR IRREGULAR VERBS CHECKLIST**

☐ Have you checked any irregular verb to make sure you have used the correct form?

☐ Have you included the correct form of *to have* (*has, have,* or *had*) with any irregular past participles you have used as verbs?

☐ Have you made yourself familiar with the irregular verbs that keep the same form for present, past, and past participle and used them properly?

☐ Have you made a note of the irregular verbs that have the same past and past participle form and used them correctly?

☐ Have you considered the irregular verbs that follow the same pattern for present, past, and past participle and used them properly?

☐ Have you memorized the irregular verbs whose past participle ends in *-n* and used them correctly?

Journal Writing

With verbs, irregular means that they don't follow predictable patterns as they change form. But in life in general, irregular has many other meanings. For instance, garments that are marked *irregular* have some defect or blemish. If it is a small problem, irregular can mean a big bargain. If a financial report is irregular, however, it means big trouble for someone. When it comes to the way we behave, irregular means unusual or other than ordinary. Consider these and other meanings of *irregular* and then write in your journal for 20 to 30 minutes on the consequences when some aspect of life doesn't conform to the typical pattern.

CHAPTER QUICK CHECK   Using Irregular Verbs Correctly

Complete each sentence in the following passage with the correct verb form. Fill in the blank with the past or perfect form (past participle plus *have, has,* or *had*) of the verb in parentheses. Refer to the list of irregular verbs in this chapter for help. Answers may vary somewhat between past and perfect forms.

(1) In 2009, *The Simpsons,* the 30-minute animated series set in the fictional community of Springfield, (become) ____became____ the longest-running prime-time series in U.S. television history. (2) The show (begin) ___began___ its run in January 1990 when the Fox network added it to its weekly lineup of shows. (3) Creator Matt Groening's characters, which first appeared in brief spots on *The Tracey Ullman Show,* quickly (win) ___won___ the affection of viewers across the United States. (4) The adventures of Homer, Marge, Lisa, Bart, and Maggie Simpson (draw) ___has drawn, drew___ consistently strong ratings over the show's time on the air. (5) Right from the start, Groening and his writers (understand) ___understood___ what fans of *The Simpsons* wanted. (6) The scathing satire of everything from business to popular culture (build) ___built___ an enormous fan base, especially among college students and young adults. (7) Even today, the writing (lose) ___has lost___ none of its satiric edge. (8) The show also (catch) ___caught, has caught___ the attention of many beyond the realm of television. (9) In fact, the creative team behind *The Simpsons* (write) ___has written, wrote___ parts for a number of celebrity guests, including former Beatle Paul McCartney, actress Michelle Pfeiffer, former British Prime Minister Tony Blair, and Dallas Mavericks owner Mark Cuban. (10) During its time on the air, *The Simpsons* (take) ___has taken___ home more than twenty Emmy Awards, clear evidence of its enduring popularity.

SUMMARY EXERCISE   Using Irregular Verbs Correctly

Complete each sentence in the following passage with the correct verb form. Fill in the blank with the past or perfect form (past participle plus *have, has,* or *had*) of the verb in parentheses. Refer to the list of irregular verbs in this chapter for help. Answers may vary somewhat between past and perfect forms.

(1) The threats and intimidation of school bullies (make) _have made, made_ life difficult for generations of middle and high school students. (2) As educators and psychologists (understand) _have understood_ for some time, many kids in this age group have a great capacity for mindless cruelty. (3) In the past, tracking down a bully (mean) _meant_ looking among the male population. (4) In recent years, though, some experts (write) _have written_ about the growth of this behavior among preteen and teenage girls.

(5) The case studies in these books and reports (make) _have made, made_ the public aware of fierce competition, great cruelty, and intense insecurity among young girls. (6) These findings (take) _took, have taken_ the public at large by surprise. (7) For years, most people (let) _let_ themselves believe that girls weren't capable of this behavior. (8) These reports prove that, regardless of their beliefs about girls and bullying, these people (be) _were_ wrong.

(9) The bullies in these stories were generally girls at the top of the pecking order who (find) _found_ the girls who most wanted to be accepted by them. (10) The girls at the top then (take) _took_ advantage of their popularity to control the behavior and loyalty of these insecure girls.

(11) Rather than act as bullies themselves, these popular girls (choose) _chose_ another tactic. (12) Capitalizing on their popularity, they often simply (hide) _hid_ behind the actions of insecure girls who desperately wanted to be accepted. (13) At the urging of the popular girls, this second group of girls (become) _became_ their agents in bullying.

(14) The two groups of girls then (begin) _began_ campaigns of negative behavior against classmates. (15) The bullying girls (hurt) _hurt_ the others by spreading rumors, name-calling, and shunning. (16) None of the victims (do) _did, had done_ anything to earn this abuse. (17) Rather, the other two groups (choose) _had chosen, chose_ to victimize this third group to maintain their own positions in this strange hierarchy.

(18) In short, the female bullies in these reports (understand) <u>understood</u> what motivated the girls to harass and emotionally terrorize their classmates. (19) Experience (show) <u>showed, had shown</u> the popular girls the consequences awaiting those at the bottom of the heap. (20) In other words, their desire to avoid being bullied themselves (drive) <u>drove</u> them to become the bullies.

FOR FURTHER EXPLORATION

1. Select one of the following subjects and use your preferred prewriting method to develop a specific focus and supporting ideas.

   - A recent news event that surprised or outraged you
   - The thing that most intimidates or scares you
   - The differences between confidence and arrogance

2. Evaluate your prewriting material, identify a focus, and create a draft of at least seven to ten sentences.

collaboration

3. Exchange your draft with a writing partner. Using the material in this chapter as a guide, evaluate the draft you receive, noting any problems with irregular verbs as well as any other weaknesses. Return the draft to the writer.

4. Revise your draft, eliminating any errors that your reader identified.

DISCOVERING CONNECTIONS

For this assignment, focus on the photo and respond to one of the following questions (or some other that the picture inspires). Explore your ideas, and then create a draft paragraph of at least seven to ten sentences, making sure to use at least two of the irregular verbs listed in this chapter. To challenge yourself, try to use one of the verbs that trouble you.

A. How do you feel about dance? What style of dancing do you like to engage in? How would you compare dance to other kinds of performance art?

B. Performing in front of a large crowd can be quite daunting for many of us. Have you ever had to perform in public? What did you do and how did you feel about the experience?

RECAP Using Irregular Verbs Correctly

Key Term in This Chapter	Definition
irregular verbs	verbs that do not form their tenses in regular, or typical, ways The past participle is used with a helping verb to form the perfect tenses.

Categories of Irregular Verbs

	Present	Past	Past Participle
All tenses use the same form	cut read	cut read	cut read
Past tense and past participle use the same form	bring teach	brought taught	brought taught
In each tense, one letter changes	begin sing	began sang	begun sung
In past tense, one letter changes; in past participle, one letter is added	grow know	grew knew	grown known

Using Discovery Online with MyWritingLab

For more practice using irregular verbs correctly, go to
www.mywritinglab.com.

CHAPTER 14

Using Passive Voice and Progressive Tenses, and Maintaining Consistency in Tense

GETTING STARTED …

Q I've heard people use the word *voice* when discussing a piece of writing, and I know that they are talking about the writer's tone and language. But what does *voice* mean when it comes to verbs? What exactly is the progressive tense? And why is being consistent in verb tense such a big deal?

A *Voice* refers to how the verb expresses the relationship with its subject. When the subject is doing the action, the verb is in the *active* voice. But when the subject is acted on, the verb is in the *passive* voice. These two options give you the chance to record a condition, situation, or individual in more exact terms. The *progressive tense*—a form of the verb *to be* plus the present participle or *-ing* form of another verb—enables you to communicate action ongoing in different times. You must maintain a consistent tense to avoid distracting your reader from what's important in your writing: your message.

Overview: Passive Voice and Progressive Tense

This chapter focuses on tenses that use some form of the irregular verb *to be* as a helping verb. The *active voice* is when the subject does the action. The *passive voice* (when the subject is acted upon) combines a form of *to be* with the *past participle* of a verb. The *progressive tense* (when action is ongoing at different times) uses a form of *to be* with the *present participle* of a verb. This chapter also emphasizes the importance of consistency in tense, which is crucial if your reader is to follow the time relationships you are communicating.

Navigating This Chapter In this chapter, you will explore

- how to form and when to use passive voice verbs
- how to form and use the progressive tenses for ongoing actions
- how to make the tense of verbs consistent throughout a paragraph

Understanding Active and Passive Voice

ESL Note
See "Sentence Basics,"
pages 483–485, for
more on the correct
placement and use of
subjects and verbs.

If the subject of a sentence performs the action, the verb is in the **active voice.** If the subject of the sentence receives the action, the verb is in the **passive voice.** To create a verb in the passive voice, add a form of *to be* to the past participle of another verb, as the chart shows.

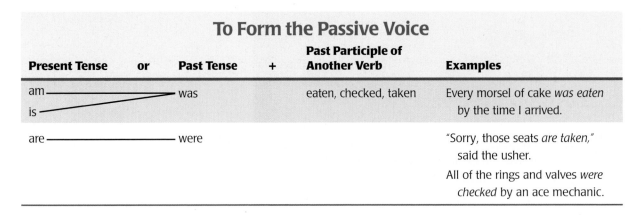

To Form the Passive Voice

Present Tense	or	Past Tense	+	Past Participle of Another Verb	Examples
am		was		eaten, checked, taken	Every morsel of cake *was eaten* by the time I arrived.
is					
are		were			"Sorry, those seats *are taken*," said the usher.
					All of the rings and valves *were checked* by an ace mechanic.

To understand an important difference between active and passive voices, consider the following examples:

ACTIVE VOICE Unfortunately, Barbara closed the corner deli for the weekend.

PASSIVE VOICE Unfortunately, the corner deli was closed for the weekend by Barbara.

In the first sentence, the verb is in the active voice because the subject (*Barbara*) performed the action (closing the deli). In the second sentence, the verb is in the passive voice. The subject (*deli*) was acted upon. After all, a deli cannot close itself. Here is another pair of examples:

ACTIVE VOICE The reporter spelled several words incorrectly in the article.

PASSIVE VOICE Several words were spelled incorrectly in the article by the reporter.

In the first sentence, the subject (*reporter*) does something (misspells words). We know who spelled the words incorrectly. Notice how the focus of the sentence shifts away from the doer in the passive voice example. When the subject *words* is acted upon, or receives the action, we no longer know who made the mistake. In most cases, you should choose the active voice because it describes things more clearly and directly and makes the communication more energetic.

Occasionally, however, you will want the focus to be on the receiver of the action rather than on the doer. Look at the pairs of sentences below, in which the passive voice is the more effective choice.

PASSIVE VOICE Last night, the windshield on my new car was smashed.

ACTIVE VOICE   Last night, someone smashed the windshield on my new car.

PASSIVE VOICE   After the heavy snowfall, school was canceled.

ACTIVE VOICE   After the heavy snowfall, the principal canceled school.

In the first pair, the passive voice version emphasizes the subject *windshield,* rather than the unknown person who damaged it. The same is true for the second pair of sentences. Knowing that school has been canceled is more important than knowing who canceled it.

Probably the best suggestion is to go first with the active voice. If as you reread the sentence, you feel the emphasis is not appropriate, try a passive version. Consider the following sentences:

PASSIVE VOICE   The referee was approached by the furious player.

ACTIVE VOICE   The furious player approached the referee.

The active voice version is clearly superior—it correctly emphasizes the angry player who initiated the argument, not the referee who was assailed.

COMPREHENSION AND PRACTICE 14.1

Passive and Active Voice

Find all uses of the passive voice in the following paragraph. To do so, first underline the subject and verb in each clause. Check to see if the subject receives the action. If it does, the verb is in the passive voice. Write a *P* above verbs in the passive voice. Use the example as a guide.

EXAMPLE
   _P
The shelves in the gift shop were dusted carefully every week.

      P

(1) The chemistry experiment was completed by most of the students
                        P

before the end of the class. (2) The results were calculated, and then the
   P

figures were submitted to the lab instructor. (3) After she reviewed the

procedures the next day, the lab instructor assigned a written lab report.
      P

(4) A groan was heard from the students when they read the assignment.

(5) Unfortunately, the students must finish their reports over their spring

semester break.

CHALLENGE 14.1

The Effectiveness of Passive versus Active Voice

1. On a separate sheet of paper, rewrite the paragraph in Comprehension and Practice 14.1 so that all verbs are in the active voice.

collaboration

2. Working with a classmate, compare your revised paragraphs and then answer the following questions about both versions of the paragraph.

    a. Who or what is the subject in each sentence?

    b. Who or what should be emphasized in each sentence?

    c. Which version of each sentence do you think is more effective? Why?

Progressive Tenses

ESL Note
See "Agreement," pages 487–489, and "Confusing Verb Forms," pages 489–491, for more on forming progressive tenses.

The **progressive tenses** are formed by adding some form of the verb *to be* to the **present participle** of another verb. For both regular and irregular verbs, you form the present participle by adding *-ing* to the basic verb form—for example, *watching, eating, driving,* as the chart shows.

To Form the Progressive Voice

Present Tense	or	Past Tense	+	Present Participle of Another Verb	Examples
am is		was		eating, checking, taking	I *am eating* less meat these days. He *was checking* the roof for leaks when it began to rain.
are		were			My cousins *were taking* swimming lessons while their pool was being built.

The progressive forms show continuing actions or situations that are or were ongoing.

    When you combine the helping verbs *am, is,* or *are* with a present participle, you create a *present progressive tense.* The helping verbs are in the present tense, so the progressive verb form indicates something that is currently ongoing, or in progress.

    Note the present progressive verbs in the following sentences.

EXAMPLES   I *am studying* algebra and geometry for the first time.

          In many cities, gangs *are driving* customers away from downtown stores.

In the first sentence, the verb is *am studying.* It indicates that the mathematical study is happening now. In the second sentence, the verb is *are driving,* and it indicates that the disruption in the downtown area is occurring now and continues.

    Verbs in the *past progressive tense* (*was* or *were* plus the present participle) show action that was ongoing at some time in the past:

EXAMPLES   The traffic light *was changing* from yellow to red when I hit the brake.

          Icicles *were forming* on the side of the cliff as we climbed.

In the first sentence, the verb *was changing* indicates that the signal was in the process of changing (not changed) when the driver applied the brake. In the second, the verb *were forming* indicates that ice development was in progress (not complete) and continuing during the climb. All these actions occurred in the past.

When you combine the helping verbs *will be* with a present participle, you create a *future progressive tense*. The helping verbs are in the future tense, so the progressive verb indicates something that will be ongoing in the future. Take a look at the future progressive verbs in the following sentences.

EXAMPLE

Forecasters predict the snow *will be falling* all through the night.

Before you know it, your daughter *will be asking* to borrow your favorite clothes.

In both sentences, the verbs indicate that the action will happen continuously in the future.

COMPREHENSION AND PRACTICE
14.2

Progressive Tenses

In each of the following sentences, a present tense verb appears in parentheses. On the line that follows each verb, write the present participle form, being sure to add an appropriate form of *to be* as a helping verb. Use the example to guide you.

EXAMPLE

The folk choir (sing) ____is singing____ at the Sunday morning service.

(1) Twitter, among the newest social networking sites, (explode) is exploding in popularity. (2) Twitter users update their status by explaining what they (do) are doing at any particular moment. (3) In the simplest sense, Twitter users (maintain) are maintaining a micro-blog, with entries of no longer than 140 characters. (4) When many users provide updates, called Tweets, they (try) are trying to be both informative and entertaining. (5) Through their tweets, sports figures like NBA superstar center Shaquille O'Neal, a regular Twitter user, report that they (attempt) are attempting to stay more connected to their fans.

COMPREHENSION AND PRACTICE
14.3

Mastering the Progressive Tense

Choose five of the following ten verbs. On a separate sheet of paper, write a paragraph of at least seven to ten sentences dealing with a disturbing or annoying conversation you had with someone. Use appropriate progressive tense forms of the verbs. Remember that these tenses call for the present participle plus a form of *to be* as a helping verb. Use the example as a guide.

| to think | to respond | to argue | to discuss | to rest |
| to call | to understand | to contact | to disagree | to try |

EXAMPLE
> to prepare
>
> *The X-ray technician is preparing the patient right now.*

CHALLENGE 14.2 Multiple Tenses

1. Choose two verbs from the list of irregular verbs in Chapter 13 (pp. 252–255) and two regular verbs. Write a sentence using each verb in the present tense, the past tense, and a progressive tense.

2. Exchange your sentences with a partner. Underline the verbs in your partner's paper, and identify the tense used in each sentence.

collaboration

Consistency in Tense

ESL Note
See "Agreement,", pages 487–489, for more on maintaining consistency in verb tense.

When you write, one of the important aspects of verb use is to maintain **consistency** in tense. Sudden switches in tense can cloud the meaning of your ideas and confuse your reader. It's simple: If you are writing about something that happened in the past, use past tense verbs throughout. If you are writing about something that is happening now or that happens habitually, use present tense verbs. If you are writing about something that will happen in the future, use future tense verbs.

Consider the different tenses of the verbs in the following pair of sentences.

EXAMPLE
> The bouncer at the door of the club *checks* licenses or other IDs. A police officer *stood* behind him in case of any trouble.

The problem is that in the first sentence, the verb *checks* is present tense, but in the second, the verb *stood* is past tense. To correct this error, make both verbs the same tense:

PRESENT
> The bouncer at the door of the club *checks* licenses or other IDs. A police officer *stands* behind him in case of any trouble.

or

PAST
> The bouncer at the door of the club *checked* licenses or other IDs. A police officer *stood* behind him in case of any trouble.

Now both versions are correct, so which tense should be used? The choice of the appropriate tense always depends on the time line you are presenting. Are you telling what happened in the past or discussing what goes on today or occurs regularly? Always have a clear sense of the chronology of the events you include before you begin to write about them.

COMPREHENSION
AND PRACTICE
14.4

Consistency in Tense

Verb tense throughout the following paragraph has been used inconsistently. Read the paragraph and underline the verbs. Then decide which tense would work best in the paragraph. Cross out the verbs that need to be changed to the tense you have chosen and write the proper versions above them, as the example shows. Present tense answers are shown.

EXAMPLE

Before too much longer, nobody will need landline phones. As a result, telephone

will disappear

poles ~~disappeared~~, changing the look of cities and towns across the country.

love

(1) My dog gives me a lot of trouble, but I still ~~loved~~ him. (2) On most days,

digs

Paco runs after my neighbor's cat and ~~will digs~~ up her flower garden.

brings

(3) When it rains, Paco rolls in the mud and ~~has brought~~ dirt into the house.

take

(4) Every afternoon when I ~~took~~ him for a walk, he drags on his leash.

beats   *welcomes*

(5) However, nothing ~~will beat~~ the good feeling I get when Paco ~~welcomed~~ me

home at the end of the day.

COMPREHENSION AND PRACTICE

14.5

Proper Verb Tenses

The sentences in the following paragraph contain the infinitive form of a verb in parentheses, followed by a blank line. Identify the verb form—past or present—appropriate for each sentence and write it on the line. Use the example to guide you.

EXAMPLE

present

When many people (to recall) _____*recall*_____ their first date, they remember

past

being both excited and nervous. They (to worry) _____*worried*_____ most about

doing something embarrassing.

present

(1) Sometimes when I (to daydream) _____*daydream*_____, I (to see)

present   *past*

_____*see*_____ the house where I grew up in the Midwest. (2) It (to stand) _____*stood*_____

on a new suburban street surrounded by prairies where pheasants (to

past

search) _____*searched*_____ for food in the grasses. (3) When my family first (to move)

past   *past*

_____*moved*_____ in, my mother (to point) _____*pointed*_____ out three large cottonwood trees in our

past

backyard. (4) Before long, those trees (to become) _____*became*_____ my own personal

past

playground. (5) Every afternoon after school, I (to spend) _____*spent*_____ hours climbing and swinging from those trees. (6) The cottonwood trees (to offer) _offered_ *past* the

perfect place for gazing across the meadows around my house. (7) One thick

trunk also (to give) _gave_ *past* me a secure seat for reading. (8) In my daydreams, I

also (to picture) _picture_ *present* the inside of my house, especially my room. (9) The

images of the green striped wallpaper and the faded green carpet (to linger)

linger *present* in my memory.

CHALLENGE 14.3 Consistent Tense and Effective Voice

1. Edit this article from a college newspaper to make verb tenses consistent with
the time frame of each particular sentence. Cross out any verbs that are incorrect, and write the correct verb forms above them. Also, revise any sentences in the passive voice that you think would be more effective in the active voice.

(1) Yesterday, a new cafeteria manager ~~begins~~ *began* his work at Western

Community College, Margaret O'Neill, dean of administration, announced.

(2) This appointment ~~will concluded~~ *concluded* a long search process.

(3) "I will cut prices and ~~increases~~ *increase* hours of operation," the new manager,

Victor Rodriguez, vowed. (4) ~~Complaints about the prices and hours at the~~ *For two semesters students had complained to the administration about the prices and early closing hours at the cafeteria.*
~~cafeteria were made to the administration for two semesters by students.~~

(5) Before the management ~~change~~ *changed*, most students boycotted the cafeteria

and ~~are refused~~ *refused* to buy any food or beverages there. (6) As a result of that

protest, student leaders have won the right to interview candidates for the

new manager position.

(7) The administration also ~~agrees~~ *agreed* to meet with a student review board

once a semester. (8) From now on, the board will bring student concerns to

the administration for action.

2. Compare your version of the article with a classmate's. Note any differences
in the way each of you corrected the sentences, and together decide on
which correction is the better choice.

collaboration

✓**VOICE, PROGRESSIVE TENSES, AND CONSISTENCY IN TENSE CHECKLIST**

☐ Have you used active voice for those sentences in which you want your reader to know immediately who is, was, or will be doing some action?

☐ Have you preferred the passive voice for any sentence in which the focus should be on the receiver of the action rather than on the subject?

☐ Have you rechecked any sentences featuring passive voice to ensure that the active voice wouldn't be a better choice?

☐ Have you used the progressive tense, including the correct form of *to be* (*am, is, are, was, were*), to signify actions or events that are ongoing in some period of time?

☐ Have you identified the general time period—past, present, or future—you are writing about and then checked all verbs to make sure that their tenses match that time?

Journal Writing

When it comes to verbs, as this chapter indicates, *active* indicates that the subject is doing the action, *passive* indicates that the subject is being acted on, and *progressive* means that the action is ongoing. But in other contexts—in other situations—these words have other meanings. For instance, consider your own day-to-day activities. What time of the day are you most or least active? Why? Have you been in a situation where you were passive when you should have been active? Why did you choose passivity? Do you wish you had acted differently now? How about your plans for the future—are they progressing as you wish they were? Are they progressing better now than they had been progressing earlier? How will they be progressing five years from now? Consider one of these questions and explore it in your journal for 20 to 30 minutes.

CHAPTER QUICK CHECK   Using Passive Voice and Progressive Tenses, and Maintaining Consistency in Tense

Each sentence in the following paragraph contains a blank line preceded by the infinitive form of a verb in parentheses. Fill in each blank with an appropriate active, passive, or progressive form of this verb. Some of the verbs are irregular, so refer to Chapter 13, pages 252–255, if you are unsure about the correct forms of these words.

(1) Although consumers don't always seem to be aware of it, product placement (to grow) ____is growing____ as a way to advertise products and services. (2) Product placement (to involve) ____involves____ integrating an item, logo, or brand name into some presentation, usually for a fee. (3) The goal of product placement is to make viewers notice the object or company name as a character (to use) ____is using____ it. (4) One of the best-known examples of product placement in a movie (to appear) ____appeared____ in Steven Spielberg's 1982 hit movie *ET.* (5) Sales of Reese's Pieces increased more than 60 percent after this candy (to use) ____was used____ in the movie to draw ET out of hiding. (6) Product placement involving FedEx and Spaulding Sporting Goods also (to play) ____played____ a major role in *Castaway,* starring Tom Hanks. (7) On television, the cars, computers, and restaurants that (to appear) ____appear____ on screen are examples of product placement, too. (8) Familiar examples of product placement on television (to include) ____include____ Apple iPods on shows like *The Office* and *Supernatural,* Jack Bauer's Ford SUV on *24,* glasses of Coca-Cola in front of the judges on *American Idol,* and Under Armour athletic apparel on *Friday Night Lights.* (9) In addition, some video games (to begin) ____are beginning____ to include product placement of everything from cell phones to fast food restaurants. (10) The frequency of this kind of advertising (to suggest) ____suggests____ that companies believe product placement works.

SUMMARY EXERCISE Using Passive Voice and Progressive Tenses, and Maintaining Consistency in Tense

Each sentence in the following essay contains a blank line preceded by the infinitive form of a verb in parentheses. Fill in each blank with an appropriate active, passive, or progressive form of this verb. Some of the verbs are irregular, so refer to Chapter 13, pages 252–255, if you are unsure about the correct forms of these words.

(1) In 2001, the world of personal transportation (to undergo) ____underwent____ an exciting change with the introduction of the first Segway Personal Transporter. (2) The device, which resembles an old-fashioned

two-wheeled lawnmower, (to make) _____made_____ its appearance after months of rumors and speculation about a blockbuster invention. (3) So far, the Segway PT hasn't yet revolutionized the world, but Segway, Inc., the company that manufactures the device, (to work) _____is working_____ hard to make this hope a reality.

(4) The Segway PT (to invent) _____was invented_____ by New Hampshire's Dean Kamen. (5) Kamen and his associates (to work) _____were working_____ on an innovative stair-climbing wheelchair called the IBOT when Kamen first envisioned the Segway. (6) Kamen (to reason) _____reasoned_____ that the same technology in the IBOT could be adapted for a personal transportation device.

(7) The Segway PT (to design) _____was designed_____ to make using it as natural as walking. (8) You step up onto the eight-inch-high platform and, in seconds, (to cruise) _____are cruising_____ along. (9) Because of the large wheels, you (to enjoy) _____enjoy_____ an especially smooth ride.

(10) The Segway PT (to control) _____is controlled_____ by the movement of the human body. (11) When you lean forward, the Segway PT (to take) _____takes_____ off. (12) To stop, you simply (to lean) _____lean_____ back. (13) While the Segway PT (to roll) _____is rolling_____, a series of internal gyroscopes keeps it from tipping over.

(14) At top speed, the Segway PT (to propel) _____propels_____ the rider at 12.5 miles per hour. (15) For this reason, Kamen (to believe) _____believes_____ that the Segway is the ideal vehicle for city streets. (16) Most states already (to permit) _____permit_____ Segway use on sidewalks. (17) In a number of major cities right now, tour companies (to employ) _____employ_____ Segways to transport tourists on sight-seeing trips.

(18) In 2009, Segway, Inc., in conjunction with General Motors, (to unveil) _____unveiled_____ a prototype two-passenger vehicle, the PUMA (Personal Urban Mobility and Accessibility), based on the same principles as the Segway

PT. (19) The PUMA (to power) ___is powered___ by powerful lithium ion batteries, and it can carry its two seated passengers 35 miles at a maximum speed of 35 mph between charges. (20) Kamen and the automaker (to hope) ___are hoping___ to have the PUMA ready for the marketplace by 2012.

FOR FURTHER EXPLORATION

1. Choose one of the following subjects and use your preferred prewriting method to develop a specific focus and ideas to support it.

   - The person you know who most needs to simplify one or more aspects of day-to-day life
   - Your definition of personal success
   - The effects that sudden prosperity—or sudden poverty—can have on people

2. Evaluate your prewriting material, identify a focus, and create a draft paragraph of at least seven to ten sentences.

collaboration

3. Exchange your draft with a writing partner. Using the material in this chapter as a guide, evaluate the draft you receive. Note any problems in the use of passive voice verbs and progressive tenses as well as inappropriate shifts in verb tense. Return the draft to the writer.

4. Revise your draft, eliminating any errors that your reader identified.

DISCOVERING CONNECTIONS

For this assignment, focus on the photo and consider one of the following questions (or some other it inspires). Explore your ideas and then create a draft paragraph of at least seven to ten sentences. If most of your sentences are in passive voice, consider changing some of them to active voice. Remember to think about what part of the sentence you want emphasized before you decide whether it should be passive or active.

A. In this image of famed cellist Yo-Yo Ma, would you say he appears to be passively or actively engaged with his audience? How can you tell?

B. Look at the joy on Yo-Yo Ma's face. Does music have the power to raise a strong emotional feeling in you or someone you know? Why do you think it holds this power?

RECAP Using Passive Voice and Progressive Tenses, and Maintaining Consistency in Tense

Key Terms in This Chapter	Definitions
active voice	a term used to describe a verb whose action is *performed* by the subject
	EXAMPLE A robber broke into my apartment.
passive voice	a term used to describe a verb whose action is *received* by the subject
	EXAMPLE My apartment was robbed.
progressive tenses	a verb form created by adding *-ing* to the basic form of regular and irregular verbs
	EXAMPLE The snow was *falling* steadily by rush hour.
	They convey actions or situations that are, were, or will be ongoing.
	EXAMPLE I *am learning* to control my temper.
	EXAMPLE Rita *was singing* at the top of her lungs.
	EXAMPLE Janet *will be using* her own bat in the softball game.
present participle	tenses formed by adding some form of *to be* to the present participle of another verb
consistency	a condition of agreement among parts
	Verb tense is consistent when it agrees throughout a piece of writing.
	INCONSISTENT I caught the ball that Eddie throws.
	CONSISTENT I caught the ball that Eddie threw.

Forming the Progressive Tenses

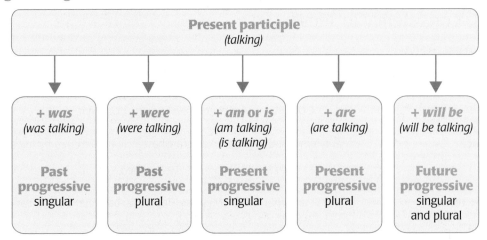

+ *was* (was talking)	+ *were* (were talking)	+ *am* or *is* (am talking) (is talking)	+ *are* (are talking)	+ *will be* (will be talking)
Past progressive singular	**Past progressive** plural	**Present progressive** singular	**Present progressive** plural	**Future progressive** singular and plural

Forming the Perfect Progressive Tenses

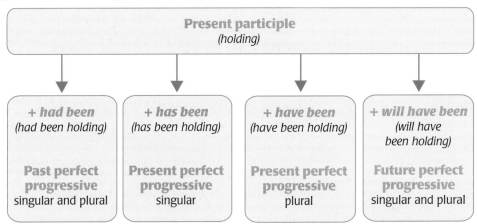

+ *had been* (had been holding)	+ *has been* (has been holding)	+ *have been* (have been holding)	+ *will have been* (will have been holding)
Past perfect progressive singular and plural	**Present perfect progressive** singular	**Present perfect progressive** plural	**Future perfect progressive** singular and plural

Using Discovery Online with MyWritingLab

For more practice using passive voice and progressive tenses, and maintaining consistency in tense, go to www.mywritinglab.com.

CHAPTER 15
Dealing with Additional Elements of Verb Use

GETTING STARTED ...

 Q Why is it so confusing to work with some irregular verbs? I'm not always sure when I should use *can* and when I should use *could*. The same thing is true about *will* or *would*. It's even worse with the different forms of *to be*.

 A It's no surprise that these verbs give you trouble. With *can* and *could* and with *will* and *would,* a number of factors determine which option is correct, including the time period involved and specific conditions or circumstances involved. And *to be* is especially challenging to use because it has more forms than any other verb. The key to selecting the correct form of any of these verbs is to identify the time and condition you're discussing, so always take a few moments to determine these factors.

Overview: Special Problems with Verbs

As the preceding chapters have shown, to write in correct sentences, you need to include a verb, choose the proper tense, and apply it consistently. You also need to steer clear of errors in verb use that can distort the meaning of what you write. Several common types of verb errors make it difficult for readers to understand what you intend to say. These errors involve confusion between *can* and *could* and between *will* and *would* and mistakes with forms of the verb *to be.*

Navigating This Chapter In this chapter, you will discover ways:

- to make the correct choice of verbs in the confusing pairs *can/could* and *will/would*
- to identify the correct form of *to be*—the most irregular of the irregular verbs

Can and *Could*

As helping verbs, *can* and *could* both mean *to be able to,* with *can* indicating present tense and *could* indicating past tense. Correctly choosing between *can* and *could* is important because depending on the form you use, the meaning of the sentence changes.

Look at these two versions of the same sentence:

EXAMPLES At this point, Sascha *can* run five miles in 30 minutes.

Last summer, Sascha *could* run five miles in 30 minutes.

As you can see, correctly choosing between *can* and *could* is important because, depending on the verb, the meaning of the sentence changes. In the first sentence, the verb indicates that Sascha *now* is able to run at that pace. In the second sentence, the verb indicates that Sascha *used to be* able to run at that pace.

In some contexts, *could* can also indicate a possibility or hope of being able to do something, as this sentence shows:

EXAMPLE Sascha wishes she *could* run five miles in 30 minutes.

In this version, Sascha isn't able to run five miles in 30 minutes, but she'd like to be able to do so.

COMPREHENSION AND PRACTICE

Correct Use of *Can* and *Could*

15.1 Each sentence in the following paragraph includes a set of parentheses containing *can* and *could*. Circle the correct verb for each sentence, using the example to guide you.

EXAMPLE Shaunna (can, could) easily pass the exam to become a firefighter.

(1) Jon (can, could) entertain everyone with his piano playing. (2) When I listen to him, I find myself wishing I (can, could) play as well. (3) I (can, could) tell that he blocks out the world around him as he plays. (4) At his last performance, the audience (can, could) see his body sway with the beat of the music, and they knew that was all he heard. (5) Only after years of practice (can, could) someone master an instrument as Jon has mastered the piano.

COMPREHENSION AND PRACTICE

Errors with *Can* and *Could*

15.2 Correct the errors in the use of *can* and *could* in the following paragraph. Cross out the incorrect word, and write the correct one above it. If a sentence is correct as written, mark it *OK*. Use the example as a guide.

EXAMPLE If I left my house at 3 P.M., ~~can~~ *could* I make it to the city before rush hour traffic clogs the highway?

(1) Today, most people who want to discard their glasses but aren't interested in LASIK surgery ~~could~~ *can* turn to a wide variety of contact lenses. (2) These lenses ~~could~~ *can* correct many common vision problems, including severe

OK
astigmatism. (3) Many brands of contact lenses can also be obtained in differ-

could
ent colors. (4) For example, if you have brown eyes, you ~~can~~ change your eye

color to various shades of blue and vice versa. (5) For sports like baseball, ten-

can
nis, and golf, you ~~could~~ purchase contact lenses that filter out certain colors.

OK
(6) With these contact lenses, you can follow the ball more easily. (7) To wake

can
up to a perfectly clear world, you ~~could~~ even purchase disposable, extended-

wear contacts and sleep with them in. (8) After wearing them for a period of

can
time, in some cases up to a month, you ~~could~~ simply throw them it away and

insert a new pair.

CHALLENGE 15.1   Evaluation of the Use of *Can* and *Could* Answers will vary.

1. Think about your skills or areas of expertise. Then, on a separate sheet of paper, write three sentences that begin: "I can _____."

2. What skills or expertise would you like to develop? On the same sheet of paper, write three sentences that begin: "I wish I could _____."

collaboration

3. Exchange your sentences with a classmate. Check the sentences you receive
to make sure that *can* and *could* have been used correctly. Put a ✓ next to
any use of these verbs that you think is incorrect and return the sentences to
the writer.

4. Check any use of *can* or *could* that your reader has questioned in your sentences, and then make any necessary changes.

Will and *Would*

Deciding between the helping verbs *will* and *would* is another choice that can be
baffling. Understanding the distinction between them is important. Both verbs indicate the future, but each links the future to a different period of time. Making the
right choice will ensure that your reader understands your meaning clearly.
    Look at the sentences below, with the verbs italicized:

PRESENT TENSE   Maria *thinks* that she *will major* in accounting.

PAST TENSE   Maria *thought* that she *would major* in accounting.

As the first sentence shows, *will* points to the future from the *present. Right now,*
Maria intends to focus on accounting at some future time. As the second sentence
shows, *would* points to the future from the *past. At an earlier time,* Maria had intended to study accounting in the future.

In some instances, *would* is also used to indicate a hope or possibility rather than a certainty, as this sentence shows:

EXAMPLE ⌈ Many people *would* feel better if they changed their diets.

As it is used in this sentence, *would* indicates the prospect of improved health, but any improvement depends on a change in eating habits.

COMPREHENSION
AND PRACTICE
15.3

Correct Use of *Will* and *Would*

Each sentence in the following paragraph includes a set of parentheses containing *will* and *would*. Circle the correct verb for each sentence, using the example to guide you.

EXAMPLE ⌈ My brother Luis hopes he (will, would) graduate in the top 10 percent of his class.

(1) The National Weather Service predicts that it (will, would) rain again this evening across the entire tri-state area. (2) If this were to happen, it (will, would) be good news for area farmers. (3) With this precipitation, many crops that might have been lost (will, would) be saved. (4) In March, the agriculture experts predicted that farmers (will, would) produce smaller than normal crops this year. (5) With this continued wet weather, it is likely that they (will, would) revise those predictions soon.

COMPREHENSION
AND PRACTICE
15.4

Errors with *Will* and *Would*

Correct the errors in the use of *will* and *would* in the following paragraph. Cross out the incorrect word, and write the correct choice above it. If a sentence is correct as written, mark it *OK*. Use the sample as a guide.

EXAMPLE ⌈
                   would
I can see why many people ~~will~~ be reluctant to move into a new apartment without signing a lease.

               would
(1) Many people ~~will~~ like to learn another language for personal or business reasons but are not sure about the best way to do so. (2) Once they check
             will   OK
around, though, they ~~would~~ find a number of options. (3) Many high schools, community organizations, and colleges have noncredit courses that will help
                                          will
them develop mastery of another language. (4) In these courses, people ~~would~~ have the opportunity to learn to read, write, and speak common phrases.

(5) After a few weeks, students ~~would~~ *will* find themselves developing a basic understanding of the language. (6) As they begin to feel more confident, they ~~would~~ *will* find their skills improving. (7) Some people would like more flexibility *OK* in terms of when they learn, however. (8) They know that formal classes ~~would~~ *will* help, but they simply can't squeeze in the time to attend. (9) For these people, self-paced language DVDs like Rosetta Stone ~~will~~ *would* allow them to learn on their own schedules. (10) Regardless of the approach they choose, people who learn a second language ~~would~~ *will* certainly expand their personal and business horizons.

CHALLENGE 15.2   Evaluation of the Use of *Will* and *Would* Answers will vary.

1. Think about some plans that you have now. Then, on a separate sheet of paper, write three sentences that begin: "I will _____."

2. Think of some plans you once had that changed or evolved in some way or consider some hope or possibility. On the same sheet of paper, write three sentences that begin: "I would _____."

collaboration

3. Exchange your sentences with a classmate. Check the sentences you receive to make sure that *will* and *would* have been used correctly. Put a ✓ next to any use of these verbs that you think is incorrect and return the sentences to the writer.

4. Check any use of *will* or *would* that your reader has questioned in your sentences, and then make any necessary changes.

Forms of *to Be*

The most irregular of the irregular verbs is the verb *to be,* and using forms of this verb properly can sometimes be difficult. Here is a table that shows the most common forms of *to be:*

Common Forms of the Verb *to Be*

When the subject is …	the present tense is …	the past tense is …	the future tense is …	the present participle is …	the past participle is …
I	am	was	will be	being	been
he, she, or it	is	was	will be	being	been
we, you, or they	are	were	will be	being	been

ESL Note
See "Sentence Basics,"
pages 483–485, "Word
Order," pages 485–486,
and "Confusing Verb
Forms," pages 489–491,
for more on the correct
use of forms of the verb
to be.

As the right side of this chart shows, not *all* the forms are irregular. *Will be, being,* and *been* are used with all subjects (although the helping verbs do change for the participles). Therefore, to master the use of the verb *to be,* focus on just those forms that *do* change. This abbreviated table will help you learn them:

When the subject is ...	the present tense is ...	the past tense is ...
I	am	was
he or she	is	was
we, you, or they	are	were

Keep these forms straight, and you'll find that you experience far fewer problems with this verb.

The following example sentences show how all the forms in the complete table above are used.

PRESENT

I *am* late.

Alonso *is* tired.

You *are* confused about the new rules. We *are* confused about them, too. They *are* also confused.

PAST

Sheila *was* tired. I *was* tired, too.

The people around the pool *were* relaxed. We *were* relaxed, and you *were,* too.

FUTURE

You *will be* glad that you are taking that self-defense class. Your family *will be* pleased, and I *will be,* too.

PRESENT PARTICIPLE

We were *being* entertained. The crowd was *being* silly. Even now, the girl in the front row is *being* silly.

The youth center has *been* planning a talent night. The performers have *been* rehearsing for a month. At first, I had *been* reluctant to try out.

Using *been* without one of the helping verbs *has, have,* or *had* is one common error in the use of *to be.* This usage can occasionally be heard in casual conversation and street talk, but it is not acceptable in college or professional writing.

Take a look at this error in the following sentences:

FAULTY

For the past two weeks, we *been* especially busy at work.

The arson suspect *been* accused of the same crime a year earlier.

Both of these units are *fragments* because they lack a complete verb. (For more on fragments and complete verbs, see Chapter 7, "Sentence Fragments," pp. 143–161.) In each sentence, *have* or *had* must be added to *been* to create a complete verb:

REVISED

For the past two weeks, we ***have*** *been* especially busy at work.

The arson suspect ***had*** *been* accused of the same crime a year earlier.

Using *be* by itself as the verb in a sentence is another common error in writing, as these examples show:

FAULTY

We *be* upset with the mess that the plumbers left in the kitchen.

He *be* the reason for this party.

Although this error also occasionally occurs in informal speech, it is not acceptable in writing for college or work. To correct this error, change *be* to another complete form of *to be,* as these versions show:

REVISED

We *are* upset with the mess that the plumbers left in the kitchen.

He *is* the reason for this party.

COMPREHENSION
AND PRACTICE

15.5

Forms of *to Be*

Supply the correct form of the verb *to be* in each sentence of the paragraph below, referring to the table on page 281 for help in choosing the correct form. Use the example to guide you.

EXAMPLE

The fishing boat __*is*__ late returning to the harbor.

(1) More than 25 years after the first Macintosh computer appeared, Apple __is__ still trying to close the sales gap between Macs and PCs. (2) Although the figures change somewhat from year to year, the percentage of Windows PCs sold annually __is__ still far larger than the percentage of Macs. (3) Price, speed, and compatibility issues __are__ just some of the reasons that consumers cite in choosing a PC over a Mac. (4) The Intel-powered iMac and the Macbook, released in 2006, __were__ attempts by Apple to attract greater number of PC users. (5) Right now, however, PCs, both laptops and desktops, __are__ often significantly less expensive than

their Macintosh counterparts, a factor that will surely keep many users from making the switch.

Correct Use of Forms of *to Be*

Some sentences in the following paragraph use *been* or *be* without a helping verb. Correct these errors by adding the appropriate helping verbs or by substituting another form of the verb *to be*. Cross out the incorrect form first, if necessary. Then write your revision in the space above the line. Use the example as a guide.

EXAMPLE

has been
The cost of living ~~been~~ increasing each year.

(1) Cloning ~~be~~ *is* a technique through which copies of living cells are made.
(2) Genetic engineers ~~been~~ *have been* involved in one type of cloning, gene cloning, since the 1970s. (3) Gene cloning ~~be~~ *is* a way to make duplicate copies of particular genes for further examination and study. (4) Dolly the sheep, created in 1997, ~~be~~ *was* the best-known example of another type, called reproductive cloning.
(5) This type of cloning ~~being~~ *is* a way to create a genetic twin of another animal. (6) The DNA ~~be~~ *is* removed from an egg cell and replaced with genetic material from an adult donor. (7) A more controversial type of cloning is therapeutic cloning. *OK* (8) The goal of therapeutic cloning ~~be~~ *is* to create cells to combat illnesses and conditions like Alzheimer's disease, heart disease, and cancer.
(9) Researchers believe that pluripotency, the unique quality of the human stem cell to adapt itself, ~~being~~ *is* the secret. (10) Therapeutic cloning ~~be~~ *is* controversial because the ideal stem cells come from a blastocyst, a five-day-old human embryo, and the harvesting process destroys the embryo.

CHALLENGE 15.3   **Evaluation of the Forms of *to Be***

1. As the discussion about forms of the verb *to be* explains, this verb is the most irregular of the irregular verbs, with forms that don't follow predictable patterns. Life is also sometimes unpredictable. Think of an event or experience that didn't unfold the way you expected it to, and, after doing some prewriting, write a paragraph of at least seven to ten sentences about it.

collaboration

2. Exchange your paragraph with a classmate. Check all forms of *to be* in the paragraph you receive to make sure that they have been used correctly. Use the listing of forms of *to be* on page 281 to guide you. Put a ✓ next to

any use of these verbs that you think is incorrect, and return the sentences to the writer.

3. Check any use of *to be* that your reader has questioned in your sentences, and then make any necessary changes.

✓ ADDITIONAL ELEMENTS OF VERB USE CHECKLIST

☐ Have you selected *can* as a helping verb to indicate actions or situations in the present?

☐ Have you used *could* as a helping verb to show actions or situations in the past or to indicate a hope or possibility of achieving some action or situation?

☐ Have you selected *will* as a helping verb to signify actions or situations that *right now* are expected to occur in the *future?*

☐ Have you used *would* as a helping verb to discuss actions or situations that *in the past* were expected to occur in the *future* or something that might happen under particular circumstances?

☐ Have you made sure you have included *have, has,* or *had* each time you have used *be* or *been* as the verb in a sentence?

Journal Writing

One verb can indicate different conditions depending on the situation. In some cases, *could* means being able to accomplish something at some earlier time. In other cases, *could* means a hope or possibility that something might be accomplished. Sometimes *would* indicates a plan for the future made in the past. Other times, *would* suggests something that might occur if something else does. Now consider circumstances in life for which you might use these verbs to describe or explain. For example, is there something that you once could do that you wish you could still do? What happened? Is it possible for you to regain this skill or ability? Or, if you could, what one event in your life would you change? Why? What difference do you think this change would make? Consider one of these questions, and explore it in your journal for 20 to 30 minutes.

CHAPTER QUICK CHECK Dealing with Additional Elements of Verb Use

The following passage contains errors in the use of *can* and *could, will* and *would,* and forms of the verb *to be.* Read the passage, and correct these errors. Cross out the incorrect word or words, and write your revision in the space above the line. Above any sentence that is correct as written, write *OK.*

        (1) History has shown that the names companies choose for products
~~could~~ ^{can} make a huge difference in the ultimate success of the product.
(2) When it comes to developing a brand name for a product, one primary
goal ~~being~~ ^{is} instant identification. (3) Usually, firms choose names for their
products that ~~be~~ ^{are} positive and upbeat. (4) That's the technique that ~~been~~ ^{has been} followed by Purina, the company that produces Beneful dog food. (5) Purina's
marketing department actually created a word that suggests *benefit* so that
people ~~will~~ ^{would} view this product in a positive light. (6) Pfizer, the makers of the
pain reliever Celebrex, had the same thing in mind and named their product
with the hopes that consumers ~~will~~ ^{would} associate their product with a celebration.
(7) Sometimes a winning product or company name ~~would~~ ^{will} appear after long
discussions and brainstorming sessions. (8) After such a session, the founders
of Google settled on this name, a misspelling of *googol*, which refers to the
number 1 followed by 100 zeroes, so that they ~~can~~ ^{could} capture the sense of something enormous. (9) A marketing firm working for Research In Motion (RIM)
suggested the name BlackBerry because somebody thought the tiny buttons
on the original device ~~will~~ ^{would} make people think of seeds on a strawberry—or, the
company ultimately decided, on a blackberry. ^{OK} (10) This brand-name game will
continue as long as new products continue to appear in the marketplace.

SUMMARY EXERCISE   Dealing with Additional Elements of Verb Use

The following essay contains errors in the use of *can* and *could, will* and *would,*
and forms of the verb *to be*. Read the passage, and correct these errors. Cross out
the incorrect word or words, and write your revision in the space above the line.
Above any sentence that is correct as written, write *OK*.

        (1) *Plagiarism* ~~being~~ ^{is} using someone else's words, opinions, or ideas in
your own writing without giving the original author credit. (2) Plagiarism
~~could~~ ^{can} easily be avoided by simply acknowledging the source of material

a writer includes in a document. (3) There be simply no excuse for stealing [is]

the words of another writer.

(4) One step that could help students understand plagiarism is to learn [can]

about a school's regulations concerning it. (5) In many cases, plagiarism means

failure in a class, and in some cases it could lead to expulsion from school. (6) [can]

Many instructors would take time in class to discuss this important ethical is- [will]

sue. (7) In my science class, for example, we been studying methods scientists [have been]

use to report their own research. (8) She made it clear that worthwhile and

ethical research could exist only if researchers credit the work that came be- [can]

fore them.

(9) I know I would have to complete many research projects and papers [will]

before I get my degree. (10) The grades for these assignments can affect my [could]

overall success in college, so I've been paying close attention. (11) I be deter- [am]

mined to make sure that I credit all my sources properly each time I complete

this kind of task.

(12) Professional writers could also have problems with plagiarism. [can]

(13) For example, a reporter will be suspended or fired for failing to give [would]

credit for material used in a story. (14) When authors of biographies or other

nonfiction texts don't acknowledge their sources correctly, they could see their [can]

professional reputations permanently tarnished.

(15) Plagiarism be an important ethical issue for fiction writers, too. (16) In [is] [OK]

general they do their best to avoid using story ideas that can be considered

someone else's intellectual property. (17) This strategy reduces the chance of

inadvertently adapting someone else's work and thinking it be their own. [is]

(18) In some ways, plagiarism be the worst kind of theft. (19) After all, [is]

when someone steals a personal possession like a watch or car, it could be re- [can]

placed. (20) When someone steals someone else's ideas and hard work, there [OK]

is no way to replace them.

FOR FURTHER EXPLORATION

1. Select one of the following subjects, and using your preferred prewriting method, develop a specific focus and supporting ideas.

   - The advantages—or consequences—of acting on impulse
   - What can undermine a good friendship
   - A time when you felt the most successful in your life

2. Evaluate your prewriting material, identify a focus, and create a draft paragraph of at least seven to ten sentences.

collaboration

3. Exchange your draft with a writing partner. Using the material in this chapter as a guide, evaluate the draft you receive. Note any problems with the use of *can* and *could, will* and *would,* and forms of *to be,* as well as any other weaknesses, and return the draft to the writer.

4. Revise your draft, eliminating any errors that your reader identified.

DISCOVERING CONNECTIONS

Look at this picture and answer one of the following questions (or another the photo inspires). Then, after exploring your ideas on this topic, create a draft paragraph of at least seven to ten sentences. To ensure that you're using the correct verb form, consider the time and condition you're writing about.

A. The police officer in the photo is female, but the figures surrounding her are male. How far do you think society has come about accepting women in what are stereotypically considered "men's professions"? In your view, is sexism still very much a problem? What leads you to this conclusion?

B. The police officer in the photo is clearly in a take-charge position. In your view, what are the biggest responsibilities that come with being in charge? What are the biggest pitfalls?

RECAP Dealing with Additional Elements of Verb Use

Verb Pairs Often Confused

can/could	helping verbs that mean *to be able to*
	Use *can* to show present tense.
	EXAMPLE Jose *can* win the contest.
	Use *could* to show past tense, or the possibility or hope of being able to do something.
	EXAMPLE If I *could* sing, then I *could* join the chorus.
will/would	helping verbs that indicate the future
	Use *will* to point to the future from the present.
	EXAMPLE Howard promises he *will* return before midnight.
	Use *would* to point to the future from the past.
	EXAMPLE Howard promised he *would* return before midnight.

The Irregular Verb *to Be*

using *to be* correctly	Always use *has, have,* or *had* with *been.*
	Never use *be* alone as a verb.
	Follow the chart below for forms of *to be.*

Common Forms of the Verb *to Be*

When the subject is ...	the present tense is ...	the past tense is ...	the future tense is ...	the present participle is ...	the past participle is ...
I	am	was	will be	being	been
he, she, or it	is	was	will be	being	been
we, you, or they	are	were	will be	being	been

Using Discovery Online with MyWritingLab

For more practice dealing with additional elements of verb use, go to www.mywritinglab.com.

Assessment: a process of evaluation designed to identify your level of mastery and help improve your performance

VERBS: CONVEYING ACTION AND TIME

The material you have completed in Part 3 focuses on **different aspects of correct verb use**. To assess your understanding of this information and your progress as a **Writer, Reader, Editor**, and **Student**, complete the following charts. First check off your level of confidence for each item, and then take the recommended action to improve your performance.

- As a **Writer**, I understand

	Confident	Moderately Confident	Not Confident
1. **subject–verb agreement** (Chapter 11)			
2. **basic tenses for regular verbs** (Chapter 12)			
3. **irregular verbs** (Chapter 13)			
4. appropriate uses of **active and passive voice**, **perfect and progressive tenses**, and **consistency in verb tense** (Chapters 12 and 14)			
5. ways to distinguish between *can* and *could* and *will* and *would* and to choose the correct forms of *to be* (Chapter 15)			

- If you are **confident**, you are all set. Move on.

- If you are **moderately confident**, review the Recaps for the appropriate chapters.

- If you are **not confident**, review the appropriate chapters, looking closely at the sample sentences, Chapter Quick Checks, and Summary exercises.

- As a **Reader**, I understand

	Confident	Moderately Confident	Not Confident
1. subject–verb agreement and the correct use of tenses and forms of verbs			
2. the purpose and usefulness of the **Chapter Q&A, Overview, Checklist**, and **Journal Writing** features			

- If you are **confident**, you are all set. Move on.

- If you are **moderately confident**, take another look at these chapter features to make sure you understand the relationship between these features and the material in the chapters.

- If you are **not confident**, reread the **Q&A** and **Overview** sections. Identify example sentences that illustrate your particular difficulty. Revisit some of the exercises and activities, and complete the **Journal Writing** assignments; then use the **Chapter Checklists** to make sure that you have made no errors in verb use.

- As an **Editor**, I understand

	Confident	Moderately Confident	Not Confident
1. how to maintain **subject–verb agreement** as well as how to recognize and correct errors in this kind of agreement (Chapter 11)			
2. how to create the **basic tenses for regular and irregular verbs** (Chapters 12 and 13)			
3. how to choose correctly between **active** and **passive voices**, use the **perfect** and **progressive tenses**, and be **consistent in verb use** (Chapters 12 and 14)			
4. how to use *can* and *could* and *will* and *would* and forms of *to be* correctly			

- If you are **confident**, you are all set. Move on.

- If you are **moderately confident**, focus on the verbs in your own draft paragraph. Make sure they all agree with their respective subjects. Consider any **passive voice** constructions to see if **active voice** versions would be better. Check any use of *can* or *could*, *will* or *would*, and forms of *to be* to make sure you have used the correct form.

- If you are **not confident** about an aspect of verb use, reexamine the examples in the appropriate chapters. Find a passage of 200 words or so in one of your textbooks or a print or online article. Highlight or circle each verb, underline its subjects, and draw a line between these two elements to emphasize agreement. Write an *A* above all active voice constructions and *P* above all passive voice versions. Put a check above each use of *can* and *could, will* and *would*, and forms of *to be*.

- As a **Student**, I understand

	Confident	Moderately Confident	Not Confident
1. the importance of careful note -taking in all my classes			
2. the need to review, amend, and correct my class notes after each class meeting			
3. the value of maintaining a response journal			

- If you are **confident**, you are all set. Move on.

- If you are **moderately confident,** review a typical set of class notes to evaluate their effectiveness. Revisit one of your entries in a response journal, noting the key points discussed in that session and your reaction to them.

- If you are **not confident**, on your next day of classes, take careful notes for all class sessions. At the end of your day, spend 30 minutes or so reviewing your notes, adjusting them as necessary. When possible, note page numbers in your textbooks or class materials where parallel discussions or explanations exist. Then write a 200- to 250- word response-journal entry for each class summarizing and emphasizing key points and reactions to class presentations and discussions.

PART 4

Sentence Elements: Striving for Precision

What subject, topic, or academic field do you prefer to write about? Which do you find most difficult to write about? Why?

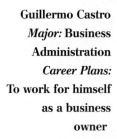

I enjoy writing about the things I live for. Basketball is on the top of my list. Not only am I actively involved in the sport, I am also a professional basketball enthusiast. I have the most trouble writing about an assigned subject or topic. When I don't have my imagination and interest to fuel me, I find it much harder.

Guillermo Castro
Major: **Business Administration**
Career Plans: **To work for himself as a business owner**

When Guillermo Castro first began college, he didn't feel that his writing skills were strong enough. "I struggled with grammar, which affected my writing. I thought I would never survive my first semester." After a semester, however, his attitude changed. "I worked hard and it paid off. I feel confident about my current writing skills. Now I can express myself, and my imagination, with confidence in my words."

What connections do you see between writing and reading? How can improving in one skill help you improve in the other?

By reading more, I have been able to learn more vocabulary because I am compelled to look up those words I don't know so I can understand what I am reading. Reading also helped me to see how the structure of the book or whatever reading material I was dealing with is set up to capture the reader. Because of reading, I was able to write better. I have noticed in college that reading, writing, and speech have all taught me to express myself in different ways—they all work together.

Leslie Ferreira
Major: **Hospitality and Tourism**
Career Plans: **To work in an upper management position or to own her own business**

Leslie Ferreira became pregnant at 14 and was unable to resume her formal education until some 44 years later. "I felt intimidated. In actuality, I had not written or read much before college. I was a novice." Within a short period of time, however, she made an important discovery. "The biggest surprise to me was to find out that I'm not a stupid person, that I have great potential." Leslie, who recently completed her bachelor's degree, also discovered that writing helped her develop a greater understanding of herself and her life. "I find it difficult sometimes when I am writing about personal subjects, but I can look at myself and learn more about who I am. It cleanses my soul, so to speak. By letting these things out, I am able to allow more positive things to come in."

How will being able to write well help you in school and on the job? What do you do to make sure that your writing is as clear, direct, and correct as possible?

Being able to write well is very important: whether you must write a speech, a letter, a report, or an informal e-mail. You have to be able to communicate your point so other people can understand what you are trying to say. To make sure that my writing is as good as it can be, I concentrate on the writing process, and how it makes writing easier. I also work on cutting back on writing errors. I am confident that I can write a good paper and have it done on a deadline without much trouble, especially if it is on a topic I like.

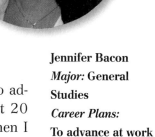

Russell Wakefield
Major: **General Studies**
Career Plans: **Undecided**

Before college, going to school was never a chore for Russell Wakefield, who admits proudly, "I had almost perfect attendance in every year of school." College has been a different experience, though. For Russell, the first member of his immediate family to attend college, the most surprising thing about attending college has been "the freedom it allows and the responsibility involved. There is so much about college that depends on the individual." Russell always considered himself a "decent writer," but thanks to a greater understanding of the writing process, he feels more comfortable and confident than ever before.

When you share a draft with another reader, how do you feel? And how do you feel when you have the opportunity to evaluate someone else's work?

The first few times I shared a draft of a writing was tough. Allowing someone else to read your personal thoughts can be intimidating. After you have done it a few times it gets easier. When you read another person's story, it helps you to realize we are all in the same boat. In the end I think this helps me become a better writer. When they tell me where they had questions or wanted more from the story, I begin to see my story through my readers' eyes.

Jennifer Bacon
Major: **General Studies**
Career Plans: **To advance at work as a medical coder**

Jennifer Bacon's initial motivation to attend college was a desire to advance at work. "I work at the hospital where I have been for the last 20 years. I started out 16 years old, washing dishes after school. Since then I have held various positions and have done okay, but if I wish to advance further, I need more education. I want to do this to make more money to provide for my family, and to feel good about myself, accomplished." Although she wasn't sure how her experience back in the classroom would be, "the biggest surprise in college is that I can really do it if I try. I didn't think this would be the case when I started." Jennifer felt that her writing skills were weak before she began her college classes, but that's all changed now: "I am not yet writing my first novel, but I do feel more comfortable."

CHAPTER 16
Working with Nouns

GETTING STARTED ...

Q Of all the words I use when I write, nouns dominate. Most of the time, I can tell whether the form is singular or plural. But I still have trouble with some singular nouns that end in *-s* such as *news* and *statistics* and some collective nouns such as *government* and *audience*. They look or seem to be plural, so I get tripped up. What can I do to avoid problems with nouns like these?

A Nouns dominate because they focus on the persons, locales, concepts, and objects of writing. For the most part, using nouns correctly is easier than you might think. The best way to avoid confusion about whether a noun is in singular or plural form is to memorize the nouns that trouble you. The task will be fairly easy since the list is likely to be small.

Overview: Words That Name

To keep the world straight, we name everything around us, and the objects we name are called **nouns.** Nouns are classified into two groups. **Common nouns** name nonspecific people or things—an executive, a state, a novel. **Proper nouns** name particular people or things—Jeremy Wright, Michigan, *Of Mice and Men*—and these are always introduced by a capital letter. Nouns also have two forms, *singular* for those nouns referring to individual persons or things and *plural* for those referring to more than one. You'll use nouns in every sentence you compose, so you need to develop a thorough understanding of them.

Navigating This Chapter In this chapter, you will learn how to:

- turn a singular noun into a plural one
- recognize singular nouns that end in *-s*
- work with collective nouns
- use cue words to identify the number of a noun

The Function and Form of Nouns

ESL Note
See "Agreement," pages 487–489, for more on nouns as subjects.

Nouns can serve as

- a **subject:**

EXAMPLE *Psychology* remains a popular choice of study for many college students.

- a **predicate nominative**, the word that answers *Who or What?* after a *linking* verb:

EXAMPLE   My best friend is an outstanding *guitarist.*

- a **direct object,** the word that answers *Whom or What?* after an *action* verb:

EXAMPLE   Caitlyn opened the *package* left on the counter.

- an **indirect object,** the word that answers *To Whom or For Whom, To What or For What?* after an *action* verb:

EXAMPLE   The sales representative gave the *woman* a brochure explaining the plasma television's warranty.

- an **object of a preposition**, the word that follows a preposition and completes a *prepositional phrase:*

EXAMPLE   The photograph on that *desk* is almost 100 years old.

- an **appositive**, a word that helps to explain or illustrate another noun:

EXAMPLE   The speaker held onto his good-luck charm, a small *keychain.*

Regardless of a noun's function, you must always select the proper form—singular or plural—for each situation. The good news, however, is that changing nouns from singular to plural is generally easy. To make most nouns plural, simply add *-s* to the singular form:

Singular	*Plural*
basketball	basketball**s**
chair	chair**s**
plan	plan**s**

Not all nouns form their plurals the same way, though. For example, to make most words that end in *-ch, -sh, -x,* or *-s* plural, you must add *-es:*

Singular	*Plural*
box	box**es**
bush	bush**es**
church	church**es**
glass	glass**es**

To make words that end in a consonant and -*y* plural, you must change the -*y* to -*i* and add -*es:*

Singular	*Plural*
baby	bab**ies**
butterfly	butterfl**ies**

To make many words that end in -*f* or -*fe* plural, you must change the ending to -*ves:*

Singular	*Plural*
half	hal**ves**
knife	kni**ves**

To make combined or hyphenated words plural, you must add -*s* to the main word:

Singular	*Plural*
maid of honor	maid**s** of honor
passerby	passer**s**by
sister-in-law	sister**s**-in-law

To make some common words plural, you must *change letters within the word:*

Singular	*Plural*
foot	f**ee**t
mouse	m**i**ce
tooth	t**ee**th
woman	wom**e**n

Some words have the same singular and plural forms:

Singular	*Plural*
antelope	**antelope**
deer	**deer**
fish	**fish**
sheep	**sheep**

Of course, other variations of plural forms exist. For example, some words that end in -*o,* such as *piano* and *radio,* form their plural by adding -*s.* Other words that end in -*o,* such as *tomato* and *hero,* form their plural by adding -*es.* Some words from foreign languages, such as *analysis* and *crisis,* form their plurals in keeping with their original language: *analyses* and *crises.*

When you are in doubt about the plural form for a noun, turn to the dictionary. It gives the plural ending in boldface for nouns that do not form a plural simply by adding -*s.*

COMPREHENSION
AND PRACTICE
16.1

The Function of Nouns

In each of the following sentences, two nouns are underlined. Using the discussion of the function of nouns to guide you, write the function of each underlined noun above it, as the example shows:

EXAMPLE

subject   *predicate nominative*
The owner of that truck is the former mayor of the city.

subject
(1) A major figure in the world of contemporary literature is Sandra

appositive
Cisneros, perhaps best known for *The House on Mango Street,* her first novel.

object of the preposition   *subject*
(2) More than 2 million copies of this work are in print, and the book is

required reading in many high school and college classrooms. (3) In the
object of the preposition   *direct object*
novel, which was first published in 1983, she discusses life in the Hispanic area

predicate nominative
of Chicago. (4) Cisneros is also the author of several volumes of poetry, a bilin-

appositive
gual children's book, and other works of fiction, including *Caramelo,* a novel

indirect object direct object
published in 2002. (5) In this book, Cisneros tells her readers the story of three

generations of the Reyes family through the words of granddaughter Celaya.

COMPREHENSION
AND PRACTICE
16.2

Plural Noun Use

Choose seven of the following nouns and on a separate sheet of paper write their plural forms. Then, on the same page, write sentences in which you use these plural forms. Use the example sentence provided as a guide.

brother-in-law	glass
wife	woman
knife	box
mouse	solo
pew	family

EXAMPLE

At the wedding I attended yesterday, the maids of honor were dressed in blue.

CHALLENGE 16.1 **Singular and Plural Forms**

1. Identify ten singular nouns in a piece of writing that you are currently working on, and list them on a separate piece of paper.

collaboration

2. Exchange your list with a classmate. On the list you receive, write the plural form of the nouns next to the singular forms, and return the list to the writer.

3. Check the accuracy of the plural forms listed on your paper, using the guidelines in this chapter and a dictionary to correct any errors.

Singular Nouns Ending in -s and Collective Nouns

Not all nouns that end in *-s* are plural. A number of singular nouns end in *-s*, including the following:

economics	mathematics	mumps	physics	statistics
ethics	measles	news	politics	

Because these words end in *-s*, it's easy to incorrectly select a plural verb form. These words are singular, however, and thus take a singular verb form, as this example shows:

EXAMPLE

In terms of academic majors, *mathematics provides* students with a background to move into several areas, including engineering, chemistry, and medicine.

ESL Note
See "Articles: *a, an,* and *the,*" pages 491–492, for more on the correct use of articles.

Collective nouns, words that stand for groups of items or people, can also be confusing in terms of number. Take a look at this list of common collective nouns:

Common Collective Nouns

audience	department	government	office
class	faculty	group	school
committee	family	herd	team
congregation	flock	jury	troop

Collective nouns generally call for a singular form of a verb, as these examples show:

EXAMPLE

Barbara's *family provides* emotional support whenever she is stressed out about her classes.

Our *team has* already won more games this season than we won for the whole season last year.

In the first sentence, the correct verb for the collective noun *family* is the singular form, *provides*. In the second sentence, the correct verb for the collective noun *team* is the singular form of the helping verb, *has*.

Cue Words That Identify Number

Some of the words you include in your sentences can help you decide whether a noun is singular or plural. When these **cue words** refer to nouns used as subjects, they can help you determine whether to use a singular or a plural form of a verb. The following words can signal that a singular noun follows.

Common Singular Cue Words

a, an	every
another	neither
each	one
either	

EXAMPLES

Each person in the photograph *looks* startled.

One luxury car in the showroom *costs* more than $55,000.

In the first sentence, the cue word *each* signals a singular subject. The singular subject *person* requires a singular verb form, *looks.* In the second sentence, the cue word *one* signals a singular subject. The singular subject *car* requires a singular verb form, *costs.*

The following cue words usually signify that a plural subject follows.

Common Plural Cue Words

all	many
both	several
few	some

EXAMPLES

Several large rabbits *feed* in my backyard every evening.

Both children in the news *come* from my neighborhood.

In the first sentence, the cue word *several* signifies a plural subject. The plural subject *rabbits* requires a plural verb form, *feed.* In the second sentence, the cue word *both* indicates a plural subject, *children,* so it requires a plural verb form, *come.*

Except for *a, an,* and *every,* these cue words are indefinite pronouns, so they may also serve as subjects. (For more on indefinite pronouns, see Chapter 17, "Using Pronouns.") Used this way, these words are usually followed by a prepositional phrase beginning with *of,* as these examples show:

SINGULAR

One of the cars in the showroom *is* my favorite shade of blue.

PLURAL

Few of the children *know* about the accident.

In the first sentence, *One* is the singular subject, requiring the singular verb *is.* In the second, *Few* is the plural subject, requiring the plural verb *know.*

COMPREHENSION AND PRACTICE

16.3

Singular Nouns Ending in *-s* and Collective Nouns

Each sentence in the following passage is preceded by a set of parentheses containing the infinitive form of a verb. On the line provided, write the correct present tense form of the verb and underline its subject. Use the example as a guide.

EXAMPLE (to stop) The flock of Canada geese _stops_ traffic when it wanders across the road.

(1) (to meet) The faculty at my college _meets_ regularly with the adminis-tration to discuss the curriculum and other matters affecting students on cam-pus. (2) (to present) At every meeting, for example, the committee on standards _presents_ a serious educational issue for discussion. (3) (to become) At least once a semester, mathematics _becomes_ the focus. (4) (to possess) Last week, the director of admissions presented a study indicating that the incoming class _possesses_ stronger math skills than previous classes. (5) (to be) In addition, the study shows that the group of students with advanced courses in math _is_ the largest ever.

Cue Word Use

Complete the following sentences. For each sentence, first circle the verb and then supply an appropriate cue word from the words listed. Use the example to guide you. With some sentences, more than one correct answer is possible.

| many | several | all |
| one | each | few |

EXAMPLE _Many_ adults (enjoy) theme parks as much as children do.

(1) Recently, _several_ students (have petitioned) the Student Senate for fund-ing to support an outdoors club. (2) _Many_ colleges in the tri-state region (offer) such clubs as a way for students to enjoy nature. (3) _Each_ activity, from hik-ing to kayaking to rock-climbing, (provides) great physical challenges. (4) _Few_ outdoor enthusiasts (are) able to resist the chance to enjoy these kinds of activi-ties. (5) Right now, _one_ trip (has been planned,) contingent on funding from the Student Senate.

CHALLENGE 16.2 Subjects That End in -*s*

1. Without consulting this chapter or a dictionary, label the nouns in the following list as either singular or plural:

dilemmas	mumps
news	apparitions
diagnoses	economics
phenomena	jury
committee	crises

collaboration

collaboration

2. Compare your list with a classmate. Consult the material in this chapter or a dictionary for any words on which you disagree.

3. Work with a classmate, and on a separate sheet of paper write sentences in which you use these nouns as subjects with appropriate present tense verbs.

✓ WORKING WITH NOUNS CHECKLIST

☐ Have you rechecked the plural nouns you've used, especially those ending in *-ch, -sh, -x, -s, -y, -f,* or *-fe,* to make sure you have formed the plural ending properly?

☐ Have you examined any plural forms of combined or hyphenated nouns and nouns requiring an internal change to ensure that you have changed the words appropriately?

☐ Have you made sure you have not added an *-s* or *-es* to any noun that has the same singular and plural form?

☐ Have you used a singular verb form with any singular noun ending in *-s* used as a subject?

☐ Have you used a singular verb form with any collective noun used as a subject?

☐ Have you focused on any cue words to make sure that you have used the nouns they identify appropriately?

Journal Writing

Nouns are words that name persons, places, things, and ideas. Common nouns name general things, and proper nouns name particular things. But what is it about those particular names? Consider your own first or last name, for example.

Is there a story associated with it? Are you named after a family member? Was your name chosen because it has some special meaning or significance? If it were easy enough to do, would you change it? Why or why not? When it comes to products and services, do you always choose a particular brand name? What are your reasons? Think of some topic associated with formal names and explore it in your journal for 20 to 30 minutes.

CHAPTER QUICK CHECK Working with Nouns

Each sentence in the following passage contains an error in noun use, including problems with plural forms, cue words, and subject–verb agreement. First, review the discussion of the number of nouns, collective nouns, and cue words. Then correct each error by crossing out the error and writing the correct form above it.

(1) All of the seemingly endless number of portable electronic devices in use today ~~owes~~ [owe] a major debt to the batteries powering them up. (2) Economics therefore ~~dictate~~ [dictates] that battery technology is a growing area of research. (3) Size, capacity, and speed of recharge are the primary ~~concernes~~ [concerns] for manufacturers. (4) Each of today's cell phones, digital cameras, MP3 players, and laptops ~~are~~ [is] generally smaller and more complex than its predecessors. (5) The challenge, then, involves figuring out how to make the ~~battery~~ [batteries] inside these devices tinier yet more powerful. (6) This group of batteries ~~need~~ [needs] to be able to handle a heavy regimen of recharging and still maintain full capacity. (7) Because of the work of researchers, the newest miniature powerhouses can be recharged hundreds of times and enjoy longer ~~lifes~~ [lives] overall. (8) As a result, fewer batteries will end up in ~~landfilles~~ [landfills], which fits in with the country's increasing focus on the environment. (9) A particularly promising group of new batteries ~~are~~ [is] powered by lithium, which weighs less and generates greater power than other materials traditionally used in batteries. (10) In fact, a research team at MIT ~~have~~ [has] developed a lithium battery that can fully recharge in a matter of seconds, perfect for power-hungry devices like cell phones, laptops, and MP3 players.

SUMMARY EXERCISE   Working with Nouns

Each sentence in the following passage contains an error in noun use, including problems with plural forms, cue words, and subject–verb agreement. First, review the discussion of the number of nouns, collective nouns, and cue words. Then correct each error by crossing out the error and writing the correct form above it.

(1) Many experts agree that athletics ~~are~~ *is* valuable for everyone. (2) Historically, ~~opportunitys~~ *opportunities* to participate in sports haven't always been as widespread, especially for females. (3) In most middle and high ~~schooles~~ *schools*, male students have long been able to participate in a wide variety of sports. (4) For most ~~woman~~ *women*, the story was different. (5) Today, however, the crowd on the playing fields and courts across the United States ~~are~~ *is* made up of both women and men.

(6) This shift to increased physical activity for all has many ~~benefites~~ *benefits*. (7) For one thing, participants generally experience improved physical ~~abilitys~~ *abilities*, including increased agility, stronger muscles, and greater stamina. (8) In many cases, these women and ~~man~~ *men* have healthier hearts and lungs as a result of their participation. (9) Most also find that their ~~leveles~~ *levels* of energy and alertness increase dramatically. (10) ~~Each~~ *Many* participants also report an increase in confidence from involvement in some sport or physical activity. (11) Whether the ~~activitys~~ *activities* are individual sports like running or team sports like basketball, people perform better when they play more. (12) When people perform better, their attitudes and ~~believes~~ *beliefs* about themselves begin to change. (13) They may therefore be better prepared to endure the frustrations and ~~difficultys~~ *difficulties* involved in mastering new tasks off the field or court.

(14) Sports often bring ~~familys~~ *families* together, too. (15) With youth sports leagues and associations, for instance, a group of parents usually ~~do~~ *does* the work to keep things running well. (16) Some parents serve as ~~coachs~~ *coaches* and referees, while others operate the snack bar or organize fund-raisers. (17) By becoming involved, these parents enjoy even more time with their ~~childs~~ *children*.

is
(18) The news ~~are~~ filled with stories of a lack of physical fitness among many

continues
Americans. (19) Meanwhile, government at every level ~~continue~~ to endorse phys-

ical activity as a means of maintaining wellness. (20) After all, physical fitness

heroes
and athletics should be about more than admiring sports ~~heros~~ from afar.

FOR FURTHER EXPLORATION

1. Choose one of the following subjects and use your preferred prewriting method to develop a specific focus and supporting ideas.

   - A lesson that you learned from your worst teacher or boss
   - The activity or task that always takes longer than you think it should
   - The best strategy you can suggest to reduce cheating among high school or college students

2. Evaluate your prewriting material, identify a focus, and create a draft paragraph of at least seven to ten sentences.

3. Exchange your draft with a writing partner. Using the material in this chapter as a guide, evaluate the draft you receive. Note any problems in the use of nouns, especially with plural forms, collective nouns, and singular nouns ending in -s. Return the draft to the writer.

collaboration

4. Revise your draft, eliminating any errors that your reader identified.

DISCOVERING CONNECTIONS

For this assignment, focus on the photo and one of these questions (or some other that the photo inspires). Explore your ideas and then create a draft paragraph of at least seven to ten sentences. When applying what you've learned about singular and plural nouns, keep in mind how the form might affect subject–verb agreement.

A. If you were involved in filmmaking, what part would you be most interested in? Why do you feel this way?

B. While the other three figures in the photo have looks of concern on their faces, the man at the camera is simply concentrating on his work. What is the best way you have found to maintain your focus when a situation suddenly becomes more complex or intense?

RECAP Working with Nouns

Key Terms in This Chapter	Definitions
noun	a word that names a person, place, thing, or idea
common noun	a noun that names a nonspecific person or thing
proper noun	a noun introduced by a capital letter that names a specific person or thing
subject	a word that answers *Who or What?* is doing the action or is being discussed
predicate nominative	a word that answers *Who or What?* after a linking verb
direct object	a word that answers *Whom or What?* after an action verb
indirect object	a word that answers *To Whom or For Whom, To What or For What?* after an action verb
object of a preposition	a word that follows a preposition, completing a prepositional phrase
appositive	a word that helps to explain or illustrate another noun
collective noun	a noun that represents a group of individuals or items Collective nouns are singular, generally calling for a singular form of a verb. EXAMPLE The *committee wants* to review the software before making a decision.
cue word	a word such as *an* or *several* that indicates whether a noun is singular or plural

Using Discovery Online with MyWritingLab

For more practice working with nouns, go to www.mywritinglab.com.

CHAPTER 17
Using Pronouns: Considering Case, Clear Pronoun–Antecedent Agreement, and Nonsexist Pronoun Usage

GETTING STARTED ...

 Q I often use pronouns when I write, but when a pronoun is supposed to function as a subject or an object, I have trouble figuring out which pronoun form to use; it is also hard to tell which form to use when I want to designate number. What can I do to make sure that I always use the proper pronoun?

A Choosing the correct pronoun for a particular situation starts with an understanding of the characteristics of the different kinds of pronouns. Personal pronouns have separate forms for subject and object. If you think of these pronouns in pairs—*I* or *me, we* or *us, he* or *him, she* or *her, they* or *them*—you'll find choosing between them easier. Keep in mind that indefinite pronouns fall into three categories: those that are always singular, those that are always plural, and those that can be either singular or plural depending on what they refer to. Take a few moments to keep these groups straight, and you'll do fine.

Overview: The Correct Pronoun Choice

Pronouns take the place of nouns. Rather than repeat a noun several times, you can add variety to your writing by substituting the noun with a recognizable and appropriate alternative. Pronouns can be classified in several groups including *demonstrative pronouns, interrogative pronouns, relative pronouns, reflexive/intensive pronouns, personal pronouns,* and *indefinite pronouns.* To use pronouns effectively, keep the following in mind: With personal pronouns consider the specific form or *case,* and with indefinite pronouns consider the *number* and *gender.* Also make sure that all pronouns *agree with* or match the words they refer to—their *antecedents.* Otherwise, the people and things the pronouns are replacing won't be clear for your reader.

Navigating This Chapter In this chapter, you will learn to:

- recognize the different types of pronouns
- understand the different cases of personal pronouns

- identify number and gender with indefinite pronouns
- ensure that pronouns and antecedents agree in number and gender

Pronoun Types

ESL Note
See "Sentence Basics,"
pages 483–485, for
more on the proper use
of pronouns.

Several types of pronouns are used in speech and writing. They can be grouped in the following classes:

- **personal pronouns,** which refer to *specific* people, places, things, and ideas

I, me, my, mine	we, us, our, ours
you, your, yours	she, he, her, him, hers, his
it, its, their, theirs	

- **indefinite pronouns,** which refer to *general* persons and things

all	each	little	nobody	others
another	either	many	none	several
any	everybody	more	no one	some
anybody	everyone	most	nothing	somebody
anyone	everything	much	one	someone
anything	few	neither	other	something
both				

- **demonstrative pronouns,** which point out *particular* people or things referred to

this	that
these	those

- **reflexive intensive pronouns,** which add emphasis to antecedents

myself	ourselves
yourself	yourselves
himself, herself, itself	themselves
oneself	

- **relative pronouns,** which introduce dependent clauses, called *relative clauses,* within a sentence

who	which
whom	that
whose	

- **interrogative pronouns,** which begin questions

Who … ?	Whom … ?	Whose … ?
Whoever … ?	Whomever … ?	Which … ?
Whichever … ?	What … ?	Whatever … ?

Using pronouns is fairly straightforward, except for two areas. The first problem is *case,* that is, which of three *forms* of a personal pronoun is called for in a specific situation. The second is the *number* of the *antecedent,* that is, whether the word the pronoun refers to is singular or plural.

Pronoun Case

The pronouns that writers use most often are **personal pronouns.** These pronouns point out *particular* people, places, things, and ideas. Take a look at the chart.

Personal Pronouns

	Subjective	**Objective**	**Possessive**
First person	I, we	me, us	my, mine, our, ours
Second person	you	you	your, yours
Third person	she, he, it, they	her, him, it, them	her, hers, his, its, their, theirs

ESL Note
See "Agreement,"
page 487–489, for
more on subject–verb
agreement.

As the chart shows, personal pronouns have three separate forms, or cases: *subjective, objective,* and *possessive.*

Subjective forms are used as subjects of sentences and as predicate nominatives, the word that answers the question *Who or What?* after a linking verb.

SUBJECT ⌐ *They* arrived five minutes before the movie began.

PREDICATE NOMINATIVE ⌐ The winner of the raffle was *she.*

Objective forms of these pronouns are used when the word serves as an *object* of some kind. For example, a *direct object* receives the action of the verb. It answers the question *What or Whom?* after the verb. An *indirect object* answers the questions *to whom, to what, for whom,* or *for what* the action of the verb is being done. The *object of the preposition* completes the meaning of the prepositional phrase. Look at these examples:

DIRECT OBJECT ⌐ As Jerry crossed the icy street, a skidding car hit *him.*

INDIRECT OBJECT ⌐ The boy's mother gave *him* the confidence to perform on stage.

OBJECT OF THE PREPOSITION ⌐ The buildings around *us* are more than 100 years old.

Possessive forms of the pronouns are used to indicate ownership, as the examples show.

EXAMPLE ⌐ Joan watched as the bicyclist crashed into *her* car.

⌐ I always carry *my* journal when I ride the bus.

To avoid problems with personal pronouns, keep several guidelines in mind.

- *Objects can't be subjects, so objective pronouns can never serve as subjects.* The exceptions to this guideline among the personal pronouns are *you* and *it,* which can serve as objects and subjects. Particularly confusing are situations when the pronoun is part of a compound subject. The solution is to check each word to make sure it could stand as a subject *by itself.*

EXAMPLE Marta, Carla, and ~~me~~ *I* had planned to go to the beach.

Here, the objective case pronoun *me* can't serve as a subject, so it must be changed to the nominative case pronoun, *I.*

- *A subject can't be an object, so subjective pronouns can never serve as objects.* Errors in the use of the objective case also occur when pronouns are used in a compound object. The solution to avoiding the problem is the same: Check each word alone to see if it can serve as an object by itself:

EXAMPLE Nobody was sure if the nurse called Karen or ~~I~~ *me*.

Here, the subjective case pronoun *I* can't stand as an object, so it must be changed to the objective case pronoun, *me.*

- *Possessive pronouns do not require an apostrophe.* Unlike possessive *nouns,* which need an *apostrophe* (')—Marcy's book, the boys' computer-game controllers—possessive pronouns don't. No apostrophe is needed because possessive pronouns are already possessive. Of all the possessive pronouns, *its* is most often a problem because the contraction for *it is* or *it has—it's—*sounds the same.

To avoid choosing the wrong form, first try using *it is.* If *it is* fits, then *it's* is correct. If *it is* doesn't work, then you need the possessive form, *its.*

FAULTY The dog ate from it's bowl.

Its too early to go running.

Here are the same sentences, this time with the correct pronouns:

REVISED The dog ate from its bowl.

It's too early to go running.

With the first sentence, you would not say, "The dog ate from *it is* bowl," so *it's* is incorrect. The proper choice is *its.* With the second sentence, *it is* does fit, so the proper choice would be *it's.*

COMPREHENSION
AND PRACTICE
17.1 **Appropriate Personal Pronoun Selection**

Fill in the blanks by supplying an appropriate personal pronoun. Then identify its case. Write *S* above subjective pronouns, *O* above objective pronouns, and *P* above possessive pronouns. Use the example to guide you.

EXAMPLE When people disagree with a law or government ruling, ___*they*___ often find

the official procedure complicated and expensive.

(1) Many people have a greater chance for financial independence than

___they___ might believe. (2) Financial analyst David Bach, author of *The*

Automatic Millionaire, argues that most of ___us___ waste money every day

on small discretionary purchases like snacks and drinks. (3) ___He___ calls

this phenomenon "The Latte Factor," after those popular but pricey coffee

drinks. (4) According to Bach, most people are unaware of how much money

___they___ actually spend each day. (5) In fact, many of ___us___ rack up

at least $10 a day for items that we could prepare or bring from home at a

fraction of the cost. (6) If we cut ___our___ expenses by $5 a day, the yearly

savings would be over $1,800. (7) In his book, Bach points out how enormous

the payoff would be if ___we___ simply invested this money in a typical

401k retirement plan. (8) According to ___his___ calculations, a simple $5 a

day over a 40-plus-year career will eventually grow to well over $1 million.

COMPREHENSION AND PRACTICE
Correct Personal Pronoun Choice

17.2 Each sentence in the following paragraph contains two sets of parentheses with a pair of personal pronouns. Circle the correct word in each pair to complete the sentences. Remember that objective pronouns can't serve as subjects, that subjective pronouns can't serve as objects, and that the possessive pronoun *its* does not have an apostrophe. Use the example as a guide.

EXAMPLE After class, Jose and (I, me) usually stay on campus to work out in the gym.

(1) Last year, my brother-in-law Billy and (I, me) taught ourselves to play

tennis, and (he, him) and I now meet early every Saturday morning for our

weekly match. (2) At first, I could barely serve to (he, him) without hitting the

net, and he couldn't keep the ball in bounds when he returned it to (I, me).

(3) Now, after (he, him) and I have been playing for a year, (it's, its) a differ-

ent story. (4) Once (he, him) and (I, me) warm up, we serve and return for almost two hours. (5) His serve is particularly hard to return because of (it's,

(its) speed and spin, but when I do get it back over the net, (he, him) and I re-

ally battle it out for the point.

CHALLENGE 17.1 **Evaluation of the Use of Personal Pronouns in Your Writing**

1. How have you used personal pronouns in your own writing? Review several paragraphs that you have written, and find three examples of each case of the personal pronouns: subjective, objective, and possessive. Write these sentences on a separate piece of paper and exchange them with a classmate.

collaboration

2. In the sentences you receive, underline any pronoun errors you find, and then return the sentences.

3. Consider your classmate's comments and, using the material in the preceding section to guide you, make any necessary adjustments in your own sentences.

Agreement in Number

One important area of agreement concerns matching singular antecedents with singular pronouns and plural antecedents with plural pronouns. As stated earlier, **antecedents** are the words a specific pronoun refers to. To make sure you have made the proper choice, first identify whether the antecedent is singular or plural. Then make sure the pronoun you have chosen matches the number of this word.

Note the pronouns and their antecedents in the following sentences:

EXAMPLES

singular antecedent   singular pronoun
The *singer* broke a string on *her* guitar.

plural antecedent   plural pronoun
Whales are very protective of *their* young.

In the first sentence, the antecedent—*singer*—is singular, so a singular personal pronoun—*her*—is used. In the second sentence, however, the antecedent is *whales,* a plural word, so *their,* a plural personal pronoun, is used.

When it comes to matching antecedents and pronouns, *collective nouns* sometimes confuse writers. Common collective nouns include words such as *class, herd, jury,* and *team.* As Chapter 16 (p. 300) explains, collective nouns represent *groups* of people or things. Nonetheless, the words themselves are generally considered *singular,* so they call for singular pronouns, as this example shows.

EXAMPLES

collective noun   singular pronoun
The *flock* of geese flew gracefully toward the South, where *it* would find a suit-

able feeding ground for summer.

As a collective noun, *flock* is a singular noun, so the proper pronoun is the singular personal pronoun *it.*

COMPREHENSION
AND PRACTICE

Agreement with Antecedents

17.3 Each sentence in the following paragraph includes a set of parentheses containing a pair of pronouns. For each sentence, underline the antecedent for the pronoun, and decide if it is singular or plural. Then circle the correct pronoun in parentheses to maintain agreement. Use the example as a guide.

EXAMPLE

The <u>tourists</u> lugged (their, her) souvenirs through the airport.

(1) The first thing <u>people</u> going to a club or a concert should do is identify (his or her, their) route of exit in case of an emergency. (2) This <u>advice</u> might seem obvious, but history has proven that (it, they) is often ignored. (3) No matter how calm a <u>crowd</u> may seem, (it, they) behaves differently in the face of danger. (4) An <u>individual</u> dealing alone with a threat like fire might manage to keep (his or her, their) cool and head for the appropriate exit. (5) Things are quite different, however, when a <u>group</u> begins to exert (its, their) influence, too often resulting in total panic and then tragedy.

COMPREHENSION
AND PRACTICE

Correct Pronoun–Antecedent Agreement

17.4 Below is a list of twelve nouns that you can use as antecedents, including several collective nouns. On a separate sheet of paper, compose a paragraph of seven to ten sentences on a concert, play, reading, or movie that you recently attended in which you use at least six of these words and pronouns to refer to them. Make sure that each pronoun you use agrees with its antecedent, as the example shows.

band	audience	singer	crowd
musicians	concert	stage crew	sound system
stage	technical staff	rock group	spotlights

EXAMPLE

The <u>quartet</u> always takes a five-minute break between <u>its</u> sets.

CHALLENGE 17.2 **Pronoun–Antecedent Agreement in a Paragraph**

collaboration

1. In each of the sentences in Comprehension and Practice 17.3, you selected the correct pronoun to agree with an antecedent. Now, working with a classmate, rewrite the paragraph on a separate sheet of paper, using the other pronoun in parentheses and then changing its antecedent. Keep in mind that you may also have to change some of the verbs to maintain subject–verb agreement.

collaboration

2. Discuss the two versions with your classmate and decide which version is better. Then, on the same paper, briefly explain your decision.

Agreement with Indefinite Pronouns

To refer to someone or something general, writers use **indefinite pronouns.** Some indefinite pronouns are always singular:

Singular Indefinite Pronouns

another	each	everything	nobody	other
anybody	either	little	no one	somebody
anyone	everybody	much	nothing	someone
anything	everyone	neither	one	something

Singular indefinite pronouns call for singular verbs, and they must also be referred to by singular pronouns, as this example shows:

EXAMPLE

Everybody exposed to the spilled chemicals **faces** the potential of damage to *her or his* lungs.

Some indefinite pronouns are always plural:

Plural Indefinite Pronouns

both	others
few	several
many	

Plural indefinite pronouns call for plural verbs, and they must also be referred to by plural pronouns, as this example shows:

EXAMPLE

Many of the students **find** it nearly impossible to pay the increase in *their* tuition without taking out loans.

Some indefinite pronouns can be either singular or plural, depending on the words to which they refer.

Indefinite Pronouns Affected by the Words That Follow Them

all	more	none
any	most	some

When you use one of these pronouns as a subject, find the word to which it refers, and check its number. If that word is singular, choose a singular form of the verb; if the word is plural, choose a plural form, as these examples show:

EXAMPLES

All of these **magazines** *focus* on style and fashion.

All of the frozen **food** in that case *carries* the same expiration date.

In the first sentence, the antecedent for *all* is the plural noun *magazines,* so the correct verb is the plural form, *focus.* In the second sentence, however, the antecedent for *all* is the singular noun *food,* so the correct verb is the singular form, *carries.*

Indefinite pronouns can be especially tricky when they serve as antecedents for another pronoun. To avoid errors in pronoun–antecedent agreement when the antecedent is an indefinite pronoun, find *both* pronouns and see if they agree. If they don't agree, change one of the pronouns to a word—noun or pronoun—that does match, as these examples show:

SINGULAR ANTECEDENT
> *Everyone* seeking a refund for the show must turn in *their* [~~their~~ *his or her*] tickets at the box office.

PLURAL ANTECEDENT
> ~~*Everyone*~~ [*Customers*] seeking a refund for the show must turn in *their* tickets at the box office.

PLURAL ANTECEDENT
> After the deadline passes, *many* of the late-paying students will lose ~~his or her~~ [*their*] chosen classes.

SINGULAR ANTECEDENT
> After the deadline passes, *each* of the late-paying students will lose ~~their~~ [*his or her*] chosen classes.

As the examples show, agreement can come about in one of two ways: (1) change the pronoun to make it agree with the antecedent, or (2) replace the antecedent with a word or words that agree with the pronoun. In your writing, make the choice that sounds best and helps you communicate your meaning most clearly.

Correct Verbs for Indefinite Pronouns

COMPREHENSION AND PRACTICE 17.5 Underline the indefinite pronouns in the sentences below and identify whether the pronoun is singular or plural. Then circle the correct verb in parentheses. Use the example and the lists of singular and plural pronouns (p. 315) to guide you.

EXAMPLE
> *Both* of my parents (is, (are)) retired.

(1) if something (S) ((is), are) not done about the traffic at the intersection near the industrial park, an accident will happen soon. (2) All (P) of the residents of that area (fears, (fear)) driving home at rush hour. (3) This concern is not surprising, since everybody (S) ((seems), seem) to be converging at this intersection. (4) Nobody (S) ((wants), want) to ask the city council to study the problem because the city lacks funding. (5) Many (P) of our residents (thinks, (think)) a recent change

S
is the answer. (6) Now, <u>anyone</u> driving to the industrial park (pays, pay) a toll

to help fund new traffic lights.

Errors in Agreement with Indefinite Pronoun Antecedent

Each sentence in the following passage contains an error in pronoun–antecedent agreement with indefinite pronouns. First underline the indefinite pronouns and their antecedents. Then cross out each error and write the correction above it, changing the verb if necessary. Use the example as a guide. More than one answer may be possible.
Answers may vary somewhat. Representative answers are shown.

EXAMPLE

<u>Everybody</u> in the calculus class passed <u>their</u> final exam.

Everybody in the calculus class passed his or her final exam.

or

All of the students in the calculus class passed their exam.

People
(1) <u>Everybody</u> should have an opportunity to participate in a parenting

class before <u>they</u> have children. (2) This kind of class is a great way for

parents or individuals
<u>anybody</u> to learn the basic skills <u>they</u> will need to care for a new baby. (3) At a

her or his
typical class, <u>one</u> of the experienced parents shares ~~their~~ knowledge and offers

tips to expectant parents. (4) <u>Few</u> of the people in these classes have ever cared

them
for a baby, so the advice reassures ~~him or her~~. (5) When the classes are over, <u>all</u>

their
of the mothers- and fathers-to-be feel prepared for the day when ~~his or her~~ bun-

dles of joy finally arrive.

Indefinite Pronoun Antecedents

Complete each of the following sentences in the space provided, making sure to supply a pronoun for the italicized antecedent. Check to be certain that the pronoun you provide agrees with the antecedent. Use the example as a guide.
Answers will vary. Representative answers are shown.

EXAMPLE

Some of the animals ___hunt by night to catch their prey off guard___.

1. *Each* of the planets in our solar system _____gets its light from the sun_____

_____.

2. *Most* of the women at the meeting were happy to _____ take their turns delivering food _____ .

3. *Nobody* likes harsh criticism, especially complaints about _____ his or her taste in clothes _____ .

4. *Both* of the babies are _____ wearing their first pair of shoes _____ .

5. Only a *few* of the survivors were able to _____ talk about the disaster they had experienced _____ .

6. The customers' food was undercooked, so *many* refused _____ to pay their checks _____ .

7. *Anyone* who wants to play a sport well must _____ give up some of his or her free time _____ .

8. *All* of the passengers were bothered by the delay, but _____ they did not complain _____ .

CHALLENGE 17.3 **Indefinite Pronouns That Change Number**

collaboration

Six indefinite pronouns—*all, any, more, most, none,* and *some*—are either singular or plural depending on what they refer to. Working with a classmate, write two sentences for each of these pronouns, using each one first as a singular word and then as a plural word.

Errors in Agreement with Demonstrative Pronouns and Adjectives

You must also maintain pronoun–antecedent agreement from sentence to sentence by using singular pronouns to refer to singular antecedents and plural pronouns to refer to plural antecedents. The correct use of the following pronouns, the **demonstrative pronouns,** plays an important role in maintaining this kind of consistency.

Demonstrative Pronouns

Singular	*Plural*
this	these
that	those

Demonstrative pronouns refer to specific persons and things. *This* and *that* are always singular and *these* and *those* are their plural forms, as these examples show.

EXAMPLES

This is a true apple, but *that* is an apple pear.

These are mandarin oranges, but *those* are tangelos.

Often demonstrative pronouns are placed next to nouns, where they answer the question *Which person, place, or thing?* In effect, they function as adjectives. Used this way, they are called **demonstrative adjectives.**

EXAMPLE

This apartment will suit me just fine.

In this usage, demonstrative adjectives agree with the noun they accompany. *Apartment* is singular, so the singular demonstrative adjective *this* agrees.

When a demonstrative pronoun or adjective begins a sentence, the antecedent is often in the previous sentence. To make sure you've used the correct demonstrative pronoun or adjective, find the antecedent. If the antecedent is singular, use *this* or *that.* If the antecedent is plural, use *these* or *those.*

Compare the antecedents and the demonstrative pronouns in the following pairs of sentences.

FAULTY

There are five major road reconstruction *projects* in the city. *This* has caused long delays for people using public transportation.

Right now, the city has instituted a 10 P.M. *curfew* at all parks and playgrounds. *Those* should be changed to give kids places to go at night.

In the first example, the demonstrative pronoun *this* is singular, which does not agree with the plural antecedent *projects.* In the second example, the plural demonstrative pronoun *those* does not agree with the singular antecedent *curfew.*

To correct these errors, change the demonstrative pronouns (and, when necessary, the verb, as in the first example) so that they match their antecedents:

REVISED

There are five major road reconstruction *projects* in the city. *These* have caused long delays for people using public transportation.

Right now, the city has instituted a 10 P.M. *curfew* at all parks and playgrounds. *This* should be changed to give kids places to go at night.

An even better strategy for eliminating these kinds of errors is to add a *clarifying word* after the pronoun, either repeating the antecedent or using a word with a similar meaning. When you do this, the pronoun serves as a demonstrative adjective, as these versions of the same pairs of sentences illustrate:

REVISED

There are five major road reconstruction *projects* in the city. These *projects* have caused long delays for people using public transportation.

Right now, the city has instituted a 10 P.M. *curfew* at all parks and playgrounds. This *rule* should be changed to give kids places to go at night.

Notice that the addition of the clarifying word, a noun, changes the role of the demonstrative pronoun. It now acts as an adjective, describing the noun next to it: *Which projects? These projects. Which rule? This rule.*

The Role of Reflexive or Intensive Pronouns

Another area of concern in maintaining pronoun–antecedent agreement involves the **reflexive** or **intensive pronouns:**

Reflexive or Intensive Pronouns

myself	oneself
yourself	ourselves
himself, herself	yourselves
itself	themselves

You use these pronouns to emphasize the words to which they refer. You should never use one unless you have also included the word to which it refers in the same sentence, as these examples show:

REFLEXIVE   Reaching across the table, Verna burned *herself* on the lit candle in the decorative lantern. *[To direct the verb's action back to the subject]*

INTENSIVE   The signal box *itself* is the cause of the many power outages. *[To emphasize a particular word]*

Keep in mind, however, that these pronouns can't serve as subjects. Should you find that you have made this error, simply replace the reflexive or intensive form with an appropriate personal pronoun, as this example shows:

EXAMPLE   Tim and *myself* played racquetball for two hours yesterday.
                              ⁱ

COMPREHENSION AND PRACTICE

17.8

Correct Demonstrative Pronoun and Adjective Choice

Each sentence in the following paragraph includes a set of parentheses containing a pair of demonstrative pronouns or adjectives. Circle the correct word, using the example to guide you.

EXAMPLE   One trip to the harbor changed my mind about (that, (those)) new water pollution laws.

(1) Each day that I put off completing and filing my taxes, the more difficult ((that), those) job gets. (2) I hate the tedium, and ((this), these) makes me delay even more. (3) All of (that, (those)) forms are piled on the desk ready to go, but I keep ignoring them. (4) The calculations are hard, and the instructions are frustrating, but (that, (those)) aren't good reasons to ignore the job. (5) I should get to work because ((this), these) is the year I hope to get a refund.

Demonstrative Pronouns and Adjectives That Agree with Antecedents

17.9 Add a second sentence to each item below, using a demonstrative pronoun or adjective that refers to the italicized antecedent in the first sentence. Use the example as a guide. Answers will vary.

EXAMPLE My sister was both *pretty and popular.* _____Those qualities made me jealous._____

1. When I was two, I was bitten by my neighbor's *pit bull.*

   _____

   _____

2. I missed the final *class* before the exam in my psychology course.

   _____

   _____

3. These running *shoes* weigh less than any others on the market.

   _____

   _____

4. I admired the museum's collection of hand-crafted wooden *toys.*

   _____

   _____

5. The rules for entering the three-on-three basketball *tournament* are posted in the student center.

   _____

   _____

Reflexive or Intensive Pronouns

17.10 Fill in the blanks in the following sentences with an appropriate reflexive or intensive pronoun from the list on page 320. Use the example as a guide.

EXAMPLE Ty finally decided to vacuum the house _____himself_____.

1. After a half hour, the tired puppy finally whimpered ___itself___ to sleep.

2. If they want reforms in insurance laws, then physicians _themselves_ need to make their case to Congress.

3. When you are tired, you may find motivating ___yourself___ to study even harder.

4. Even though she is the manager, tonight Beverly ___herself___ will join the rest of the workers in cleaning the shelves.

5. When my friends and I go out for a night, we spend as much time making ___ourselves___ laugh as we do dancing.

CHALLENGE 17.4   Correct Use of Demonstrative Pronouns and Adjectives

1. The sentences below contain errors in pronoun–antecedent agreement. In each sentence, cross out the incorrect demonstrative pronoun or adjective. Above it, write one that matches the italicized antecedent. Remember that the antecedent may be positioned before or after the demonstrative pronoun. Also change the noun following the demonstrative adjective if necessary. Use the example to guide you.

EXAMPLE   *Rabbits* used to be made into fur coats, but now it's unfashionable to use
~~these animals~~
~~this animal~~ for clothing.

(1) Some *days* it doesn't pay to get out of bed, and today was one of ~~that~~ *those* days. (2) In the morning, my car's *battery was dead,* but I solved ~~these~~ *this* *problem* by replacing it for $55. (3) On top of ~~these~~ *this* *expense,* I had to have a garage tow my car—another $50. (4) I finally arrived at work, only to be told, "~~These~~ *This* will be your last *week*—you are being laid off." (5) ~~That~~ *Those* are just *three* disasters from my terrible day.

2. Now write a paragraph of at least seven to ten sentences in which you describe a day of your own that you would just as soon forget.

3. Exchange your paragraph with a classmate. On the paper you receive, underline any demonstrative pronouns and circle any errors in agreement. Then return the paper to its writer.

collaboration

4. Using the material in the preceding section to guide you, correct any errors identified in your paragraph.

Agreement in *That, Who,* and *Which* Clauses

As Chapter 8, "Subordination," explains, the pronouns *that, who,* and *which* may also introduce a subordinate clause that describes an antecedent. These pronouns are called **relative pronouns.** The verb in a *that, who,* or *which* clause must agree with the antecedent. If the antecedent is singular, then the verb in the *that, who,* or *which* clause must be singular. If the antecedent is plural, however, then the verb must also be plural. Consider the following sentence:

EXAMPLE

⌐——— subordinate clause ———⌐

The candidates *who run for president* spend too much time and money on image.

The antecedent *candidates* is plural. The clause describing *candidates* is *who run for president.* The verb in the clause is *run,* the plural form.

Find the antecedents for the italicized clauses in the following sentences:

FAULTY

The rooms *that faces the beach* are all taken.

My favorite shirt, *which are made of silk,* is now almost ten years old.

In the first sentence, the antecedent for the *that* clause is the plural noun *rooms,* but the verb in the clause is *faces,* a singular form. In the second sentence, the antecedent for the *which* clause is the singular noun *shirt,* which does not agree with the plural verb *are* in the *which* clause.

To correct these kinds of errors in agreement, simply change the verbs in the subordinate clauses.

REVISED

The *rooms* that *face* the beach are all taken.

My favorite *shirt,* which *is* made of silk, is now almost ten years old.

COMPREHENSION
AND PRACTICE
17.11

Agreement with *That, Who,* and *Which* Clauses

The italicized clauses in the following paragraph contain errors in agreement. Correct each error by underlining the antecedent and then changing the verb in the clause. Cross out the incorrect verb, and write the correct one above it. Use the example as a guide.

EXAMPLE

                                                    are
My teacher asks <u>students</u> who *is̶ late for class* to enter the classroom as quietly

as possible.

(1) Whether on regular broadcast channels, cable stations, or HBO or

                                                                have
some other pay-per-view venue, television <u>programs</u> *that h̶a̶s̶ adult content*

                                                                are
should air after 10:00 P.M. (2) Young <u>children,</u> *who i̶s̶ generally awake earlier in*

the evening, should not be exposed to violence, profanity, and sexual situations.

(3) Up to now, <u>research</u> *that* ~~*study*~~ ^{studies} *the effects of these programs on children* has

produced mixed results. (4) Still, most <u>parents</u>, *who, after all,* ~~*knows*~~ ^{know} *their chil-*

dren best, generally agree on the unsuitability of this material for kids. (5) In

their view, television <u>programs</u> *that* ~~*focuses*~~ ^{focus} *on the mature interests of adults* may

harm their children's development.

CHALLENGE 17.5   Subordinate Clause–Antecedent Agreement

1. On a separate sheet of paper, write six present tense sentences, two each with
   a *that, which,* and *who* clause.

collaboration

2. Exchange your sentences with a classmate. On the paper you receive, check
   for agreement problems between the main and subordinate clauses. Put a ✓
   next to any word you think needs to be changed, and return the sentences to
   the writer.

3. Review your classmate's comments, and make any necessary changes to your
   sentences.

Problems with Gender in Pronoun–Antecedent Agreement

Gender refers to whether a word is *feminine* or *masculine.* The gender of a pronoun must agree with the gender of its antecedent. Feminine words call for feminine pronouns, and masculine words require masculine pronouns.

In English, maintaining agreement in gender is fairly simple. Unlike many
other languages, English requires that you consider gender only when you are
writing about people and animals. The pronoun *it* is used to refer to all other kinds
of singular nouns, and *they* is used to refer to all plural nouns. Therefore, you don't
have to be concerned with gender except when you are using the following pronouns that refer to singular nouns:

Masculine Pronouns	*Feminine Pronouns*
he	she
him	her
his	hers

Consider the problems in agreement between the antecedents and the pronouns in these sentences:

FAULTY   Film star *Denzel Washington* got *her* start on the television show *St. Elsewhere.*

The *woman* left the house with no money in *his* purse.

In the first sentence, the antecedent is *Denzel Washington,* and its pronoun is *her.* However, Denzel Washington is a man, so the pronoun should be masculine. There is also an error in agreement in the second sentence. The antecedent (*woman*) is feminine, but the pronoun (*his*) is masculine.

To eliminate this type of error in agreement, simply change the pronoun so it matches the gender of its antecedent:

REVISED Film star *Denzel Washington* got *his* start on the television show *St. Elsewhere.*

The *woman* left the house with no money in *her* purse.

Avoidance of Sexist Language

As you are matching antecedents and pronouns, you need to avoid using **sexist language,** any wording that inappropriately or unnecessarily identifies gender. A word such as *foreman* is sexist because it excludes women, suggesting that only a man could perform such a job. A better choice would be the nonsexist word *supervisor.*

Problems with sexist language sometimes arise when writers try to match antecedents such as *each, everybody,* and *someone* with singular pronouns. For many years, it was acceptable to use *he, him,* or *his* to represent *all* people, as this sentence shows:

FAULTY *Everyone* should have *his* vision checked once a year.

Today, however, using only a masculine pronoun to refer to a word like *everyone* is considered sexist.

There are two main ways to avoid using sexist language in these instances. One option is to use *both* a feminine and a masculine pronoun connected by *or,* as shown below:

REVISED *Everyone* should have *his or her* vision checked once a year.

The second option—and often the better choice—is to make both the pronoun and its antecedent plural. This may require replacing the antecedent with a different word or phrase. Look at this version of the sentence, with both pronoun and antecedent plural:

REVISED *People* should have *their* vision checked once a year.

In this instance, the plural noun *people* is a better choice than the singular pronoun *everyone.* It allows the writer to avoid the issue of gender altogether.

COMPREHENSION AND PRACTICE

Agreement with Gender and Avoidance of Sexist Language

17.12 The sentences in the paragraph below contain errors in agreement or sexist language. Underline both the antecedents and the incorrect pronouns referring to them. Then rewrite each sentence on a separate sheet of paper, making any changes you need to correct the error. Use the example to guide you.

EXAMPLE

Anybody attending the club had to have his hand stamped.

Students attending the club had to have their hands stamped.

or

Anybody attending the club had to have his or her hand stamped.

(1) Ida Minerva Tarbell was a newspaperman who left her mark on the field of investigative journalism. (2) Everyone who studies the history of magazines should include Tarbell on his list of influential writers. (3) Tarbell reported for *McClure's Magazine* on his investigation of Standard Oil. (4) Tarbell's articles exposed the company's corrupt practices, and it helped break the Standard Oil Trust. (5) Any reporter today should be proud if he can follow in Ida Tarbell's footsteps.

COMPREHENSION
AND PRACTICE
17.13

Nonsexist Language

On a separate piece of paper, rewrite the following sentences, correcting each gender error in two different ways. Be sure to avoid sexist language in your revisions. Use the example as a guide.

EXAMPLE

Everybody in the office will be asked to submit his vacation plans.

Everybody in the office will be asked to submit his or her vacation plans.

or

Employees will be asked to submit their vacation plans.

1. Every passenger must sit in his seat until the pilot shuts off the "fasten seat belt" sign.

2. Anyone who is late will have to pay extra for his ticket.

3. Nobody should be unprepared for his first day of class.

4. Each customer will be asked for his opinion.

5. Someone who works in sales should know his product well.

6. A police officer must be prepared to risk his life when on duty.

7. It makes sense for a doctor to know a little about his patients' lives.

8. Every one of the candidates must complete his nomination forms.

COMPREHENSION
AND PRACTICE
17.14

Sexist Language

Below is a list of eight sexist words. Write a neutral substitute next to each one, being careful not to use another equally sexist word in its place. For example, don't replace *policeman* with *policewoman*. Next, on a separate sheet of paper, compose a sentence for each substitution.

Answers may vary. Suitable responses are shown.

1. chairman _____ chairperson _____

2. mailman _____ mail carrier _____

3. manpower _____ people power _____

4. fireman _____ firefighter _____

5. serviceman _____ serviceperson _____

6. maid _____ household help _____

7. poetess _____ poet _____

8. stewardess _____ flight attendant _____

CHALLENGE 17.6 Analysis of Sexist Language

1. Consider the sexist terms listed in the previous exercise or others you have read or heard. What effect do you think such words have on people? Write a paragraph of at least seven to ten sentences in which you address your own attitudes concerning the possible effects of sexist language.

collaboration

2. Exchange your paragraph with a classmate. Compare your attitudes about sexist language and together prepare a brief summary of your similarities and differences to be shared with the class.

✓USING PRONOUNS CHECKLIST

☐ Have you made sure that you have used subjective case personal pronouns only as subjects and objective case pronouns only as objects?

☐ Have you made sure that you have used possessive case personal pronouns without apostrophes, paying particular attention to the use of *its?*

☐ Have you checked the number of the personal and indefinite pronouns you have used to make sure they are the correct choice for the situation?

☐ Have you used singular pronouns as antecedents for any collective nouns?

Journal Writing

When it comes to number, most pronouns can be easily identified as singular or plural. But as page 315 points out, six indefinite pronouns can be either singular or plural depending on what they refer to. What have you found in your experiences that changes dramatically depending on the circumstances? For example, do you project one image at school or work and another at home? Why? Do you have a friend who treats you differently from the way he or she treats other friends? How does that make you feel? Does your campus, city, or neighborhood take on a very different look or atmosphere after dark? What causes the change? Which do you like better? Why? Consider one of these topics or one related to them, and explore it in your journal for 20 to 30 minutes.

CHAPTER QUICK CHECK   Using Pronouns

The following passage contains errors in pronoun–antecedent agreement and sexist language. Make corrections by crossing out the incorrect words and writing the correct versions above them. Put *OK* above any sentence without an error.
Answers may vary somewhat.

(1) With America's increasing thirst for energy, many people see hybrid cars as the best chance for the United States to reduce ~~their~~ *its* dependence on imported oil. (2) Hybrid cars differ from any other kind of vehicle on the road today because of ~~its~~ *their* fuel system. *OK* (3) Hybrid vehicles rely on a combination of a smaller gasoline engine and a constantly recharging battery system. (4) As a

result, hybrids still have plenty of horsepower, but it enjoys *[they enjoy]* mileage of up to 50 mpg under optimum conditions. (5) ~~Salesmen~~ *[Sales representatives]* for Toyota, Honda, and Ford have been selling hybrids, including trucks and SUVs, for a number of years already, with luxury car makers Mercedes, Lexus, and BMW now offering hybrids as well. (6) Until recently, ~~everybody hasn't~~ *[consumers haven't]* immediately thought of hybrids when they need a new car, so purchases of hybrids still represent only a small fraction of total sales. (7) One reason for ~~that~~ *[these]* relatively low sales figures is that hybrid models cost thousands more than traditional gas engine versions of the same vehicle. (8) In addition, many consumers still think in terms of internal combustion engines only, so ~~he or she is~~ *[they are]* unsure about performance and maintenance issues associated with hybrids. (9) Backed by new tax credits and other incentives, however, hybrids could greatly increase ~~its~~ *[their]* market share in the coming years. (10) The United States must break ~~it's~~ *[its]* dependence on foreign oil, and to do so, more hybrids need to be in America's fast lane.

SUMMARY EXERCISE Using Pronouns

The following passage contains errors in pronoun–antecedent agreement and sexist language. Make corrections by crossing out the incorrect words and writing the correct versions above them. Put *OK* above any sentence without an error.
Answers may vary somewhat.

(1) The planet Mars, which ~~are~~ *[is]* one of our closest neighbors in the solar system, remains an enticing enigma. (2) Researchers have regularly focused attention on Mars, raising many questions about ~~these~~ *[this]* planet. (3) *[OK]* Perhaps the most persistent question concerns the possibility of life on Mars.

(4) Some of the scientists who ~~is~~ *[are]* studying the Red Planet believe that it was once quite different from what it is today. (5) According to ~~they~~ *[them]*, Mars was at one time a warm planet like Earth, with water and an atmosphere.

they

(6) After all, photographs of Mars show enormous canyons, and ~~it~~ also

reveal
~~reveals~~ areas that appear to be dried-up lakes or river beds. (7) But ~~this~~ ex-
these

perts still aren't sure what happened to the water.

they know
(8) Other researchers believe that ~~she knows~~ where the water went.

(9) These scientists believe that enormous asteroids hit Mars billions of

they
years ago, and ~~it~~ changed the planet's atmosphere and appearance.

it
(10) The impact was so severe that ~~they~~ caused huge amounts of water

within the planet and asteroids to vaporize. (11) The condensed vapor

it
rained down on the planet, and ~~they~~ carved deep crevices into the surface.

these
(12) It was ~~this~~ physical characteristics that some early astronomers mis-

took as canals.

experts agree
(13) In terms of what life might be found on Mars, ~~everyone agrees~~

OK
that they aren't expecting to find little green people. (14) Instead, some sci-

entists theorize that life may exist in the form of bacterial organisms.

They
(15) ~~It~~ could be living in a frozen mixture of water, rock, and sand beneath

the surface of Mars.

(16) Since 2004, NASA's Mars rovers, Spirit and Opportunity, have

their
been exploring the Red Planet, and ~~its~~ performance has been nothing short

of amazing. (17) For years longer than anyone ever had hoped for, these

they have
robotic crafts have transmitted stunning panoramic photos, and ~~it has~~ ex-

amined the chemical composition of the planet's rocks, soil, and dust.

these
(18) In their travels, ~~this~~ rolling laboratories have come across bedrock,

OK
evidence of the existence of seas sometime in the past. (19) In 2008,

NASA's Phoenix Mars lander parachuted down to the arctic area of the

planet and began digging into the Martian soil. (20) The analysis of this

it's
soil identified two different types of ice deposits, so ~~its~~ increasingly likely

that the idea of life on Mars is not merely the subject of science fiction.

FOR FURTHER EXPLORATION

1. Choose one of the following subjects and use your preferred prewriting method to develop a specific focus and ideas to support it.

   - How you tolerate frustration
   - The power of optimistic thinking
   - A change in a rule, law, or policy that would immediately make your life easier or less complicated

2. Evaluate your prewriting material, identify a focus, and create a draft paragraph of at least seven to ten sentences.

collaboration

3. Exchange your draft with a writing partner. Using the material in this chapter as a guide, evaluate the draft you receive. Note any problems with pronoun use as well as any other weaknesses, and return the draft to the writer.

4. Revise your draft, eliminating any errors that your reader identified.

DISCOVERING CONNECTIONS

For this assignment, focus on the photo and consider one of these questions (or some other that the picture suggests). Explore your ideas and then create a draft paragraph of at least seven to ten sentences. Be sure your pronouns and antecedents match throughout.

A. In your view, what is the single most important quality someone who works with children must possess? Why do you feel this way?

B. These children are proudly displaying their artwork. What was your favorite activity when you were that age? What in particular made it so enjoyable?

Using Pronouns: Considering Case, Clear Pronoun–Antecedent Agreement, and Nonsexist Pronoun Usage

Key Terms in This Chapter	Definitions
pronoun	a word used in place of a noun

> **EXAMPLE** Larry picked up the *CD player* and shook *it*.

personal pronoun	a pronoun that specifies a particular person, place, thing, or idea. Personal pronouns have three separate forms, or cases, to show person.

Personal Pronouns Case

	Subjective	Objective	Possessive
First person	I, we	me, us	my, mine, our, ours
Second person	you	you	your, yours
Third person	she, he, it, they	her, him, it, them	her, hers, his, its, their, theirs

antecedent	the word or words to which a pronoun refers. Singular antecedents call for singular pronouns; plural antecedents call for plural pronouns.

> **EXAMPLE** The little *boy* dropped *his* hat.

Indefinite pronoun antecedents must agree with their pronouns.

> **EXAMPLE** *Everyone* who has a student ID will receive 25 percent off *her or his* purchase.

indefinite pronoun	a pronoun used to refer to someone or something in general

Singular Indefinite Pronouns

another	each	everything	nobody	other
anybody	either	little	no one	somebody
anyone	everybody	much	nothing	someone
anything	everyone	neither	one	something

Plural Indefinite Pronouns

both	others
few	several
many	

Indefinite Pronouns Affected by the Words That Follow Them

all	more	none
any	most	some

Key Terms in This Chapter	Definitions
demonstrative pronoun/ demonstrative adjective	singular: *this, that* plural: *these, those* If a demonstrative pronoun begins a sentence, find the antecedent in the preceding sentence. A demonstrative pronoun placed next to a noun is then called a *demonstrative adjective.* **EXAMPLE** Some CDs in *that box* are damaged. *Those* should be discarded.
reflexive/intensive pronoun	a combination of a personal pronoun with *-self* or *-selves: myself, yourself, himself, herself, itself, ourselves, yourselves, themselves* Reflexive or intensive pronouns are used for emphasis (Liz *herself* answered the question) or to direct the action of the verb back to the subject (Peter allowed *himself* a period of rest).
relative pronoun	*that, who, which, whom, whose* A relative pronoun introduces a clause that describes an antecedent; the verb in the clause must agree with the antecedent. **EXAMPLE** The nurse who *is* addressing my class this morning graduated from this college.
interrogative pronoun	What … ? Whatever … ? Which … ? Whichever … ? Who … ? Whoever … ? Whom … ? Whomever … ? Whose … ? An interrogative pronoun introduces a question. **EXAMPLE** *What* is the problem?
gender	refers to whether a word is masculine or feminine Pronouns must match the gender of their antecedents.
sexist language	language that inappropriately excludes one gender Try using plural antecedents and pronouns instead. **EXAMPLE** *All bicyclists* using the municipal bike path must wear *their* helmets.

Pronoun Agreement Chart

Type	Gender	Number	
		Singular	*Plural*
personal pronouns			
subject pronouns		I	we
		you	you
	masculine	he	
	feminine	she	
	neutral	it	they
object pronouns		me	us
		you	you
	masculine	him	
	feminine	her	
	neutral	it	them
possessive pronouns		my, mine	our, ours
		your, yours	your, yours
	masculine	his	
	feminine	her, hers	
	neutral	its	their, theirs

Type	Number		
	Singular		*Plural*
indefinite pronouns	another	much	both
	anybody	neither	few
	anyone	nobody	many
	anything	no one	others
	each	nothing	several
	either	one	
	everybody	other	
	everyone	somebody	
	everything	someone	
	little	something	
	Indefinite pronouns that can be either singular *or* plural: all, none, most, any, some, more		
demonstrative pronouns	this		these
	that		those
relative pronouns	who		who
	which		which
	that		that

Using Discovery Online with MyWritingLab

For more practice using pronouns, go to www.mywritinglab.com.

CHAPTER 18
Working with Adjectives and Adverbs: Using Modifiers Effectively

GETTING STARTED ...

 Q I know it's important when I write to make sure that my ideas are clear, vivid, and strong. How can adjectives and adverbs help me make this happen? And when I use adjectives and adverbs, how can I make sure I use them correctly?

 A Adjectives and adverbs modify or describe other words, amplifying and spelling out their meanings for your reader. To ensure that you use them correctly, concentrate on the most likely problem spots. Making comparisons with the wrong form of a descriptive word is one common problem. Using two negatives, words such as *not* or *never,* in the same subject–verb unit is another. Putting a modifier in the wrong position in a sentence is also a concern. As you compose and revise, if you monitor your sentences for these problem spots and learn how to correct them, you should be fine.

Overview: Building Precise Detail with Modifiers

To make their ideas more precise and informative, writers turn to *adjectives* and *adverbs,* words that *modify* or describe other words. Adjectives modify nouns and pronouns, and adverbs modify verbs, adjectives, and other adverbs. These modifiers are among a writer's most powerful tools because they create memorable images in readers' minds, providing not only clarity but also excitement. They paint a more vibrant picture, bringing an action or event into sharper focus for the reader. Adjectives and adverbs also pinpoint the degree to which another word possesses the quality described—that is, to make comparisons. The key to using modifiers correctly is to recognize the forms that modifiers take.

Navigating This Chapter This chapter will introduce you to these forms of modifiers and help you discover how to use them. You will learn about:

- the roles of adjectives and adverbs as modifiers
- the positive, comparative, and superlative forms of modifiers
- the forms of commonly confused modifiers and common irregular modifiers
- ways to avoid double negatives
- ways to avoid errors with *-ing* modifiers

The Positive Form of Adjectives and Adverbs

An **adjective** describes a noun or pronoun by telling *which one, how many,* or *what kind:*

EXAMPLES

which one?	what kind?	how many?
the first desk	*antique* desk	*one* desk

ESL Note
See "Sentence Basics," pages 483–485, for more on the correct placement of adjectives and adverbs.

An **adverb** describes a verb, adjective, or other adverb by telling *how, when, where, to what extent,* or *how much:*

EXAMPLES

how?	when?	where?
She ran *quickly.*	She ran *daily.*	She ran *here.*

to what extent?	how much?
She ran *very* quickly.	She ran *enough.*

Both adjectives and adverbs have more than one form. The *positive* form is used to modify a single word. Look at these sentences:

EXAMPLES

adverb
Austin talked *quietly.*

adjective
Ava owns *two* computers.

In the first sentence, the adverb *quietly* modifies the verb *talked,* explaining how Austin talked. In the second sentence, the adjective *two* modifies the noun *computers,* telling how many computers Ava owns.

With the positive form of modifiers, you use a special category of adjectives called *articles.* There are just three articles: *a, an,* and *the.* You use *a* before a non-specific word beginning with a consonant sound: *a television.* You use *an* before a nonspecific word beginning with a vowel sound: *an apple.* You use *the* before a specific word: *the dictionary.* These words help identify noun or pronoun is being discussed. Often they appear in combination with other adjectives, in usages that call for an article, as this example shows:

EXAMPLE

article and adjective
Tori washes *the blue* car every other Thursday.

COMPREHENSION
AND PRACTICE
18.1

The Positive Form of Modifiers

In the sentences below, circle the adjectives (including articles), and underline the adverbs. Use the example to guide you.

EXAMPLE

(One) program I never miss is (the evening) news.

(1) Hamsters make (great) pets for (young) children to raise. (2) The (small) animals thrive efficiently as long as you provide (a small) amount of food and (clean) water daily. (3) Hamsters can easily live in (a simple) cage or (glass) aquarium.

(4) For exercise they scurry <u>quickly</u> in⟨exercise⟩wheels, explore⟨plastic⟩tunnels, or shred cardboard to make nests. (5) <u>Never</u> keep ⟨a⟩ male and ⟨a⟩ female in ⟨the same⟩ enclosure, however, or you will <u>inevitably</u> have ⟨a huge⟩ family of hamsters.

CHALLENGE 18.1   The Use of the Positive Form of Modifiers to Improve Your Writing

1. Use ten or more of the modifiers in the list below to write a paragraph of at least seven to ten sentences about the scariest or spookiest place you have ever visited. After you have finished your paragraph, circle the adjectives and articles, and underline the adverbs.

dark	slowly	the	chillingly	clammy
musty	dismal	carefully	mournfully	dark
anxiously	quiet	icy	dreadful	a

collaboration

2. Exchange your paragraph with a classmate. Copy the paragraph on a separate sheet of paper, leaving out all adjectives and adverbs (except for articles). Read both versions again, and, on the same paper, briefly explain how the modifiers enhance, illustrate, or clarify the ideas in the writing.

The Comparative Form of Adjectives and Adverbs

Adjectives and adverbs may be used to show the degree or extent to which the modified word possesses a certain quality. When modifiers are used to compare or contrast two things or actions, their forms change. Look at the **comparative forms** in the following sentences:

EXAMPLES

adjective
This movie starring Ben Stiller is *more hilarious* than his last one.

adverb
At that restaurant, the dishwashers work *harder* than the waitstaff.

In the first sentence, the modifier *more hilarious* indicates which one of two movies is funnier. In the second sentence, the modifier *harder* specifies how one group of employees works compared to another.

Forming the comparative of most modifiers is simple. Use one of these two methods, depending on the number of syllables in the modifier.

1. For words of *one syllable,* add *-er* to the positive form.

Positive	*Comparative*
clean	clean**er**
loud	loud**er**
fast	fast**er**

2. For modifiers of *more than two syllables,* put *more* before the modifier.

Positive	Comparative
extravagant	**more** extravagant
enjoyable	**more** enjoyable
awkwardly	**more** awkwardly

Things are more complicated with modifiers of exactly *two* syllables, however, because there is no automatic way to know whether to add *-er* or *more* to form the comparative. Some two-syllable modifiers form their comparative by dropping a *-y* from the end of the positive form, changing it to *-i,* and then adding *-er:*

Positive	Comparative
angry	angri**er**
hungry	hungri**er**
happy	happi**er**

Other two-syllable modifiers form their comparative by placing *more* before them:

Positive	Comparative
anxious	**more** anxious
helpful	**more** helpful
promptly	**more** promptly

When it comes to two-syllable modifiers, the rule is simple: If you aren't absolutely sure, check in a dictionary. It often lists the correct way to form the comparative of two-syllable modifiers.

One point to remember: *Never* add both *-er* and *more* to the same modifier. It is never correct to write *more prouder* or *more humider. Always* use one method or the other.

COMPREHENSION
AND PRACTICE

18.2

The Comparative Form of Modifiers

In the following paragraph, comparative forms of modifiers are italicized. Some are incorrect. Cross out each incorrect form, and write the correct form above it. If a sentence is correct as written, mark it *OK.* Use the example as a guide.

EXAMPLE

more closely
Some movie sequels follow the original film ~~closer~~ than others.

OK
(1) As odd as it sounds, my friend Jill is almost two inches *taller* than her

lighter
identical twin Julia. (2) Also, both have brown eyes, but Jill's eyes are *~~more light~~*

lower
than Julia's. (3) Both girls can sing well, but Jill has a *~~more low~~* voice than Julia.

(4) Whenever they sing together, Jill sings the low notes while Julia takes the

higher   prettier
~~more high~~ notes. (5) Many people think that Julia is the *~~more pretty~~* of the two.

OK

(6) Maybe that's why she is the *more outgoing* of the sisters. (7) In most social

quieter   more unlikely

settings, Jill is usually *more quiet.* (8) She is *unlikelier* to strike up a conversation

with someone she doesn't know.

CHALLENGE 18.2   **The Use of the Comparative Form of Modifiers in Your Writing**

collaboration

collaboration

1. Make a list of the positive form of at least ten modifiers.

2. Exchange your list with a classmate. On the list you receive, change the positive form of the modifiers to the comparative form.

3. Working with your partner, choose five comparative form modifiers from each of your lists and write sentences in which you use these modifiers.

The Superlative Form of Adjectives and Adverbs

ESL Note
See "Articles: *a, an,* and *the,*" pages 491–492, for more on the use of articles with the superlative form.

The **superlative form** of an adjective or adverb is used to compare *more than two* things. As with the comparative, the superlative of most adjectives and adverbs is formed in one of two ways: (1) by adding *-est* or (2) by placing *most* in front of the modifier. Look at these examples:

EXAMPLES

adjective

Of all the new video releases, the one starring Will Smith is the *newest.*

adverb

Kathryn and Jody danced the *most gracefully* of all the contestants.

In the first sentence, the superlative *newest* indicates which video among several is the most recent. In the second sentence, the superlative *most gracefully* explains how Kathryn and Jody's dancing compared to that of several other contestants.

To form the superlative of any one-syllable modifier, simply add *-est* to the positive form:

Positive	*Superlative*
bright	bright**est**
slow	slow**est**
young	young**est**

To form the superlative of words of *more than two syllables,* add *most* before the modifier:

Positive	*Superlative*
considerate	**most** considerate
frightening	**most** frightening
unfortunately	**most** unfortunately

There is also no automatic way to tell how to form the superlative of a two-syllable modifier. Some two-syllable modifiers form their superlatives by adding *-est*. Notice in the following examples that a modifier ending in a *consonant + y* requires a spelling change:

Positive	Superlative
heavy	heavi**est**
easy	easi**est**
simple	simpl**est**

Other two-syllable modifiers form their superlatives by the addition of *most:*

Positive	Superlative
eager	**most** eager
private	**most** private
famous	**most** famous

You can always use a dictionary to check for the correct way to form the superlatives of two-syllable modifiers.

As with comparative forms, *never* use both methods of forming the superlative with the same modifier. It is *never* correct to write *most smallest* or *most curiousest. Always* use one method or the other but never both.

COMPREHENSION AND PRACTICE

18.3

The Superlative Form of Modifiers

Following the guidelines above for forming superlatives, revise the sentences below by changing the positive modifier in parentheses to the superlative. Write the superlative form above the positive one. Use the example to guide you.

EXAMPLE   *most frightening*
The dream I had last night was the (frightening) one I ever had.

(1) The way movies are shown has been one of the (fast) [*fastest*] changing aspects of the film business. (2) One of the (early) [*earliest*] ways to view movies was to look in a peephole at film passing in front of a lightbulb. (3) The kinetoscope, one of the first movie projectors, was developed by one of the world's (famous) [*most famous*] inventors, Thomas Edison. (4) By the early 1900s, going to the local nickelodeon was the (popular) [*most popular*] way to see movies. (5) From France, Edison brought the (new) [*newest*] way to view a movie: projected on a wall for many people to watch together. (6) Today, one of the (innovative) [*most innovative*] developments in the film business is the ability to download a movie directly to a computer for viewing.

CHALLENGE 18.3   The Use of the Superlative Form of Modifiers in Your Writing

1. A fun book to explore is the *Guinness Book of World Records,* a collection of astonishing records from around the world. Visit your local or college library or go online, and examine the entries in this book or another book of records. Write down three odd, amazing, or extraordinary facts that you find interesting using the superlative form of modifiers. For example, X company has the greatest annual sales, X is the tallest building in the world, X is the longest snake.

collaboration

2. Compare your findings with a classmate. Together, decide which of the six facts is the most extreme and why you feel this way.

Irregular and Confusing Modifiers

ESL Note
See "Confusing Words," pages 493–494, for more on potentially confusing modifiers.

A number of modifiers have both adjective and adverb forms, which can be confusing to you as a writer. Here is a list of commonly confused modifiers:

Commonly Confused Modifiers

Adjective	*Adverb*
awful	awfully
bad	badly
good	well
poor	poorly
quick	quickly
quiet	quietly
real	really
worse	worst

Take a look at the italicized modifiers in the following examples:

FAULTY

Matt is *real* unhappy with his new work-study assignment.

Caitlyn ran across the playground *quick.*

In the first sentence, the adverb form of the modifier is needed to indicate *to what extent* Matt is unhappy, and in the second, the adverb form is needed to indicate *how* Caitlyn ran across the playground.

REVISED

Matt is *really* unhappy with his new work-study assignment.

Caitlyn ran across the playground *quickly.*

Other modifiers that can lead to errors in writing are the comparative and superlative forms of *bad—worse* and *worst.* The problem is that in informal speech, *worse* and *worst* can sound almost the same. As a result, it's easy to choose the wrong form when you write.

Look at these examples:

FAULTY

> At the beginning of the course, Leo had *worst* accounting skills than Flo.
>
> The *worse* part of the evening was when my car was towed away.

The first sentence compares the accounting skills of *two* students, so the comparative form—*worse*—should be used, not the superlative. The second sentence pinpoints the *least pleasant* part of a night that had many parts, so the superlative form—*worst*—is needed:

REVISED

> At the beginning of the course, Leo had *worse* accounting skills than Flo.
>
> The *worst* part of the evening was when my car was towed away.

Choosing between *good* and *well* and between *bad* and *badly* probably represents the biggest puzzle for most writers. *Good* and *bad* are adjectives—they modify people, locales, sensations, and so on. *Badly* and *well* are adverbs—they describe *how* something is done. One trick is to memorize a pair of simple sentences like the following, in which the words are used correctly, and then to repeat them to yourself whenever you use one of the words:

EXAMPLE

> Shannon is a *good* cook. He cooks *well.*

EXAMPLE

> Billie is a *bad* singer. She sings *badly.*

An additional complication for you as a writer is that the following modifiers are *irregular*, meaning that they don't form their comparatives and superlatives in the standard ways explained earlier:

Common Irregular Modifiers

Positive	Comparative	Superlative
bad (adjective)	worse	worst
badly (adverb)	worse	worst
good (adjective)	better	best
well (adverb)	better	best
little	less	least
much	more	most

As this list shows, two commonly confused pairs—*good* and *well* and *bad* and *badly*—share the same comparative and superlative forms.

As you do with other modifiers, use the comparative form when you are talking about two and the superlative when you are discussing more than two. Look at the following examples:

adjective

EXAMPLES   That new nightclub has *less* room than the club across the street.

Of all the rides at that amusement park, I enjoyed the roller coaster the *most.*

adverb

In the first sentence, the comparative form *less* sizes up two clubs. In the second, the superlative form *most* tells how much the roller coaster was enjoyed compared to at least two other rides.

COMPREHENSION AND PRACTICE 18.4

Errors with Confusing Modifier Pairs

This short letter, written by a distressed young man to his girlfriend, contains some incorrect choices among frequently confused modifiers. Help him out by correcting his errors. Cross out each incorrect form, and write the correct one above it. Use the example to guide you.

worst

EXAMPLE   Of all the runners in the race, he has the worse lane position.

Dear Leslie,

awfully

(1) I'm awful sorry about spilling grape soda on your dress last night at the

worst

party. (2) I want you to know that it really wasn't my fault. (3) The worse part

is that you won't believe me. (4) That obnoxious woman who had the argu-

quickly

ment with Karrie backed into me so quick that I didn't have time to react.

quietly

(5) Afterward, you quiet sat with a spreading purple stain on your dress, and

worse

you wouldn't even look at me. (6) That was worst than if you had yelled and

badly

screamed at me. (7) I just had the feeling that you thought I behaved bad, but,

honestly, it was an accident. (8) I know that this whole thing has turned into a

real mess, but if we talk about it, I think we can work it out.

Love, Dan

COMPREHENSION AND PRACTICE 18.5

Errors with Irregular Modifiers

The following paragraph contains some errors in the use of irregular modifiers. Cross out each incorrect modifier, and write the correct form above it. If a sentence is correct as written, mark it *OK.* Use the example to guide you.

most

EXAMPLE   Of all of my professors, Mr. Feeney, my economics instructor, is the more helpful.

(1) Of all the places I've ever lived, my current apartment is definitely the ~~better~~ [best] one. (2) The apartment itself had been remodeled before I moved in, so there was ~~least~~ [little] that I had to do myself. (3) The owners had decorated ~~good~~ [well], too, with wallpaper, paint, and carpeting that matched. (4) I can't believe how lucky I am, especially when I think about how ~~badly~~ [bad] my last place was [OK]. (5) For one thing, the apartment was tiny, with only a small bedroom and an equally small living room, kitchenette, and bathroom. (6) ~~Most~~ [More] annoying than the small size of the apartment was its overall condition. (7) The paint on the ceiling was peeling, and the walls were in no ~~best~~ [better] shape. (8) But the ~~worse~~ [worst] thing was the stained yellow and green carpeting. (9) It had been installed ~~bad~~ [badly] as well, so there were several wrinkles that ran the length of the living room. (10) My new apartment costs me a little more each month, but I know I am getting a ~~best~~ [better] place for the money.

CHALLENGE 18.4 The Use of Irregular Modifiers in Your Writing

1. To practice using the comparative and superlative forms of irregular modifiers, write five interview questions to ask a writing partner, each of which includes one of the following words: *worse, worst, better, best, less, least, more, most.* Use the example as a guide.

EXAMPLE Do you like action movies *more* than comedies?

collaboration

2. Interview your classmate, taking notes on his or her responses. Then write a brief "Getting to Know … " feature about your partner to share with the entire class.

Double Negatives

ESL Note
See "Double Negatives," page 493, for more on avoiding double negatives.

Another potential complication with modifiers involves expressing negatives correctly. *No, not,* and *never* are modifiers that express *negation*—the idea of *no.* Modifiers such as *scarcely, hardly,* and *barely* also suggest negation because they imply that there is almost none. In addition, a few pronouns such as *nowhere, nothing, nobody, no one,* and *none* also add negative emphasis to a thought.

When you use two of these negative words together in the same phrase or sentence, you create an error called a **double negative.** Although double negatives can be heard in casual conversation and street talk, they aren't acceptable in college or professional writing.

Avoid errors by checking your sentences to make sure you have only one negative in each subject–verb unit. Find the negatives in these examples:

FAULTY

My best friend has not had no luck in finding a good part-time job.

The quality-control department couldn't do nothing to speed up production.

The first sentence contains two negatives: *not* and *no.* The second sentence also has two negatives: *couldn't* (could + *not*) and *nothing.* Often, contractions such as *couldn't* confuse writers. Because contractions combine words and omit letters, it's easy to forget that they can contain negatives.

Eliminating double negatives is easy. Simply delete one of the negatives or change it to a positive form.

REVISED

My best friend has had *no* luck in finding a good part-time job.

or

My best friend has *not* had *any* luck in finding a good part-time job.

REVISED

The quality-control department could do *nothing* to speed up production.

or

The quality-control department *couldn't* do *anything* to speed up production.

Each of these sentences expresses the writer's real point correctly, with a single negative. Notice how the writer eliminated one negative in the first sentence of each pair. In the second sentence of each pair, one negative is changed to a positive form: *no* luck → *any* luck, and *nothing* → *anything*. Both strategies are equally correct and effective.

COMPREHENSION
AND PRACTICE
18.6

Revision to Eliminate Double Negatives

Read the paragraph below, and underline any double negatives you find. If a sentence is correct as written, mark it *OK.* On a separate sheet of paper, revise the faulty sentences to eliminate the double negatives. Use the example as a guide.

EXAMPLE

I wouldn't never want to have to go through high school again.

I would never want to have to go through high school again.

or

I wouldn't want to have to go through high school again.

(1) Once alligators lived away from humans in Florida and avoided them—not no more! (2) In earlier years, people didn't have no reason to fear the gators. (3) These residents felt secure because they never saw none. (4) Now the creatures aren't no strangers, as they frequently find their way into people's yards, garages, pools, and even their houses. OK (5) Experts feel that one of the major reasons for their increased appearances is that some people are feeding the alligators. (6) Feeding these reptiles is illegal, but these people don't seem to know no better. (7) Providing food for them isn't no joke because it makes the gators link humans with food. (8) When a hungry gator comes to call, home owners don't have no choice but to call a professional trapper.

CHALLENGE 18.5   **Problems Caused by Double Negatives**

1. If you listen carefully, you'll often hear double negatives, for instance, in informal conversation or music. For a week (or for another time period that your instructor assigns), write down examples of double negatives you hear or read.

collaboration

2. Bring your list to class and, working with a classmate, compare the occasions and situations during which you noticed double negatives being used.

Problems with *-ing* Modifiers

ESL Note
See "Word Order," pages 485–486, for more on avoiding dangling and misplaced modifiers.

Another kind of modifier that can be troublesome is the present participle of a verb, the *-ing* form. As Chapter 14, "Using Passive Voice and Progressive Tenses, and Maintaining Consistency in Tense," showed, words ending in *-ing* function as verbs in a sentence as long as they are preceded by a helping verb of some type, as this example shows:

EXAMPLES   The toddler was *bouncing* around the room gleefully.

Without a helping verb, however, the *-ing* word switches roles, in some cases functioning as a modifier. Look at these examples:

EXAMPLES   *Dancing* in the end zone, Alex celebrated his game-winning play.

The officer on the scene tried to calm the *crying* accident victims.

In the first sentence, *dancing* describes *Alex,* and in the second, *crying* describes *victims.*

Employing an *-ing* modifier to combine the ideas in two brief sentences can often be a good strategy to make your writing flow more smoothly. Look at the pairs of sentences in these examples:

CHOPPY

┌─── -ing phrase ───┐
The workers were sitting under the highway overpass. They were on a break.

┌─── -ing phrase ───┐
I was talking quietly to the frightened child. I tried to get him to tell me his street address.

The two sentences in each example are correct, but they are choppy. To eliminate this choppiness, combine the sentences, putting the *-ing* word and any other necessary phrasing next to the word referred to, as these versions show:

COMBINED

modifier
Sitting under the highway overpass, the *workers* were on a break.

modifier
Talking quietly to the frightened child, *I* tried to get him to tell me his street address.

In the first example, *Sitting* now modifies the *workers*, and in the second, *Talking* modifies *I*.

Also, always make sure that the word the *-ing* modifier is next to is the word it describes so that your meaning is clear for the reader. Otherwise, you will end up with a misplaced modifier, phrasing that will likely distract or confuse your reader, as this example shows:

MISPLACED MODIFIER

Hanging from the top of the building, Del saw the old flag.

Arranged this way, with the *-ing* modifier closer to *Del* than to *flag*, the sentence seems to suggest that Del, not the flag, is hanging from the top of the building. To correct this kind of error, you can either (1) move the *-ing* modifier next to the word it describes, or (2) reword the sentence, as these corrected versions show:

CLEAR

Del saw the old flag *hanging* from the top of the building.

or

Hanging from the top of the building, the old flag looked faded to Del.

At the same time, make sure that you have included the word that the *-ing* modifier actually describes. When you fail to do so, the result is a *dangling modifier* that makes the sentence awkward and unclear, as this example illustrates:

DANGLING MODIFIER

Taking a fast shower, my phone began to ring.

As worded, the sentence suggests that the *phone*, not the writer of the sentence, was taking a shower. To eliminate a dangling modifier, include the word that the *-ing* modifier describes or restate the sentence in some way to make its meaning clear, as these examples show:

CLEAR

Taking a fast shower, I could hear my phone begin to ring.

or

As I took a fast shower, my phone began to ring.

COMPREHENSION AND PRACTICE 18.7

Problems with *-ing* Modifiers

To avoid errors when you use *-ing* modifiers, you need to identify both the *-ing* modifier and the word it modifies. In the sentences below, underline the *-ing* modifier, and draw an arrow from it to the word that it *appears* to modify. Use the example to guide you. Then, on a separate sheet of paper, rewrite any sentences with misplaced modifiers to clarify their meaning, using the guidelines and examples on pages 346–348.

EXAMPLE

Putting the last dishes in place, the table was finally set.

(1) Barking loudly, I couldn't catch my dog, Mugwump. (2) Out of the corner of my eye, I saw Mugwump run down the beach dragging a leash. (3) Getting overexcited and playful, the trainer had told me Mugwump didn't yet understand how to obey. (4) Sure enough, now here I was, chasing after a runaway dog. (5) Laughing, I turned away and hoped Mugwump would follow. (6) Hearing the approach of paws, Mugwump started to run back at top speed. (7) I felt good, winning the game this time. (8) Putting my supper in the microwave, Mugwump sat happily in front of the couch.

CHALLENGE 18.6 Modifier Use to Combine Sentences

1. Combine the following pairs of sentences to eliminate the choppiness. Convert the first sentence to an *-ing* modifier, including any words from the first sentence that you think are necessary, and then make any other changes in phrasing that would make the resulting sentence more effective. Follow the examples and guidelines on pages 346–348.
   a. The baby was sitting quietly in her highchair. The baby waited for her oatmeal.
   b. The customers were waiting to get into the movie theater. The customers grew impatient.

> c. Jenny was skiing too fast. She hit a large bump and fell.
>
> d. I was shopping for a DVD player. I saw my old friend Richard.
>
> e. The sky was growing suddenly dark. It started to look threatening.

collaboration

2. Working with a classmate, compare how each of you revised the sentences. Discuss which versions are most effective and why.

✓ WORKING WITH ADJECTIVES AND ADVERBS CHECKLIST

☐ Have you chosen the comparative form for any modifiers used to compare *two* people or things?

☐ Have you chosen the superlative form of any modifiers used to *compare more than two* people or things?

☐ Have you double-checked the forms of any irregular modifiers you have used?

☐ Have you chosen the proper form of any modifiers used from the list of commonly confused modifiers like *good/well?*

☐ Have you used only one negative word in each subject–verb unit?

☐ Have you placed *-ing* modifiers next to the words they modify?

Journal Writing

Adjectives and adverbs add clarity and specificity to your writing. When you include modifiers in your writing, you *enhance* it, turning something general into something distinct and particular. Now think in terms of your day-to-day life: What enhances it now? Is it a personal relationship of some kind? Or is it school, your job, or some hobby or other interest? What *could* enhance it if you had the opportunity? Why would it make a difference for you? Consider some aspect of this subject, and then explore it for 20 to 30 minutes in your journal.

CHAPTER QUICK CHECK   Working with Adjectives and Adverbs

The following passage contains errors involving incorrect forms of adjectives and adverbs, double negatives, and misplaced modifiers. First, underline all the modifiers and articles in the sentences below. Then cross out each error and write the correct form above it. For misplaced modifiers, you may need to insert new words or cross out an entire clause and rewrite it. You may also be able to correct any double negatives in more than one way.

      (1) For millions of people across the United States, the day ~~quick~~ *quickly* becomes a

mess as soon as they reach traffic-clogged streets and highways. (2) To alleviate

traffic problems, cities have adopted many strategies, the ~~popularest~~ *most popular* of which include subways and busing. (3) Unfortunately, these strategies generally

~~any~~

haven't resulted in ~~no~~ serious reduction of traffic. (4) Of the possible solutions,

most

traveling by monorail seems to possess the ~~more~~ potential to ease these traffic

quieter

woes. (5) Monorail systems are ~~more quiet~~ and better for the environment than

any other system. (6) Until now, cities haven't considered the monorail as a

real   best

~~really~~ solution to traffic congestion. (7) In fact, the ~~better~~ known monorail sys-

tem in the United States isn't in a city at all. (8) Disney World in Orlando,

longer

Florida, has a monorail system that is several miles ~~longest~~ than any existing U.S.

any

monorail. (9) But now Disney World doesn't have ~~no~~ monopoly on monorails

because in 2004, Las Vegas, Nevada, joined the club. (10) Costing almost $90

million a mile, ~~company official hope that~~ the 3.9-mile monorail could someday

be the first choice for tourists traveling up and down the Vegas Strip.

SUMMARY EXERCISE Working with Adjectives, Adverbs, and Other Modifiers

The following passage contains errors involving incorrect forms of adjectives and adverbs, double negatives, and misplaced modifiers. First, underline all the modifiers and articles in the sentences below. Then cross out each error and write the correct form above it. For misplaced modifiers, you may need to insert new words or cross out an entire clause and rewrite it. You may also be able to correct any double negatives in more than one way.

(1) Anthropologists continue to scour the world in their search for remains of

oldest

the ~~most old~~ prehumans, some of whom lived many millions of years ago.

(2) Over the last several decades, teams in different parts of Africa have discov-

ered teeth, skull fragments, and other bones of ancient human ancestors. (3) The

clearly

fossils show ~~clear~~ that they were hominids, which means that they walked upright.

Because this creature had this ability   an

(4) ~~Having this ability,~~ anthropologists know it is not ~~no~~ ancestor of modern apes.

most famous

(5) One of the ~~famousest~~ prehuman fossils, "Lucy," was discovered over

thirty years ago. (6) ~~Buried in Ethiopia,~~ anthropologists found nearly half of the skeleton of this human ancestor buried in Ethiopia. (7) The fossilized re-

mains, which date back at least 3.2 million years, were from a female of

about 25. (8) ~~Looking something like a chimpanzee~~, the scientists who dis-
Although this being looked something like a chimpanzee

covered her showed that, unlike chimps, Lucy walked upright.

(9) When they examine fossils, anthropologists consider a number of signs

before deciding that they are ~~actual~~ from a human ancestor. (10) Fossil teeth,
actually

for example, merit ~~real~~ close attention. (11) Big, broad molars and thick tooth
really

enamel indicate not ~~no~~ ape but a prehuman specimen. (12) Common ances-
an

tors of both apes and humans also had little ears, big canine teeth, and small

heads, so these characteristics are examined ~~careful~~.
carefully

(13) The work involved in uncovering fossils is ~~awful~~ tedious. (14) The
awfully

members of a research team must painstakingly unearth the ~~most small~~
smallest

pieces of fossil. (15) They must work ~~slow~~ and ~~deliberate~~ to uncover a bone
slowly   *deliberately*

and remove it from the dry earth and rocks. (16) When dig sites are in ex-

tremely hot and dry regions, workers often can't get ~~no~~ relief from the severe
any

conditions.

(17) Perhaps the ~~more~~ well-known family associated with anthropology is
most

the Leakey family, including today's standard bearers, Maeve Leakey and her

daughter Louise. (18) Following a tradition established by Mary and Louis

Leakey, the parents of Maeve's husband, Richard, ~~Africa is their center of~~
Richard and Maeve and, later, Louise have made Africa the center of exploration

~~exploration~~. (19) Their team has uncovered a number of significant fossils, in-

cluding Maeve Leakey's 1995 discovery in Kenya of teeth and bones that are

4.2 million years old. (20) These remains are among the ~~most old~~ prehuman fos-
oldest

sils, including *Kenyanthropus platyops,* or flat-faced man of Kenya, the hominid

discovered by Louise in 2001 that she believed might replace Lucy as the

ultimate human ancestor.

FOR FURTHER EXPLORATION

1. Select one of the following subjects, and, using your preferred prewriting method, develop a specific focus and supporting ideas.

   - The possible value of making mistakes
   - A time when you took a risk and it paid off—or it didn't
   - The most creative person you know or have learned about

2. Evaluate your prewriting material, identify a focus, and create a draft paragraph of at least seven to ten sentences.

collaboration

3. Exchange your draft with a writing partner. Using the material in this chapter as a guide, evaluate the draft you receive. Note any problems with the use of the different forms of adjectives and adverbs as well as with irregular modifiers, -*ing* modifiers, and double negatives. Check for any other weaknesses, and then return the draft to the writer.

4. Revise your draft, eliminating any errors that your reader identified.

DISCOVERING CONNECTIONS

For this assignment, think about this picture and one of the following questions (or another that the photo inspires). Then, after exploring your ideas on this topic, create a draft paragraph of at least seven to ten sentences. Highlight all the modifiers you use in each of your sentences and double-check them to ensure you've used the correct form of the word.

A. The individuals in this photo are practicing yoga, a meditative stretching exercise that looks easier said than done. What kind of physical and mental discipline do you think is required to practice yoga? Have you ever taken a yoga class? What was it like? How did it make you feel?

B. Many experts say that daily exercise boosts energy and mental well-being. In your view, what's the best way to maintain your physical and mental health? What kind of exercise do you practice and what are the benefits? When appropriate, try using the comparative form of adjectives and adverbs to amplify your points.

RECAP Using Modifiers

Key Terms in This Chapter	Definitions
adjective	a word that describes a noun or pronoun
	tells *which one, how many, what kind*
adverb	a word that describes verbs, adjectives, and other adverbs
	tells *how, when, where, to what extent, how much*
comparative form	a modifier used to compare two things
	EXAMPLE *more* handsome, hung*rier*
superlative form	a modifier used to compare more than two things
	EXAMPLE *most* considerate, slow*est*
double negative	incorrect use of two negative words in the same phrase or sentence
	Do not use two of these words in a single sentence: *not, no, never, nowhere, nobody, nothing, no one, none, scarcely, hardly, barely.*
	EXAMPLE Nobody should bring nothing flammable.
	REVISED Nobody should bring anything flammable.

Forming Modifiers

Positive form	Comparative form	Superlative form
one-syllable word	positive form + *-er*	positive form + *-est*
brave	*braver*	*bravest*
words of three or more syllables	*more* + positive form	*most* + positive form
enjoyable	*more enjoyable*	*most enjoyable*
some two-syllable words	change *-y* to *-i* + *-er*	change *-y* to *-i* + *-est*
funny	*funnier*	*funniest*
other two-syllable words	*more* + positive form	*most* + positive form
famous	*more famous*	*most famous*

Common Irregular Modifiers

Positive form	Comparative form	Superlative form
bad (adjective)	worse	worst
badly (adverb)	worse	worst
good (adjective)	better	best
well (adverb)	better	best
little	less	least
much	more	most

Using Discovery Online with MyWritingLab

For more practice with adjectives and adverbs, go to www.mywritinglab.com.

Assessment: a process of evaluation designed to identify your level of mastery and help improve your performance

SENTENCE ELEMENTS: STRIVING FOR PRECISION

The material you have completed in Part 4 focuses on the use of **nouns** and **pronouns** as well as on **adjectives, adverbs,** and other **modifiers**. To assess your understanding of this information and your progress as a **Writer, Reader, Editor,** and **Student,** complete the following charts. First check off your level of confidence for each item, and then take the recommended action to improve your performance.

- As a **Writer**, I understand

	Confident	Moderately Confident	Not Confident
1. the correct use of **nouns** (Chapter 16)			
2. **pronoun case; pronoun–antecedent agreement** with **indefinite pronouns, demonstrative pronouns,** and **subordinate clauses;** the correct use of **reflexive pronouns;** and issues of **gender** and **sexist language** (Chapter 17)			
3. the role of **adjectives** and **adverbs,** correct spellings of **comparative** and **superlative forms, commonly confused** and **irregular modifiers, double negatives,** and *-ing* **modifiers** (Chapter 18)			

- If you are **confident**, you are all set. Move on.

- If you are **moderately confident**, review the Recaps for the appropriate chapters.

- If you are **not confident**, review the appropriate chapters, looking closely at the sample sentences, Chapter Quick Checks, and Summary exercises.

- As a **Reader**, I understand

	Confident	Moderately Confident	Not Confident
1. noun and pronoun use, various kinds of pronoun–antecedent agreement, sexist language, comparative and superlative forms of adjectives and adverbs, frequently confused and irregular modifiers, double negatives, and -*ing* modifiers			
2. the purpose and usefulness of the **Chapter Q&A**, **Overview**, **Checklist**, and **Journal Writing** features			

- If you are **confident**, you are all set. Move on.

- If you are **moderately confident,** take another look at these chapter features to make sure you understand the relationship between these features and the material in the chapter.

- If you are **not confident**, reread the **Q&A** and **Overview** sections. Identify example sentences that illustrate your particular difficulty. Revisit some of the exercises and activities, and complete the **Journal Writing** assignment; then use the **Chapter Checklist** to make sure that you have made no errors in your use of nouns, pronouns, adjectives, adverbs, or other modifiers.

- As an **Editor**, I understand

	Confident	Moderately Confident	Not Confident
1. how to form the plurals of nouns and deal with singular nouns ending in -*s* and collective nouns (Chapter 16)			
2. how to choose the appropriate case of personal pronouns; ensure pronoun–antecedent agreement with indefinite pronouns, demonstrative pronouns, and subordinate clauses; use reflexive pronouns; and avoid sexist language (Chapter 17)			

	Confident	Moderately Confident	Not Confident
3. how to use and spell the comparative and superlative forms of adjectives and adverbs, deal with commonly confused and irregular modifiers, avoid double negatives, and use *-ing* modifiers correctly (Chapter 18)			

- If you are **confident**, you are all set. Move on.

- If you are **moderately confident,** focus on the nouns, pronouns, and various modifiers in your own draft paragraph. Evaluate all plural forms, singular nouns ending in *-s,* and collective nouns. Take another look at all pronouns, considering the case of all personal pronouns as well as pronoun–antecedent agreement and sexist language. Check all positive and superlative modifiers as well as any *-ing* modifiers while also looking for any double negatives.

- If you are **not confident**, choose and complete—or do again—select exercises dealing with the area of concern you have identified. Find a passage of 200 words or so in one of your textbooks or a print or on-line article. Highlight all plural and collective nouns and all singular nouns ending in *-s.* Underline all pronouns, drawing a line from the pronoun to its antecedent. Circle all modifiers, putting *C* above all comparative forms and *S* above all superlative forms. Put a check next to any *-ing* modifier.

- As a **Student**, I understand

	Confident	Moderately Confident	Not Confident
1. the importance of examining the college catalog when considering classes for the next semester			
2. the value of establishing a long-term plan for my academic or professional future			
3. the need to visit the college advisement center or meet with my academic adviser to prepare class registration			

- If you are **confident**, you are all set. Move on.

- If you are **moderately confident**, check your college calendar—available online and in the college catalog—for specific dates related to college transfer and employment fairs, academic advisement, and class registration.

- If you are **not confident**, on your next day of classes, write down the location of your campus advisement and career center. If you have been assigned an academic adviser but don't know that person's name, check with Student Services and then make an appointment for an individual meeting with your adviser to discuss your current and future classes.

PART 5

Consistency Workshop: Aiming for Correctness

How do you adjust to in-class or timed writing situations? In general, how would you rate the writing you produce under these circumstances versus the writing you produce when you can spread the work out?

Simply knowing how to approach a writing situation has helped me produce what is necessary when I write for other classes. Timed writing is a bit harder for me, but knowing the basics of writing helps me produce a successful piece of writing. Prewriting helps me gather scattered thoughts and guides me to complete any writing assignment I face.

Marcy Gagnon
Major:
Small Business Management
Career Plans:
To be an entrepreneur

Before Marcy Gagnon began college, she felt that her writing skills were poor, "and I most certainly had no idea how to approach something like a basic essay." Her time as a college student has made her more confident, however. "The biggest surprise is how much I have actually learned, not only on an academic scale but also on a personal level. I have been amazed at how much continuing my education has improved my life and given me opportunities that I never thought were available to me." In particular, she feels that her writing has improved dramatically: "Now, I enjoy writing, and I am confident that I have the basic skills to approach a project or a writing task. Being able to write well has helped me in all my college courses, and my skills have become an asset in everyday living."

When you write a paragraph, an essay, a term paper, or a letter—what do you find easier to create, the opening or the closing?

For me the easier part is always the closing. When I write I might have three or four opening paragraphs that I have to choose from. Because the closing paragraph often restates the opening paragraph, I find it easier to come up with an effective closer.

Brian Levesque
Major:
Web Design and Media Arts
Career Plans:
To open his own graphic design center

When Brian Levesque was in high school, college was not a part of his goals for the future. Instead, he took a physically demanding full-time job and became the father of two children, the first when he was eighteen and the second a year and a half later. But a work injury changed his plans. "After almost four years at my job, I hurt my back. I decided to go back to school and acquire a new skill, so I could get a job that is more relaxed and not so physical." Although Brian was initially concerned about his writing skills, he now feels confident "to take on any writing assignment." He fully recognizes that if he writes well, his "boss or teacher will always remember my name because of my writing." Brian's decision to return to school was also personal: "I … want that college degree to show my children that they could do it, too."

How do you approach different types of writing assignments—for example, a personal paragraph or essay, a letter of application, a research paper, and so on?

I write with a different tone and style depending on the topic and the audience. When I write research papers for chemistry, psychology, or biology, I use the APA format. It is more scientific and fact-based writing. In other classes, MLA format is usually used for research papers. A personal paragraph or essay usually expresses personal experiences and opinions. I think that writing in different styles makes writing interesting.

Born and raised in South Korea, Mi Carnaghan found that the most surprising thing about attending college in the United States was the wide variety of students attending classes with her. "I was surprised by the differences in age groups, experiences, and attitudes. I didn't expect such a diverse group of classmates." Mi was unable to attend college immediately after high school because she needed to work, but "interacting at work with college graduates and people who speak and write English well motivated me to go to college." Before she began her classes, she felt uncertain about her writing skills. "It had been some time since I had needed to complete any formal writing, and English is my second language." Now she feels more comfortable with writing, and she is determined to continue to improve. "I want to improve my writing skills, graduate from college, and start a career, and being able to write well is directly related to my success in school and on the job."

Mi Carnaghan
Major:
Early Childhood Education
Career Plans:
To become a registered nurse

How would you describe your overall approach to writing? What makes it successful for you?

I quickly brainstorm and then place my ideas in a certain order and start writing. In timed situations, I get nervous and rush a lot. Spreading out work is more comfortable—no rush, I can take my time, and just write. I find the opening easier—the closing is like restating the opening. With revising, it depends on the length of the writing and how thorough it needs to be. For example, a research paper would take more time to be revised, and the same for a letter of application.

"Writing well," Frank Stephenson says, "shows character." The middle child of three, Frank is the first among his immediate family to attend college. "I started slowly, taking off a year after high school, then taking one or two classes, and then eventually full time." One pleasant discovery Frank has made about college is flexibility in scheduling. "I like being able to choose classes, times, and days I attend school." This flexibility has helped Frank balance his studies, work responsibilities, and involvement in intercollegiate basketball. Before he began his college classes, Frank assessed his writing abilities as "not too good." Now, however, Frank views his writing differently, saying simply, "I feel a lot better."

Frank Stephenson
Major:
Liberal Arts and Sciences
Career Plans:
To become a teacher and coach

CHAPTER 19
Maintaining Parallelism

GETTING STARTED ...

 Q Sometimes when I write about related ideas in pairs or in a series, the items or ideas don't seem to *match*. What am I doing wrong? Is there a strategy I can follow to make sure that all the items and ideas go together correctly?

 A When pairs or series of items match or *sound right*, they are *parallel*. In order to go together or match, elements must follow the same form. If one element begins with a preposition or ends in *-ing*, any item connected to it must follow the same pattern. To connect pairs and items in a series, use conjunctions such as *and, or, not only/but also,* and *either/or*. Find one of these conjunctions in your writing and identify the elements it is connecting. Make sure the second item and any others that follow match the first in form or structure. The resulting unit will *sound* correct and *be* correct.

Overview: Creating Balance in Writing

When discussing similar or related ideas in the same sentence, you must make sure that the ideas are expressed in a *parallel*, or similar, form. The easiest way to think about **parallelism** is to picture a seesaw or an old-fashioned scale. To keep everything balanced, you need to place objects of similar weight at each end. When you write, you balance out pairs or groups of connected ideas by presenting them in a similar form. If your connected items don't match, your reader can become distracted from the main point of your sentence. Maintaining parallelism in your writing is therefore an important strategy for expressing yourself clearly.

Navigating This Chapter In this chapter you will learn ways to balance:

- individual words in a series
- phrases in a series
- words linked by pairs of correlative conjunctions

Keeping Individual Words in a Series Parallel

Whenever you connect individual words in a series, make sure that the words are similar parts of speech. For example, it's correct to connect nouns to other nouns, pronouns to other pronouns, verbs to other verbs, adjectives to other adjectives, and adverbs to other adverbs. But it's *incorrect* to connect *different* types of words. You

ESL Note
See "Word Order,"
pages 485–486, for
more on presenting
items in a series and
"Agreement," pages
487–489, for more on
presenting verbs in
a series.

can't connect nouns to adverbs, for example, or verbs to adjectives. The exception concerns nouns and pronouns. These two parts of speech *can* be connected because pronouns refer to or are used in place of nouns.

In English, *conjunctions* are the words we use to connect other words. *And* and *or* are the most common conjunctions. Therefore, one way to make sure that you have maintained parallelism is to look at every sentence that contains *and* or *or*. Then double-check the words they connect to make sure they are similar parts of speech.

Look at the words that are connected in the following examples:

EXAMPLES

Her favorite jeans were *old* **and** *torn.*

To keep fit, you should *walk, run,* **or** *swim* three times a week.

In the first sentence, the conjunction *and* is connecting two *adjectives: old* and *torn.* In the second, the conjunction *or* connects three *verbs: walk, run,* and *swim.* The structure of each series of words is therefore *parallel.*

Now look at these examples:

FAULTY

Lauren didn't take an art course because she wasn't interested in *sketching* **or** *to create paintings.*

Shark attacks can be *quick, unexpected,* **and** *they are deadly.*

In the first sentence, the conjunction *or* is connecting *sketching,* a gerund, and *to create paintings,* an infinitive phrase. Infinitives and gerunds are different types of *verbals*—verb forms that act as other parts of speech—so they don't match. In addition, the one-word and three-word units are not balanced in length, so there is a problem with parallelism. In the second sentence, the conjunction *and* connects *quick* and *unexpected,* two adjectives, to *they are deadly,* a clause. Only the adjectives match, so this sentence also lacks a parallel structure.

To correct this faulty parallelism, simply change the parts of speech that do not match, as these versions show:

REVISED

Lauren didn't take an art course because she wasn't interested in *sketching* **or** *painting.*

Shark attacks can be *quick, unexpected,* **and** *deadly.*

In the first sentence, the infinitive phrase *to create paintings* is changed to *painting,* a gerund, so that it matches *sketching.* In the second example, the clause *they can be deadly* is shortened to a single adjective, *deadly,* which matches the adjectives *quick* and *unexpected.*

COMPREHENSION AND PRACTICE 19.1

Parallelism with Individual Words

Complete each of the following sentences by adding a word that completes the thought and maintains parallel structure. Use the example to guide you.

Answers will vary.

EXAMPLE Men and _____*women*_____ have significantly different life spans.

(1) The impulse to shoplift hits both wealthy and _____ peo-ple. (2) According to some psychologists, certain adults may shoplift because they are angry, anxious, or _____. (3) For them, shoplifting is a kind of protest against the expensive and _____ task that shopping of-ten becomes. (4) These shoppers become irrationally irritated with poorly paid salesclerks and cashiers who, they feel, are inattentive or _____ to customers. (5) Of course, some other shoplifters appear to be taking revenge on merchants for poor-quality products or _____. (6) The most experienced shoplifters move quickly and _____ (7) Once they have stolen the merchandise, they quickly conceal it in their pocket or _____. (8) Despite the presence of store detectives and _____, they often succeed in sneaking the item out of the store.

CHALLENGE 19.1   Analysis of Parallel Structure

1. The following passage discusses acid rain and its effects. As you read the ma-terial, underline all parallel elements, circling the conjunctions that provide the connection.

Acid rain actually begins after fossil fuels like oil (or) coal have been burned. Once the fuel has been expended, leftover gases drift out as exhaust (and) rise up into the atmosphere. Two of the elements in the leftover gases, sulfur dioxide (and) nitrogen oxide, go through a chemical change (and) become sulfuric acid and nitric acid. The property damage from acid rain can be exten-sive. It can corrode paint, metal, (or) architectural stone. In some older cities in the Northeast, acid rain has eroded some priceless monuments, statues, (and) stone carvings beyond repair. Furthermore, acid rain is a silent threat because its effects are gradual (and) cumulative.

collaboration

2. Compare your answers with a classmate's, and make any necessary corrections to your own answers.

Keeping Phrases in a Series Parallel

Whenever you connect two phrases, or *groups of words*, with a conjunction, the phrases must also be parallel. In other words, they must contain the same word forms. For example, it's correct to connect *prepositional phrases* with other *prepositional phrases*. It's also correct to connect *-ing verbal phrases* to other *-ing verbal phrases*, and *infinitive phrases (to eat, to dream)* to other *infinitive phrases.*

To check parallelism for phrases, follow the same process you use for individual words. First find every *and* or *or* in your sentences. Then, if you've used these conjunctions to connect phrases, make sure the phrases match.

Consider the connected phrases in these examples:

EXAMPLES

Steve knew his missing media card was in the closet, under the couch, **or** behind the bookcase.

Roberta wants to major in accounting **and** to take as many Spanish courses as possible.

In the first sentence, *or* is connecting two prepositional phrases—*in the closet* and *under the couch*—with a third one, *behind the bookcase.* In the second sentence, *and* is connecting two infinitive phrases: *to major in accounting* and *to take as many Spanish courses as possible.* The structure of each sentence is therefore *parallel.*

Now consider the connected phrases in these faulty examples:

FAULTY

The greatest challenges for me in school are *keeping up with my homework* **and** *to study for exams.*

I get parts for my old motorcycle *through catalogs, calling junk dealers,* **or** *at flea markets.*

In the first sentence, *and* connects a gerund phrase, *keeping up with my homework,* to an infinitive phrase, *to study for exams.* These phrases don't match, so they are not parallel. In the second, *or* connects two prepositional phrases, *through catalogs* and *at flea markets* to a verbal phrase, *calling junk dealers.* The verbal phrase does not match the other two.

To make the elements in these sentences parallel, change one so that it matches the word or words to which it is connected. Take a look at these corrected versions of the sentences about school difficulties:

REVISED

The greatest challenges for me in school are *keeping* up with my homework **and** *studying* for exams.

or

The greatest challenges for me in school are to *keep* up with my homework **and** to *study* for exams.

In the first corrected version, *and* is now connecting two *-ing* phrases. In the second version, *and* is now connecting two infinitive phrases. Both phrases match, so these sentences are now parallel.

Now look at these corrected versions of the sentence about purchasing motorcycle parts:

REVISED

I get parts for my old motorcycle *through* catalogs, *from* junk dealers, **or** *at* flea markets.

or

I get parts for my old motorcycle by *checking* through catalogs, *calling* junk dealers, **or** *going* to flea markets.

In the first of these corrected versions, *or* is now connecting three prepositional phrases. In the second version, *or* is connecting three verbal phrases. Each group of phrases now matches, so the structure of each sentence is parallel.

COMPREHENSION
AND PRACTICE
19.2

Parallelism with Phrases

Circle the conjunctions in each sentence below. Then underline the items that each conjunction connects. If the items are not parallel, change one so that the connected phrases match in form. There may be more than one way to correct each sentence, as this example shows. Answers may vary.

EXAMPLES

The shoppers rushed through the door, hurried across the lobby, (and) they ~~went~~
ran
running for the sale.

or

           went rushing   hurrying
The shoppers ~~rushed~~ through the door, ~~hurried~~ across the lobby, (and) ~~they went~~

running for the sale.

(1) Last week I attended a program about sex discrimination (and) about
sexual harassment
~~harassing people sexually~~. (2) The speaker began by showing a movie (and)
leading
~~she led~~ a discussion about what we had seen. (3) I learned that many people
                              how to get information about it
don't know what harassment is, ~~getting information about it is difficult,~~ (or) where

to go for help. (4) We discovered that solutions for discrimination at work (and)
admitting
school include ~~to admit~~ discrimination exists, attending educational programs,
keeping
(and) ~~to keep~~ the lines of communication open. (5) At the end of the program, the
applauded
audience ~~was applauding~~ the speaker (and) asked the sponsors to have her return.

COMPREHENSION
AND PRACTICE

Phrases to Maintain Parallelism

19.3   Complete the following sentences by adding phrases that complete the thought and maintain sentence parallelism. Use the sample as a guide. Answers will vary.

EXAMPLE   My best friend enjoys running, hiking, and _____*swimming*_____

_____.

1. My husband's cooking pleasures include shopping for the freshest ingredients, hunting down hard-to-find spices, and _____

_____.

2. Unfortunately, some of his other activities include messing up the kitchen and

_____.

3. During the holiday season, he bakes dozens of cookies, arranges them on gift platters, and _____

_____.

4. The cookies are perfectly baked, beautifully decorated, and _____

_____.

5. Afterward, however, I'm the one who has to scrub the bowls and pots, put away all of the ingredients, and _____

_____.

6. According to him, a master chef shouldn't have to be bothered with mopping the floor or _____

_____.

7. Once, when I insisted that he clean up after himself, I found the sugar in the refrigerator, the mixer in the attic, and _____

_____.

8. Another consequence of his baking is that I always eat too many cookies, gain too many pounds, and _____

_____.

CHALLENGE 19.2 Evaluation of Parallel Structure

1. Comprehension and Practice 19.3 discusses food preparation. Think of a memorable experience you had that involved cooking or eating a meal, and then write about it in a paragraph of at least seven to ten sentences.

collaboration

2. Exchange your paragraph with a classmate. On the paper you receive, underline the connected items, and evaluate the parallelism. Put a ✓ above any element that you believe doesn't match the item or items to which it is connected, and return the paper to the writer.

3. Evaluate your classmate's analysis of parallelism in your paragraph, and then make any necessary corrections.

Parallelism with Correlative Conjunctions

Certain pairs of connecting words, known as **correlative conjunctions**, also call for parallel structure:

either + or	both + and	whether + or
neither + nor	not only + but also	

These pairs are especially useful to you as a writer because they enable you to focus on two ideas in the same sentence. Take a look at these examples:

EXAMPLES

I enjoy **both** *mountain biking* **and** *in-line skating.*

The problem with that printer is **either** *a paper jam* **or** *a software issue.*

The first example features *both–and.* Each word in the pair is followed by a participle and its modifier, *mountain bik**ing*** and *in-line skat**ing***, so they are parallel. The second example features *either–or* connecting nouns plus their modifiers—*a paper jam* and *a software issue*—so these elements are parallel.
Now look at these faulty examples:

FAULTY

The salesclerk was **not only** *rude* **but also** *her work was completed slowly.*

The security guard had **neither** *a flashlight* **nor** *did he have a two-way radio.*

In the first sentence, the ideas connected by *not only–but also* aren't parallel. *Rude* is an adjective, but *her work was completed slowly* is a clause that could stand on its own as a sentence. In the second sentence, the words connected by *neither–nor—a flashlight* and *did he have a two-way radio*—aren't parallel either.
Eliminating this faulty parallelism is easy. Simply change the form of the more awkwardly expressed item to match the more concise one.

REVISED

The salesclerk was **not only** *rude* **but also** *slow.*

The security guard had **neither** *a flashlight* **nor** *a two-way radio.*

COMPREHENSION
AND PRACTICE
19.4

Errors with Parallel Structure Involving Correlative Conjunctions

Each sentence in the following paragraph has an error in parallelism involving correlative conjunctions. Circle the pair of connecting words in each sentence, and underline the words that they connect. Then, on a separate piece of paper, rewrite the sentences to make them parallel. Remember that there may be more than one correct version, as the following example shows. Answers will vary.

EXAMPLE

To our surprise, (neither) the falling snow (nor) the wind that was howling caused the ski lift to close.

To our surprise, neither the falling snow nor the howling wind caused the ski lift to close.

or

To our surprise, neither the snow that was falling nor the wind that was howling caused the ski lift to close.

(1) On most Saturday mornings, I go down to Riverfront Park and (either) sketch (or) to paint. (2) These hobbies occupy (not only) my hands (but also) I have to use my mind. (3) I really enjoy these activities because they are (both) inexpensive (and) these hobbies are easy to learn. (4) (Whether) I am completing a previously started work (or) a new one is ready to be started by me, I always find myself completely relaxed. (5) The top benefit of these activities are that I (not only) have fun (but also) developing my artistic abilities.

COMPREHENSION
AND PRACTICE
19.5

Problems with Special Parallel Structure

Complete the following sentences by adding an appropriate connecting word or phrase. Use the example to guide you. Answers may vary.

EXAMPLE

_____*Not only*_____ is drag racing dangerous, _____*but*_____ it is _____*also*_____ illegal.

1. Oprah Winfrey, host of the award-winning daytime program *The Oprah Winfrey Show*, is <u>not only</u> famous <u>but also</u> loved by millions of fans all over the world.

2. When Winfrey began her radio broadcasting career at age nineteen in Nashville, Tennessee, she had <u>neither</u> experience <u>nor</u> any formal education in journalism.

3. She decided to enroll at Tennessee State University, where she studied <u>both</u> speech <u>and</u> the performance arts.

4. In her sophomore year at Tennessee State, Winfrey switched broadcast mediums and became the first African-American news anchor at Nashville's WTVF-TV. Now she had <u>both</u> radio experience <u>and</u> broadcast television work under her belt.

5. It was not long before Winfrey had to make a choice: <u>either</u> stick with television <u>or</u> return to radio.

6. Winfrey chose television, and this proved to be the right choice. After making the decision to remain a television journalist, Winfrey was offered <u>not only</u> her own local talk show, called *People Are Talking*, <u>but also</u> an opportunity for great success.

7. Because she wanted her talk show to be less formal than other talk shows, Winfrey used <u>neither</u> traditional interview techniques <u>nor</u> high-profile guest lists.

8. With an Oscar nomination for her role in *The Color Purple*, Winfrey had to decide <u>whether</u> to focus on acting <u>or</u> to concentrate on television, which has made her the single most powerful woman on television.

CHALLENGE 19.3   Parallel Structure in a Famous Passage

1. Read the following passages from Abraham Lincoln's "Gettysburg Address," given at the consecration of the Gettysburg National Cemetery.

> Four score (and) seven years ago our fathers brought forth upon this continent, a new nation, conceived in Liberty, (and) dedicated to the proposition that all men are created equal....

> But, in a larger sense, we cannot dedicate—we cannot consecrate—we cannot hallow this ground. The brave men, living (and) dead, who struggled here, have consecrated it, far above our poor power to add (or) detract. The world will little note, (nor) long remember, what we say here, (but) it can never forget

what they did here….We here highly resolve <u>that these dead shall not have died in vain;</u> <u>that this nation, under God, shall have a new birth of freedom,</u> (and) <u>that government of the people, by the people, for the people, shall not perish from the earth.</u>

collaboration

2. Working with a classmate, underline the parallel elements in the passage, and circle the conjunctions that connect them.

3. On a separate piece of paper, briefly explain how the parallel structure helped Lincoln communicate his ideas to his audience.

✓ MAINTAINING PARALLELISM CHECKLIST

☐ Have you checked any individual words connected by the conjunctions *and, or,* or *but* to make sure they match in form?

☐ Have you checked any prepositional phrases connected by the conjunctions *and, or,* or *but* to make sure they match in form?

☐ Have you checked any *-ing* verbal phrases connected by the conjunctions *and, or,* or *but* to make sure they match in form?

☐ Have you checked any infinitive phrases connected by the conjunctions *and, or,* or *but* to make sure they match in form?

☐ Have you checked any units connected by pairs of correlative conjunctions such as *not only–but also* and *either–or* to make sure they match in form?

Journal Writing

Maintaining correct parallelism involves making sure that related elements match in form. When things match in a sentence–or in life–it's easy to recognize. Do you know twins, for instance, or people who look enough alike to be twins? Are their actions as similar as their appearance? Or have you been to two places that look quite different on the surface but are actually very similar? Think of one of these subjects or some other aspect related to similarities, and then explore it for 20 to 30 minutes in your journal.

CHAPTER QUICK CHECK   Maintaining Parallelism

Revise the following paragraph, making sure that similar or related ideas are expressed in parallel form. Cross out words, phrases, or clauses that aren't parallel, and write your revisions above them.

(1) Americans have a big thirst, and today they have a wide variety of beverages, both hot and ~~some of them are~~ cold, available to help them quench it. (2) Consumers can often find the coffee they are looking for at a convenience store, ~~they can go to~~ small neighborhood bistros, or at mall kiosks. (3) Major chains like Starbucks, Dunkin' Donuts, and ~~then there is~~ Seattle's Best have franchises spread across the country. (4) Here, consumers can enjoy not only a wide variety of regular and flavored coffee but also ~~they can enjoy~~ specialty coffee, including café au lait and espresso. (5) Visitors can see customers savoring rich coffees, enjoying various hot and cold whipped coffee drinks, and _{drinking} ~~to drink~~ fruit-flavored frozen drinks. (6) Carbonated beverages have traditionally made up a large share of the soft-drink market, both caffeinated colas like Coke and Pepsi and citrus-flavored sodas like Sprite and Seven-up ~~make up a good portion~~, too. (7) Today, sports drinks have become increasingly popular for active people, whether they are competing in some athletic activity or _{doing yard work} ~~yard work is being completed by them~~. (8) These kinds of drinks are designed to restore some of the minerals, ~~they restore~~ electrolytes, and other nutrients lost during physical activities. (9) But the beverage of choice for more and more people, either while exercising or ~~when they are~~ relaxing, is also the most basic drink: water. (10) Bottles of water are now commonplace in homes, ~~they are~~ in offices, and in classrooms across the country, a development few would have imagined a decade ago.

SUMMARY EXERCISE   Maintaining Parallelism

Revise the following essay, making sure that similar or related ideas are expressed in parallel form. Cross out words, phrases, or clauses that aren't parallel, and write your revisions above them.

(1) I had to decide last summer whether to look for another job or _{to go} ~~going~~ back to school. (2) I think I made the best decision for both me and ~~it was good for~~ my family.

(3) After I was laid off in June, I tried to find either a ~~job where I could~~ [full-time job] ~~work full-time~~ or two part-time jobs. (4) Employers kept telling me I needed new computer skills, more experience, or ~~having a college degree would help~~ [a college degree]. (5) A lot of the jobs I applied for were either temporary or only ~~a few hours a week open to me~~ [part time]. (6) Furthermore, these jobs had low pay and ~~benefits didn't exist~~ [no benefits]. (7) In most cases, the places where I applied either rejected me right away or ~~a call was made a day later~~ [called a day later] to turn me down.

(8) I decided that if I went back to school, my confidence would increase and ~~an improvement in my job prospects would exist~~ [my job prospects would improve]. (9) I also felt it would be good for my children to see me striving for a better life and ~~to make progress~~ [progressing]. (10) With a better education, I would feel better about myself and ~~an improvement in our standard of living would occur~~ [improve our standard of living]. (11) Still, I wasn't sure I could apply for school, ~~finding~~ [find] an appropriate part-time job, arrange for childcare, and keep my sanity.

(12) My thoughts of going to college were both exciting and ~~I was intimidated~~ [intimidating]. (13) I wasn't sure how I would be able to take care of my kids, ~~keeping~~ [keep] up with household responsibilities, and study. (14) I worried how my kids would handle my absence while I attended classes on some weeknights and ~~a class would be attended by me every Saturday~~ [every Saturday]. (15) The kids would have to prepare some of their own meals and ~~their help would be needed~~ [help] with the laundry. (16) In addition, we would all have to be a bit more tolerant about occasional dirty dishes, dust on the floors, and ~~beds might not always be made~~ [unmade beds].

(17) Once I finally made the decision to take classes, I felt hopeful and ~~happiness~~ [happy]. (18) I am determined that neither my fears about failure nor ~~will I let~~ my natural pessimism will keep me from achieving this goal. (19) In a few years, I will be able to get a better job and ~~giving~~ [give] my children the life they deserve. (20) As long as I work hard, stay organized, and ~~remaining~~ [remain] focused, I'll make it.

FOR FURTHER EXPLORATION

1. Choose one of the following subjects and use your preferred prewriting method to develop a specific focus and ideas to support it.

   - A famous saying, proverb, or maxim that you think is accurate—or one that you think isn't—and why
   - A concern or fear you have about the direction the future may take
   - A time when you were caught in a lie

2. Evaluate your prewriting material, identify a focus, and create a draft paragraph of at least seven to ten sentences.

collaboration

3. Exchange your draft with a writing partner. Using the material in this chapter as a guide, evaluate the draft you receive. Note any problems with parallelism, and return the draft to the writer.

4. Revise your draft, eliminating any errors that your reader identified.

DISCOVERING CONNECTIONS

For this assignment, focus on the photo and one of the following questions (or some other that the photo inspires). Explore your ideas, and then create a draft paragraph of at least seven to ten sentences. Remember to check for parallelism between phrases as well as individual words.

A. An official in any sport is supposed to ensure fairness. Was there a time, either during a game or just in your life in general, when you were treated unfairly? What were the circumstances? What happened as a result?

B. Most people can recall a game or competition of some kind that stands out because of a key incident. What comes to mind for you? What role, if any, did you play? If you could change something about that event, what would it be? Why?

RECAP Maintaining Parallelism

Key Terms in This Chapter	Definition
parallelism	a balanced structure in writing, achieved by expressing similar or related ideas in the same grammatical form
	Individual words that are connected by a conjunction should be parallel.
	EXAMPLE My office is *messy* **and** *dusty.*
	Phrases that are connected by a conjunction should be parallel.
	EXAMPLE I like to *bake pies* **and** *decorate cakes.*
	Words that follow pairs of correlative conjunctions should be parallel.
	EXAMPLE The forecast was for **either** *heavy snow* **or** *freezing rain.*
correlative conjunctions	connecting words used in pairs: *both/and, either/or, neither/nor, not only/but also, whether/or*

The Basics of Parallelism

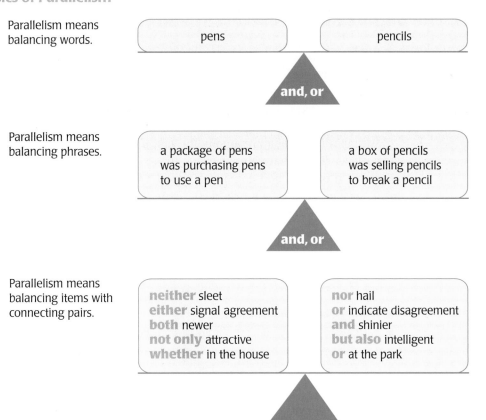

Parallelism means balancing words.

pens   pencils

and, or

Parallelism means balancing phrases.

a package of pens   a box of pencils
was purchasing pens   was selling pencils
to use a pen   to break a pencil

and, or

Parallelism means balancing items with connecting pairs.

neither sleet   **nor** hail
either signal agreement **or** indicate disagreement
both newer   **and** shinier
not only attractive   **but also** intelligent
whether in the house   **or** at the park

Using Discovery Online with MyWritingLab

PEARSON mywritinglab

For more practice with parallelism, go to www.mywritinglab.com.

CHAPTER 20
Mastering Spelling

GETTING STARTED ...

Q I've really tried to improve my spelling and learn all the rules, but I still have so much trouble spelling correctly. Why is spelling in English so complicated?

A The fact is that no set of rules can cover every word. For one thing, English has been drawn from a number of other languages. Also, some words have silent letters, so they aren't spelled the way they sound. Some words have plural forms that are spelled in vastly different ways from the singular forms. And some words are spelled the same way in both the singular and plural forms. Even the rules we have can be problems because many rules have exceptions, and these exceptions are the words that often cause difficulties.

Overview: The Importance of Correct Spelling

Spelling English words can be difficult for many reasons. For instance, many English words don't follow consistent spelling patterns. Other words, such as *pneumonia* and *though,* are not spelled the way they sound. Furthermore, some words, such as *there, their,* and *they're,* sound the same but are spelled differently and have different meanings.

Mistakes in spelling are among the first things a reader notices. They distract your reader from what you are trying to say, definitely making your writing less effective. Instructors and employers expect you to spell correctly, and when you make spelling errors, they will likely judge the quality of your thinking and reasoning harshly. Therefore, you must make developing a greater mastery of spelling a priority.

Navigating This Chapter In this chapter you'll discover strategies to help you ensure that you spell words correctly. You will learn:

- some basic spelling rules
- different meanings and spellings of commonly confused words

Forming Plurals

As Chapter 16, "Working with Nouns," showed, you can form the plural of most nouns by adding *-s* to the singular form:

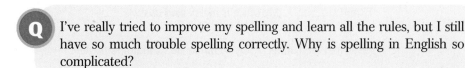

helicopter	helicopter**s**	cat	cat**s**	television	television**s**

Nouns That End in -*ch*, -*sh*, -*x*, and -*s*   For nouns ending in -*ch*, -*sh*, -*x*, and -*s*, form the plural by adding -*es*:

church   church**es**   bush   bush**es**   box   box**es**

Nouns That End in -*y*   For nouns ending in -*y* preceded by a *vowel* (*a, e, i, o, u*), form the plural by adding -*s*:

toy   toy**s**   play   play**s**   key   key**s**

For nouns ending in -*y* preceded by a *consonant* (non-vowel letter), form the plural by changing the -*y* to -*i* and adding -*es*:

story   stor**ies**   baby   bab**ies**   butterfly   butterfl**ies**

Compound Nouns   Most combined or compound nouns form the plural by adding -*s* to the *main* word:

runner up   runner**s** up   maid of honor   maid**s** of honor
brother-in-law   brother**s**-in-law

Words from Other Languages   With some words from other languages, you form the plural in keeping with the original language. The following Latin words form the plural by changing the final -*i* to -*e*:

analysis   analys**es**   crisis   cris**es**   thesis   thes**es**

Nouns That End in -*o*   Some nouns share the same ending but form their plurals differently. For nouns that end in -*o*, for instance, the plural form depends on one of three things:

- If the noun ends in a vowel plus -*o*, add -*s* to form the plural:

  patio   patio**s**   stereo   stereo**s**   radio   radio**s**

- If the noun ends in a consonant plus -*o*, add -*es* to form the plural:

  tomato   tomato**es**   hero   hero**es**   veto   veto**es**

- Nouns ending in -*o* that refer to music are an exception. They form the plural by adding -*s*:

  piano   piano**s**   soprano   soprano**s**   solo   solo**s**

Nouns That End in -*f* and -*fe*   Nouns that share the -*f* or -*fe* ending also may have different plural forms. For most of these nouns, you form the plural by simply adding -*s*:

belief   belief**s**   chief   chief**s**   roof   roof**s**

However, some nouns with this same ending form the plural by changing the -*f* or -*fe* to -*v* and adding -*es:*

half   hal**ves**   wife   wi**ves**   leaf   lea**ves**

Irregular Nouns   For some common irregular nouns, you form the plural by changing letters within the word:

woman   wom**e**n   tooth   t**ee**th   mouse   m**ice**

Nouns That Have the Same Singular and Plural Forms   Finally, a few nouns have the same singular and plural forms:

sheep   sheep   deer   deer   antelope   antelope

If you are not sure how a noun forms the plural, consult a dictionary. The dictionary lists the plural ending for words that do not form plurals simply by adding -*s.*

COMPREHENSION
AND PRACTICE
20.1

Plurals

Using the guidelines in the preceding section or a dictionary, change the italicized singular words in the paragraph below to their correct plural forms. Write your answers above the italicized words. Use the example to guide you.

EXAMPLE
tomatoes
We'll raise *tomato* in the garden.

families   possibilities
(1) Most *family* consider a number of *possibility* when it comes to vacations.
alternatives
(2) Camping is among the best *alternative* available to them, especially if
children
they want their *child* to experience the great outdoors. (3) With the constant
echoes
smell of pine and the *echo* of wild birds, even small, regional camping areas
cities
seem miles away from the *city* around them. (4) At National Parks like
wolves deer
Yellowstone, campers can see *wolf, deer*, and bears in their natural setting.
backpacks
(5) Tents, *backpack*, and sleeping bags are available at a reasonable cost, so
opportunities
even those on a tight budget can enjoy the *opportunity* that camping presents.

COMPREHENSION
AND PRACTICE
20.2

Improper Plurals

Each of the following sentences contains an incorrectly spelled plural form. Cross out the incorrect spelling, and write the correct one above it. Use the example as a guide.

EXAMPLE

To the frustration of homeowners who want to keep their lawns clean, many

leaves

oak ~~leafs~~ remain on the trees long into the winter.

(1) When my cultural studies instructor told the class we would be visiting

societies

three area historical ~~societys~~, I practically groaned. (2) The last thing I wanted to

boxes

do was waste time looking at display cases and ~~boxs~~ full of old junk. (3) I could-

stories

n't have been more surprised by how interesting I found the ~~storys~~ behind the

different items in the collections. (4) For instance, one case contained about

keys

100 types of ~~keyes~~, some from colonial times. (5) Another display included var-

knives

ious decorative ~~knifes~~ set with precious stones. (6) Apparently they were used

chiefs

by the ~~chiefes~~ of a long-ago fraternal organization as they initiated new mem-

bers. (7) Some of the items, including rare books and china, came from two

churches

~~churchs~~ and several stores that were destroyed when a tornado hit the city in

butterflies

1900. (8) One of the most elaborate displays is a large collection of ~~butterflys~~

that belonged to a minister who died in the storm. (9) The minister had been a

countries

missionary in several ~~countrys~~, and at every stop he caught and preserved dif-

heroes

ferent specimens. (10) In the case of this display, the real ~~heros~~ were the cura-

tors who convinced the minister's widow to donate the collection so the entire

community could enjoy it.

CHALLENGE 20.1   Plural Noun Forms

collaboration

Working with a partner, choose a reading from the selections in Part 6. On a separate sheet of paper, identify and list ten singular nouns. Then change these
nouns to their plural forms.

Prefixes and Suffixes

Prefixes and suffixes are units of one or more letters that you add to nouns,
verbs, adjectives, and adverbs to change their meanings. A **prefix** is a unit such
as *un-*, *dis-*, or *semi-* that you add to the *beginning* of a word. A **suffix** is a unit
such as *-ness*, *-able*, or *-ous* that you add to the *end* of a word.

When you add a prefix to a word, you *don't* change the spelling of the word:

necessary   **un**necessary   agree   **dis**agree

spell   **mis**spell   conscious   **semi**conscious

Suffixes -*ly* and -*ness*   When you add the suffixes -*ly* and -*ness* to a word, you *usually* don't change the spelling of the word:

usual   usual**ly**   rare   rare**ly**   mean   mean**ness**

Exception   One exception to this rule is the word *true*. When you add -*ly* to *true*, you drop the -*e:* tru**ly**.

However, for words of more than one syllable that end in -*y*, you change the -*y* to -*i* before adding the -*ly* or -*ness:*

happy   happ**iness**   easy   eas**ily**   crazy   craz**iness**

For other suffixes, however, you may have to change the spelling of the word itself.

Words That End in -*y*   For words ending in -*y*, change the -*y* to -*i* before adding a suffix:

worry   worr**ied**   modify   modif**ied**   identify   identif**ied**

However, if the suffix begins with -*i*, keep the -*y:*

worry   worry**ing**   modify   modify**ing**   identify   identify**ing**

Words That End in -*e*   When the word ends in -*e* and the suffix begins with a *vowel*, drop the final -*e* before adding the suffix:

hope   hop**ing**   approve   approv**al**   fame   fam**ous**

If the suffix begins with a *consonant*, keep the final -*e:*

care   care**less**   safe   safe**ty**   arrange   arrange**ment**

Exceptions   Here are several exceptions to these guidelines. You will need to memorize them.

notice   notice**able**   mile   mile**age**   peace   peace**able**

argue   argu**ment**   whole   whol**ly**   judge   judg**ment**

COMPREHENSION AND PRACTICE

20.3 **Prefixes and Suffixes**

Add the prefix or suffix in parentheses to each italicized word in the paragraph below. Write the new word in the space above. Check the guidelines in the section above for help. Use the example as a guide.

EXAMPLE   We are *hope* (ing) for warm weather during our vacation.
hoping

(1) Some men and women are *leave* (ing) or downsizing their careers to
leaving
find *happy* (ness) at home *raise* (ing) their children. (2) These people say they
happiness   *raising*
made this choice because they felt *guilt* (y) and (dis) *appoint* (ed) about *miss* (ing)
guilty   *disappointed*   *missing*
their children's first years of life. (3) Now, however, some of them are often
worry (ed) about *make* (ing) ends meet. (4) In order to support their families
worried   *making*
comfort (able) (ly), many of these parents will *probable* (ly) have to supplement
comfortably   *probably*
their incomes by adding part-time work. (5) Many people may (dis) *agree* with
disagree
the *arrange* (ment) these men and women have made. (6) Nevertheless, these
arrangement
parents find that *devote* (ing) this time to childrearing is both important and
devoting
fulfill (ing).
fulfilling

COMPREHENSION AND PRACTICE
20.4

Meanings with and without Prefixes or Suffixes

Adding a prefix or suffix changes the meaning of a word. To help you discover how the meaning can change, choose five words from among those used as examples on pages 379–380. On a separate sheet of paper, write them both with and without the suffix or prefix. Then write brief definitions of the words with and without the prefix or suffix. For example, *conscious* means "alert and awake"; *semiconscious* means "partially alert and awake."

CHALLENGE 20.2

Suffix Use

1. On a separate piece of paper, add the suffixes in parentheses to the following eight words. Make any spelling changes necessary. Then write a sentence using each of the words.

finish (ed)	refer (ed)
occur (ed)	judge (ment)
snowy (est)	create (ed)
hammer (ed)	notice (able)

collaboration

2. Exchange your work with a classmate. Check the spelling of the list you receive and underline any misspelled words you find. Return the sentences to the writer.

Doubling the Final Consonant

To add a suffix that begins with a vowel to a word that ends in a consonant, do you double that final consonant? The answer depends on the word itself.

One-Syllable Words   If the word has one syllable, and the letter before the final consonant is a *single vowel*, double that consonant before adding a suffix beginning with a vowel:

> stop   stop**ping**   plan   plan**ned**   fat   fat**test**

However, if the final consonant is preceded by a consonant (as in warn) or more than one vowel (as in eat), just add the suffix beginning with a vowel:

> warn   warn**ed**   eat   eat**en**   sail   sail**ing**

Words of Two or More Syllables   What do you do if a word ends in a single consonant preceded by a single vowel, but the word has *more than one syllable?* If the *accent*, or emphasis, is on the *last syllable*, double the final consonant before adding the suffix. (Say the word out loud to identify which syllable is *accented*.)

> begin   begin**ning**   admit   admit**ted**   occur   occur**rences**

If the accent is *not* on the last syllable, simply add the suffix:

> travel   travel**ed**   suffer   suffer**ed**   abandon   abandon**ing**

COMPREHENSION
AND PRACTICE
20.5 **To Double the Final Consonant or Not**

In each sentence below, add the suffixes in parentheses to the italicized words. Write the new word above the italicized word. Refer to the rules in the section above to help you decide whether to double the final consonant of the original word. Use the example as a guide.

EXAMPLE

fattest

Aunt Sophie always picks out the *fat* (est) turkey for Thanksgiving dinner.

(1) I have always *enjoy* (ed) [enjoyed] Robert Frost's well-known poem "*Stop* (ing) [Stopping] by Woods on a Snowy Evening." (2) I wanted to read it at the *begin* (ing) [beginning] of the poetry slam my class was *sponsor* (ing) [sponsoring]. (3) However, because a huge snowstorm *occur* (ed) [occurred] on that day, the event was *cancel* (ed) [canceled]. (4) The poem is about a man who *linger* (ed) [lingered] for a brief time on a winter night as he was *travel* (ing) [traveling] to his

destination miles away. (5) Like the speaker in the poem, I too have *talk* (ed) ^talked^
myself into going on, even when I might have *prefer* (ed) to disappear, at least ^preferred^
for a short while.

CHALLENGE 20.3 **Analysis of Accented Syllables**

1. It can be a challenge to decide which syllable of a word is accented. Make two copies of at least five lines of a song lyric, a favorite poem, or even a nursery rhyme. Read the piece aloud. Do the words have a beat or a rhythm? Is it regular? On one copy, put a ´ above the syllable that should be accented in each multisyllable word.

collaboration

2. Give a classmate the second copy of the lines you have been working on. On the paper you receive, use a ´ to mark the syllable that should be accented in each multisyllable word, and then return the passage to your classmate.

collaboration

3. Compare your version of each passage with your classmate's version. Discuss any differences and together decide which answer is correct. Consult a dictionary if necessary.

Words with *ie* or *ei* Combinations

Another challenge for writers is spelling words with *ie* or *ei* combinations correctly. The basic rule, taught to millions of school children each year, is this:

> *I* before *e*
> Except after *c*
> And when sounded like *a*
> As in *neighbor* or *weigh.*

This simple rule offers guidance for spelling many words with *ie* or *ei* combinations. For example, in these common words, *i* comes before *e*:

bel**ie**ve   n**ie**ce   f**ie**ld   ach**ie**ve

But for others of these words, *e* comes before *i* when these letters come after *c*, as in these common words:

rec**ei**ve   conc**ei**ve

Or the *e* comes before the *i* because the two letters together are pronounced like *a:*

eight   v**ei**n

Exceptions   There are a number of exceptions to this rule. *Either, neither, leisure, seize,* and *weird* feature *ei* combinations even though these letters *don't* follow *c*. Also, *species, ancient, glacier, proficient, society,* and *science* contain an *ie* combination even though these letters *do* follow *c*. You should therefore take the time to memorize the spelling of the words with *ie* and *ei* combinations that you use most often.

<table>
<tr><td>COMPREHENSION AND PRACTICE

20.6</td><td>

Words with *ie* or *ei* Combinations

Each of the sentences below contains a word with an *ie* or *ei* combination. Underline each of these words and check the spelling. If the word is spelled incorrectly, cross it out, and write the correct version above it. If the word is spelled correctly, write *OK* after it. Use the example to guide you.

</td></tr>
</table>

EXAMPLE

ancient
When she looked at the ~~ancient~~ artifacts, she felt as if she had slipped back in time.

experience
(1) After my recent ~~expereince~~, I think some people should never be able to get a license to drive. (2) I had just finished some shopping at the mall and
OK
had stopped at the booth in the parking garage to get my receipt. (3) I was
brief
at the booth for only a ~~breif~~ time, but the driver behind me started honking
believe
his horn and yelling out his window. (4) I can't be sure, but I ~~beleive~~ that he
Neither
was no older than seventeen. (5) ~~Niether~~ the attendant nor I could calm this driver down. (6) He finally backed up, squeezed his car around mine, and
piece
roared out of the lot, taking a ~~peice~~ of the gate in front of the exit with him.
OK   weird
(7) I was relieved that he didn't hit my car. (8) The ~~wierd~~ thing is that the attendant recognized the driver, so the police were able to make an arrest in about fifteen minutes.

CHALLENGE 20.4   Recognition and Use of Correctly Spelled Words with *ie* or *ei*

collaboration

Here is a list of words containing *ie* or *ei* combinations. Working with a classmate, check the spelling of each word. If the word is misspelled, write the correct version on the line next to it. If it is correct, write *OK*. Choose five of the words, and on a separate sheet of paper use them correctly in sentences.

cheif	chief	cieling	ceiling
protien	protein	yeild	yield
height	OK	anceint	ancient
acheive	achieve	reciept	receipt
beige	OK	frieght	freight
foriegn	foreign	sufficeint	sufficient

Confusing Endings and Incorrect Forms

Words That End in *-ceed, -cede, -sede*　*Proceed, concede,* and *supersede* are examples of words with endings that sound the same but that are spelled differently. To make sure you always use the correct ending, remember the following:

- Only one word in English ends in *-sede.*

  super**sede**

- Only three words in English end in *-ceed.*

  pro**ceed**　　　　ex**ceed**　　　　suc**ceed**

- All other words with this sound end in *-cede.*

  pre**cede**　　con**cede**　　re**cede**　　inter**cede**

Contractions That Confuse　Often a word's sound can cause difficulty with spelling. The contractions for *would have, could have,* and *should have* are good examples. *Would've, could've,* and *should've* sound like the incorrect forms *would of, could of,* and *should of.* Rather than risk making a mistake, avoid these contractions in your writing.

Also, don't trust your ear when it comes to the common expressions *used to* and *supposed to.* In both cases, the final *-d* is almost silent, so it's easy to write the forms incorrectly: *use to* and *suppose to.* Therefore, even though you might not hear the *-d,* always add it when you write these expressions.

COMPREHENSION AND PRACTICE 20.7 **Confusing Endings and Incorrect Forms**

Correct any incorrect forms or words with incorrect endings in the paragraph below. Cross out the incorrect word, and write the correct one above it. If a sentence contains no error, write *OK* above it. Use the example to guide you.

EXAMPLE　I sat on the sand and watched the tide ~~receed~~. *recede*

(1) Until fairly recently, a significant number of people ~~use~~ *used* to smoke.

(2) Now that extensive research has shown that smoking causes cancer and leads to numerous other health problems, these same people clearly know that they're not ~~suppose~~ *supposed* to smoke. (3) Many middle-aged and elderly smokers would ~~of~~ *have* quit much earlier if they had fully realized the dangers. (4) If they had, they could ~~of~~ *have* added years to their lives. (5) Once studies in the 1960s began to show that smoking ~~was~~ *is* a definite health hazard, the federal government

have
should of considered a complete ban on all tobacco products. (6) Of course, al-

proceed
though they now know how bad smoking is, some people procede with this

have
dangerous habit. (7) My uncle should of quit when the doctor said he was de-

OK
veloping a heart problem. (8) He tried a few times, but he never could suc-

ceed in kicking the habit.

CHALLENGE 20.5 **Words with Confusing Endings**

1. Look up the definitions of the following words in a dictionary, and then write the words and their definitions on a separate sheet of paper.

intercede	precede	concede
supersede	exceed	recede

collaboration

2. Working with a classmate, use each of these words correctly in a sentence.

Commonly Confused Words

ESL Note
See "Spelling," pages 492–494, for more on the correct spelling of commonly confused words.

Homonyms can deceive our ears because these words sound alike but have different spellings and different meanings, such as *threw* and *through*. The following pages provide a list of some homonyms and other commonly confused word pairs and trios.

Commonly Confused Words

Words	Definitions	Examples
accept	to take or receive	The patient wouldn't *accept* any visitors.
except	to leave out; excluding, but	*Except* for his fiancé, he refused to let anyone in.
advice	opinions, suggestions (a noun)	The lawyer gave me sound *advice*.
advise	to give suggestions or guide (a verb)	I asked her to *advise* me of my rights.
affect	to influence, stir emotions (a verb)	Any amount of stress *affects* Paul.
effect	a result, something brought about by a cause (a noun)	The most noticeable *effect* is irritability.
among	within a group	For a minute, the toddler stood *among* her four friends.
between	within two, indicating individual relationships	Then she took a seat *between* two smaller children.

Commonly Confused Words *(continued)*

Words	Definitions	Examples
brake	a device for stopping forward motion; to come to a halt	I jammed on the *brake* when the light changed.
break	to shatter; pause	I hit the windshield, but it didn't *break*.
buy	to purchase	Tim tried to *buy* a ticket to the concert in person.
by	near; no later than; through	Unfortunately, tickets must be ordered *by* mail.
can	be physically able	Once the cast is removed, my sister *can* test her leg.
may	have permission	Then she *may* be able to do more things for herself.
choose	to decide or select (present tense)	I will *choose* my classes more carefully next time.
chose	decided or selected (past tense)	Last semester, I *chose* my classes without enough planning.
conscience	inner sense of right and wrong	My *conscience* still bothers me.
conscious	aware, awake	I'm especially *conscious* of the way I treated my younger brother.
council	a group formally working together	The town *council* rejected the developer's proposal.
counsel	give advice; also, legal representative	The town manager tried to *counsel* against the rejection, but she failed.
desert	(1) to abandon	People began to *desert* the picnic.
	(2) a dry, arid, sandy place	The park was as hot as a *desert*.
dessert	final part of a meal	The picnic *dessert* was untouched.
fewer	refers to items that can be counted	During December, I have *fewer* asthma attacks.
less	refers to amounts or quantities that can't be counted	I also have *less* difficulty with allergies in general.
fine	(1) excellent, very good	Last night, the Houston Rockets finally had a *fine* game.
	(2) money paid as a penalty	Players who failed to hustle faced hefty *fines*.
find	(1) to discover, come upon	This treat seemed to help them *find* the basket consistently.
	(2) something found or discovered	The antique vase was a great *find*.
good	used to describe people, places, things,	Andrea has proven to be a *good* boss.
well	used to describe the performance of some action	When people perform their jobs *well*, she makes a point to acknowledge their work.

(continued)

Commonly Confused Words *(continued)*

Words	Definitions	Examples
hear	to take in sounds by ear	Can you *hear* that noise?
here	in this place, at this point	I think it's coming from right *here*.
hole	an empty spot	A spark burned a *hole* in the carpet.
whole	complete	The *whole* carpet has to be replaced.
its	possessive form of *it*	The mustang broke free from *its* handlers.
it's	contraction for *it is* or *it has*	*It's* dangerous to handle wild animals.
knew	understood (past tense)	I *knew* what that noise meant.
new	recent, not old	I'd have to buy a *new* muffler.
know	to understand (present tense)	Most people *know* how to exercise.
no	negative, the opposite of *yes*	The problem is they have *no* discipline.
lay	to place down, spread out	To complete the assembly, *lay* the desk on its side.
lie	to rest or recline; also, to tell an untruth	As it *lies* on its side, gently tap the casters into the ends of the legs.
lead	(1) to go first, direct (present tense, rhymes with *bead*)	The manager told Brian to *lead* the team to victory.
	(2) soft metal, graphite (rhymes with *bed*)	Brian took the *lead* warm-up ring off his bat.
led	went first, directed (past tense)	He swung and *led* off the inning with a double to center field.
loose	not tight	During the warmer months, I wear *loose* clothing.
lose	misplace; fail, not win	I still sweat and *lose* weight, though.
mine	belonging to me	That old shirt is *mine*.
mind	(1) intellect	(1) Happy memories come to *mind* whenever wear it.
	(2) to object to, be careful of	(2) *Mind* your manners when you eat.
of	stemming from; connected with or to	The best day *of* the vacation was our day at Wet 'n' Wild.
off	away from; no longer on	Riding the steep water slide felt like dropping *off* a cliff.
passed	went beyond or by (past tense)	The speeding car *passed* a police car.
past	time gone by, former time	*Past* experience may not teach speeders to slow down.
precede	to come before	An overture will *precede* the first act.
proceed	to go on	After the play, *proceed* to the cast party.
principal	(1) individual in charge	She hopes to become a middle school *principal*.
	(2) primary	Her *principal* goal is to maintain a positive environment for learning.
principle	guideline, rule, or law	In her view, the most important *principle* for educators is to reinforce the positive.

Commonly Confused Words *(continued)*

Words	Definitions	Examples
quiet	not noisy; solitude	The room was completely *quiet*.
quite	very; really	We were *quite* surprised by the party.
than	used in comparisons	Eddie is a much better runner *than* Billy.
then	next; at that time	Each day, they warm up and *then* they race.
their	possessive form of *they*	The protesters are devoted to *their* cause.
there	that place or position; function word introducing a sentence	*There* were twenty police officers watching from over *there*.
they're	contraction for *they are*	*They're* staying on the picket line all night.
though	despite; however	*Though* they all may fail, they all will try.
thought	idea; process of reasoning	I *thought* hard about his meaning.
threw	tossed, hurled (past tense)	A child *threw* a rock at the passing car.
through	in one side and out the other; from beginning to end	The rock went *through* the driver's window.
to	(1) in the direction of, toward (2) used to form infinitives	She handed the receipt *to* the clerk. The clerk refused *to* give a refund.
too	also; excessively	The receipt was *too* illegible.
two	the whole number between one and three	The warranty had expired *two* months ago.
waist	middle part of the body	David constantly worries abut his expanding *waist*.
waste	use up needlessly; leftover material	If he'd stick with a diet, he wouldn't *waste* so much time worrying.
weak	not strong, feeble	The muscles of the broken arm are *weak*.
week	seven days	Furthermore, even after a *week*, the pain is still strong.
weather	atmospheric conditions	The *weather* this past summer was unusually hot.
whether	indicating alternatives	Winter will come *whether* we like it or not.
were	past tense of *are*	Last week we *were* unable to go see the movie.
we're	contraction for *we are*	*We're* finally going to go tonight, however.

(continued)

Commonly Confused Words *(continued)*

Words	Definitions	Examples
where	Indicates or raises a question about a specific direction or location	The theater is in the mall *where* we met.
wear	have on (clothing)	We usually *wear* casual clothes when we go out.
who's	contraction for *who is* or *who has*	*Who's* supposed to drive the carpool?
whose	possessive form of *who*	I can never remember *whose* turn it is.
your	possessive form of *you*	I left *your* gift in the living room.
you're	contraction for *you are*	I think *you're* really going to like it.

COMPREHENSION AND PRACTICE 20.8

Correct Choices with Commonly Confused Words

Circle the correct word from the pair in parentheses. Refer to the preceding list of commonly confused words, and use the meaning of the sentence to guide you. Use the example as a guide.

EXAMPLE   The taxi driver had to (brake, break) suddenly.

(1) Most of us (know, no) from experience that stress can (lead, led) to (quiet, quite) a lot of frustration. (2) For instance, (your, you're) ready to leave the house (accept, except) you can't find (your, you're) car keys. (3) (Its, It's) in (your, you're) (mind, mine) that you (threw, through) them over (their, there) on the kitchen counter last night. (4) (Weather, Whether) you find them or not is important because (of, off) the job interview facing you in an hour. (5) At this point, you simply want to find your keys, not (hear, here) any (advice, advise) about how not to (loose, lose) things.

COMPREHENSION AND PRACTICE 20.9

Proper Use of Commonly Confused Words

The paragraph below contains a number of commonly confused words used incorrectly. Using the list in this chapter and the meaning of each sentence itself, decide which words are wrong. Cross out the incorrect words, and write correct ones above them. Use the example to guide you.

EXAMPLE   The world record for the mile has proven to be a hard mark to ~~brake~~. *break*

(1) ~~Weather~~ (Whether) they are sports fans or not, people around the world know one name: Tiger Woods. (2) The popularity of this golfer has had a widespread ~~affect~~ (effect) on golf, attracting a ~~hole~~ (whole) new audience for the sport. (3) Tiger ~~choose~~ (chose) to become a professional golfer in the late summer of 1996 after considering the ~~advise~~ (advice) of coaches and family members. (4) Since ~~than~~ (then), he has gone on to win ~~quiet~~ (quite) an impressive number of professional tournaments, including the Masters Championship and the PGA Championship four times each and the British Open and U.S Open three times each. (5) Born in 1975, Tiger, ~~who's~~ (whose) actual name is Eldrick Woods, grew up in California, in a town situated between the ~~dessert~~ (desert) and Los Angeles. (6) Even ~~thought~~ (though) he was only six months old at the time, Tiger made his first ~~brake~~ (break) into golf by watching his father hit golf balls into a net. (7) The ~~affect~~ (effect) on the precocious golfer was demonstrated ~~buy~~ (by) his perfect imitation of his father's swing. (8) When he was five, Tiger hit his first ~~whole~~ (hole) in one, ~~to~~ (too). (9) It took only a few short years for fame to ~~fine~~ (find) Tiger and for this athlete to become widely ~~excepted~~ (accepted) as a genuine golf prodigy. (10) Even after a nine-month absence from the links in 2008 because of leg surgery, Tiger remains one ~~off~~ (of) professional golf's top players, something that his early supporters always ~~new~~ (knew) would happen.

COMPREHENSION
AND PRACTICE
20.10

Correct Use of Commonly Confused Words

On a separate sheet of paper, write ten sentences using each of the following commonly confused words once. Be sure to use each word correctly for the meaning of the sentence. Answers will vary.

1. affect	6. then
2. effect	7. knew
3. your	8. new
4. you're	9. who's
5. than	10. whose

Maintaining a Personal Spelling Dictionary

As noted in Chapter 4 (pp. 89–90), the spell check feature that accompanies most word-processing programs is a valuable tool, but it isn't a foolproof way to avoid spelling errors. Spell checkers can identify *many* spelling mistakes, marking those that don't match the spelling in the software's dictionary and offering alternatives. However, they can't always tell if you are using the wrong homonym or a word that is only similar to the one you want. While you should take full advantage of all the tools your computer software has, you still need to learn the rules—and the exceptions to those rules. This knowledge, coupled with computer tools, will help you master spelling.

You should also develop and maintain *your own spelling dictionary*. Setting up this kind of dictionary is easy, especially if you prepare it as a computer document that you can change:

- Make a list—in alphabetical order—of the words that you know you have trouble spelling, leaving two or three lines between words.
- Whenever you discover that you have misspelled a word in your notes or in a paragraph or essay you have written, add that word to the list, maintaining alphabetical order. If you keep your dictionary on a computer, simply insert the new words, and then print out a new list.
- Review the list frequently, especially as you are completing drafts of a paper, so that you can master the spelling of these words.

In addition to the commonly confused words presented earlier, many—if not most—of the words you have trouble with are probably on the following list of frequently misspelled words. To make this list work for you, read through it, marking the ones that you misspell. Then add them to the list you have already started, and you will be well on your way to having your own complete personal spelling dictionary.

Commonly Misspelled Words

A

absence	acquired	all right	answer	assented
academic	acre	a lot	Antarctic	association
acceptance	across	although	anxious	athlete
accident	actual	aluminum	apologize	attacked
accidentally	actually	always	apparatus	attempt
accommodate	address	amateur	apparent	attendance
accompany	administration	among	appreciate	attorney
accomplish	advertise	amount	approach	authority
accumulate	again	analysis	approval	auxiliary
accurate	agreeable	analyze	argument	available
accustom	aisle	angel	arrival	awful
ache	alcohol	angle	article	awkward
achieve		angry	ascended	
acquaintance		anonymous		

Commonly Misspelled Words *(continued)*

B

bachelor	bathe	believe	boundaries	bureau
balance	beautiful	benefit	breath	bury
bargain	because	biscuits	breathe	business
basically	beginning	bookkeeping	brilliant	
bath	belief	bottom	Britain	

C

cafeteria	cereal	cocoa	committee	convenience
calendar	certain	collect	company	cooperate
campaign	change	colonel	comparative	cooperation
cannot	characteristic	color	competent	corporation
careful	cheap	colossal	competitive	correspondence
careless	chief	column	conceivable	courteous
catastrophe	children	comedy	condition	courtesy
category	church	comfortable	consistent	criticize
ceiling	cigarette	commitment	continuous	curriculum
cemetery	circuit	committed		

D

daily	definitely	diameter	discuss	dominate
daughter	definition	diary	disease	doubt
dealt	dependent	different	disgust	dozen
debt	describe	direction	distance	drowned
deceased	description	disappointment	distinction	duplicate
decision	despair	disastrous	distinguish	
defense	despise	discipline	dominant	

E

earliest	emergency	environment	essential	exhausted
efficiency	emphasis	equip	exaggerated	existence
efficient	emphasize	equipment	excellent	experience
eligible	employee	equipped	excessive	extraordinary
embarrass	envelop	especially	excitable	extremely
embarrassment	envelope			

F

fallacy	February	flery	fourth	fulfill
familiar	feminine	foreign	freight	further
fascinate	fictitious	forty	frequent	futile
fatigue				

G

garden	genuine	gracious	guarantee	guest
gauge	ghost	grammar	guardian	guidance
general	government	grateful	guess	gymnasium
generally				

(continued)

Commonly Misspelled Words *(continued)*

H

handicapped	height	humor	hygiene	hypocrite
handkerchief	hoping	humorous	hypocrisy	

I

illiterate	incidentally	inevitable	intelligence	irresistible
imaginative	incredible	infinite	interest	irreverent
immediately	independent	inquiry	interfere	island
immigrant	indictment	instead	interpret	isle
important				

J

jealousy	jewelry	judgment

K

kitchen	knowledge	knuckles

L

language	leave	lengthen	library	literature
later	legitimate	lesson	license	livelihood
latter	leisure	letter	lieutenant	lounge
laugh	length	liable	lightning	luxury

M

machinery	mathematics	miniature	missile	mortgage
maintain	measure	minimum	misspell	mountain
maintenance	mechanical	minute	mistake	muscle
marriage	medicine	miscellaneous	moderate	mustache
marry	medieval	mischief	month	mutual
marvelous	merchandise	mischievous	morning	mysterious

N

naturally	necessity	nickel	noticeable	nuisance
necessary	negotiate	niece		

O

obedience	occurrence	omit	opportunity	organization
obstacle	official	opinion	oppose	original
occasion	often	opponent	optimism	ought
occurred				

P

pamphlet	peasant	perseverance	picnic	preferred
parallel	peculiar	personality	piece	prejudice
paralyze	perceive	perspiration	pleasant	preparation
parentheses	percentage	persuade	politics	presence
participant	perform	phase	possess	pressure
particularly	performance	phenomenon	possibility	primitive
pastime	permanent	physical	practically	priority
patience	permitted	physician	precisely	privilege

Commonly Misspelled Words *(continued)*

p *(continued)*

probably	professor	psychology	pursuing
procedure	protein	publicity	pursuit

Q

qualified	quantity	quarter	question	questionnaire
quality				

R

readily	recipient	reign	removal	residence
realize	recognize	relevant	renewal	resistance
really	recommendation	relieve	repeat	responsibility
reasonably	reference	remember	repetition	restaurant
receipt	referring	remembrance	requirement	rhythm
receive	regretting	reminisce	reservoir	ridiculous

S

salary	sergeant	specimen	strategy	sufficient
sandwich	severely	statistics	strength	summarize
scenery	similar	statue	stretch	superior
schedule	solemn	stature	subsidize	surprise
scissors	sophisticated	statute	substantial	surprising
secretary	sophomore	stomach	substitute	susceptible
sensible	souvenir	straight	subtle	suspicion
separate				

T

technique	thorough	tournament	transferring	tremendous
temperament	thoroughly	tragedy	travel	truly
temperature	through	traitor	traveled	Tuesday
tendency	tomorrow	transfer	treasure	typical
theory	tongue			

U

unanimous	urgent	useful	utensil

V

vacancy	valuable	vein	villain	visibility
vacuum	vane	vicinity	violence	visitor
vain	vegetable			

W

warrant	Wednesday	weird	writing	written

Y

yesterday

Z

zealous

COMPREHENSION
AND PRACTICE
20.11

Correct Use of Commonly Misspelled Words

1. Here is series of words from the list of Commonly Misspelled Words on pages 392–395. Some of these words are spelled correctly, and some are not. Without consulting the list, evaluate the spelling. If you believe the spelling of a word is correct, write *OK* in the space provided. If you believe the word is incorrectly spelled, cross out the incorrect form and write the correct version in the space.

abcense	absence	although	OK	
cafateria	cafeteria	differant	different	
corespondence	correspondence	disipline	discipline	
commitee	committee	seperate	separate	
exxagerate	exaggerate	Febuary	February	
independant	independent	responsability	responsibility	
scissors	OK	salery	salary	
schedule	OK	imediately	immediately	
Wenesday	Wednesday	requirement	OK	

2. Check the changes you have made against the list of commonly misspelled words. If you have made any mistakes, add these words to your personal spelling list.

CHALLENGE 20.6 **Analyzing Your Methods of Checking for Spelling Errors**

1. How have you proofread for possible spelling errors in writing you have completed up to this point? Write a paragraph of at least seven to ten sentences in which you explain the methods, rules, guidelines, or helpful hints you follow when you proofread.

collaboration

2. Exchange your paragraph with a classmate. Make a note of any part of the process that you have in common. If your classmate's paragraph contains a step that would help you become a better proofreader, add it to the process outlined in your own paragraph.

✓ SPELLING CHECKLIST

☐ Have you checked the endings of the plurals you have used, especially for words ending in *-ch, -sh, -x, -s, -y, -o,* and *-f* or *-fe*?

☐ Have you checked the plural forms of compound nouns, foreign words, irregular nouns, and words that have only one form?

❏ Have you checked the spelling of any words to which a prefix or suffix has been added, especially those that are exceptions to the rules?

❏ Have you evaluated the spelling of words that end in a single consonant preceded by a single vowel to determine whether the final letter should be doubled before adding an ending?

❏ Have you checked the spelling of words with -ie combinations, especially the exceptions, words with confusing endings, and words with confusing contractions?

❏ Have you checked the spelling of any words from the list of commonly confused words to ensure that you've made the correct choice and from the list of commonly misspelled words to make sure you've avoided error?

Journal Writing

Spelling a word correctly is a matter of using the correct combination of letters in the proper order. Change the combination or adjust the order, and the spelling is no longer correct. Combination and order play important roles in other aspects of life. For example, the right combination of players or workers makes a winning team. Change this combination, and suddenly everything can change. Try to play a song without seeing the music ahead of time, and you'll find it a very different experience than if you played it after studying and practicing the piece. Consider some aspect of combination or order, and then explore it for 20 to 30 minutes in your journal.

CHAPTER QUICK CHECK Mastering Spelling

The following passage contains a number of misspelled words and incorrect word choices. Using the guidelines and examples in the chapter and your personal spelling dictionary as a guide, find and cross out the errors. Write the correct version above the incorrect one.

(1) The story of Rubin "Hurricane" Carter is an almost ~~unbeleivable~~ *unbelievable* tale

of injustice. (2) Carter spent twenty years in a maximum security prison, half

of it in solitary confinement, for a triple murder that he hadn't ~~commited~~ *committed*.

(3) In 1966, this contender for the ~~middlewieght~~ *middleweight* boxing crown was arrested

and charged with a triple homicide in Paterson, New Jersey. (4) Despite his un-

wavering assertion of innocence, Carter was convicted and ~~than~~ *then* sentenced to three life terms, just narrowly escaping the electric chair. (5) But by the mid-

their
1970s, the state's two key witnesses against Carter admitted that ~~there~~

testimony was false. (6) This fact, along with the publication of Carter's autobi-

ography and the hit song about the case by folk rocker Bob Dylan, enabled

hear
the world to ~~here~~ about Carter's situation. (7) Finally, after two retrials, a judge

in 1988 declared that Carter's original conviction had been based on shoddy

prejudice   Through
evidence and ~~predjudice~~, and Carter once again tasted freedom. (8) ~~Threw~~

the 2000 release of *Hurricane,* a major motion picture starring Denzel

Washington as Carter, another generation learned the story of this sad inci-

dent in the American justice system. (9) Now in his seventies, Carter works on

traveled
the behalf of the wrongfully accused and has ~~travelled~~ the country lecturing

on hope and tolerance. (10) Despite his years of false imprisonment, he re-

fuses to give in to anger and bitterness, just as he refused to allow the system

break
to ~~brake~~ his spirit.

SUMMARY EXERCISE Mastering Spelling

The following passage contains a number of misspelled words and incorrect word
choices. Using the guidelines and examples in the chapter and your personal
spelling dictionary as a guide, find and cross out the errors. Write the correct version above the incorrect one.

accept   variety
(1) Some children refuse to ~~except~~ other children for a ~~vareity~~ of reasons.

there   whose
(2) As a result, ~~their~~ are many people ~~who's~~ memories of childhood are simply

negative.

friends   believe   they're
(3) Children need to have ~~freinds~~ and to ~~beleive~~ that ~~their~~ liked. (4) When

admitted   abandoned
they are first ~~admited~~ to school, many children may even feel ~~abandonned~~

recede
when their parents leave them at school. (5) Their self-confidence may ~~receed~~

new   friendly
even more if they aren't happy in their ~~knew~~ surroundings. (6) One ~~freindly~~

effect   whole
face can have a positive ~~affect~~ on a child's ~~hole~~ day.

(7) ~~Weather~~ or not children are ~~excepted~~ may depend on ~~there~~ looks or
Whether   *accepted*   *their*

thinner   *than*
mannerisms. (8) For example, some children are ~~thiner~~ or taller ~~then~~ their

noticeable
classmates, and so they are more ~~noticable~~. (9) If students have a speech or

deficiency   *extremely quiet*
hearing ~~deficeincy~~, they may be ~~extremly quite~~ or shy. (10) Children from

learning   *choose*
other cultures who are ~~learnning~~ English often ~~chose~~ to remain silent in class.

whose   *language*
(11) They are afraid that kids ~~who's~~ native ~~langage~~ is English will make fun of

their
~~thier~~ accents.

clothes   *wear*
(12) For other kids, the problem is the ~~cloths~~ they ~~where~~. (13) These chil-

embarrassed   *their*
dren often feel ~~embarased~~ because ~~there~~ clothing comes from discount stores.

Unfortunately their *families*   *too*
(14) ~~Unfotunatly~~, ~~there familys~~ are ~~to~~ poor to purchase the latest styles and fads.

succeed
(15) Of course, some school children ~~succede~~ in spite of these painful

experiences   *they're*   *find* *friend*
~~expereinces~~. (16) Sometimes ~~their~~ lucky enough to ~~fine~~ a ~~freind~~ who is good at

identifying
~~identifing~~ the best in everyone. (17) When my family moved to a new city, I

through   *quite*
went ~~threw~~ some difficulty at school, but I was ~~quiet~~ lucky. (18) Within a

week   *science*   *they're*
~~weak~~, a couple of kids in my ~~sceince~~ class reached out to me, and ~~their~~ still my

though   *buddies*
friends today. (19) On most days, just the ~~though~~ of the fun my school ~~buddys~~

hoping
and I had makes me smile. (20) I am ~~hopeing~~ that when I have children, they

choose
will ~~chose~~ to reach out to others.

FOR FURTHER EXPLORATION

1. Choose one of the following subjects and use your preferred prewriting method to develop a specific focus and supporting ideas.

   - Your definition of common sense
   - A time you witnessed an argument or confrontation about something that you found to be silly or insignificant
   - Ways that a lack of logic or poor planning can complicate one's life

2. Evaluate your prewriting material, identify a focus, and create a draft paragraph of at least seven to ten sentences.

3. Exchange your draft with a writing partner. Using the material in this chapter as a guide, evaluate the draft you receive. Note any problems with spelling as well as any other weaknesses, and return the draft to the writer.

collaboration

4. Revise your draft, eliminating any errors that your reader identified.

DISCOVERING CONNECTIONS

For this assignment, think about this photo and one of the following questions (or another it suggests). After exploring your ideas on this topic, create a draft paragraph of at least seven to ten sentences. Check your spelling carefully, especially your plurals and commonly confused and misspelled words.

A. Habitat for Humanity is a volunteer organization dedicated to building affordable housing for those in need. How do you feel about such an organization? Have you ever volunteered for such an organization before? Describe your experience.

B. Homelessness is a pervasive problem in the United States and throughout the world. Describe the homeless situation in your city and town. Do you think enough is being done to help the homeless where you live? What policies would you propose to help alleviate or eliminate homelessness?

RECAP Mastering Spelling

Key Terms in This Chapter	Definitions
prefix	the letter or letters added to the beginning of a word that change its meaning: *un-, dis-, semi-, re-, il-, ex-*
	EXAMPLE **un**able, **re**run
suffix	the letter or letters added to the end of a word that change its meaning: *-ness, -able, -ous, -ly, -er, -ed, -ing*
	EXAMPLE sad**ness**, danger**ous**

Spelling Guidelines for Adding Prefixes and Suffixes

Check the dictionary for exceptions to these general guidelines.	
To add a prefix	prefix + word (no spelling change)
	dis + agree = **dis**agree
To add *-ly* or *-ness*	word + *-ly* or *-ness* (usually no spelling change)
	mean + ness = mean**ness**
	change *-y* to *-i* before adding *-ly* or *-ness*
	happy + ness = happ**iness**

To add -*ed*	change -*y* to -*i* before adding -*ed*
	worry + ed = worr**ied**
To add a suffix that begins with a vowel	drop -*e* at the end of a word before adding the suffix
	hope + ing = hop**ing**
	double the final consonant if
	• the word has one syllable
	plan + ed = plan**ned**
	• the accent is on the last syllable of a word with two or more syllables
	begin + ing = begin**ning**
	• the final consonant is preceded by a single vowel
	fat + est = fat**test**
To add a suffix that begins with a consonant	keep -*e* at the end of the word
	safe + ty = safe**ty**

Using Discovery Online with MyWritingLab

For more practice with spelling, go to www.mywritinglab.com.

CHAPTER 21
Using Commas

GETTING STARTED ...

Q Of all the punctuation marks I use, I feel the least confident about the comma. Why is comma use so hard? What's the best way to make sure I include commas when I'm supposed to and do not when they aren't needed?

A Commas represent pauses. In speech, we pause in the middle of saying something for a number of reasons—to take a breath, to emphasize some point, even to figure out what to say next. These pauses in speech are not always easy to detect in writing, which makes deciding when to use a comma tricky. Sometimes no comma is needed because no pausing or slowing down is called for or needed. The good news here is that comma use falls into seven main categories. If the comma you're contemplating using doesn't fit into one of these seven categories, you probably don't need it.

Overview: When Commas Are Needed

When you speak, you include brief, natural pauses within your sentences to make your meaning clear. In writing, you use punctuation to indicate those pauses. Of the three pausing punctuation marks, the **comma** is the one you'll use most frequently. It is also the most troublesome one because it serves so many different purposes, making it difficult sometimes to determine when and where to use commas. It makes sense, then, to focus on the specific instances when commas are needed.

Navigating This Chapter In this chapter you will learn:

- seven functions of commas
- guidelines to determine when a comma is needed
- guidelines to help you decide where to place commas

Comma Function 1

ELS Note
See "Punctuation and Capitalization," pages 494–496, for more on this aspect of comma use.

To indicate a pause between two simple sentences connected by a coordinating conjunction

As Chapter 9, "Coordination," showed, one way to combine two simple sentences is to link them using a comma and coordinating conjunction such as *and* or *but*. The conjunction provides the connection, and the comma provides the necessary pause between the clauses, as these examples show:

EXAMPLES
Those sunglasses are attractive, but they are too expensive.

The back door flew open, and four huskies raced out.

Commas and Coordinating Conjunctions

Read the following sentences, and place a comma where needed to indicate a pause between clauses joined by a coordinating conjunction. Use the example to guide you.

EXAMPLE
Michael and his twin sister both took the class, but she was the only one who passed.

(1) Many health care professionals in the United States are studying the effects of a sedentary lifestyle on children, and most are deeply concerned about their findings. (2) Levels of obesity among elementary school children is at an all-time high, but the public seems relatively unconcerned about this finding. (3) According to one theory, children are spending increasingly longer periods in front of the television or computer, for they find these two devices simply irresistible. (4) According to another theory, children are eating more prepared and fast foods, and portion sizes are larger than ever before. (5) Researchers may not agree on the primary cause of the problem, but they all agree with the need to encourage lifestyle changes among the very young.

Compound Sentence Completion

In the space provided, complete the following compound sentences by adding a comma, a coordinating conjunction (*and, but, yet, nor, so, or*), and an independent clause. Remember that the clause you add must be a complete thought with a subject and verb. Use the example as a guide. Answers will vary.

EXAMPLE
After the holidays, I discovered to my regret that I had lost my ATM card
_____, so I immediately called my bank_____.

1. The amount of violence in the media today has many people upset

_____.

2. Violence in the media is often blamed for violent crimes _____

_____.

3. Sociologists and psychologists are studying the effects of violent media on the

    human brain _____ .

4. An increasing number of these studies have focused on the effects of violent

    programming on children _____ .

5. With violent crimes committed by children on the rise, violent TV shows,

    movies, and video games have often been blamed _____

    _____ .

6. Some young offenders blame their actions on violence in the media _____

    _____ .

7. Recent attention to this link between violent media and violent crime has in-

    spired laws designed to limit violence in the media _____

    _____ .

8. In the view of some people, all violence should be banned from the media

    _____ .

Comma Function 2

ESL Note
See "Punctuation and
Capitalization," pages
494–496, for more on
this aspect of comma
use.

To separate items in a series

Commas also indicate the natural pauses in your speech when you are listing more than two items. The series of items may consist of words, phrases, or even clauses. Look at these examples, and say them out loud:

EXAMPLES

Georgie bought paint, tape, rollers, and brushes.

Jack's eighty-year-old grandfather still drives his truck, plays the piano, and walks five miles every day.

In the first sentence, the commas are needed to separate the various one-word items Georgie purchased. In the second, the commas separate phrases that describe the activities of Jack's elderly grandfather. Without the commas, the sentence would not be understandable.

If you have only two items in a series, however, don't use a comma. Just use the conjunctions *and, or,* or *but* to connect the items.

EXAMPLES Liz enjoys dancing *and* singing.

Please bring canned goods *or* cleaning supplies to the food bank.

COMPREHENSION
AND PRACTICE

Commas in a Series

21.3 In the following sentences, fill in the banks with items to complete the series. Each item may consist of more than one word. If you see three blanks, provide three items and the commas needed to separate them. If you see only two blanks, provide only the two items—no commas are needed. Use the example as a guide.
Answers will vary.

EXAMPLE At the end of the month, I have a number of bills to pay, including

_____ my rent, _____ _____ credit card charges, _____ and

_____ tuition bill _____ .

(1) Before leaving on vacation, my wife and I always have a lot to do, for

example _____ _____

and _____ . (2) If it's a summer vacation, we

pack _____ _____ and

_____ . (3) The two youngest kids always insist on

bringing along more than they need, including _____

and _____ . (4) My wife gathers her supply of maps

of _____ _____ and

_____ . (5) Of course, I have to clean out the stockpile

of junk in the car, and I always find things like _____

_____ and _____ .

(6) Our teenage daughter insists on packing all of her beauty products, such as

_____ _____ and

_____ . (7) Our twelve-year-old son, on the

other hand, has to be pushed to pack some bare essentials like

_____ _____ and

_____ . (8) Winter trips can be even more

complicated, especially around the holidays, because we have to pack gifts

for _____ _____ and

_____.

Comma Function 3

To separate an introductory phrase from the rest of the sentence

Sometimes a sentence begins with an introductory phrase that describes a time, place, or condition. If that phrase is four or more words long, separate it from the rest of the sentence with a comma as these examples show:

EXAMPLES

At the entrance to the mall, several people were handing out Earth Day flyers.

Within the shelter of the old barn, Katie and Madison waited for the storm to end.

In each case, the introductory phrase consists of more than four words, so a comma is needed between the phrase and the rest of the sentence.

For introductory phrases of fewer than four words, you need to look at the sentence, read it out loud, and ask yourself this question: *Would the meaning of my sentence be clearer with a comma?* If the answer is yes, always include the comma.

Look at the two sentences below, and read them out loud. Do they need commas?

CLEAR   After supper Kathy and John dropped by.

CONFUSING   Overall workers at the factory performed better in the redesigned production area.

The first sentence is clear without any comma between the introductory phrase *After supper* and the rest of the sentence. But the second sentence is confusing because the word *overall* has two possible meanings. It can mean "taken as a whole" or "covering all jobs within the workplace." A comma makes it clear that *overall* here means "taken as a whole."

CLEAR   *Overall,* workers at the factory performed better in the redesigned production area.

COMPREHENSION
AND PRACTICE

21.4

Commas after Introductory Phrases

Place commas where they are needed in the following sentences to separate introductory phrases from the rest of the sentence. If a sentence is correct, write *OK* above it. Use the example as a guide.

EXAMPLE | In my extended family, twins are fairly common.

(1) Month after month and year after year, my city keeps growing. (2) For most of the city's population that increasing size means a faster pace of life and more stress.(3) By evening most city dwellers are more than ready to enter the familiar cocoon of their neighborhoods. (4) With a stable and welcoming environment, your own block gives you a place to belong and to be safe. (5) As a result of a huge buildup of industry, some neighborhoods in my city are becoming less desirable.(6) In some places the streets are growing noisier and dirtier. (7) Without motivation to stay, many families are moving to the quieter and cleaner suburbs. (8) Referred to as urban flight, this phenomenon has definitely contributed to an economic decline in my city.

Comma Function 4

To set off an introductory subordinate clause

As Chapter 8, "Subordination," showed, a subordinate clause may be joined to a main clause to indicate the relationship between the two thoughts. If the subordinate clause comes *first* in the sentence, set it off with a comma.

EXAMPLE | *Until I actually saw Mount Rushmore,* I couldn't understand what all the fuss was about.

The subordinate clause *Until I actually saw Mount Rushmore* sets the reader up for the surprise the writer implies in the main clause. The comma indicates the necessary pause between the two clauses.

When the subordinate clause follows the main clause, however, no comma is needed:

EXAMPLE | We didn't mention the lost necklace *until we had found it again.*

COMPREHENSION AND PRACTICE

Commas with Introductory Subordinate Clauses

21.5 In the following paragraph, find the subordinate clauses. Set off each introductory subordinate clause with a comma. If a sentence needs no comma added, write *OK* above it. Use the example to guide you.

EXAMPLE | When people have limited financial resources, they have to make sacrifices.

(1) As community colleges have grown⌄they have continued to serve many functions. (2) Because so many communities now have community colleges⌄more students across the United States have a far less expensive alternative to a four-year college or university education. (3) Community colleges [OK] specialize in addressing the needs of students who have not been part of the academic mainstream. (4) While they pursue courses in their major⌄students can also take basic courses to bring them up to speed in math and composition. (5) Although community colleges generally have open-door admissions policies⌄they still have rigorous academic standards. [OK] (6) Regardless of their backgrounds, students are expected to meet these standards. (7) If students want to succeed in the classroom⌄they must be diligent and committed. (8) Even though community colleges are primarily teaching institutions⌄many instructors are also accomplished scholars in their academic or professional fields.

Comma Function 5

ESL Note
See "Punctuation and Capitalization," pages 494–496, for more on this aspect of comma use.

To set off word groups that would otherwise interrupt the flow of the sentence

Sometimes a word, phrase, or clause within a sentence describes something just named or emphasizes a thought or action. When these additions interrupt the main flow of the action in the sentence, they require pauses. Use commas *before* and *after* these interrupters to set them off from the rest of the sentence.

Take a look at this sentence:

EXAMPLE

The L.A. Shuffle, which is the fifth action film of the summer, has already made $70 million.

Here, the clause *which is the fifth action film of the summer* describes the subject of the sentence: *The L.A. Shuffle.* At the same time, this clause separates the subject from the verb phrase that shows what the subject did. Because it interrupts the flow of the action in the sentence, the words are set off by commas before and after.

Consider this sentence:

EXAMPLE

The biggest reason to promote sex education, *however,* is threat of STDs.

In this example, the word *however* interrupts the main thought of the sentence. It falls into a category called *parenthetical expressions,* or side remarks, that are injected into a sentence to qualify or emphasize the idea. Other examples include *nevertheless, in my opinion, by the way, in fact,* and *as a matter of fact.* Because they interrupt sentence flow, parenthetical expressions need to be set off by commas.

Now take a look at this sentence:

EXAMPLE

The utility shed, *a rickety building behind our apartment complex,* is infested with rats.

Here an *appositive phrase* interrupts the flow of the sentence. An appositive phrase renames a noun or pronoun in a sentence, in this case, *shed.* In almost all cases, appositive phrases should be set off by commas, as this example shows. (See Chapter 7, "Sentence Fragments," for a more complete discussion of appositives.)

Finally, consider this sentence:

EXAMPLE

I called to tell you, *Andrea,* that your dress is ready.

The example illustrates a kind of interrupter called a *noun of direct address,* in which the person being spoken to is also identified by name. A noun of direct address, such as *Andrea* in this sentence, is set off by commas.

Of course, all these types of interrupters may also appear at the beginning or the end of a sentence. When an interrupter begins a sentence, place a comma after it, and when one ends a sentence, place a comma before it, as these examples show:

EXAMPLES

In my opinion, the food processor is a great invention.

My in-laws won a cruise, *a dream vacation in the Caribbean.*

COMPREHENSION
AND PRACTICE
21.6

Words, Phrases, or Clauses That Interrupt Sentence Flow

In the sentences below, insert commas where they are necessary. If a sentence is punctuated correctly, write *OK* above it. Use the example as a guide.

EXAMPLE

The weather over the last month, rain almost every day, has hurt the tourist industry badly.

(1) Stand-up comedians, people who voluntarily try to make a bunch of strangers laugh, have one of the most stressful jobs in the world. (2) Even airline pilots, with the heavy responsibility they carry, get some "downtime" while they work. (3) Comedians, however, have to be "on" every second. (4) They have to have perfect timing, an instinctive sense of when to throw in the punch line, in order to succeed. (5) Fortunately, club audiences, most of whom are already in a good mood, can be easy to please. (6) Every now and then,

comedians, especially before they have become established, have to deal with a hostile audience. (7) Heckling, which seems to get nastier as the evening progresses, is enough to drive newcomers out of the business. (8) Those who hang in there and profit from their mistakes, however, often become sought-after headliners.

Comma Function 6

To set off a direct quotation from the rest of the sentence

Writers use quotation marks to show when they are using someone else's exact words. The quote, and therefore the quotation marks, can appear at the beginning, at the end, or in the middle of a sentence. It all depends on where you place the *attribution,* the part that identifies the speaker.

If the attribution comes at the beginning of the sentence, place a comma *after* it, as this example shows:

EXAMPLE *Woody said,* "This argument is pretty silly."
┌─ attribution ─┐

If the attribution comes at the end of the sentence, place the comma *at the end of the quotation,* within the closing quotation mark, as this version shows:

EXAMPLE "This argument is pretty silly," *Woody said.*
┌─ attribution ─┐

If the attribution appears in the middle of the quotation, place one comma *within the first closing quotation mark* and a second comma *after the attribution,* as this version shows:

EXAMPLE "This argument," *Woody said,* "is pretty silly."
┌─ attribution ─┐

Note that in all three locations, the quotation begins with a capital letter and is surrounded by quotation marks. See page 424 for further discussion about quotation marks.

COMPREHENSION AND PRACTICE

Commas with Quotation Marks

21.7 In each sentence below, underline the attribution. Place commas where they are needed to help separate the attribution from the exact words of the speaker. Use the example to guide you.

EXAMPLE "I have a terrible headache," I complained.

(1) "I'm going to quit smoking this year," Joe said yesterday. (2) He looked serious as he declared, "I'm going to take one day at a time, but I'm determined to make it work this time."

(3) "The nicotine patch has helped plenty of smokers," I told him. (4) "Maybe using that would help you, too," I said, "or chewing nicotine gum."

(5) Joe smiled and said, "Thanks for the suggestions—and your support."

Comma Use in Quotations

Write two alternative sentences for each quotation below by moving the attribution to other locations in the sentence. Be careful to punctuate your sentences correctly. Use the example as a guide.

EXAMPLE

The little girl sobbed, "I lost it, but I don't know where."

a. "I lost it," the little girl sobbed, "but I don't know where."

b. "I lost it, but I don't know where," the little girl sobbed.

1. "You do that one more time," the mother warned, "and you'll be sent to your room."

   The mother warned, "You do that one more time, and you'll be sent to your room."

   "You do that one more time, and you'll be sent to your room," the mother warned.

2. "I hate it when I can't find my keys," she said irritably.

   She said irritably, "I hate it when I can't find my keys."

   "I hate it," she said irritably, "when I can't find my keys."

3. He shouted above the clamor, "Ladies and gentlemen, please remain calm!"

   "Ladies and gentlemen, please remain calm!" he shouted above the clamor.

   "Ladies and gentlemen," he shouted above the clamor, "please remain calm!"

_____

_____

4. "You can do it if you just try a little harder," she encouraged.

   She encouraged, "You can do it if you just try a little harder."

   "You can do it," she encouraged, "if you just try a little harder."

_____

_____

5. "There are no seats left for this showing," the manager explained, "but we can sell you advance tickets for the 9 o'clock show."

   The manager explained, "There are no seats left for this showing, but we can sell you

   advance tickets for the 9 o'clock show."

   "There are no seats left for this showing, but we can sell you advance tickets for the 9

   o'clock show," the manager explained.

Comma Function 7

To punctuate dates and addresses

Commas are also used to separate items in dates and addresses. In the example below, note that commas separate the parts of the date and follow the last item in the date:

EXAMPLE On Friday, June 30, 1915, my great-grandfather arrived in America.

Commas also separate the items in an address or multiple-part place-name, as this example shows:

EXAMPLE Eventually, his father moved the family to 692 Whipple Street, River City, Maryland.

No comma is placed before the zip code in an address, as this sentence shows:

EXAMPLE Our address has changed to Route 79, Thaxton, Virginia 24174.

Finally, if a single element of an address or part of a date is preceded by a preposition, then no comma is needed, as this example illustrates:

EXAMPLE   The sales manager drives to Fort Wayne on Wednesday.

COMPREHENSION
AND PRACTICE
   21.9

Commas in Dates and Addresses

Insert commas where they are needed to set off dates and addresses in the following sentences. Use the example to guide you.

EXAMPLE   Our first date was on March 13, 2003, in Elberton, Georgia.

(1) We would like to invite you to our parents' 50th wedding anniversary on Saturday, April 16, 2011, at 2 P.M. (2) They will renew their wedding vows in front of family and friends at the Hawthorne Chapel, 2575 South Wells Avenue, St. Paul, Minnesota. (3) You are cordially invited to a reception to be held afterward at the home of Sharon and Keith Balster, 1977 Tallchief Drive, Shakopee, Minnesota. (4) We would appreciate a response, addressed to Ms. Rebecca Brauer, P. O. Box 550, Tempe, Arizona 41342, by January 15, 2011, so that we can plan appropriately. (5) In place of gifts, we ask that you write a brief passage about your friendship with Edith and Roy during their years in Tempe, Arizona, and Minneapolis, Minnesoa, which we will include in a memory book for them.

COMPREHENSION
AND PRACTICE
   21.10

Multiple Comma Use with Dates and Addresses

Correct the punctuation in the following sentences. If commas are needed, insert them. If commas are used incorrectly, cross them out. Use the example as a guide.

EXAMPLE   My aunt and uncle opened a small bakery sometime in July, or early August, in St. Louis, Missouri.

(1) While my best friend was spending his summer on a construction crew, I was biking through the Midwestern, states, marveling at the sights. (2) I suppose he never got the postcards I sent him at 405A, Ninth Street, Ada, Ohio, 45810. (3) It amazed me how many Midwestern towns borrowed their names from glamorous cities, like Geneva, Illinois, and Paris, Missouri. (4) River, towns along

the Mississippi, for example, Camanche, Iowa, and Prairie du Chien, Wisconsin, have an old-fashioned, feel. (5) By Wednesday, August 10, I had covered 500 miles, of my 650-mile journey.

CHALLENGE 21.1 **Analysis of Comma Functions in a Paragraph by a Professional Writer**

collaboration

collaboration

1. Choose a passage of 150 to 200 words from one of your textbooks or a magazine, newspaper, or online essay. Copy it over on a separate sheet of paper, but don't include any of the commas the original contains.

2. Exchange your passage with a classmate. On the paper you receive, insert commas where they are needed, using the guidelines in this chapter to guide you. Then return the paper to your classmate.

3. Referring to the original passage for accuracy, check the commas your classmate has added. Circle any errors and, working with your classmate, review the comma functions involved.

✓ USING COMMAS CHECKLIST

☐ Have you used a comma following the conjunction joining two simple sentences to indicate the needed pause?

☐ Have you used a comma to separate items in a series and to set off an introductory passage of four or more words at the beginning of a sentence?

☐ Have you used a comma to set off an introductory subordinate clause introduced by a subordinating conjunction?

☐ Have you used a comma *before* and *after* any word or group of words interrupting the flow of a sentence?

☐ Have you used a comma to set off a direct quotation from the rest of a sentence?

☐ Have you used commas to separate the elements in dates and addresses appearing in the middle of a sentence, including one after the last element?

Journal Writing

Commas perform several functions. If you reduce them to one primary purpose, you could say that they keep things *separated* within a sentence. In terms of life in general, *separated* doesn't carry much of a positive connotation. It suggests people or things that are kept apart or divided in some way. However, the word doesn't necessarily mean something negative. For example, some synonyms for *separate* are *independent, distinct,* and *individual.* Consider one meaning for *separate*—positive or negative—and think of it in terms of something you have read about, experienced, or witnessed. Then explore it for 20 to 30 minutes in your journal.

CHAPTER QUICK CHECK   Using Commas

Commas are missing from the following passage. Review the seven functions of commas, and then proofread the passage and add the necessary commas.

(1) Except for a select group of scholars, most people have never had the chance to examine priceless illustrated manuscripts, all created before the invention of the printing press. (2) Only a relatively small number of these manuscripts exist, and age makes them highly fragile, so most are kept locked away, often under climate-controlled conditions. (3) Unlike the researchers involved in this specialized field, most people have seen only illustrations or copies of these beautiful documents in textbooks, museums, or specialized journals. (4) A software system, *Turning the Pages*, which is owned by the British Library, is changing this, however. (5) Although users don't actually touch or turn these electronic pages, they can virtually handle, touch, and turn them by running a finger across the page pictured on the screen, causing the page to flip to the next page. (6) As with a real page, the virtual page reacts if the user stops short of the end of the page, and it slips back to the original position. (7) The image on the screen is an exact digital image of the original page, so it includes colorful paintings of birds, biblical scenes, and everyday medieval life. (8) The software has some special features, including audio clips, all of which the creators of the original manuscripts could never possibly have imagined. (9) For example, because the entire page has been digitized, a touch of the screen at any point enlarges words, icons, or images, which means the viewer can study them in close detail as well. (10) Since the introduction of *Turning the Pages* in 2004 and then *Turning the Pages 2.0* in 2007, a wide variety of texts have been recorded in this way, including a fifth-century Buddhist work, a collection of Leonardo da Vinci's drawings, poet William Blake's notebooks, and Mozart's musical diary.

SUMMARY EXERCISE   Using Commas

Commas are missing from the following passage. Review the seven functions of commas, and then proofread the passage and add the necessary commas.

(1) In my neighborhood, which extends over two city blocks, we have both helpful and annoying neighbors. (2) Everyone gets along well, however, because we all have learned to accept each other as we are.

(3) Lionel, Marilyn, and their two sons are kind and helpful neighbors. (4) When it snows, for example, Lionel and his boys are the first ones outside shoveling out the walkways, cars, and parking spaces of the people on their street. (5) The other neighbors, some of whom are elderly, sick, or disabled, truly appreciate their kindness. (6) On one occasion that I recall, Marilyn brought me homemade vegetable soup when I had the flu. (7) On a fairly regular basis, she invites neighbors for dinner, and she always brings us extra tomatoes, peppers, and cucumbers from her garden. (8) The boys, who are named Dominique and Gerald, love to play basketball and street hockey. (9) About a year and a half ago, they broke my car window, but they told me about the accident, apologized, and paid to replace it themselves.

(10) Across the street, though, we have other neighbors who can be annoying, even if they don't mean to be. (11) Each morning before 7, I wake up hearing the father, Eric, yelling and whistling for his dog to come in. (12) When I asked him why he had to make so much noise so early, he just said, "Because I have to go to work, Laura, and get the dog in before I leave." (13) To keep peace in the neighborhood, I put up with this early alarm clock, but I'm not happy about it. (14) At least on the weekends and during Eric's vacation, I can sleep without this unwelcome interruption.

(15) Sometimes late at night, Eric's daughter, Rose, plays her guitar, an electric one with an amplifier, very loudly. (16) As she tries to imitate Jimi Hendrix, Carlos Santana, and Eddie Van Halen, I just can't fall asleep. (17) I don't complain too much, however, because Rose entertains us with her music at our summer block parties, and her performances are the most popular among the neighbors.

(18) From time to time‸I probably annoy my neighbors as much as they annoy me‸so I try to be patient. (19) In addition to my personal loudness‸ my family also occasionally engages in a passionate argument‸hosts a raucous party‸or plays the television at top volume. (20) Unless neighbors look for the best in each other‸they won't get along at all‸and the neighborhood will become a far less attractive place to live.

FOR FURTHER EXPLORATION

1. Select one of the following subjects, and, using your preferred prewriting method, develop a specific focus and supporting ideas.

   - What qualifies as hard work to you
   - How you would fare if you had to face a world without the technological advances you now depend on
   - A childhood fear or belief that you now find amusing

2. Evaluate your prewriting material, identify a focus, and create a draft paragraph of at least seven to ten sentences.

collaboration

3. Exchange your draft with a writing partner. Using the material in this chapter as a guide, evaluate the draft you receive. Note any mistakes in the use of commas. Check for any other weaknesses, and then return the draft to the writer.

4. Revise your draft, eliminating any errors that your reader identified.

DISCOVERING CONNECTIONS

For this assignment, think about this picture and one of the following questions (or another the photo suggests). Then, after exploring your ideas on this topic, create a draft paragraph of at least seven to ten sentences. Think carefully about each pause in your writing, making sure to avoid mistakes in comma usage.

A. Have you ever thought of a career in writing? What types of writing professions intrigue you? Why? If not, what is it about writing that makes you hesitant about a career in which writing plays a major role?

B. How often do you write in a day? Before you answer this question, think carefully about all the different types of writing you do in your everyday life: e-mailing, text messaging, blogging, Twittering, posting on Facebook. How are these writing tasks different from the other types of writing you complete for your classes?

RECAP Using Commas

Key Term in This Chapter	Definition
comma	a punctuation mark that indicates a pause within a sentence

Seven Comma Functions

to indicate a pause between two simple sentences connected by a coordinating conjunction

> **EXAMPLE**   I bought new shoes, but they don't fit.

to separate the items in a series

> **EXAMPLE**   Math, chemistry, and anatomy are required courses in my major field.

to separate an introductory phrase from the rest of the sentence

> **EXAMPLE**   In almost every North American home, a TV blares for hours a day.

to set off an introductory subordinate clause

> **EXAMPLE**   Before I pay this bill, I want an itemized list of expenses.

to set off word groups that would otherwise interrupt the flow of the sentence

> **EXAMPLE**   These shoes, which I bought on sale, don't fit.

to set off a direct quotation from the rest of the sentence

> **EXAMPLE**   "That book," said Luis, "was made into a movie."

to punctuate dates and addresses

> **EXAMPLE**   The wedding will be held on Saturday, August 10, in Kansas City, Missouri.

Using Discovery Online with MyWritingLab

For more practice with commas, go to www.mywritinglab.com.

CHAPTER 22
Using Punctuation Properly

GETTING STARTED ...

 Q I would like to be more confident about choosing the right punctuation mark for a particular situation, especially with end punctuation, semicolons, and colons. I also really have trouble with the apostrophe in *it's* and *its*. Is there a fast way to stop confusing these two words?

 A Yes, working with punctuation marks can occasionally be confusing. Here's the secret: how do the marks *function*? Do they signal an ending, a connection, a pause, or ownership? Once you identify the function, you can determine the mark that performs that function. And when trying to eliminate your confusion with *its* and *it's*, slow down. As soon as you write either version, stop and substitute *it is* or *it has* in the sentence. If the sentence makes sense with *it is* or *it has,* then use *it's*. If not, use *its*.

Overview: The Role of Punctuation

Listen to any conversation around you. You can hear people start, pause, and change the tone and pitch of their voices as they tell their stories. In writing, **punctuation**—the system of symbols that substitutes for all these starts, stops, and changes—clarifies your message for your reader. Mastering punctuation will enable you to avoid writing sentences that are confusing or ambiguous.

Navigating This Chapter This chapter helps you discover how to use punctuation effectively and correctly in your writing. You will learn how to use:

- periods, question marks, and exclamation points, which signal the end of a thought
- colons and semicolons, which indicate a pause within a thought
- quotation marks, which indicate a person's exact words
- apostrophes, which indicate ownership or take the place of letters left out in contractions

Periods, Question Marks, and Exclamation Points

ESL Note
See "Punctuation and Capitalization," pages 494–496, for more on the proper use of end punctuation.

To indicate the end of a thought, use one of three punctuation marks. When a sentence makes a statement (rather than asks a question or makes an exclamation), use a **period** to indicate a stop in the flow of words. Most of the sentences you write call for a period. Look at these examples:

EXAMPLES

The audience at the theater laughed loudly at the movie.

Carol speaks three languages.

Periods also serve other purposes in writing. For example, a period is used to separate dollars and cents in monetary amounts: $79.56. A period is also used with many abbreviations and most initials:

Mr. (Mister)	etc. (et cetera)	P.M. (post meridian)
Dr. (Doctor)	D. H. Lawrence	M.D. (medical doctor)
Lt. (Lieutenant)	W. H. Auden	Ave. (Avenue)

When a sentence expresses a question directly, use a **question mark**:

EXAMPLES

When will the party start?

Why did Erick choose to major in accounting?

But if the question is *indirect,* don't use a question mark. An indirect question is *embedded* within a statement and so requires a period.

EXAMPLES

Doug asked when the party would start.

I wondered why Erick chose to major in accounting.

When a sentence expresses strong excitement or emotion, use an **exclamation point**:

EXAMPLES

Don't touch that wire!

The truck driver had just seriously injured another driver, and all he could think about was his insurance rates!

One danger with exclamation points is the temptation to overuse them. Don't rely on exclamation points to spice up your writing. Instead, reserve them for those few occasions when you need to demonstrate profound excitement or emotion.

COMPREHENSION **Use of End Punctuation**
AND PRACTICE
22.1 Place the appropriate punctuation mark at the end of each of the following sentences. Use the example to guide you.

EXAMPLE

When are you going to the laundromat __?__

    (1) Do you know that the tradition of sending manufactured Christmas cards is over 135 years old __?__ (2) Louis Prang, who had a business in Boston, printed cards from 1875 until 1890 __.__ (3) Early Christmas card decorations included flower designs and arrangements, and today a number of Internet sites allow you to send beautiful and entertaining e-cards __.__ (4) Some of my friends do not believe that a simple thing like sending an e-card is worth the time and trouble __.__ (5) However, I love sending and receiving holiday greetings __!__

**COMPREHENSION
AND PRACTICE**

Errors in End Punctuation

22.2   The following paragraph contains errors in the use of the period, question mark, and exclamation point. Cross out the incorrect punctuation marks, and write the correct ones in the space above. If a sentence is punctuated correctly, mark *OK* above its end mark. Use the example as a guide.

EXAMPLE

Where did the family move¿ᵖ

    (1) Anyone who has spent time with an infant knows that the care of new-born babies is demanding work! (2) For one thing, babies need to eat a lot more frequently than older children and adults. (3) You might ask why this is so? (4) The reason is that a baby's stomach can hold only small amounts of milk at a time! (5) Babies become hungry very quickly, and when they do, watch out¡ (6) How is it possible for such a tiny person to make so much noise¿ (7) The pressure becomes even more difficult if the baby gets sick. (8) You don't have to be a pediatrician to figure out that something is wrong!

CHALLENGE 22.1   Correct End Punctuation

1. Choose a paragraph of at least seven to ten sentences from one of your text-books or one of your own paragraphs. Copy these sentences on a separate sheet of paper, but omit the punctuation at the end of each sentence.

2. Exchange sentences with a classmate. On the paper you receive, add the appropriate end punctuation marks, and return the paper to your classmate.

collaboration

3. Evaluate the end punctuation your classmate has added, and, after comparing this version with the original, make any necessary corrections.

Colons and Semicolons

In some instances, you need to indicate a pause *within* a sentence. In many of these cases, you rely on **colons** and **semicolons.**

When you want to signal readers about the importance of information coming up, use a colon. The material *before* the colon should be able to stand on its own as a sentence, preparing the reader for the material following the colon.

The material after the colon may be an explanation, an announcement or a list. Look at these examples:

EXAMPLES

The reason for Doreen's strange behavior was suddenly clear: she had lost her job days earlier.

So far, I've chosen three courses for next semester: Graphic Design 100, American civilization, and business mathematics.

In the first example, the colon introduces an explanation. In the second example, the colon introduces a list.

As Chapter 9, "Coordination," and Chapter 10, "Comma Splices and Run-On Sentences," explained, a semicolon has the same power to connect as a coordinating conjunction and a comma. Because this mark of pausing punctuation calls attention to the connection between subject–verb units, use a semicolon when the units are closely related.

Consider these examples:

EXAMPLES

The day had been long and hot; all I wanted to do was go for a swim.

For months Peter had avoided speaking to Valerie; now he had no choice.

In the first example, the semicolon connects the two simple sentences, as the ideas they express are closely related. It emphasizes *why* taking a swim was so important. In the second example, the semicolon not only connects the related ideas but also adds drama to the description of Peter's situation.

You can also place a *conjunctive adverb* such as *finally, however,* or *then* after the semicolon to suggest a relationship or condition and highlight the relationship between the two thoughts. (For a complete listing of common conjunctive adverbs, see p. 179) Remember that conjunctive adverbs are NOT conjunctions—they are adverbs, so they cannot serve as connectors by themselves. Always use a semicolon *before* the conjunctive adverb in order to connect the sentences (or a period, if you want to use a conjunctive adverb but still have separate sentences).

Look at these examples:

ESL Note
See "Punctuation and Capitalization," pages 494–496, for more on the proper use of semicolons.

EXAMPLES

The manager was hoping to reopen the store today; *however,* carbon monoxide levels were still too high.

The lifeguards continued to search in the water for the missing man; *meanwhile,* volunteers searched the grounds around the lake.

In the first example, the conjunctive adverb *however* indicates that something happened to disrupt the plans spelled out in the first part of the sentence. In the second example, the conjunctive adverb *meanwhile* specifies that something else was going on at the same time as the action described in the first part of the sentence.

Colons and Semicolons

Decide which type of pausing punctuation—a colon or a semicolon—is correct in each of the following sentences. Then insert either a colon or a semicolon where needed. Use the example as a guide.

EXAMPLE

I have identified three steps in my writing process _____:_____ exploring, composing, and organizing.

(1) People who enroll in college usually look forward to their courses _____;_____ however, some of the required subjects don't hold the same appeal for all people. (2) For example, some college students find the prospect of studying literature intimidating for several reasons _____:_____ difficulty of the language, relevance of the poems and plays, and complexity of the subject matter. (3) Math can also cause anxiety _____;_____ I get nervous just hearing the word *equations*. (4) Nevertheless, required courses are important _____:_____ a general education helps give students a new perspective on their career interests. (5) Core courses also build a college community in one way in particular _____:_____ students who share knowledge about a subject can share other ideas, too.

Errors in Colon and Semicolon Use

In the following paragraph, correct the errors in the use of colons and semicolons. Cross out the incorrect punctuation mark and write the correct one in the space above. If there is no error in the use of colons or semicolons in a sentence, put *OK* in front of it. Use the example to guide you.

EXAMPLE

After two hours of work, we finally discovered the cause of the blackout : a frayed wire.

(1) Our Fourth of July picnic features a great spread of delicious food; barbecued chicken, cold salads, hot dogs and burgers, and homemade cake and pies. (2) Early on the holiday morning, my family heads to Echo Lake; we

have managed to set up at the same barbecue pit five years in a row.
OK
(3) Somebody always brings a CD player and lots of different kinds of music:

Motown, classic rock, R&B, even some crossover and alternative country.

(4) We love all kinds of music; therefore, you hear a bit of just about every-
OK
thing at our Independence Day get-togethers. (5) The older folks prefer the

music of Motown and classic rockers: Marvin Gaye, Santana, the Beatles, Sly

and the Family Stone, and Aretha Franklin. (6) Soon, however, the sound

gives way to a more modern beat; U2, Black-Eyed Peas, and Beyoncé. (7)

Once everybody has eaten, the best part of the party gets going; some serious

dancing performances. (8) A space is cleared in the grass; then the dancers

start to move.

CHALLENGE 22.2   Analysis of the Use of Semicolons

collaboration

1. Make a list of the sentences in Comprehension and Practice 22.3 and 22.4 in which semicolons connect two clauses. Rewrite each of them on a separate sheet of paper, creating two distinct sentences.

2. Working with a classmate, decide whether the original sentence or the two-sentence revision is better. Then briefly explain your reasoning for your decisions.

Quotation Marks

To indicate someone's exact words—a direct quotation—enclose the passage in **quotation marks.** Look at the following example:

EXAMPLE

The customer service representative said, *"You are responsible for the first $50 charged to a stolen credit card."*

The italicized section is a direct quotation, so the passage is enclosed in quotation marks. As this sentence shows, the first word of a direct quotation is always capitalized. If the quote ends the sentence, as it does here, place a comma *before* the opening quotation mark, and place the end punctuation for the sentence *within* the closing quotation mark.

But if the quote begins the sentence, replace the ending period of the quote with a comma. Place the ending punctuation for the sentence after the attribution—the "she said" portion—as this version shows:

EXAMPLE

"You are responsible for the first $50 charged to a stolen credit card," the customer service representative said.

And if the quote that begins a sentence is a direct question, use a question mark within the quotation and then put a period after the attribution, as this version shows:

EXAMPLE

"Are you sure you understand what I have just told you?" the customer service representative asked.

By the way, when you include the interchange between two or more speakers—called **dialogue**—in your writing, begin a new paragraph each time the speaker changes.

EXAMPLE

Miranda asked, *"How long will the drive take?"*

"It should take only about an hour," Jack replied.

Unlike direct quotations, *indirect quotations* are the *restatement* of someone else's words. Because this restatement *doesn't present the person's exact words,* you don't use quotation marks. Look at this version of the first example sentence:

EXAMPLE

The customer service representative said *that I was responsible for the first $50 charged to my stolen credit card.*

The italicized section is a restatement of the direct quotation, not the person's actual words. Therefore, no quotation marks are needed.

You also use quotation marks to indicate the titles of published short texts that are generally part of a larger document, for example, short stories, articles in periodicals, songs from a CD, chapters from a book, an episode from a TV show, and so on:

EXAMPLES

Article: "The Last Leisure Suit"   **Poem:** "Collage"   **Song:** "Vertigo"

Book Chapter: "The Famous Incident of the Stilts"   **TV Episode:** "Do-Over"

COMPREHENSION AND PRACTICE

22.5

Direct and Indirect Quotations

In the following sentences, insert quotation marks where they are needed. Some sentences are indirect quotations, and indirect quotations do not need quotation marks. Use the example as a guide.

EXAMPLE

As she ran across the street, Alisse yelled, "I'll see you next week!"

(1) "I can't believe how rude the salesperson in that jewelry store was!" Dawn exclaimed. (2) I was about to ask her to tell me what happened, but she kept on talking. (3) "First, she looked at me as if I was going to steal something," Dawn continued, "and then she didn't come to the counter to help me."

(4) "I've had that happen to me, too," I replied. (5) We compared notes, and we said that some clerks assume we can't afford to buy anything because of our age and the way we dress.

Evaluation of Direct and Indirect Quotations

Some of the following sentences include direct quotations without quotation marks, while others include indirect quotations. If the sentence contains a direct quotation, rewrite it on a separate piece of paper, adding the needed quotation marks. If the sentence contains an indirect quotation, rewrite it on a separate sheet of paper, changing it into a direct quotation. Use the example as a guide. Answers will vary.

EXAMPLE

As the defendant emerged from the courthouse, the reporters hurried after him to ask whether he was ready to give a statement.

As the defendant emerged from the courthouse, the reporters hurried after him. They asked, "Are you ready to give a statement, sir?"

1. Confucius, a philosopher who lived in ancient China, is famous for saying that it is only the wisest and the stupidest who cannot change.

2. Once, a boy asked Confucius what the definition of wisdom is.

3. Confucius answered him, Devotion to one's duties as a subject and respect for the spirits while keeping them at a distance. This may be called wisdom.

4. As a sign of respect for Confucius' own wisdom and insight, the ancient Chinese did not address Confucius by his name. Instead they would say Greetings, Grand Master K'ung.

5. Because the teachings of Confucius are more practical and ethical than religious, followers of Confucianism discuss the teachings by saying things like, It is the way of the ancients.

CHALLENGE 22.3 Correct Punctuation and Format for Dialogue

1. Think of a brief discussion you have had with a sales representative or with a friend or relative about making a purchase. Write a paragraph of at least seven to ten sentences in which you re-create this discussion, using both direct and indirect quotations, and then make a copy of your paragraph in which you eliminate the quotation marks.

2. Exchange your paragraph with a classmate. On the paper you receive, insert quotation marks where they are needed and make sure a new paragraph begins when speakers change. Return the paper to the writer.

collaboration

3. Check your classmate's revision of your paragraph for correctness. Make any additional changes or corrections in the use of quotation marks.

Apostrophes

One of the most useful—and most often used—marks of punctuation is the **apostrophe.** Apostrophes show ownership, or possession, in nouns.

To change a *singular* noun into a possessive form, add an apostrophe and -*s:*

a boy**'s** shoe   an actor**'s** costume   a giraffe**'s** neck

Add an apostrophe and an -*s* even for singular words that already end in -*s:*

Jacques**'s** problem   boss**'s** concerns   witness**'s** response

If the resulting possessive form is awkward, you have another option: Use a prepositional phrase to replace it. In other words, instead of writing *Descartes's works,* write *the works of Descartes.*

To make most plural nouns possessive, simply add an apostrophe:

those boys**'** shoes   several actors**'** costumes   all giraffes**'** necks

Some plural words don't end in -*s.* Make these words possessive by adding an apostrophe and -*s* to the plural noun:

people**'s** lives   children**'s** toys   women**'s** issues

Apostrophes are also used to signify letters left out in a *contraction,* a word created by combining two words. They may also replace numbers omitted in dates. Look at these sentences, with the contractions italicized:

EXAMPLES

The new key *wouldn't* open the lock.
We'll never forget the blizzard of *'03.*

In the first example, the contraction *wouldn't* is used instead of *would not.* In the second, the contraction *we'll* is used in place of *we will;* *'03* represents *2003.*

Here is a list of other common contractions:

ESL Note
See "Confusing Verb Forms," pages 489–491, for more on the correct use of apostrophes in contractions.

Common Contractions

are**n't** (are not)	he**'d** (he would)	should**'ve** (should have)
can**'t** (cannot)	I**'m** (I am)	should**n't** (should not)
could**n't** (could not)	I**'ll** (I will)	that**'s** (that is)
did**n't** (did not)	I**'d** (I would)	they**'re** (they are)
do**n't** (do not)	is**n't** (is not)	they**'ll** (they will)
does**n't** (does not)	it**'s** (it has)	who**'s** (who has)
had**n't** (had not)	it**'s** (it is)	who**'s** (who is)
has**n't** (has not)	it**'ll** (it will)	wo**n't** (will not)
have**n't** (have not)	she**'s** (she has)	you**'re** (you are)
he**'s** (he has)	she**'s** (she is)	you**'ll** (you will)
he**'s** (he is)	she**'ll** (she will)	you**'d** (you would)
he**'ll** (he will)	she**'d** (she would)	

In every case except one, the letters in a contraction follow the same order as in the original two words. The exception is the contraction for *will not: won't.*

COMPREHENSION
AND PRACTICE

22.7

Apostrophes

Correct each italicized noun below that is meant to show ownership or possession. Cross out the unpunctuated form and write the correctly punctuated possessive form above it. For each italicized pair of words, create a contraction. Cross out the word pairs, and write the contraction above them. Use the example to guide you.

EXAMPLE

I'm
~~I am~~ planning to join my friends to play cards at ~~Chriss~~ *Chris's* apartment on Saturday.

(1) My ~~mothers~~ *mother's* stories about shopping for ~~childrens~~ *children's* shoes when my brothers and sisters and I were young make her laugh now, but that ~~was not~~ *wasn't* always the case. (2) ~~She would~~ *She'd* put off the expensive trip to the shoe store as long as possible, but then ~~we would~~ *we'd* all outgrow our shoes at the same time. (3) Mom says she ~~will not~~ *won't* ever forget the expressions on sales ~~representatives~~ *representatives'* faces when all five of us would troop into the store. (4) The boys always wanted just sneakers, so ~~Moms~~ *Mom's* biggest challenge was buying ~~girls~~ *girls'* shoes. (5) Mom thinks ~~it is~~ *it's* odd that I like to hear stories about these stressful moments in our ~~familys~~ *family's* past.

COMPREHENSION
AND PRACTICE

22.8

Errors with Apostrophes

The following paragraph contains some words that need an apostrophe, either because they are contractions or because they show ownership. Cross out any words that need an apostrophe. Write the correct version in the space above the incorrect one. Use the example as a guide.

EXAMPLE

there's   *can't*   *it's*
If ~~theres~~ one thing I ~~cant~~ stand, ~~its~~ hot, muggy weather.

(1) Children who ~~havent~~ *haven't* been taught how to behave in a restaurant challenge ~~everyones~~ *everyone's* patience. (2) Of course, ~~its~~ *it's* not the ~~childrens~~ *children's* fault, but rather their ~~parents~~ *parents'* fault. (3) Children, even very small children, can behave very well if ~~theyve~~ *they've* been shown how. (4) The most inconsiderate parents are those who allow their kids to roam around the restaurant, bother other people, and get in the ~~servers~~ *servers'* way. (5) ~~Im~~ *I'm* always amazed by parents who pay so little attention to their

children. (6) Slightly better are the parents who manage to keep their children in

their seats but who ~~dont~~ [don't] keep their ~~childrens~~ [children's] noise level within reasonable lim-

its. (7) ~~Ive~~ [I've] left some restaurants without even taking a seat if the place seemed

too noisy. (8) ~~Its~~ [It's] not that I dislike children, but I ~~cant~~ [can't] enjoy a meal in a restau-

rant that has had ~~it's~~ [its] atmosphere disrupted by bratty kids.

COMPREHENSION
AND PRACTICE
22.9

Correct Use of Contractions and Possessives

The italicized phrases in the following sentences can be simplified using apostrophes to create possessive forms or contractions. Cross out each of these phrases. Above the crossed-out phrase write a new version, using an apostrophe to create a possessive noun or a contraction. Use the example to guide you.

EXAMPLE The bus *~~does not~~* [doesn't] stop at *~~the childcare center of my daughter~~* [my daughter's childcare center].

(1) Adults often complain about *~~the teen fashions of today~~* [today's teen fashions]. (2) Those people must have forgotten *~~the criticism of their own parents~~* [their own parents' criticism] about their clothing and hairstyles. (3) *~~The clothes of teens~~* [Teens' clothes] in the 1970s and 1980s included things like designer jeans, leg warmers, bike shorts, and anything that reflected the punk music scene. (4) *~~The favorite outfit that belonged to my aunt~~* [My aunt's favorite outfit] consisted of a Bon Jovi concert T-shirt, ripped Jordache jeans, and Converse high-top sneakers. (5) My uncle says *~~he will~~* [he'll] never be allowed to forget the green parachute pants he wore for days at a time. (6) *~~The hairstyles of yesterday could not~~* [Yesterday's hairstyles couldn't] have pleased many parents, either. (7) For example, *~~the hair of many young males~~* [many young males' hair] was cut in the infamous mullet style, with shorter hair on the sides and long, often stringy sections hanging down in the back, over the collar. (8) Generations *~~are not~~* [aren't] all that different after all, and *~~the individuality of young~~* [young people's individuality] people will always be expressed through fashion.

CHALLENGE 22.4   Correct Use of *Its* and *It's*

1. The list of common contractions on page 427 shows that the contractions of *it has* and *it is* are written as *it's*. To show ownership, the form without the apostrophe—*its*—is used: a picture and *its* frame. Write ten sentences, five using *its* and five using *it's* but without including the apostrophes.

collaboration

2. Exchange your sentences with a classmate. Add apostrophes where needed in the paper you received, and then return it to the writer.

3. Check the apostrophes your classmate has added for correctness. Make any additional changes or corrections in the use of apostrophes.

✔ PUNCTUATION CHECKLIST

☐ Have you examined each sentence to see whether it makes a statement, asks a question, or shows great excitement or emotion, and then chosen the appropriate mark of end punctuation?

☐ Have you rechecked to ensure that no question marks have been used with *indirect* questions?

☐ Have you used a colon when you had to signal that significant information follows in a sentence?

☐ Have you used a semicolon, with or without a conjunctive adverb, to connect related simple sentences?

☐ Have you used quotation marks with direct quotations only?

☐ Have you checked the apostrophes used to signal ownership and to form contractions, paying particular attention to *it's*?

Journal Writing

Punctuation is the system of marks that signal stops, pauses, direct address, announcements, combinations, and ownership. Of course, if punctuation as we know it didn't exist, all these concepts would still exist in life. We start and stop activities, relationships, and behaviors. We pause to consider things or take a break from activities. We have conversations, we talk with others and listen to what they have to say, and we announce important events. We provide connections between people and between things, and we assert custody or ownership of other elements in our lives. Focus on one of these topics, and then take 20 to 30 minutes to explore it in your journal.

CHAPTER QUICK CHECK Using Punctuation Properly

In the following passage, many necessary punctuation marks are missing. Supply an appropriate mark of end punctuation—period, question mark, or exclamation point—for each sentence. You may also need to add a colon or semicolon, quotation marks, or apostrophes within a sentence. With any incorrect use of *its* or *it's,* cross out the word and write the correct version above it.

(1) When I think back to my childhood, I have one serious regret: my failure to take advantage of free guitar lessons offered in the sixth grade. (2) I can still remember the day when the school's music teacher, Ms. Souza, asked, "Is there anyone here who would like to learn to play the guitar?" (3) For a few minutes, the class didn't respond, and then finally one of the girls raised her hand and asked what the charge would be. (4) Ms. Souza's answer was astonishing: a superintendent's grant would pay for the lessons and instrument rental! (5) I'd always wanted to learn to play the guitar; still, I was afraid that somebody might make fun of me. (6) What would my friends' attitudes be if I didn't just stare at Ms. Souza as we all usually did? (7) When nobody spoke up, Ms. Souza said, "If nobody here wants to do this, I'll offer the chance to my other students." (8) It's funny, but I knew that I shouldn't have rejected her generous offer. (9) She was offering me the chance I'd always hoped for; however, I didn't want anyone to think I was a nerd. (10) If I could go back in time, I'd stand up for myself, regardless of what my friends' attitudes might have been.

SUMMARY EXERCISE   Using Punctuation Properly

In the following passage, many necessary punctuation marks are missing. Supply an appropriate mark of end punctuation—period, question mark, or exclamation point—for each sentence. You may also need to add a colon or semicolon, quotation marks, or apostrophes within a sentence. For any incorrect use of *its* or *it's,* cross out the word and write the correct version above it.

(1) If things go as I've planned, I'm finally going to get organized. (2) Maybe I'll even manage to keep these New Year's resolutions: to balance my checkbook, clean my desk, and keep better track of appointments. (3) For the last month, I've really been thinking about this goal and it's [its] importance in my life.

(4) Often, my desk looks as if its [it's] been in a tornado. (5) "How can you live with this mess?" my husband asks me at least once a week. (6) The truth is that I dont know where to start. (7) Its [It's] as if Im afraid to start; nevertheless, I am going

to fight this feeling. (8) I dont have a choice because I've lost or misplaced so many important things I really need appointment cards, letters, and phone numbers.

(9) One thing I shouldve started to do a long time ago is use the calendar feature on my cell phone (10) Its certainly easy enough I just never seemed to get around to it (11) Ill use it to list my assignments or appointments, and I wont have to worry about forgetting any important dates (12) What could be simpler (13) When I mentioned this plan to my husband, he smiled and said, "Haven't I been suggesting that to you for months

(14) Im also going to start keeping lists every Sunday, Ill write down the tasks to complete for each day of that week (15) Its a good way to avoid feeling overwhelmed, and thats been a major problem for me (16) Ive made the following promise to myself to take care of at least one item on my list every day

(17) Whose fault is it that Im so unorganized (18) I wont blame anyone else I take full responsibility (19) Someone much wiser than I am once said, "Never put off until tomorrow what you can do today. (20) Im planning to follow that advice from now on

FOR FURTHER EXPLORATION

1. Choose one of the following subjects and use your preferred prewriting method to develop a specific focus and supporting ideas.

   - A time when you accomplished more than you had believed you were physically or emotionally capable of
   - What it means to be truly independent
   - A person you consider to be an outstanding motivator

2. Evaluate your prewriting material, identify a focus, and create a draft paragraph of at least seven to ten sentences.

collaboration

3. Exchange your draft with a writing partner. Using the material in this chapter as a guide, evaluate the draft you receive. Note any problems with the use of end punctuation, semicolons and colons, quotation marks, and apostrophes. Return the draft to the writer.

4. Revise your draft, eliminating any errors that your reader identified.

DISCOVERING CONNECTIONS

For this assignment, focus on the photo and consider one of the following questions (or another that the picture inspires). Explore your ideas and then create a draft paragraph of at least seven to ten sentences. Try to include, at least once, all the punctuation marks you learned about in this chapter.

A. President Obama believes that higher enrollment in college math and science programs will lead to the development of new jobs for this and future generations. What do you think parents and teachers can do to encourage young people to devote their energies to mastering math and science?

B. In popular culture, scientists and mathematicians are often portrayed as people who are slightly eccentric and out of the mainstream. Such characterizations are of course inaccurate—but it is true that each of us might engage in an activity, interest, or pursuit that others consider "unusual." What do you think some of these activities might be and why do you think they are deemed "out of the mainstream"?

RECAP Using Punctuation Properly

Key Terms in This Chapter	Definitions
punctuation	the system of symbols that signal starts, stops, and pauses in writing
period	used to indicate a stop at the end of a sentence, to separate dollars and cents in monetary amounts, and to show abbreviations and initials
	EXAMPLE The pharmacy bill was $129.42.
question mark	used at the end of a sentence to indicate a direct question
	EXAMPLE Did the baseball game go into extra innings?
exclamation point	used at the end of a sentence to express strong emotion
	EXAMPLE That fire is hot!
colon	marks a pause within a sentence and prepares for following words that explain, announce, or list
	EXAMPLE After the storm, the town was devastated: broken windows, flooded roads, fallen wires.

semicolon	connects simple sentences and calls attention to the connection
	EXAMPLE The boys were fighting again; one of them got hurt.
quotation marks	used to set off someone's exact words
	not used with indirect quotations, a restatement of someone else's words
	EXAMPLE "Who is your favorite movie star?" Whitney asked, after I told her that I love watching movies.
dialogue	the interchange between two or more speakers in direct quotation form
apostrophe	used to show ownership or possession in nouns and to signify letters left out in a contraction
	EXAMPLE I haven't seen Brian's new car yet.

To Form the Possessive

add **'s** to singular nouns	the bike of the boy → the boy**'s** bike
add **'** to plural nouns	the bikes of the two boys → the two boys' bikes
add **'s** to irregular plural nouns	the issues of women → women**'s** issues

Using Discovery Online with MyWritingLab

For more practice with punctuation, go to www.mywritinglab.com.

CHAPTER 23
Capitalizing Correctly

GETTING STARTED ...

 Sometimes I don't capitalize words that need it, and other times I capitalize words that don't need it. Why is capitalization so difficult sometimes? How can I make sure that I am capitalizing only the words that need to be capitalized?

 Because we talk a great deal more than we write, it is easy to overlook capitalization rules. In conversation, capitalization is not an issue. So when you prepare to write, the best strategy for remembering the rules of capitalization is simple: determine whether the word is common or proper. Common nouns don't call for capitalization, but proper nouns do. And a word that begins a sentence is *always* capitalized.

Overview: Proper Capitalization

In writing, certain words stand out because they begin with capital letters. This system of emphasis is called **capitalization.** A capital letter announces a *particular* person, place, or thing rather than a member of a general class of persons, places, or things. To use capitalization properly, you need to understand some broad guidelines about this system.

Navigating This Chapter This chapter presents capitalization guidelines and shows you how to apply them. You will learn:

- when words should be capitalized
- when words should not be capitalized

When Words Should Be Capitalized

According to the basic rules of standard English usage, always capitalize

- the first word in a sentence:

EXAMPLES

The sunflowers in the center of the vacant lot caught her attention.

When will Nancy arrive?

- the proper names of people, things, and places, including specific holidays, countries, states, cities, bodies of water, parks, historical periods or events, months, days of the week, planets, races, religions, and nationalities:

Michael McNally	Latino	Vietnam War
Italian Renaissance	Thursday	Irish
Uranus	Yellowstone National Park	Lake Huron
Asia	Buddhist	Mississippi
December	Mother's Day	Los Angeles

Note that the first letter after *Mc* in a surname is also usually capitalized.

- the months and days of the week, but NOT the seasons

EXAMPLE Annual employee reviews must be completed by the second **M**onday in **J**une, before the official start of **s**ummer.

- the personal pronoun *I*:

EXAMPLE Jada and **I** made plans to meet after class.

- a word that designates a family relationship when you use that word as part of, or as a substitute for, a specific name, but NOT when it is used as a basic word of identification or as a general descriptor:

EXAMPLE Gregory loves his talks with **G**randma and **U**ncle Glenn, but not as much as his **s**ister does.

- formal titles such as *doctor, senator, mayor,* and so on, when you use them in conjunction with a person's name but NOT when you use them as a basic word of identification or as a general descriptor:

EXAMPLE **R**epresentative Marshall promised to lower taxes and to consult more regularly with **r**epresentatives from other districts.

- words such as *street, avenue,* and *boulevard* when they are part of a specific address:

EXAMPLES 49 Richmond **S**treet   5 Washington Court   1450 Spencer **D**rive

- words such as *South* and *West* when they designate specific sections of a country but NOT when they simply designate a direction:

EXAMPLE Every year, his girlfriend, who lives in the **S**outh, drives almost 1,000 miles **n**orth to go skiing.

- all main words of the names of languages and specific course names but NOT the names of basic school subjects or classes in general:

EXAMPLE Next semester, I plan to take **S**panish III, **W**riting 102, and a **p**sychology course.

- the first word and all main words in the titles of books, poems, newspapers, magazines, television shows, movies, and so on:

EXAMPLES

Pride and Prejudice   *Los Angeles Times*   *National Geographic*

No Country for Old Men   "**O**de on a **G**recian Urn"   *The Daily Show*

- brand names, companies, clubs, and associations:

EXAMPLES

Nike   **A**pple **C**omputer, **I**nc.

New **Y**ork **R**unners **C**lub   **N**ational **O**rganization for **W**omen

Keebler   **B**ose

- all letters of abbreviations of proper names and acronyms:

EXAMPLES

NEH (National Endowment for the Humanities)   **ABC** (American Broadcasting Corporation)

IBM (International Business Machines)   **NASA** (National Aeronautics and Space Administration)

- the first letters of the beginning of a correspondence, called the *salutation,* and the first word of the ending, called the *complimentary close:*

Common Salutations	*Common Complimentary Closings*
Dear **M**r. James:	**S**incerely,
Greetings **T**erry,	**R**espectfully,

COMPREHENSION
AND PRACTICE **Words Needing Capitalization**

23.1 Decide which words in the following paragraph should be capitalized. Cross out each incorrect lowercase letter, and write a capital letter above it. Refer to the guidelines in this chapter and the following example to help you.

EXAMPLE

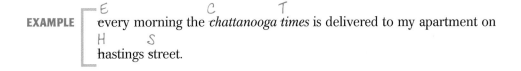

every morning the *chattanooga times* is delivered to my apartment on hastings street.

(1) *war of the worlds,* [W W] a big-budget movie released in summer of 2005, is not the most famous theatrical performance to carry that name. (2) a [A] 1938 cbs [CBS] radio broadcast of *war of the worlds on the mercury theater on the air* [W W T M T] caused widespread panic among thousands in the radio audience. (3) american [A] performer, director, and writer orson welles [O W] produced this radio play, based on the science fiction novel by english writer h. g. wells. [E H G W] (4) For the radio broadcast from new york city [N Y C] at 8 P.M. on halloween, [H] welles [W] changed the location of the fictional attack from england [E] to the u. s. [U S] (5) many [M] people who had been listening to *edgar bergen and charlie mccarthy* [E B C M C] on an nbc [NBC] station missed the disclaimers about the fictional nature of the show. (6) as [A] a result, they believed that aliens were invading new jersey [N J] and fled from their homes, jamming streets and highways of major cities. (7) because [B] of the hysteria that *war of the worlds* [W W] caused, the fcc [FCC] eventually prohibited performances of fictional events that the public might mistakenly believe to be actual. (8) for [F] the wisconsin-born welles, [W W] this cbs [CBS] broadcast made him a household name and paved the way for his masterpiece film, *citizen kane.* [C K]

COMPREHENSION
AND PRACTICE

Errors with Words Needing Capitalization

23.2   In the following passage, capitalize letters where necessary in each sentence. Cross out each incorrect lowercase letter, and write the capital above it. Use the example to guide you.

EXAMPLE   From the forests of the northwest [N] to the beaches of florida, [F] the united states [U S] is overflowing with great vacation sites.

(1) Last year, mom, dad, kevin, [M D K] and i [I] took a driving tour of the southwest, [S] including new mexico, arizona, [N M A] and nevada. [N] (2) The grand canyon [G C] was a high-light, and i [I] nearly wore out my nike [N] sandals and minolta [M] camera hiking and taking pictures. (3) On the fourth of july, [F J] we celebrated my birthday in tucson, [T]

arizona. (4) Kevin sent gramma postcards at 1529 whispering pines lane, aurora, illinois, even though she was staying at green lake in wisconsin that week. (5) It rained on tuesday, the day we had scheduled to see the saguaro national monument. (6) While our parents read magazines like *time, newsweek,* and *esquire* and watched hbo, kevin and i visited el con regional mall. (7) With my birthday money, i bought italian sandals and some shorts at the gap. (8) On our final day of the trip, we heard the arizona governor speak at a special event held at the university of arizona.

[Editing marks above words indicate capital letters: A-arizona; G-gramma, W-whispering, P-pines, L-lane; A-aurora, I-illinois, G-green, L-lake, W-wisconsin; T-tuesday, S-saguaro; N-national, M-monument, T-time, N-newsweek; E-esquire, HBO-hbo, K-kevin, I-i, E C R-el con regional, M-mall; I-i, I-italian, G-gap; A-arizona; U-university, A-arizona]

COMPREHENSION AND PRACTICE 23.3

More Words Needing Capitalization

The underlined words in the following sentences are general and so don't need to be capitalized. Cross out the underlined words and then, above them, write appropriate, specific words that *do* call for capitalization. Use the following example to guide you. Answers will vary.

EXAMPLE

The Sears Tower
That building is one of the tallest buildings in the world.

1. The mayor met with the striking city workers in the municipal building.

2. My uncle always carves the turkey at our holiday feast.

3. The street is a one-way street.

4. That movie is a very enjoyable romantic comedy.

5. The leaf-raking month has arrived at last.

6. She would be homesick if she moved away from her hometown.

7. They all speak the same language.

8. I earned an A in that course because my paper on a major war was so impressive.

CHALLENGE 23.1 The Importance of Capitalization

1. Download an article from the front page of an online newspaper, and circle the words that are capitalized. Bring the article to class and exchange it with a classmate. On a separate sheet of paper, write the capitalized words your class-mate has circled. Beside each, explain why the word should be capitalized.

2. Write a posting to your favorite blog, praising or criticizing the blogger for his or her latest entry.

collaboration

3. Exchange your posting with a classmate. Check the posting you receive for correct use of capitals. Underline any words that you believe have a mistake in capitalization and return the posting to the writer.

4. Check the notations your classmate has provided, and make any necessary changes to your posting.

✓ CAPITALIZING CORRECTLY CHECKLIST

☐ Have you capitalized the first word in each sentence and the pronoun *I*?

☐ Have you capitalized the proper names and titles of people and places, including countries, states, cities, bodies of water, parks, and planets?

☐ Have you capitalized the proper names of specific things and events, including days of the week, geographical areas, months, holidays, religions, races, historical periods or occurrences, and nationalities?

☐ Have you capitalized the titles of books, periodicals, movies, television shows, clubs, academic courses, languages, brand names, and abbreviations of the proper names of organizations and businesses?

☐ Have you used lowercase letters for the names of all nonspecific people, places, events, titles, compass directions, and academic subjects?

Journal Writing

Capitalizing a word distinguishes it, making it stand out from words naming someone or something general. But that doesn't mean that words that aren't capitalized aren't important. For instance, *grandparent* is a nonspecific word. So are words such as *love, career, success, time, intelligence, talent, education,* and *vacation.* Choose one of these words or select some other, and then explore its importance or significance for 20 to 30 minutes in your journal.

CHAPTER QUICK CHECK   Capitalizing Correctly

The following sentences contain a number of capitalization errors. Cross out the capital letter of any incorrectly capitalized word, inserting the lowercase version above it. Cross out the lowercase letter of any word that should be capitalized, inserting the capital version above it.

(1) Whether it is called highland road estates or riverview gardens, the
       H   R   E   R   G

name chosen for a Housing Development can play an important role in its
                  h   d

success. (2) When Construction Executives consider what to call their Developments, they often try to capture some special quality of the surrounding area. (3) For example, if a Developer is building an Apartment Complex on the shores of lake springfield, calling the development lakeview acres highlights the advantages of the location. (4) With Condominiums at the foot of a Mountain in a ski area, a name like black diamond run conjures up a vision of skiers racing down snow-covered slopes. (5) Naming a housing development pine cone preserve because it is near a State Forest underscores the beauty inherent in the Locale. (6) developers must also make sure that they don't choose a name of some well-known Corporation or Product. (7) Names like gateway heights or rolex villas would not be acceptable because they might infringe on corporate Trademarks or Copyrights. (8) Unfortunately, some Real Estate Companies aren't always completely honest when they assign names to their Housing Units. (9) Not every Development named ocean echo cottages or desert view gardens is within sight of the Ocean or Desert. (10) as with so many other Consumer Issues, a potential buyer must investigate things fully before actually making such a significant Financial Investment.

SUMMARY EXERCISE   Capitalizing Correctly

The following essay contains a number of capitalization errors. Cross out the capital letter of any incorrectly capitalized word, inserting the lowercase version above it. Cross out the lowercase letter of any word that should be capitalized, inserting the capital version above it.

(1) Many americans are motivated to follow Sports, judging by the large number of long-established Sports Rivalries. (2) some of these Team matchups on both the College and Professional level go back more than 100 years. (3) Because so many sporting events are Nationally televised today, rivalries

that were once only Regional now attract the attention of Sports Enthusiasts across the u. s.

(4) Several College Football rivalries are among the oldest in organized american Sports. (5) For example, harvard and yale first played each other in Football in 1875, and army first played navy in 1890. (6) The Annual battle between ohio state university and michigan state university goes back to 1897. (7) other long-standing Opponents include the university of Florida gators and the Florida State seminoles, and the University of texas longhorns and the University of oklahoma sooners.

(8) Similar rivalries can be found in the national Hockey league, the national basketball Association, the National football league, and Major league Baseball. (9) In the nhl, canada's toronto Maple leafs and montreal canadiens, both members of the "original six" of Professional Hockey, play every game against each other like it's the stanley cup final.

(10) In Professional Basketball, the bi-coastal rivalry between the Los Angeles lakers and the Boston celtics dominated the nba for many years. (11) their games especially captivated the attention of the Public in the 1960s when the Celtics's bill russell battled the Lakers's wilt chamberlain. (12) Interest in the Contests between these Teams was rekindled in the 1980s when Boston's larry bird clashed with Los Angeles's earvin "magic" johnson, and again more recently with teams led by the Celt's Coach, doc Rivers, and the lakers's coach, Phil Jackson.

(13) devotees of Professional Football enjoy a number of rivalries between n f l teams, some of which have existed as long as the League has. (14) Fans in wisconsin look forward every year to the big Match-up between their green bay Packers and the chicago bears. (15) Washington redskins fans feel the same way about the dallas cowboys, and Followers of the Cleveland browns take particular interest when their team is facing the pittsburgh steelers.

(16) Major ~~l~~league ~~b~~baseball is home to some of the most enduring ~~R~~rivalries in all of ~~S~~sports, for instance, the ~~n~~national ~~l~~league's ~~st~~St. Louis Cardinals and Chicago ~~c~~cubs. (17) ~~c~~Contests between two former ~~new york~~New York ~~city~~City teams, the Los Angeles ~~d~~dodgers and the San Francisco ~~g~~giants, always attract great attention as well.

(18) But the rivalry between the ~~american~~American ~~league~~league's Boston Red ~~sox~~Sox and the New York ~~y~~yankees, which began even before the Sox traded ~~babe ruth~~Babe Ruth to the ~~p~~pinstripes, ranks right at the top. (19) ~~i~~In terms of ~~world series~~World Series appearances and ~~V~~victories, New York has the edge over Boston. (20) Still, when the ~~r~~red ~~s~~sox and ~~y~~yankees square off, sports fans across the ~~C~~country tune in to witness another clash in one of the greatest of all ~~S~~sports ~~R~~rivalries.

FOR FURTHER EXPLORATION

1. Choose one of the following subjects and use your preferred prewriting method to develop a specific focus and supporting ideas.

   - The single funniest incident you have ever witnessed or experienced
   - A time when saying the right thing completely changed a situation
   - Someone you know who regularly speaks without thinking or considering the impact careless words can have

2. Evaluate your prewriting material, identify a focus, and create a draft paragraph of at least seven to ten sentences.

3. Exchange your draft with a writing partner. Using the material in this chapter as a guide, evaluate the draft you receive. Note any problems with capitalization as well as any other weaknesses, and return the draft to the writer.

collaboration

4. Revise your draft, eliminating any errors that your reader identified.

DISCOVERING CONNECTIONS

For this assignment, focus on the photo and one of the following questions (or another that the photo inspires). Explore your ideas and then create a draft paragraph of at least seven to ten sentences. Remember the rules for capitalization: Have you capitalized the first word of all your sentences? Did you remember to capitalize all your proper nouns? Do these nouns agree with their verbs?

A. The type of work depicted in the photo on the next page is typically performed by forensic specialists, medical examiners, crime scene investigators, and laboratory analysts. Could you see yourself as a professional in this field? Why or why not?

B. Perhaps the bones in this picture are from people who donated their bodies to science. What's your opinion? Would you agree to donate your body to a medical school or research facility? Why do you feel this way? How about organ donation? According to some recent estimates, less than 40 percent of licensed drivers have registered as organ donors. What do you think keeps more people from signing on?

RECAP Capitalizing Correctly

Key Term in This Chapter	Definition
capitalization	the emphasis given to words by beginning them with a capital letter
Do Capitalize:	first word in a sentence
	EXAMPLE **T**he accident created a traffic jam.
	proper names of people, things, and places
	EXAMPLE **S**usan and **I** leave on **T**uesday to visit **C**hicago.
	words that designate family relationships when part of or a substitute for a specific name
	EXAMPLE On my birthday, **A**unt Margaret sent me $10.
	formal titles used in conjunction with a person's name
	EXAMPLE Send a letter about the bridge repairs to **S**enator Dayton.
	words that are part of a specific address or a specific section of a country
	EXAMPLE **K**ennedy **S**treet is a common street name in the **N**ortheast.
	main words in specific academic subjects, languages, and titles
	EXAMPLE I stopped studying for my **S**panish and **E**conomics 205 finals to watch a *Seinfeld* rerun.
	brand names, company and association names, and abbreviations for proper names
	EXAMPLE Does **M**icrosoft make software for both **IBM** and **M**acintosh computers?

Key Term in This Chapter	Definition
	first letters of the salutation and complimentary closing of a letter
	EXAMPLE **D**ear **S**ir, **S**incerely yours
Do Not Capitalize:	words that designate a family relationship
	EXAMPLE She vacations with her **m**om and **d**ad.
	titles if they aren't used with a person's name
	EXAMPLE Martina is **p**resident of the **s**tudent **g**overning **b**ody.
	words that designate a direction
	EXAMPLE Travel **s**outheast for five blocks.
	general school subjects
	EXAMPLE Most colleges require three years of **m**ath and **s**cience.
	seasons of the year
	EXAMPLE For once, **s**pring came early.

Using Discovery Online with MyWritingLab

For more practice with capitalization, go to www.mywritinglab.com.

Assessment: a process of evaluation designed to identify your level of mastery and help improve your performance

CONSISTENCY WORKSHOP: AIMING FOR CORRECTNESS

The material you have completed in Part 5 concentrates on **parallelism; spelling; commas; punctuation—periods, question marks, exclamation points, colons, semicolons, quotation marks,** and **apostrophes;** and **capitalization.** To assess your understanding of this information and your progress as a **Writer, Reader, Editor,** and **Student,** complete the following charts. First check off your level of confidence for each item, and then take the recommended action to improve your performance.

- As a **Writer,** I understand

	Confident	Moderately Confident	Not Confident
1. the guidelines of **proper parallelism** (Chapter 19)			
2. the guidelines of **correct spelling** (Chapter 20)			
3. the **seven functions of commas** (Chapter 21)			
4. the correct use of **periods, question marks, exclamation points, colons, semicolons, quotation marks,** and **apostrophes** (Chapter 22)			
5. the rules of **capitalization** (Chapter 23)			

- If you are **confident,** you are all set. Move on.

- If you are **moderately confident,** review the Overviews and Recaps for the appropriate chapters.

- If you are **not confident,** go through the appropriate chapters again, carefully rereading the rules, example sentences, and lists plus the Chapter Quick Checks and Summary exercises.

- As a **Reader,** I understand

  - If you are **confident,** you are all set. Move on.

  - If you are **moderately confident,** reexamine these chapter features to reinforce your understanding of the connection between these elements and the subject matter of the different chapters.

	Confident	Moderately Confident	Not Confident
1. the analysis provided about how to maintain correct parallelism, spelling, punctuation, and capitalization and *-ing* modifiers			
2. the purpose and usefulness of the various **Chapter Q&A's**, **Overviews**, **lists** of **rules** and **examples**, **Checklists**, and **Journal Writing** sections			

- If you are **not confident**, revisit these components. Start with the **Q&A** and **Overview** sections, seeing if the issues discussed match your own concerns. Go through the lists and examples to identify specific problem spots and copy them on paper or in a computer file. Complete the **Journal Writing** assignments and then use the appropriate **Chapter Checklists** to check your knowledge of the information.

- As an **Editor**, I understand

	Confident	Moderately Confident	Not Confident
1. how to recognize and correct problems with parallelism (Chapter 19)			
2. how to find and fix errors in spelling (Chapter 20)			
3. how to spot and eliminate errors in comma use (Chapter 21)			
4. how to recognize and correct mistakes in the use of periods, question marks, exclamation points, colons, semicolons, quotation marks, and apostrophes (Chapter 22)			
5. how to identify and correct errors in capitalization (Chapter 23)			

- If you are **confident,** you are all set. Move on.

- If you are **moderately confident,** closely examine a draft on which you are currently working. After reviewing the rules and guidelines, reread your draft four separate times, once each to check for correct parallelism, spelling, use of punctuation, and capitalization.

- If you are **not confident,** review completed exercises, noting the correct way to eliminate specific errors. Select a passage of 200 words or so in one of your textbooks or a print or online article. Highlight or circle any element in the text that presents the correct form of the aspect of parallelism, spelling, punctuation, or capitalization that you find challenging.

- As a **Student,** I understand

	Confident	Moderately Confident	Not Confident
1. the need to keep on schedule and not fall behind in my work during the final weeks of the semester			
2. all end-of-semester assignments—papers, presentations, lab reports, activity logs, and portfolios—that must be completed and the dates when they must be submitted			
3. the preparation necessary for final examinations, exit conferences, and so on			

- If you are **confident,** you are all set. Move on.

- If you are **moderately confident,** check your syllabi, class notes, and online postings concerning course requirements for the remaining time of the semester, any culminating course activities or papers, and the type and nature of your final examinations.

- If you are **not confident,** prepare a two-column handwritten chart or computer spreadsheet. Label the first column **End-of-Semester Schedule,** and in this column list, course by course, all remaining papers, quizzes, projects, and so on, and their due dates. Label the second column **Final Examination/Evaluation Preparation,** and in this column list the dates and locations for all final examinations, presentations, exit conferences, and so on. List the type and scope of each final evaluation as well as your specific plans to prepare for it—scheduled study times and particular study techniques.

PART 6

Discovering Connections through Reading

Navigating This Section This section of the text will help you discover:

- active reading strategies
- additional subjects for writing
- new writing techniques

Overview: Active Reading Strategies

Active reading is a technique through which a reader interacts closely with the words on the page. Writers read actively to react to the ideas other authors have developed and to discover the strategies they have used to express those ideas. When you use active reading to examine what other authors have written, you will improve your own writing.

This section of the text includes writings by students and professional authors. Questions follow each selection to help you consider and respond to the ideas presented and to discover the ways those ideas and your own experiences are connected. At the same time, they will lead you to employ in your own writing the different techniques these other writers have used.

Taking Notes

Learning to write well involves experience and practice. In the same way, the more you practice active reading, the more skilled you will become. One important learning strategy is to take notes—to record in writing your responses, questions, and comments about what you read. Your instructor may ask you to record in a journal what you discover by reading. Some readers make notes in the margins of the pages they are reading or mark sections with self-stick notes or highlighters for later reference. Still others keep responses in a computer file or on tape. Whatever method or methods you use, cultivate the habit of taking notes on the most significant points you discover as you read. Your notes will help you prepare for discussions with your classmates and explore ideas for your own writing assignments.

Five Steps to Active Reading

As you read each selection, follow these five steps. Be sure to record your responses to these questions as you read.

1. **Establish the context.** What's going on? Who is involved? When did it happen? Where? How? Why? The answers to these questions, the ones that news stories generally answer in their opening sentences, provide the *context*—the significant elements—of a piece of writing. As you read, ask these questions to identify the essential details of the reading.

2. **Discover the organization.** How many paragraphs are in the writing? Does the selection have a beginning, a middle, and an end? How does the author connect these sections? As you read, note where each section begins and

ends. Usually, you will find the author's main idea in the beginning of the writing, or the *introduction*. The middle often develops the main idea through supporting examples or details. This section is known as the *body*. At the end, the author usually restates the main point and explains the significance of the piece in the *conclusion*.

As you read, highlight or record in your journal
- parts of the reading that state the author's main idea
- evidence that supports that idea
- the author's conclusions about the subject

3. **Explore the main ideas.**   Try to identify the main idea or topic sentence of each paragraph. Are there sentences or paragraphs that confuse you or sections that you don't understand? Make note of these to discuss with your instructor or classmates. Active reading does not mean you have to find all the answers, but it does require that you ask questions. Next, take special note of supporting information that helps you understand the writer's points. What details catch your eye? Why are these effective?

4. **Respond to the ideas.**   What do you think of the selection? Why do you think the way you do? Do you agree with the ideas the author has expressed? Are you familiar with the context or the ideas in the reading? Does the author present an experience or a view of the world that is new to you? Your answers to these questions will help you greatly in understanding the writing. As you talk or write about the piece, you will also be making sense of it. Remember as you read that a good piece of writing touches the reader. When you read, identify what the writer has done to make this happen. The better able you are to find out how a writer has reached you, the better prepared you'll be to reach your own reader.

5. **Read again.**   Active reading is both challenging and rewarding. It also usually requires that you read a piece of writing more than once. You'll no doubt discover some elements or aspects in a second reading that you missed in the first. Regardless of what they are, those elements or aspects help to make the writing successful. Therefore, they are worth exploring so that you will be able to use similar elements in your own writing.

Active Reading Illustrated

Here is a brief excerpt from David Feldman's book *Do Penguins Have Knees? An Imponderables Book*. This book provides answers to questions about both unusual and mundane matters related to the world around us. The following passage discusses the economic purposes of and strategies behind mail-in refunds and coupons. The annotations that accompany the excerpt illustrate how active reading can help you. Through active reading, you can discover the meaning of the reading as well as the techniques the writer has used to express that meaning.

Main Idea: topic sentence — In many cases, the cash reward for mail-in refunds is higher than those for coupons, **[Context: What]** but the lower redemption rates make mail-ins cheaper in the long run. As Robert A. Grayson, **[Context: Who]** publisher of *The Journal of Consumer Marketing*, [explains], "The promotion looks as big but doesn't cost as much," **[Context: Why]** particularly if consumers purchase the goods and neglect to ever send for the rebate.

Main Idea: topic sentence — But cost isn't the primary consideration in implementing a mail-in rather than a coupon campaign. **[Context: Why]** The choice is really a strategic decision dictated by whom the marketer is trying to attract. Thomas L. **[Context: Who]** Ruble, consumer response manager of the Louis Rich Company, explains:

[Context: Why] Coupons are used to stimulate new business—to encourage first-time buyers. **[Context: Who]** Mail-in refunds, on the other hand, encourage continuity among the established **[Context: Who]** customer base. Mail-ins also encourage established customers to purchase multiple packages.

Main Idea: topic sentence — Mail-in refunds are also most effective for products, including foods, sold outside of grocery stores. **[Context: Who]** Supermarkets are geared for the paperwork involved **[Context: Why]** in processing coupons. But a family-run hardware or **[Context: Who]** camera store might not know how to receive compensation for the refund on a package of batteries or be **[Context: Why]** willing to put up with the nuisance of doing so.

Main Idea: topic sentence

One other crucial point. By making you fill out personal information for the refund, the marketer now has in its possession your name and address. Most companies retain this information in databases, and then can ply you with direct-mail campaigns.

Context why

(From Feldman, David. Do Penguins Have Knees? An Imponderables Book. New York: Harper Perennial, 1991. 188. Print.)

So that's why some companies choose coupons and some select rebates. Both strategies make us buy more! Therefore, it's about $$$!

As the annotations show, active reading focuses on the key elements in the writing. For one thing, it helps to identify the *context,* showing *who* would adopt a coupon campaign (*a supermarket*) and *who* would follow a mail-in refund strategy (*a company pushing products not sold in supermarkets*). At the same time, it shows *who* among consumers would be the targets of such campaigns and *what* motivates manufacturers to choose one of the options (*attracting new customers versus holding on to longtime buyers*). Finally, it explains *why* one method is generally cheaper than the other. (*People often redeem coupons but don't always mail away for rebates.*)

Besides helping you to establish the context, active reading highlights the main ideas as expressed in the *topic sentences* and the *supporting sentences.* Furthermore, when you *respond* to the reading, you focus more completely on the significance or meaning of the passage. Understanding how a writer communicates ideas to a reader enables you to communicate your own ideas more effectively to your reader.

To Be an All-American Girl

Elizabeth Wong

Elizabeth Wong, the daughter of immigrant parents, is a writer and playwright. This essay, first printed in the Los Angeles Times *in 1989, explores her memories about learning the "language of [her] heritage." As you read, see what you discover about what it means "[t]o Be an All-American Girl."*

1   It's still there, the Chinese school on Yale Street where my brother and I used to go. Despite the new coat of paint and the high wire fence, the school I knew 10 years ago remains remarkably, stoically the same.

2   Every day at 5 P.M., instead of playing with our fourth- and fifth-grade friends or sneaking out to the empty lot to hunt ghosts and animal bones, my brother and I had to go to Chinese school. No amount of kicking, screaming, or pleading could dissuade my mother, who was solidly determined to have us learn the language of our heritage.

3   Forcibly, she walked us the seven long, hilly blocks from our home to school, depositing our defiant tearful faces before the stern principal. My only memory of him is that he swayed on his heels like a palm tree, and he always clasped his impatient twitching hands behind his back. I recognized him as a repressed maniacal child killer, and knew that if we ever saw his hands we'd be in big trouble.

4   We all sat in little chairs in an empty auditorium. The room smelled like Chinese medicine, an imported faraway mustiness. Like ancient mothballs or dirty closets. I hated that smell. I favored crisp new scents. Like the soft French perfume that my American teacher wore in public school.

5   There was a stage far to the right, flanked by an American flag and the flag of the Nationalist Republic of China, which was also red, white and blue but not as pretty.

6   Although the emphasis at the school was mainly language—speaking, reading, writing—the lessons always began with an exercise in politeness. With the entrance of the teacher, the best student would tap a bell and everyone would get up, kowtow, and chant, "Sing san ho," the phonetic for "How are you, teacher?"

7   Being ten years old, I had better things to learn than ideographs copied painstakingly in lines that ran right to left from the tip of a *moc but,* a real ink pen that had to be held in an awkward way if blotches were to be avoided. After all, I could do the multiplication tables, name the satellites of Mars, and write reports on "Little Women" and "Black Beauty." Nancy Drew, my favorite book heroine, never spoke Chinese.

8   The language was a source of embarrassment. More times than not, I had tried to disassociate myself from the nagging loud voice that followed me wherever I wandered in the nearby American supermarket outside Chinatown. The voice belonged to my grandmother, a fragile woman in her seventies who could outshout the best of the street vendors. Her humor was raunchy, her Chinese rhythmless, patternless. It was quick, it was loud, it was unbeautiful. It was not like the quiet, lilting romance of French or the gentle refinement of the American South. Chinese sounded pedestrian. Public.

9   In Chinatown, the comings and goings of hundreds of Chinese on their daily tasks sounded chaotic and frenzied. I did not want to be thought of as mad, as talking gibberish. When I spoke English, people nodded at me, smiled sweetly, said encouraging words. Even the people in my culture would cluck and say that I'd do well in life. "My, doesn't she move her lips fast," they would say, meaning that I'd be able to keep up with the world outside Chinatown.

10   My brother was even more fanatical than I about speaking English. He was especially hard on my mother, criticizing her, often cruelly, for her pidgin speech—smatterings of Chinese scattered like chop suey in her conversation. "It's not 'What it is,' Mom," he'd say in exasperation. "It's 'What *is* it, what *is* it, what *is* it!' " Sometimes Mom might leave out an occasional "the" or "a," or perhaps a verb of being. He would stop her in midsentence: "Say it again, Mom. Say it right." When he tripped over his own tongue, he'd blame it on her: "See, Mom, it's all your fault. You set a bad example."

11   What infuriated my mother most was when my brother cornered her on her consonants, especially "r." My father had played a cruel joke on Mom by assigning her an American name that her tongue wouldn't allow her to say. No matter how hard she tried, "Ruth" always ended up "Luth" or "Roof."

12   After two years of writing with a *moc but* and reciting words with multiples of meanings, I finally was granted a cultural divorce. I was permitted to stop Chinese school.

13   I thought of myself as multicultural. I preferred tacos to egg rolls; I enjoyed Cinco de Mayo more than Chinese New Year.

14   At last, I was one of you; I wasn't one of them.

15   Sadly, I still am.

EXPLORING THE READING THROUGH DISCUSSION

1. Where did the author and her brother have to go every day after school? Why?

2. Why was the Chinese language a "source of embarrassment" to Wong?

3. What does Wong mean by the "cultural divorce" granted to her after two years of Chinese school?

4. Who are the people Wong refers to as *you* and *them* at the end of her essay? Why is she sad to be "one of them"? Did she always feel this way?

5. Wong writes about the sights, sounds, and smells she remembers from her childhood. Find three of these sensory descriptions, and underline or highlight them. In your view, which detail is most effective? Why do you feel this way?

DEVELOPING VOCABULARY

List at least three words in this selection that are new to you. Looking for clues in the context, the sentences surrounding the words you have chosen, write what you think is a good definition for each word. Then look up each word in the dictionary, and write the correct dictionary definition next to your original definition.

DISCOVERING CONNECTIONS THROUGH WRITING

1. Have you or someone you know well had to learn English as a second language? Write about that experience. Here are some questions to help you explore the topic: What was difficult about learning a new language? Have you ever felt embarrassed or frustrated when trying to speak or write? How do you react when someone trips over his or her own tongue?

2. Most children have had the experience of being embarrassed by parents and family members. What are some causes? Can you recall a time when a family

member embarrassed you—or when you embarrassed your own child or another child? Tell the story.

3. Who are Americans? How would you recognize an American? Here's what Michael Dorris, a Native American, wrote about these questions:

> The answer is clear: to be Americans means to be not the clone of the people next door. I fly back from any homogeneous country, from a place where every person I see is blond, or black, or belongs to only one religion, and then disembark at JFK. I revel in the cadence of many accents, catch a ride to the city with a Nigerian–American or Russian–American cab driver. Eat Thai food at a Greek restaurant next to a table of Chinese–American conventioneers from Alabama. Get directions from an Iranian–American cop and drink a cup of Turkish coffee served by a Navajo student at Fordham who's majoring in Japanese literature. Argue with everybody about everything. I'm home.

What does Michael Dorris love about America? Do you think Elizabeth Wong would agree with him? Do you agree with him? Write about your response to one or more of these questions.

Education

Malcolm X

In this selection from The Autobiography of Malcolm X, *coauthored by Alex Haley, Malcolm X explores how his studies during his time in prison affected him. As a result of reading about his experience, what do you discover about the power of writing?*

1   It was because of my letters that I happened to stumble upon starting to acquire some kind of a homemade education.

2   I became increasingly frustrated at not being able to express what I wanted to convey in letters that I wrote, especially those to Mr. Elijah Muhammad. In the street, I had been the most articulate hustler out there—I had commanded attention when I said something. But now, trying to write simple English, I not only wasn't articulate, I wasn't even functional. How would I sound writing in slang, the way I would *say* it, something such as, "Look, daddy, let me pull your coat about a cat, Elijah Muhammad—"

3   Many who today hear me somewhere in person, or on television, or those who read something I've said, will think I went to school far beyond the eighth grade. This impression is due entirely to my prison studies.

4   It had really begun back in the Charlestown Prison, when Bimbi first made me feel envy of his stock of knowledge. Bimbi had always taken charge of any conversations he was in, and I had tried to emulate him. But every book I picked up had few sentences which didn't contain anywhere from one to nearly all of the words that might as well have been in Chinese. When I just skipped those words, of course, I really ended up with little idea of what the book said. So I had come to the Norfolk Prison Colony still going through only book-reading motions. Pretty

soon, I would have quit even these motions, unless I had received the motivation that I did.

5   I saw that the best thing I could do was get hold of a dictionary—to study, to learn some words. I was lucky enough to reason also that I should try to improve my penmanship. It was sad. I couldn't even write in a straight line. It was both ideas together that moved me to request a dictionary along with some tablets and pencils from the Norfolk Prison Colony school.

6   I spent two days just riffling uncertainly through the dictionary's pages. I'd never realized so many words existed! I didn't know *which* words I needed to learn. Finally, just to start some kind of action, I began copying.

7   In my slow, painstaking, ragged handwriting, I copied into my tablet everything printed on that first page, down to the punctuation marks.

8   I believe it took me a day. Then, aloud, I read back, to myself, everything I'd written on the tablet. Over and over, aloud, to myself, I read my own handwriting.

9   I woke up the next morning, thinking about those words—immensely proud to realize that not only had I written so much at one time, but I'd written words that I never knew were in the world. Moreover, with a little effort, I also could remember what many of these words meant. I reviewed the words whose meanings I didn't remember. Funny thing, from the dictionary first page right now, that "aardvark" springs to my mind. The dictionary had a picture of it, a long-tailed, long-eared, burrowing African mammal, which lives off termites caught by sticking out its tongue as an anteater does for ants.

10   I was so fascinated that I went on—I copied the dictionary's next page. And the same experience came when I studied that. With every succeeding page, I also learned of people and places and events from history. Actually the dictionary is like a miniature encyclopedia. Finally the dictionary's A section had filled a whole tablet—and I went on into the B's. That was the way I started copying what eventually became the entire dictionary. It went a lot faster after so much practice helped me to pick up handwriting speed. Between what I wrote in my tablet, and writing letters, during the rest of my time in prison I would guess I wrote a million words.

11   I suppose it was inevitable that as my word-base broadened, I could for the first time pick up a book and read and now begin to understand what the book was saying. Anyone who has read a great deal can imagine the new world that opened. Let me tell you something: from then until I left that prison, in every free moment I had, if I was not reading in the library, I was reading on my bunk. You couldn't have gotten me out of books with a wedge. Between Mr. Muhammad's teachings, my correspondence, my visitors—usually Ella and Reginald—and my reading of books, months passed without my even thinking about being imprisoned. In fact, up to then, I never had been so truly free in my life.

EXPLORING THE READING THROUGH DISCUSSION

1. Malcolm X writes about being articulate when speaking and being articulate when writing. What is the difference? Why do you think there is a difference?

2. Why would someone think Malcolm X went to school beyond the eighth grade after hearing him speak?

3. Malcolm X copied the entire dictionary when he was in prison. Why did he do that, and what did he learn as a result?

4. Reread the last sentence in this selection and then explain what you think Malcolm X meant.

5. Find synonyms for the following words from the reading: *convey, functional, emulate, inevitable, correspondence.* Why do you think the author chose to use these particular words?

DEVELOPING VOCABULARY

List at least three words in this selection that are new to you. Looking for clues in the context, the sentences surrounding the words you have chosen, write what you think is a good definition for each word. Then look up each word in the dictionary, and write the correct dictionary definition next to your original definition.

DISCOVERING CONNECTIONS THROUGH WRITING

1. Later in his book Malcolm X writes that he preferred "to read in the total isolation of [his] own room," and that he'd read after "lights out" by the light from the prison corridor "until three or four every morning." Describe your own reading habits. Use these questions to help you explore this topic: Do you like to read? Why? Where is your favorite place to read? What do you like to read?

2. What do you remember about learning to read and write? Explore your memories, and write about what you recall. Here are some questions to help you remember: Were you in school? Did someone in your family or a friend help you? Did you want to learn? Why? What was difficult about learning to read? Do you remember a favorite book that you read or that was read to you?

3. In this excerpt, Malcolm X devotes his attention to the concept of becoming an educated person. Write about what you think an educated person should know, or explain what you think are the benefits of education.

Becoming a Writer

Russell Baker

Near the end of his memoir, Growing Up, *Pulitzer prize–winning columnist Russell Baker recalls worrying about what he would do after graduating from high school. As you read this selection from his book, consider who or what has influenced your decision about what career paths to explore.*

1   The only thing that truly interested me was writing, and I knew that sixteen-year-olds did not come out of high school and become writers. I thought of writing as something to be done only by the rich. It was so obviously not real work, not a job at which you could earn a living. Still, I had begun to think of myself as a writer. It was the only thing for which I seemed to have the smallest talent, and, silly though it sounded when I told people I'd like to be a writer, it gave me a way of thinking about myself which satisfied my need to have an identity.

2   The notion of becoming a writer had flickered off and on in my head since the Belleville days, but it wasn't until my third year in high school that the possibility took hold. Until then, I'd been bored by everything associated with English courses. I found English grammar dull and baffling. I hated the assignments to turn out "compositions," and went at them like heavy labor, turning out leaden, lackluster paragraphs that were agonies for teachers to read and for me to write. The classics thrust on me to read seemed as deadening as chloroform.

3   When our class was assigned to Mr. Fleagle for third-year English I anticipated another grim year in that dreariest of subjects. Mr. Fleagle was notorious among city students for dullness and inability to inspire. He was said to be stuffy, dull, and hopelessly out of date. To me he looked to be sixty or seventy and prim to a fault. He wore primly severe eyeglasses, his wavy hair was primly cut and primly combed. He wore prim vested suits with neckties blocked primly against the collar buttons of his primly straight nose, and a prim manner of speaking that was so correct, so gentlemanly, that he seemed a comic antique.

4   I anticipated a listless, unfruitful year with Mr. Fleagle and for a long time was not disappointed. We read *Macbeth*. Mr. Fleagle loved *Macbeth* and wanted us to love it too, but he lacked the gift of infecting others with his own passion. He tried to convey the murderous ferocity of Lady Macbeth one day by reading aloud the passage that concludes:

> … I have given suck, and know
> How tender 'tis to love the babe that milks me.
> I would, while it was smiling in my face,
> Have plucked my nipple from his boneless gums …

The idea of prim Mr. Fleagle plucking his nipple from boneless gums was too much for the class. We burst into gasps of irrepressible snickering. Mr. Fleagle stopped.

5   "There is nothing funny, boys, about giving suck to a babe. It is the—the very essence of motherhood, don't you see."

6   He constantly sprinkled his sentences with "don't you see." It wasn't a question but an exclamation of mild surprise at our ignorance. "Your pronoun needs an antecedent, don't you see," he would say, very primly. "The purpose of the Porter's scene, boys, is to provide comic relief from the horror, don't you see."

7   Late in the year we tackled the informal essay. "The essay, don't you see, is the … " My mind went numb. Of all forms of writing, none seemed so boring as the essay. Naturally we would have to write informal essays. Mr. Fleagle distributed a homework sheet offering us a choice of topics. None was quite so simpleminded as "What I Did on My Summer Vacation," but most seemed to be almost as dull. I took the list home and dawdled until the night before the essay was due. Sprawled on the sofa, I finally faced up to the grim task, took the list out of my notebook, and scanned it. The topic on which my eye stopped was "The Art of Eating Spaghetti."

8   This title produced an extraordinary sequence of mental images. Surging up out of the depths of memory came a vivid recollection of a night in Belleville when all of us were seated around the supper table—Uncle Allen, my mother, Uncle Charlie, Doris, Uncle Hal—and Aunt Pat served spaghetti for supper. Neither Doris nor I had ever eaten spaghetti, and none of the adults had enough experience to be good at it. All the good humor of Uncle Allen's house reawakened in my mind as I recalled the laughing arguments we had that night about the socially respectable method for moving spaghetti from plate to mouth.

9   Suddenly I wanted to write about that, about the warmth and good feeling of it, but I wanted to put it down simply for my own joy, not for Mr. Fleagle. It was a moment I wanted to recapture and hold for myself. I wanted to relive the pleasure of an evening at New Street. To write it as I wanted, however, would violate all the rules of formal composition I'd learned in school, and Mr. Fleagle would surely give it a failing grade. Never mind. I would write something else for Mr. Fleagle after I had written this thing for myself.

10   When I finished it the night was half gone and there was no time left to compose a proper, respectable essay for Mr. Fleagle. There was no choice next morning but to turn in my private reminiscence of Belleville. Two days passed before Mr. Fleagle returned the graded papers, and he returned everyone's but mine. I was bracing myself for a command to report to Mr. Fleagle immediately after school for discipline when I saw him lift my paper from his desk and rap for the class's attention.

11   "Now, boys," he said, "I want to read you an essay. This is titled 'The Art of Eating Spaghetti.'"

12   And he started to read. My words! He was reading *my words* out loud to the entire class. What's more, the entire class was listening. Listening attentively. Then somebody laughed, then the entire class was laughing, and not in contempt and ridicule, but with openhearted enjoyment. Even Mr. Fleagle stopped two or three times to repress a small prim smile.

13   I did my best to avoid showing pleasure, but what I was feeling was pure ecstasy at this startling demonstration that my words had the power to make people laugh. In the eleventh grade, at the eleventh hour as it were, I had discovered a calling. It was the happiest moment of my entire school career. When Mr. Fleagle finished he put the final seal on my happiness by saying "Now that, boys, is an essay, don't you see. It's—don't you see—it's of the very essence of the essay, don't you see. Congratulations, Mr. Baker."

14   For the first time, light shone on a possibility. It wasn't a very heartening possibility, to be sure. Writing couldn't lead to a job after high school, and it was hardly honest work, but Mr. Fleagle had opened a door for me. After that I ranked Mr. Fleagle among the finest teachers in the school.

EXPLORING THE READING THROUGH DISCUSSION

1. The author believed he had not turned in "a proper, respectable essay," and would be reprimanded, but instead he was praised. Why do you think his readers enjoyed his writing?

2. What was Baker's opinion about English classes when he was a student? What happened in his third year of high school to change his mind?

3. Why did the topic of "The Art of Eating Spaghetti" motivate him to write? Why did he enjoy writing his essay?

4. How did Baker's classmates and Mr. Fleagle respond to his writing? Why was that feedback important to him?

5. Find and list the adjectives Baker uses to describe Mr. Fleagle throughout the writing. Why does the author's opinion of his teacher change?

DEVELOPING VOCABULARY

List any words in this selection that are new to you. Write your understanding of each word from the context. Then look up each word in the dictionary, and write the definition that you think best fits the meaning in this writing.

DISCOVERING CONNECTIONS THROUGH WRITING

1. Baker's story describes a turning point in his life, a time when he "discovered a calling" and "light shone on a possibility." Have you had an experience when you discovered a new possibility in your life? Write a story of your own turning point.

2. As a young man, the author incorrectly believed that writing was "obviously not real work, not a job at which you could earn a living." In what job or career do you see writing well as essential to success? What about this field calls for solid writing skills. Provide a clear thesis and plenty of examples to support this main idea.

3. Russell Baker brings his memory of Mr. Fleagle to life with details about his physical appearance, his actions, and his language. Write your own character description of someone you know well using descriptive language so that your readers can see your own impression of this person.

Complaining

Maya Angelou

In her book Wouldn't Take Nothing for My Journey Now, *Maya Angelou explores her life and what her experiences, friendships, and relationships have taught her. As you read this chapter from the book, see what useful advice you can discover.*

1   When my grandmother was raising me in Stamps, Arkansas, she had a particular routine when people who were known to be whiners entered her store. Whenever she saw a known complainer coming, she would call me from whatever I was doing and say conspiratorially, "Sister, come inside. Come." Of course I would obey.

2   My grandmother would ask the customer, "How are you doing today, Brother Thomas?" And the person would reply, "Not so good." There would be a distinct whine in the voice. "Not so good today, Sister Henderson. You see, it's this summer. It's this summer heat. I just hate it. Oh, I hate it so much. It just frazzles me up and frazzles me down. I just hate the heat. It's almost killing me." Then my grandmother would stand stoically, her arms folded, and mumble, "Uh-huh, uh-huh." And she would cut her eyes at me to make certain that I had heard the lamentation.

3   At another time a whiner would mewl, "I hate plowing. That packed-down dirt ain't got no reasoning, and mules ain't got good sense. ... Sure ain't. It's killing me. I can't ever seem to get done. My feet and my hands stay sore, and I get dirt in my eyes and up my nose. I just can't stand it." And my grandmother, again stoically with her arms folded, would say, "Uh-huh, uh-huh," and then look at me and nod.

4   As soon as the complainer was out of the store, my grandmother would call me to stand in front of her. And then she would say the same thing she had said at least a thousand times, it seemed to me. "Sister, did you hear what Brother So-and-So or Sister Much to Do complained about? You heard that?" And I would nod. Mamma would continue, "Sister, there are people who went to sleep all over the world last night, poor and rich and white and black, but they will never wake again. Sister, those who expected to rise did not, their beds became their cooling boards, and their blankets became their winding sheets. And those dead folks would give anything, anything at all for just five minutes of this weather or ten minutes of that plowing that person was grumbling about. So you watch yourself about complaining, Sister. What you're supposed to do when you don't like a thing is change it. If you can't change it, change the way you think about it. Don't complain."

5   It is said that persons have few teachable moments in their lives. Mamma seemed to have caught me at each one I had between the age of three and thirteen. Whining is not only graceless, but can be dangerous. It can alert a brute that a victim is in the neighborhood.

EXPLORING THE READING THROUGH DISCUSSION

1. What was Mamma's routine when whiners entered her store?

2. Instead of complaining, what did Mamma suggest people do? Do you agree with her advice?

3. According to Angelou, why is whining dangerous?

4. Read the whiners' words out loud. What tone of voice do you use? Does written language have a tone as spoken words do? Explain.

5. Find and underline or highlight the transition words Angelou uses in this essay. How do they help her readers understand her experience and the lesson it taught her?

DEVELOPING VOCABULARY

List at least three words in this selection that are new to you. Looking for clues in the context, the sentences surrounding the words you have chosen, write what you think is a good definition for each word. Then look up each word in the dictionary, and write the correct dictionary definition next to your original definition.

DISCOVERING CONNECTIONS THROUGH WRITING

1. What is one change you would like to make in your job, or in a personal relationship, or in another aspect of your life? Write a plan for making that change.

2. What is a "teachable moment"? Write about a time you learned something at a teachable moment in your own life.

3. Besides whining, what other bad habits do people have that annoy you? For example, do you live with a sloppy person? Do you know someone who is always borrowing money or someone who is habitually late? Describe a person or a situation that helps your reader understand what annoys you and why.

Baseball

Annie Dillard

Have you ever felt as if you were an outsider? If so, you might understand Annie Dillard's frustration at being prohibited from playing a sport she loved, not because of her ability but because of her gender. As you read this selection from her book An American Childhood, *think about your own experience with sports as a spectator or player.*

1   On Tuesday summer evenings I rode my bike a mile down Braddock Avenue to a park where I watched Little League teams play ball. Little League teams did not accept girls, a ruling I looked into for several years in succession. I parked my bike and hung outside the chain-link fence and watched and rooted and got mad and hollered, "Idiot, catch the ball!" "Play's at first!" Maybe some coach would say, "Okay, sweetheart, if you know it all, you go in there." I thought of disguising myself. None of this was funny. I simply wanted to play the game earnestly, on a diamond, until it was over, with eighteen players who knew what they were doing, and an umpire. My parents were sympathetic, if amused, and not eager to make an issue of it.

At school we played softball. No bunting, no stealing. I had settled on second base, a spot Bill Mazeroski would later sanctify: lots of action, lots of talk, and especially a chance to turn the double play. Dumb softball: so much better than no ball at all, I reluctantly grew to love it. As I got older, and the prospect of having anything to do with your Ricky up the street became out of the question, I had to remind myself with all loyalty and nostalgia, how a baseball, a real baseball, felt.

2   A baseball weighted your hand just so, and fit it. Its red stitches, its good leather and hardness like skin over bone, seemed to call forth a skill both easy and precise. On the catch—the grounder, the fly, the line drive—you could snag a baseball in your mitt, where it stayed, snap, like a mouse locked in its trap, not like some pumpkin of a softball you merely halted, with a terrible sound like a splat. You could curl your fingers around a baseball, and throw it in a straight line. When you hit it with a bat it cracked—and your heart cracked, too, at the sound. It took a grass stain nicely, stayed round, smelled good, and lived lashed in your mitt all winter, hibernating.

3   There was no call for overhand pitches in softball; all my training was useless. I was playing with twenty-five girls, some of whom did not, on the face of it, care overly about the game at hand. I waited out by second and hoped for a play to the plate.

EXPLORING THE READING THROUGH DISCUSSION

1. What is Annie Dillard's attitude about being denied the chance to play Little League baseball? What evidence in her writing helps you understand her tone?

2. Since a legal ruling in 1974, Little League Baseball teams have not excluded girls. At the same time, Little League Softball was created for girls only. If these opportunities had existed when Dillard was a girl in the 1950s, which sport do you think she would have played? Why?

3. Earlier in the memoir from which this excerpt is taken, Dillard writes about playing a "two-handed baseball game" of catch with a friend, Ricky. Yet here she writes that continuing that relationship as she got older would be "out of the question." Speculate a bit: why do you think she rules out such a relationship in the future?

4. What qualities of a baseball does Annie Dillard praise? In addition to seeing the baseball, what other senses does she use to describe it?

5. Find examples of specific language in the writing that demonstrates Dillard's knowledge of baseball. Why does she include these terms instead of more general words?

DEVELOPING VOCABULARY

List any words in this selection that are new to you. Write your understanding of each word from the context. Then look up each word in the dictionary, and write the definition that you think best fits the meaning in this writing.

DISCOVERING CONNECTIONS THROUGH WRITING

1. In the selection above, Annie Dillard mentions Bill Mazeroski, a second baseman now enshrined in the Baseball Hall of Fame in Cooperstown, New York. Is there an athlete whose skills and accomplishments you admire? Write about him or her and include specific details to show readers why you rank this athlete highly.

2. If you have played a team sport, think in terms of a memorable experience and write about it . In addition to learning the rules and new physical skills, what lessons did you learn about yourself and other people that you could apply to life off the field or court?

3. When Dillard was not allowed to play baseball, her parents "were sympathetic, if amused, and not eager to make an issue of it." Do you think they were correct to respond in this way? Write to persuade readers that parents should—or should not be—actively involved in their children's sports teams or other activities as coaches or spectators. Consider using emphatic order to organize your main ideas.

The Pleasures of the Text

Charles McGrath

How much time do you spend sending and replying to text messages every day? In this essay, originally published in the New York Times Magazine *in 2006, Charles McGrath defines the language of text messaging and explores how we use this form of communication. As you read, think about the various ways you communicate at work, in school, or with friends and family.*

1   There used to be an ad on subway cars, next to the ones for bail bondsmen and hemorrhoid creams, that said: "if u cn rd ths u cn gt a gd job & mo pa." The ad was promoting a kind of stenography that is now extinct, presumably. Who uses stenographers anymore? But the notion that there might be value in easily understood shorthand has proved to be prescient. If u cn rd these days, and, just as important, if your thumbs are nimble enough so that u cn als snd, you can conduct your entire emotional life just by transmitting and receiving messages on the screen of your cellphone. You can flirt there, arrange a date, break up, and—in Malaysia at least—even get a divorce.

2   Shorthand contractions, along with letter-number homophones ("gr8" and "2moro," for example), emoticons (like the tiresome colon-and-parenthesis smiley face) and acronyms (like the ubiquitous "lol," for "laughing out loud"), constitute the language of text-messaging—or txt msg, to use the term that txt msgrs prefer. Text-messaging is a refinement of computer instant-messaging, which came into vogue five or six years ago. But because the typical cellphone screen can accommodate no more than 160 characters, and because the phone touchpad is far less versatile than the computer keyboard, text-messaging puts an even greater premium on concision. Here, for example, is a text-message version of "Paradise Lost" disseminated by some scholars in England: "Devl kikd outa hevn coz jelus of jesus&strts war. pd'off wiv god so corupts man (md by god) wiv apel. devl stays serpnt 4hole life&man ruind. Woe un2mnkind."

3   As such messages go, that one is fairly straightforward and unadorned. There is also an entire code book of acronyms and abbreviations, ranging from CWOT (complete waste of time) to DLTBBB (don't let the bedbugs bite). And emoticonography has progressed way beyond the smiley-face stage, and now includes hieroglyphics to indicate drooling, for example (: -) …), as well as secrecy (:X), Hitler (/.#( ), and the rose (@{rcub};--). Keep these in mind; we'll need them later.

4   As with any language, efficiency isn't everything. There's also the issue of style. Among inventive users, and younger ones especially, text-messaging has taken on many of the characteristics of hip-hop, with so much of which it conveniently overlaps—in the substitution of "z" for "s," for example, "a," for "er" and "d" for "th." Like hip-hop, text-messaging is what the scholars call "performative"; it's writing that aspires to the condition of speech. And sometimes when it makes abundant use of emoticons, it strives not for clarity so much as a kind of rebus-like cleverness, in which showing off is part of the point. A text-messaging version of "Paradise Lost"—or of the prologue, anyway—that tries for a little more shnizzle might go like this: "Sing hvnly mewz dat on d :X mtntp inspyrd dat shepherd hu 1st tot d chozn seed in d begnin hw d hvn n erth @{rcub};-- outa chaos."

5   Not that there is much call for Miltonic messaging these days. To use the scholarly jargon again, text-messaging is "lateral" rather than "penetrative," and the medium encourages blandness and even mindlessness. On the Internet there are several Web sites that function as virtual Hallmark stores and offer ready-made text messages of breathtaking banality. There are even ready-made Dear John letters, enabling you to dump someone without actually speaking to him or her. Far from being considered rude, in Britain this has proved to be a particularly popular way of ending a relationship—a little more thoughtful than leaving an e-mail message but not nearly as messy as breaking up in person—and it's also catching on over here.

6   Compared with the rest of the world, Americans are actually laggards when it comes to text-messaging. This is partly for technical reasons. Because we don't have a single, national phone company, there are several competing and incompatible wireless technologies in use, and at the same time actual voice calls are far cheaper here than in most places, so there is less incentive for texting. But in many developing countries, mobile-phone technology has so far outstripped land-line availability that cellphones are the preferred, and sometimes the only, means of communication, and text messages are cheaper than voice ones. The most avid text-messagers are clustered in Southeast Asia, particularly in Singapore and the Philippines.

7   There are also cultural reasons for the spread of text-messaging elsewhere. The Chinese language is particularly well-suited to the telephone keypad, because in Mandarin the names of the numbers are so close to the sounds of certain words; to say "I love you," for example, all you have to do is press 520. (For "drop dead," it's 748.) In China, moreover, many people believe that to leave voice mail is rude, and it's a loss of face to make a call to someone important and have it answered by an underling. Text messages preserve everyone's dignity by eliminating the human voice.

8   This may be the universal attraction of text-messaging, in fact: it's a kind of avoidance mechanism that preserves the feeling of communication—the immediacy—without, for the most part, the burden of actual intimacy or substance. The great majority of text messages are of the "Hey, how are you, whassup?" variety, and they're sent sometimes when messenger and recipient are within speaking distance of each other—across classrooms, say, or from one row of a stadium to another. They're little electronic waves and nods that, just like real waves and nods, aren't meant to do much more than establish a connection—or disconnection, as the case may be—without getting into specifics.

9   "We're all wired together" is the collective message, and we'll signal again in a couple of minutes, not to say anything, probably, but just to make sure the lines are still working. The most depressing thing about the communications revolution is that when at last we have succeeded in making it possible for anyone to reach anyone else anywhere and at any time, it turns out that we really don't have much we want to say.

EXPLORING THE READING THROUGH DISCUSSION

1. What is the author's opinion about text messaging? Identify the specific sentences in his writing as evidence.

2. Do you agree with McGrath's view about this method of communication? Explain why or why not, using examples from your own experience as evidence.

3. What are the elements that "constitute the language of text-messaging" that the author describes in the beginning of his essay? Can you think of other examples in addition to the ones he provides?

4. How does text messaging in the United States compare with the practice in other parts of the world? According to McGrath, what are some reasons for these differences?

5. Can you translate into standard written English one of the examples of text message language that McGrath provides? How is a translation different from the original? Which do you prefer and why?

DEVELOPING VOCABULARY

List any words in this selection that are new to you. Write your understanding of each word from the context. Then look up each word in the dictionary, and write the definition that you think best fits the meaning in this writing.

DISCOVERING CONNECTIONS THROUGH WRITING

1. Other than text messaging, social networking sites such as MySpace, Facebook, and Twitter as well as blogging help individuals stay "wired together." Do you use any of these sites? If so, which ones? Create an essay to help readers understand the benefits of these online communities.

2. Write about one or more situations when you have been distracted, annoyed, or even endangered by someone's use of text messaging in a public setting, such as a restaurant, business, classroom, or car. Remember to amplify your statements to help your readers understand your specific points.

3. Charles McGrath states that the language of texting "has taken on many of the characteristics of hip-hop," and that in both of these forms of communication, the way we write is similar to the way we speak. How much do you know about hip-hop? Write a definition of that term as you understand it, and provide specific examples to support your ideas as McGrath does.

Remembering India

Elsa "Chachi" Maldonado (student)

In this essay, Elsa Maldonado remembers and honors her sister, India. Although some subjects can be difficult to write about, see whether you can discover as you read how writing can help to bring order to strong thoughts and feelings.

1   My sister, Carmen, and I were very close. We were inseparable until her untimely death. I can remember thinking at the time of her death that someone made a mistake. That was not my sister they found lying on the eighteenth floor of the Ringe Tower Projects in Cambridge, Massachusetts. Clearly, it had to be someone else's sister. My sister, Carmen, better known as India, was an outgoing, loving person who had no known enemy. I could not understand why anyone would want to take her away from us.

2   I can remember when I was about eight years old, my mother, Lucy, had to work two jobs in order to provide food, clothing, and shelter for my brothers, sister, and me. It wasn't easy for her, but she did her best to keep us all together as a family. The oldest child was India, and at the age of fourteen, she was the primary caregiver while Mom was away at work. Although I didn't understand at the time, I now realize how difficult it must have been for India to stay at home when she really wanted to be out with her friends. Sometimes her friends used to come over to our house and ask if she wanted to go hang out with them at the park. India would look over her shoulder only to find my brothers and me staring at her. She would then look back at her friends and tell them she was sorry, but

she had to baby-sit. I can remember my brothers and me letting out a sigh of relief, knowing that she was not going to leave us alone—not that she ever did.

3   My sister never let the "I'm in charge" status go to her head. Whenever she
wanted us to pick up our toys or put the dishes away, she would say to us, "O.K. guys,
it's time to pick up after ourselves." She would even pick up our mess, even if she
didn't join us in making the mess. One time, during one of our usual cleaning routines,
I asked my sister how it felt to be the boss in charge of all of us. She replied by saying,
"I don't know. I'm only your big sister looking out for you guys." Afterwards, my brothers and I decided to go play in our room. As I was leaving the living room, I looked
back at my sister, who had decided to watch television. I noticed she had a big smile
on her face as she turned to look back at me, saying, "I'll tell you what, though—it feels
great to be a big sister." I smiled back and left the room to join my brothers.

4   India made sure that our days were not boring while in her care. Every day she
would bring home a bag of penny candies that she picked up on her way home
from school. When she walked in the door, we would greet her, and she would tell
us in a low tone of voice who the birthday person was for the day. My brothers and
I knew that India would have a small paper bag full of candy stashed away somewhere in the house, so we tried to be on our best behavior. We loved our mother,
but sometimes we couldn't wait for Mom to go to work so we could spread the
candy on top of the kitchen table and sing "Happy Birthday" to the birthday person. The candy was saved until our school work was completed and the dishes
were cleaned and put away. With a birthday candle melting over the cream of a
cupcake, we sang "Happy Birthday" off key. These parties were kept secret from
my mother because she would never have allowed us to eat so much candy. After
the party, my sister would impose her golden rules, which were that we had to
brush our teeth and give each other a hug and a kiss. Of course, we gave her an extra kiss and hug, so she could pass it on to Mom when she got home.

5   When India was around sixteen, Mom started working one full-time job, so
India's baby-sitting services were no longer needed. However, I believe that the
time she spent baby-sitting us brought us all closer to each other. Even when she
wasn't baby-sitting me, India and I spent a great deal of time together. We shared
each other's secrets. She taught me how to play handball, how to keep up-to-date
with dances, how to put on makeup and how to keep a diary, among other things.
I even used her baby-sitting techniques when I started baby-sitting.

6   India's death left us all in disbelief, horror, and sadness. Although my sister is no
longer with us physically, the love, laughter, caring, and joy that she inspired within
our hearts will last a lifetime. Nothing, not even her untimely death, can destroy that.

EXPLORING THE READING THROUGH DISCUSSION

1. Elsa doesn't include the specific circumstances of India's death in this essay.
    Should the author have included that information? Explain.

2. Was India a good "primary caregiver" of her brothers and sister? What evi-
    dence does the author provide?

3. How did India feel about caring for her siblings? How do you know?

4. In your view, what is the biggest lesson Elsa learned from her sister?

5. Essays should have effective introduction and conclusion paragraphs. Do you
    think these paragraphs in this essay are effective? Why?

DEVELOPING VOCABULARY

List at least three words in this selection that are new to you. Looking for clues in the context, the sentences surrounding the words you have chosen, write what you think is a good definition for each word. Then look up each word in the dictionary, and write the correct dictionary definition next to your original definition.

DISCOVERING CONNECTIONS THROUGH WRITING

1. Using Elsa Maldonado's essay as a model, write a memoir of someone you know and love. Be sure to identify a focus for your writing. Begin by exploring your memories through prewriting.

2. As Elsa explains, India spent a significant amount of time as a babysitter. Drawing on your experiences and beliefs, write a guide for babysitters. Include as many specific tips and ideas as you can.

3. India was given a lot of responsibility as a young teenager. How much do you think children should be asked to do to help at home? What do they gain from the experience? Refer to this essay or your own experiences to support your ideas.

"Forget the past. No one becomes successful in the past."

Peter LeComte (student)

In this essay, Peter LeComte uses examples from his life to help explain his understanding of a quotation. As you read, what examples from your own experience can you discover that support or conflict with Peter's conclusions?

1   If we examine the grammar within this quotation, we can attempt to grasp the meaning of the words. No one *becomes* successful in the past; this is not saying that no one *became* successful in the past, but that the past is *our* past, and people become successful in *their* present. So what this statement has at its core is that you can never go back and alter what you believe to be past mistakes. We cannot undo what has already been done. If we wish to live a full life, we have to do it now. There is no use wallowing in our past mistakes.

2   Many people berate themselves over mistakes they have made in the past. Unfortunately, too many people never get past the anger stage. Of course, I am not exempt from this. As recently as this past Saturday, I found it difficult to forget the past. When I went to bed on Friday night, I set the alarm for 8:20. It should have given me plenty of time to get to work. Unbeknownst to me, I had inadvertently set it on P.M. rather than A.M. Needless to say, when I awoke at twenty-five past nine, I realized the error I had made the night before. When I arrived at work, I was nearly forty-five minutes late. Throughout the work day, the fact that I was late festered in the back of my mind. I was unable to put aside my anger and simply do my job. Thus, my work suffered.

3   I find this to be a perfect example, at least in my life, of being unable to free oneself from the past. In retrospect, I realize that had I just accepted the fact that I was late, I could have had a much more productive and enjoyable day. If we are able to grasp this linear concept of the past being the past while we are still in the situation, we can do our best to forgive ourselves and simply get on with our lives.

4   In this quotation, success does not necessarily pertain to finances. Success is something you achieve when you live your life the way you truly want to. I'll be honest. I do not want to continue to deny myself happiness right now because I never went to a high school prom, or because I quit playing hockey. These things just don't make sense. If I am upset that I don't play hockey, I could go get my stick and my skates and go and play. Sitting around being angry about not playing won't get me out on the ice.

5   When we make mistakes, and believe me, we all have regrets, we are powerless to rectify these past events. If we caused harm to another person, we cannot undo the pain we have caused; we can only ask for forgiveness from those we have hurt. The people we have hurt might include ourselves.

6   By letting go of the past, we become free from it, and we can live in the present, where we belong. I know we belong here because this is where we are. If we don't choose to let go of the past, we will continue to harbor resentment toward the present. We will continue to remember the pain we have lived, and our future will be filled with pain as well.

EXPLORING THE READING THROUGH DISCUSSION

1. Peter LeComte writes, "We cannot undo what has already been done." Do you agree with him or are there times that we can act to rectify mistakes already made? What leads you to this belief?

2. According to the author, how can anger about our own mistakes affect our lives?

3. How do you react when you realize that you have made a mistake? How does your reaction compare with the author's?

4. What is Peter's definition of success? Do you agree with his view? Why or why not?

5. Identify the life mistakes the author writes about in his essay. Which example provides the strongest support for the thesis of the essay? Why do you feel this way?

DEVELOPING VOCABULARY

List any words in this selection that are new to you. Write your understanding of each word from the context. Then look up each word in the dictionary, and write the definition that you think best fits the meaning in this writing.

DISCOVERING CONNECTIONS THROUGH WRITING

1. Choose a quotation, as Peter did, and explain what the words mean to you. Be sure to let readers know why the quotation is important to you.

2. In his essay, Peter offers his own definition of success. Now, write your own definition of success. Include examples of success to help readers understand your definition.

3. Write about a time when you were able to let go of the past and live in the present or about a time that, try as you might, you just couldn't.

Differences in Child Rearing in Russia and the United States

Svetlana Melamedman (student)

Writers can help readers understand something new by comparing it to something familiar. As you read this essay by Svetlana Melamedman, you will discover how children are raised in Russia. Consider how the Russian approach is similar to or different from the way you were brought up.

1   Sometimes I ask myself, "Am I ready to face the responsibility of raising a child?" Right now, my answer is no. It's not just because I am young but also because I have not decided which way I should raise my baby: American or Russian. Every country has a different system for the upbringing and education of young children. I know two ways, the Russian and American, but I'm not sure which one I prefer. They are so different in terms of attitudes about childbirth, education, and relationships with extended family.

2   One major difference between life in Russia and the United States is what happens before babies are born. In Russia, before women give birth, people don't talk about the babies or speculate about their future or sex. Also, nobody buys presents before babies are born. It is considered bad luck, and everyone believes in it. In my country, instead of trying to help women who are giving birth, men go shopping for baby clothes and other things. In addition, women and their babies are kept in a hospital for about a week while the new mothers are taught how to take care of their babies.

3   On the other hand, in the United States, before women give birth, people freely discuss the babies that are coming. Often, mothers are given baby showers. There are no restrictions on who can come to the parties, and when they are over, both mother and babies have received presents before the birth. Here, it is not considered to be bad luck if you want to know the gender of the baby. Also, in the U.S., moms and sometimes dads take classes in how to have and care for a baby. In addition, women and their babies are sent home within a day of birth.

4   Another important difference to me is the way children are educated in the two countries. In Russia, after spending their first three years home with their mothers, children begin formal schooling. They leave their parents and go to full-time day care, and then to kindergarten, and after that to elementary school, all usually run by the government. Every class has between twenty and twenty-five people. When kids turn seven years old, they go to a school that is located right near their house. Parents accompany their kids on the way to school for just a half year. After that, they go by themselves. Children attend five or six classes every day and study six days a week. They do their homework by themselves while their parents are at work. At night, parents will often check their work. Children stay in this system for ten years. After completing the last grade, they can choose a university or institute.

5   The American system is somewhat different. Before many children in the U.S. begin school, they have spent time with babysitters or day care providers. Preschool is not a requirement for U.S. students as it is in Russia. When they start school in kindergarten, children often have to travel to and from the school by bus. After school, they do their homework with babysitters or parents. Schools in the U.S. have three levels, elementary, middle, and high school, and it takes twelve years to complete them. Then, if they want and have done well in school, they can go on to college or a technical school of some kind.

6   Another major difference for kids in Russia and those in the U.S. is the relationships children have with their extended families. In Russia, not many children spend time with family members other than their siblings and parents. Sometimes children don't even know about aunts or uncles or cousins until later in their lives. Houses and apartments are often arranged so that they share a big playground. Neighborhoods aren't private places, and kids from the houses nearby gather in the playground to play together. In the summer months, almost all kids go to camps or small villages to visit grandparents. Children therefore have many friends because they spend a lot of time separate from their families. This independence helps to make them more confident.

7   In my opinion, America is perfect in terms of family relationships. From the time most babies are born, their relationships with their extended families are usually closer than they are in Russia. U.S. children are more likely to know and spend time with cousins and other members of their extended families than kids in Russia do. Spending time at a summer camp isn't as common here as it is in Russia, so children spend their summers with family members, too.

8   As you can see, there are serious differences in the way things are done in the two countries, and they leave me with many questions. What is the right way for me to raise my child? I hope in the future that I am able figure out whether the Russian system or the U.S. system will be right for my baby and me.

EXPLORING THE READING THROUGH DISCUSSION

1. Svetlana Melamedman writes about three important aspects of raising a child. What are they? What do you think are the most important aspects of child rearing?

2. What, if any, ideas about child rearing in Russia do you find surprising?

3. Are there any Russian practices that you think you might prefer to those you are more familiar with in the United States? Why? Do you have experience with other practices not mentioned in the essay?

4. Do you think that the author presents a balanced view of each country's practices? Explain your answer.

5. An essay should include both an introduction and a conclusion. In your view does Svetlana provide an effective introduction and conclusion? Explain.

DEVELOPING VOCABULARY

List any words in this selection that are new to you. Write your understanding of each word from the context. Then look up each word in the dictionary, and write the definition that you think best fits the meaning in this writing.

DISCOVERING CONNECTIONS THROUGH WRITING

1. In the beginning of her essay, Svetlana asks herself an important question. Her answer is "no." When do you think a person is "ready to face the responsibility of raising a child"? Write about at least three reasons why you think someone could answer "yes."

2. If you could do so, how would you change the education requirements for children? For example, should children begin their formal education earlier or spend more hours in school each week? As you write, consider the reasons you would propose the changes and what positive effects the changes would create.

3. How did you spend your summers as a child? Did you attend camp or spend time with your relatives? Did you have a summer job or help with family responsibilities? Write about at least three of your summer activities, or tell the story of your happiest summer memory.

I Do Remember You

Soledad A. Munoz-Vilugron (student)

In her essay, Soledad Munoz-Vilugron writes about an object she treasures because of the memories it helps her recall. Explore the memories that are important to you. What priceless objects help you stay connected to these significant moments in your past?

1   Because of their significance in our lives, priceless objects are among the most wonderful things someone could have. It's not the price, nor its beauty that matters, but the memories those objects bring back to us. My priceless object is a portrait of my favorite poet, Pablo Neruda, whose poems have captivated me since I was in high school. The picture was given to me by my grandmother whom I have also admired for much longer.

2   Six years ago, when I was still living in Chile, my grandmother and I took a trip to different museums in Chile. One of the many we visited was Pablo Neruda's house. His house lay on a greenish-rocked hill, from where you could see the infinite horizon of the Pacific Ocean. Its panoramic view astonished us. From every single room of the house, you were able to see the furious waves fighting against the rocks sculpted by the salty water. And there we were, my grandmother and I, enjoying the salty smell of the ocean while venerating the scenery that surrounded us. I felt as if I was in paradise. In front of me I had this marvelous ocean that looked as if it were coming for me to take me with it. The ocean sounded like a plane ready to take off, full of power, ready to meet his beloved one, the sand. There she was waiting, peacefully and patiently, for her ocean to take part of her with him.

3   Located right next to Neruda's house was the souvenir store, which if it weren't for the sign that said "souvenirs" and a picture of Neruda hanging from one of the windows, we wouldn't ever have found. As we walked in, we were surrounded by the different aromas. It was the smell of sea, the books and the red wood shelves conjugated in that camouflaged place. After being distracted by all this, my grandmother focused her attention on a black and white portrait of

Neruda. In this picture Neruda looks like he was an adventurous, strong but humble man. She picked it for me. I think she knew I was going to need something to remember her when I moved to the States.

4   I was nineteen years old when I moved to the States. One of the things that I brought with me was the picture my grandmother bought for me at Neruda's museum. I needed something to hold on to, in case I got home sick or felt lonely. By looking at that picture I'm still able to relive every moment of that trip. The smell of the ocean, the souvenir store, the scenery, my grandmother's voice, laugh, and face. I just close my eyes to transport myself to Neruda's home. I remember everything, every single detail that she and I experienced. I wonder if grandma does too. No, she doesn't. She has Alzheimer's now. And that's fine because she gave me the most beautiful and priceless object a person could ever have, a picture that is full of smell, laughs, words, and most of all my grandmother who is the protagonist of my most loved object and memory. I had the pleasure of being with her when I was still someone familiar to her.

EXPLORING THE READING THROUGH DISCUSSION

1. Why is the author's photograph of Pablo Neruda a "priceless object"?

2. What are two places that the photograph helps her to remember?

3. In addition to having the opportunity to visit her favorite poet's home, why was the trip to this museum important to the author?

4. Why doesn't Soledad include details in this essay about Pablo Neruda and the poems that he wrote? With the help of a librarian, or by searching the Internet, find a brief biography about this poet and write a paragraph of at least seven to ten sentences in which you summarize his life and accomplishments. Be sure also to record and cite the source of your information.

5. Find examples in the writing of details that relate to our senses of sight, smell, and hearing. Why is it important for the author to include these details in her writing?

DEVELOPING VOCABULARY

List any words in this selection that are new to you. Write your understanding of each word from the context. Then look up each word in the dictionary, and write the definition that you think best fits the meaning in this writing.

DISCOVERING CONNECTIONS THROUGH WRITING

1. Describe an object you own that is priceless to you because of its significance. As this author did, use specific language to help readers visualize the object.

2. Do you have a favorite photograph that brings back the sights, sounds, or smells of a place or time? Write a story about a memory that the photograph helps you relive. Be sure to include sensory words to bring your story to life.

3. Have you experienced a vacation during which you saw and enjoyed some of the beauty of the natural world or visited an historic place or cultural landmark? Write about this trip. If it's appropriate, use chronological order to organize the events of your visit.

Moving to America

Pranee Vincent (student)

Change often comes with challenges. The secret, as author Pranee Vincent explains, is to face up to the challenges and find ways to adapt. When she moved from Thailand to the United States, Pranee took a risk that led first to discoveries and then to adjustments to a life quite different from the one to which she had been accustomed. As you read, consider how you embrace and adapt to changes in your own life.

1   Have you ever thought about moving to another country? I never did until I met my husband who was from America. A few years ago, I had to make an important decision whether or not to move to America or stay in my native country of Thailand. Eventually, I made the decision to move to America with my husband. I left everything behind such as my family, friends, job, culture, and traditional Thai food. Starting a new life in America was not easy for me because I had to deal with learning a new language, trying to understand a new culture, getting used to the climate, and acquiring a taste for American food. All of this made me question whether or not I was capable of adapting to this new environment.

2   After I moved to America, a difficult obstacle for me to overcome was learning the English language. Even though I learned basic English while going to college in my country, I did not understand how to apply basic English in a daily conversation. I also had trouble understanding the American accent. When I was speaking with Americans, they did not understand me as well because I have a very strong Thai accent. Even now, living in America for several years, I still have trouble understanding certain Americans, especially those from down South. However, I am still working on my English skills such as writing, reading, and speaking. I hope one day I will be able to speak, read, and write English fluently.

3   Also, I had to adjust myself to the cold weather. I came from a tropical country. There is no snow in Thailand and only two seasons, the rainy season and dry season. I never experienced fall, winter, or spring. The first year I was in America I found that winter was exceedingly cold for me. My husband had to keep the house's temperature between seventy-five to eighty degrees to keep me warm. It helped me survive the first winter. Even after three years I still find American winters extremely cold, but my body has adjusted, and I am used to it now. I am able to reduce the temperature of my house to seventy-two degrees in the winter, and I feel semi-comfortable this year.

4   Another big obstacle I had to overcome was trying to understand American culture. I felt a total sense of "culture shock" after first arriving in America. For example, Americans wear shoes in their homes, which is considered very unsanitary in my country. They also greet each other by shaking hands, kissing, or hugging each other, which is very inappropriate in my culture. We greet each other by bowing and smiling. We never touch someone we just met. The first time I saw Americans greet by hugging, kissing, or by shaking hands I felt very uncomfortable, especially when people I first met gave me a hug. I remembered when I first met my husband's family. My mother-in-law, my husband's nieces and a nephew, and my brother-in-law all gave me a hug upon first seeing me. I felt very uncomfortable because in my country we don't greet that way. However, after living in

America for a while, I realized that this is the appropriate way to greet someone and it's just a part of American culture.

5   The last obstacle I had to overcome was acquiring a taste for American food. It is totally different than Thai food. For instance, Thai food is very hot and spicy. It is low in fat and calories because we do not use cheese or butter in Thai dishes; we instead use a lot of herbs, spices, fruits, and vegetables. American food is the exact opposite and is very high in fat and calories because they use a lot of cheese and butter while making American dishes. I found that even Thai restaurants in America were not really cooking true Thai food. They all put an American spin on their dishes making them taste less spicy and sweeter for the American palate. This is not original Thai food and tasted terrible to me. I thought I wouldn't survive here because I did not like American food, and all the Thai restaurants I went to were not cooking real Thai food. All I ate was Thai spicy noodles, which I bought while visiting Chinatown in Boston. However, my husband kept making me try different types of foods from the area. I found that I really like Portuguese food. I discovered that I loved the taste of linguiça, cacoila, and kale soup, which I found to be slightly spicy. Over time I began to eat more and more American foods. Now, I enjoy eating everything from pepperoni pizza to hot dogs.

6   In summary, I would like to say that although I had a difficult transition when I first came to America, it was worth it because of all the good experiences I have had. I have met many nice people and learned all about a new culture. I am also in the process of learning a new language. Looking back on all my experiences, I realize that I am capable of adapting to a new environment. I feel this overall experience has made me a stronger person, and I am glad to say that America is now my second home.

EXPLORING THE READING THROUGH DISCUSSION

1. What differences in lifestyle and culture made moving to the United States difficult for Pranee Vincent?

2. What do you think would be the biggest obstacle for you if you were to move to another country? Why?

3. What did the author do to meet the challenges she faced? Who helped her learn to adapt to her new environment?

4. Choose one paragraph and underline the topic sentence. How do the other sentences in this paragraph support or explain this topic sentence?

5. As Chapter 5 explains, essays have three sections: the introduction, the body, and the conclusion. Identify the three parts of an essay in "Moving to America." Of these sections, which do you think is the strongest and most successful? Why do you feel this way?

DEVELOPING VOCABULARY

List any words in this selection that are new to you. Write your understanding of each word from the context. Then look up each word in the dictionary, and write the definition that you think best fits the meaning in this writing.

DISCOVERING CONNECTIONS THROUGH WRITING

1. Pranee did not care for the new tastes she found in America. Describe your favorite food or cuisine. Let readers know why you like the food by providing details about how the food tastes, smells, and looks.

2. Would you prefer to live in a hot or a cold environment? Use your favorite prewriting technique to explore your preferences, and write about them.

3. Have you ever had to adapt to a new environment? You might have moved to a new neighborhood, from a rural area to the city, to a new school or job, or even, as Pranee has done, from one country to another. Explain the challenges you faced and how you met them. Be sure to include enough specific details and examples so that readers understand these obstacles. You may want to consider using the emphatic order of arrangement.

The Old Store

Valeri L. Cappiello (student)

Did you have a favorite place to hang out with friends when you were a child? Valeri Cappiello shares her memories of a place that was "magical" and that still holds a place in her heart and mind even though it has changed. As you read, what do you discover about your own childhood memories?

1   When I was a child, there was a favorite place all the neighborhood kids loved to go. It was the Chartley Country Store in Rehoboth, Massachusetts, but we called it the covered wagon. I remember it was a single, small brown country store, and everything seemed old and simple. The floors were old and dirty looking. There was one cash register, and it was on top of a worn-out, cracked wooden counter.

2   It was a convenience store, but we kids thought of it as the candy store. We would come out with small brown paper bags filled with penny candy such as fireballs and chocolate covered coins. The people and atmosphere were always warm and friendly.

3   We would sit outside the store with our bags of candy, and it was like we were in our own magical world. We also rode our bikes to the covered wagon when we were old enough. That was a big deal to us, and we would hang out together outside the store when it was still okay to loiter!

4   I've always held a special place for that store inside my heart, and when I was sixteen years old, I got my first job there. I was a cashier who did different odd jobs. That old floor was not fun to mop because it always seemed dirty. It didn't matter how many times I emptied the dirty water. It was always black and dirty. The floor washing was an important job because they also specialized in meats, and the floor needed to remain sanitary. However, I did love the atmosphere and the people I worked with. I really gained some special friendships in that old place. When I was 19, I went to live in Providence, RI, near Katherine Gibbs School where I attended for one year. It was sad to leave my first job I loved so much.

5   I can still remember how sad and empty I felt when I heard they tore the old store down. The owners were building a shopping plaza next door to where the store had been, and they were going to incorporate Chartley Country Store, which would become Chartley Country Plaza. It didn't seem right or possible because I had known that building all my life. It was like an old, comfortable home, and now it was gone.

6   Our childhood covered wagon was gone, and now there were a few restaurants, a hair cutting place, and Chartley Country Store, which was not the same at all. It was not by itself anymore because now it was like a strip mall, and the store was just another meat/convenience store.

7   It is now so neat, clean, and large. It is no longer a homey atmosphere in my eyes but rather an impersonal business with customers coming and going. Moreover, it is not a place to hang out with paper bags of penny candy and neighbors.

8   I still go in from time to time, usually when I am in Rehoboth visiting my parents. I will sometimes get a meat bundle or a sub and say hello to the owner if he is there. However, the old crowd is gone along with the store, and I miss that. It is amazing to me how things in this world can change so drastically, but they remain instilled in our hearts and minds forever.

EXPLORING THE READING THROUGH DISCUSSION

1. How is the new Chartley Country Plaza different from the covered wagon? List as many details as you can to show the difference.

2. Why did the author enjoy going to the store as a child? Why was it a special place?

3. The author and her friends "would hang out together outside the store when it was still okay to loiter." Do you think children "hang out" at the new store? Why?

4. Why do you think the owners of the store made the changes that they did?

5. Do you think the language in this essay is effective? Explain why. Point out at least two examples as evidence.

DEVELOPING VOCABULARY

List at least three words in this selection that are new to you. Looking for clues in the context, the sentences surrounding the words you have chosen, write what you think is a good definition for each word. Then look up each word in the dictionary, and write the correct dictionary definition next to your original definition.

DISCOVERING CONNECTIONS THROUGH WRITING

1. Do you have a special place that you keep in your heart and mind even though it may have changed over the years? Describe that place so that readers understand why it was—and is—special to you.

2. Is the new shopping plaza that the author describes an improvement for her neighborhood? Why do you think so? What types of business and shopping areas do you like to visit?

3. In her writing, Valeri discusses her first job at "the covered wagon." Do you recall your first job? Describe what you did and what you did or did not enjoy about the job.

"Why Couldn't I Have Been Named Ashley?"
Imma Achilike

In her essay that won second place in the 2004 Kaplan/Newsweek "My Turn" Essay Competition, Imma Achilike discovers the origin of her name, and with that knowledge she gains a new sense of herself. What do you know about your own name and its meaning?

1   "Ashley!" exclaimed Mrs. Renfro, and simultaneously three heads whipped around at attention towards the perturbed teacher. At the same time, all three Ashleys proudly replied, "Yes, ma'am?"

2   When I was a fourth grader, I remember sitting in class that day just before the bell rang for dismissal. I remember thinking of all the names in the world, how I could have possibly been stuck with such an alien one. I thought about all the popular kids in the class. I figured that I wasn't popular because of my weird name. I put some things together in my mind and came up with a plausible equation: COOL NAME = POPULARITY. The dismissal bell rang. As I mechanically walked out to catch my ride, I thought to myself, "Why couldn't I have been named Ashley?"

3   I was born, on July 7th, 1986, in Texas. I was the first American-born Nigerian in both of my parents' families. I was my parents' first joy, and in their joy, they gave me the name that would haunt me for the rest of my life, Immaculeta Uzoma Achilike.

4   The first time I actually became aware of my name was on the first day of first grade. I went to school loaded with all my school supplies and excited to see all of my old kindergarten friends. I couldn't wait to see who my new teacher was. As I walked into the classroom, all my friends pushed up to me, cooing my name: "Imma, Imma I missed you so much." The teacher walked in with the attendance sheet. She told everyone to quiet down so she could call roll. Before she started, she said something I thought would have never applied to me. She said, "Before I call roll, I apologize if I mispronounce anyone's name," with a very apologetic look on her face. She looked down at the attendance sheet, paused for a minute, and then looked up with an extremely puzzled look on her face. I remember thinking that there was probably some weird name before mine, although my name was always the first name to be called in kindergarten. Suddenly, my palms started sweating and then she began to hopelessly stutter my name, "Im-Immaculet Archliki, I mean, Achei ... " Here, I interrupted. My ears burned with embarrassment and droplets of perspiration formed on my nose. "Did I say it right?" she said with the same apologetic look on her face. Before I responded, the laughs that the other kids in class had been holding back suddenly exploded, like a volatile vial of glycerin, into peals of laughter. One kid thought it was so funny his chubby face started turning red and I could see a tear gradually making its way down his face. I found myself wishing I could sink into the ground and never come back. I hated being the laughing stock.

5   I never really recovered from the shock of that day. From that day forward, the first day of school was always my most feared day. I didn't know what to do; all I could do was to tell my teachers, "I go by Imma."

6   I felt so alone when all the other girls in my class had sparkly, pink pencils with their names printed on them. You know, the ones they sell in the stores along with name-embossed sharpeners, rulers, and pencil pouches. Every year I searched through and rummaged around that rack at the store, but I could never find a pencil with my name on it.

7   The summer of my seventh-grade year, my family and I took a vacation to our "home" in Nigeria, where my parents were born. My cousin and I were playing cards, talking girl talk, and relating our most embarrassing moments. Each tried to see whose story could top whose. I told one story of how I wet the bed at a sleep-over, and she told me how she had farted in class during a test. That was a hoot. Then, I told her the story of how I was laughed at because of my weird name. I thought it was pretty funny, but she didn't laugh. She had the most serious look on her face, then she asked me, "Immaculeta Uzoma Achilike, do you know what your name means?" I shook my head at her and that's when she started laughing. I thought she was making fun of me, and as I started to leave she said: "Immaculeta means 'purity,' 'Uzoma' means 'the good road' and … " having heard her words, I stopped walking away and turned around in amazement. "What does Achilike mean?" I asked. After a long pause she calmly said, "Archilike means 'to rule without force.'" I was astonished and pleased. I never knew what my name meant.

8   My name is Immaculeta Uzoma Achilike. I am the daughter of first-generation Nigerian immigrants. I am the daughter of hardworking and brave parents. My name means "to rule without force." My grandfather was a wealthy man of generous character. When I say my name in Nigeria, people know me as the grand-daughter of a wealthy man of generous character. They know me by my name. There my name is not embossed on any pencil or vanity plate. It is etched in the minds of the people.

My name is Immaculeta Uzoma Achilike.

EXPLORING THE READING THROUGH DISCUSSION

1. How much do you think names matter? Explain.

2. When does the author first become aware of her name? What happens?

3. Why is it important for Imma to find a pencil with her name on it? Why does she change her mind later?

4. Why do you think that her parents named her Immaculeta Uzoma and not Ashley or another more popular name? Did they make the right decision?

5. Is this story told in chronological order? Do you agree with the author's choice to organize her essay the way that she did? Why?

DEVELOPING VOCABULARY

List at least three words in this selection that are new to you. Looking for clues in the context, the sentences surrounding the words you have chosen, write what you think is a good definition for each word. Then look up each word in the dictionary, and write the correct dictionary definition next to your original definition.

DISCOVERING CONNECTIONS THROUGH WRITING

1. Write about your own name and what it means to you. Consider the following or other questions in your response. What do you know about the meaning or origin of your own name? Were you named to honor someone? Does your family or first name have a special meaning for you? Do you prefer to use a nickname? If you have named a child, explain why you chose the name that you did.

2. The first day of school is often a memorable one, whether it is the first day of a new school, or middle or high school or even college. What is your recollection of the first day of one of your school years? Was it a happy day or a "most feared day" as it was for this author?

3. Everyone has had an experience when, as Imma writes, "I found myself wishing I could sink into the ground and never come back. ... " Write about your own most embarrassing moment.

Tips for ESL Writers

If you can speak and write in at least one language other than English, consider yourself fortunate. In a multicultural country such as the United States and in a world in which most major corporations are multinational, your knowledge of more than one language is definitely an advantage.

However, nonnative writers often experience trouble with those aspects of English that are different from their primary language. Mastering the rules of English grammar, usage, sentence structure, and word order will help you overcome communication difficulties, as will learning the guidelines concerning correct capitalization, article use, spelling, and punctuation. You must also consider the structure and logic of texts written in English, which are often very different from texts in your language group and culture.

Remember: your ultimate goal is to communicate your ideas fully to your reader. It's not realistic to expect to have the same level of expertise and the same comfort level with English that you have with your primary language—at least not right away. But learning the elements, patterns, and approaches of standard written English will help you on your journey toward mastery.

Sentence Basics

- Make sure each sentence has a subject and a verb. If a group of words does not have both, it does not express a complete idea.

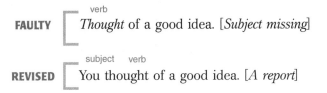

FAULTY   verb
Thought of a good idea. [*Subject missing*]

REVISED   subject   verb
You thought of a good idea. [*A report*]

In writing, the subject can be an implied *you* only if you are issuing a command.

EXAMPLE   subject   verb
[*You*] *Think* of a good idea! [*A command*]

For more information about the role and importance of subjects and verbs, see Chapter 6, "Subjects and Verbs," Chapter 7, "Sentence Fragments," and Chapter 11, "Maintaining Subject–Verb Agreement."

- Make sure that when you use *is* and *are* that they are linked to a subject. The words *there* and *here* sometimes *appear* in the normal location of a subject at the beginning of a sentence. However, *there* and *here* are adverbs, so they can't act as subjects. In such cases, the actual subject is found after the verb. (Usually, in English, the subject comes before the verb.)

FAULTY [*Is* a good place to eat near here. [*Subject missing*]

REVISED [
substitute verb   subject
There is a good *place* to eat near here. [There *signals subject after verb.*]

or

location   verb   subject
Near here is a good *place* to eat.

For more information on this aspect of verb use, see the section "Forms of to Be" on pages 281–285 in Chapter 15, "Dealing with Additional Elements of Verb Use," and "Sentences Beginning with There and Here" on pages 217–219 in Chapter 11, "Maintaining Subject–Verb Agreement."

- In English sentences, the word *there* with some form of the verb *to be* is commonly followed by a noun. The noun may have modifiers, or it may be followed by a word or phrases that specify a place.

EXAMPLES [
noun ┌──── modifier ────┐
There will be a new *student entering class today.*

┌─noun─┐ place
There is *no one here.*

noun ┌── place ──┐
There are three *cars in the lot.*

- The pronoun *it* with the verb *to be* is frequently followed by an adjective, an adjective with a modifier, an identification, or an expression of time, weather, or distance.

EXAMPLES [
adjective
It is *hot.*

adjective ┌──── modifier ────┐
It is *hot outside and inside.*

┌──── identification ────┐
What is this? It is *my English book.*

┌──────── time ────────┐
It is *eleven o'clock on Wednesday morning.*

┌──weather──┐
It is *cold and rainy.*

┌──────── distance ────────┐
It is *twenty miles from school to home.*

The word *there* should *not* be used in these expressions.

FAULTY   There is long. There has been a long time.

REVISED   *It* is long. *It* has been a long time.

Word Order

- In most English sentences, the *subject comes first, followed by the verb.*

FAULTY
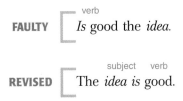
verb
Is good the *idea.*

REVISED
subject   verb
The *idea is* good.

- Adjectives, even strings of adjectives, usually come *before* nouns. *See Chapter 18, "Working with Adjectives and Adverbs: Using Modifiers Correctly," for more information about adjectives.*

FAULTY
noun   adjectives
The *man* is talking—*tall, thin,* and *handsome.*

REVISED
adjectives   noun
The *tall, thin, handsome man* is talking.

See Chapter 18, "Working with Adjectives and Adverbs: Using Modifiers Correctly," for more information about adjectives.

- Clauses that modify a noun, however, usually come immediately *after* the noun if they begin with *who, whom, whose, which,* or *that.*

FAULTY
noun   modifier
The *man* is talking *who won the award.*

REVISED
noun   modifier
The *man who won the award* is talking.

- Verb forms ending in *-ed* or *-ing* and serving as modifiers generally go after a noun they identify. That is, they follow the noun if they add essential identifying information to the sentence. However, they can go either immediately before or immediately after a noun about which they add extra information. Take a look at the following example, in which the *-ing* modifier is necessary to tell *which man:*

FAULTY
modifier   which man?
Sitting next to you, the *man* is blind.

REVISED
noun   identifying modifier
The *man sitting next to you* is blind.

Now consider the following sentence, in which the *-ing* modifier adds extra information:

EXAMPLE

┌─── modifier ───┐ ┌ noun ┐
Forgetting his promise, John left the building without locking the garage door.

- If the modifier is necessary to identify the noun, you don't use commas to separate it from the noun. If the modifier adds information about the noun, but the sentence makes sense without it, then set the modifier off with commas.

EXAMPLE

My *friend Frank* works hard.

In this sentence, the modifier is needed to identify which friend—*my friend Frank,* not *my friend Tom*—so no commas are needed.

EXAMPLE

┌ noun ┐ ┌─── modifier ───┐
Frank, who lives next door, works hard.

The modifier in this sentence provides extra information, so it needs commas. *For more on using commas in this way, see "Comma Function 5" on pages 408–409 in Chapter 21, "Using Commas."*

- Adverbs are usually placed *after to be* verbs (is/are/was/were) but *before* other one-word verbs.

EXAMPLES

verb adverb
They *are often* late.

adverb verb
Birds *usually arrive* in the spring.

For more information on using adverbs, see "The Positive Form of Modifiers" on pages 336–337 in Chapter 18, "Working with Adjectives and Adverbs: Using Modifiers Effectively."

- Adverbs often go *between* verbs that have two parts (verb phrases).

EXAMPLE

helping verb adverb verb
They *have often arrived* late.

- Pronouns that rename the subject in the same sentence are unnecessary and confusing. Even when a long modifier separates the subject from the verb, the word order alone makes the main idea of the sentence clear.

FAULTY

subject modifier subject verb
The *place* where they studied *it was* old.

REVISED

subject ┌── modifier ──┐ verb
The *place* where they studied *was* old.

Agreement

- Make the *subject and verb agree* in number. Be especially careful about collective nouns, such as *family* and *class,* and words that specify uncountable things, such as *sugar* and *water. For more on subject–verb agreement, see "The Function and Form of Nouns" on pages 296–300 in Chapter 16, "Working with Nouns," and Chapter 11, "Maintaining Subject–Verb Agreement."*

- You can count *fingers, books,* or *students,* so they are called *count* words. You cannot count *freedom, advice,* or *machinery,* so they are called *noncount.* Noncount words *always* take a *singular verb* and *a singular pronoun reference.*

noncount plural   plural
noun   verb   pronoun plural
                            reference verb

FAULTY   *Sugar make* the recipe better. *They are* tasty.

noncount singular   singular
noun   verb   pronoun singular
                            reference verb

REVISED   *Sugar makes* the recipe better. *It is* tasty.

- Some words are count words with one meaning and noncount with another meaning.

EXAMPLES   Three *chickens are* in the yard. [*Countable animals*]

                  Chicken is good with white wine. [*Noncountable meat*]

                  Three pieces of *chicken is* enough. [*Quantity of noncountable meat*]

As the last examples show, some aspects of noncount words can be measured. You can count the number of *lumps* of sugar, *cups* of milk, *tablespoons* of flour, or *gallons* of water, but you cannot say *ten sugars, three milks, two flours,* and *four waters* as a complete grammatical form.

count
noun

EXAMPLES   Twelve *cups are* necessary because we have twelve guests. [*12 items*]

                 noncount
quantity + noun

                  Two cups of *water is* sufficient. [*A measurement of a noncount noun*]

noncount   count
noun   noun

EXAMPLES   Ten *dollars is* enough. [*Amount*] Ten dollar *bills are* enough. [*Number*]

noncount   count
noun   noun

                  My *luggage is* heavy. [*Amount*] My two *bags are* heavy. [*Number*]

                 noncount
quantity + noun

FAULTY   Ten gallons of *gasoline are* all I need.

REVISED
> quantity + noncount noun
> Ten gallons of *gasoline is* all I need.

Quantities like *pounds, quarts, minutes, dollars,* and *gallons* can be numbered, but because they are collective nouns, you must use the *singular verb. For more information, see the section "The Function and Form of Nouns" on pages 296–300 in Chapter 16, "Working with Nouns."*

- Adjectives are *always* singular.

FAULTY
> the *talls* men; the *six-year-olds* children

REVISED
> the *tall* men; the six-year-*old* children

- Adjectives that end in *-ing* are active, while adjectives that end in *-ed* are passive.

EXAMPLE
> James is *boring.*

This adjective is formed from the active verb. It shows the effect that James has on others—he makes them feel bored.

EXAMPLE
> James is *bored.*

This adjective is derived from the passive verb. It shows the effect something has on James—something makes him feel bored.

For more on using adjectives, see "Understanding Active and Passive Voice" on pages 264–266 in Chapter 14, "Using Passive Voice and Progressive Tenses, and Maintaining Consistency in Tenses," and "Problems with -ing Modifiers" on pages 346–349 in Chapter 18, "Working with Adjectives and Adverbs: Using Modifiers Effectively."

- A single phrase or clause serving as a subject takes a singular verb.

FAULTY
> phrase as subject ⌐ verb   clause as subject ⌐ verb
> *Understanding the rules are* hard. *That they must be followed are* clear.

REVISED
> phrase as subject ⌐ verb   clause as subject ⌐ verb
> *Understanding the rules is* hard. *That they must be followed is* clear.

- *Verb tenses* of verbs connected in a series with commas should agree in their form.

FAULTY
> The child *was running, jumped,* and *has skipped.* [*Mixed tense forms*]

REVISED
> The child *ran, jumped,* and *skipped.* [*All past tense forms*]

For more on this aspect of verb use, see Chapter 19, "Maintaining Parallelism."

- Use the present or present perfect tense, not the future tense, in a subordinate clause whose main clause is future tense.

FAULTY

⌐────── subordinate clause ──────⌐ ⌐─ main clause ─⌐
After I will do my homework, I will go out.

REVISED

⌐────── subordinate clause ──────⌐ ⌐─ main clause ─⌐
After I have done my homework, I will go out.

See "Consistency in Tense" on pages 268–271 in Chapter 14, "Using Passive Voice and Progressive Tenses, and Maintaining Consistency in Tense," for more information on keeping the voice of tense consistent.

Confusing Verb Forms

- Don't omit the *-s* in third person singular present tense verb forms.

FAULTY He *come* here every day.

REVISED He *comes* here every day.

For more on this aspect of verb use, see "The Present Tense" on pages 237–239 in Chapter 12, "Forming Basic Tenses for Regular Verbs."

- Memorize the irregular verbs. Some pairs of irregular verbs—for example, *lie/lay, rise/raise,* and *sit/set*—can be confusing, but remembering which takes an object and which does not will help you distinguish between them. The verbs *lie, rise,* and *sit* never have an object. The verbs *lay, raise,* and *set* do take an object.

No Object	*Object*
She lay in the sun.	She laid *her books* on the floor.
The sun rises every morning.	They raised *the flag.*
He sat in the chair.	He set *the table* for four.

For more on this aspect of verb use, see Chapter 13, "Using Irregular Verbs Correctly."

- Use *complete* passive verb forms; combine a form of *to be* with the past participle of another verb.

FAULTY His work finished.

REVISED His work *was* finished. *[Add form of* to be*]*

or

He finished his work. *[Transform to active voice]*

For more information on this aspect of verb use, see "Understanding Active and Passive Voice" on pages 264–266 in Chapter 14, "Using Passive Voice and Progressive Tenses, and Maintaining Consistency in Tense."

- Use *-'s* to make contractions with *is* and *has*, but shorten *has* only when it is a helping verb.

FAULTY She's some money.

REVISED She has some money.

- To avoid sounding too informal, don't rely too heavily on contractions like *she's*. Use *she is* instead.

INFORMAL She's ready to help.

FORMAL She is ready to help.

- Verbs describing a completed mental process (*believe, consider, forget, know, remember, think, understand*), a consistent preference (*drink, swim, eat*), a state of being (*am, appear, have, seem, remember, forget, love*), or perceptions (*feel, hear, see, taste*) can *never* be progressive. If the verb refers to an incomplete process, it can be progressive.

EXAMPLES I *consider* my choice good. [*An already completed decision*]

I *am considering* going. [*A decision-making process not yet complete*]

I *think* she should be president. [*A completed intellectual position*]

I *am thinking* about what to do this summer. [*An incomplete thought process*]

I *drink* coffee. [*A consistent preference*]

I *am drinking* coffee. [*An incomplete action*]

FAULTY I *am seeing* you. I *am liking* you, but I *am loving* cheeseburgers.

REVISED I *see* you. I *like* you, but I *love* cheeseburgers.

For more on this aspect of verb use, see "Progressive Tenses" on pages 266–268 in Chapter 14, "Using Passive Voice and Progressive Tenses, and Maintaining Consistency in Tense."

- *Do* and *make* do *not* mean the same thing in English. *Do* often refers to action that is mechanical or specific. *Make* often refers to action that is creative or general: The teacher *makes* up the exercise (creative), but the student *does* the exercise (mechanical). No clear rule explains the difference, so you will just have to memorize this usage.

Mostly Mechanical or Specific	*Mostly Creative or General*
do the dishes	make the bed
do the homework	make an impression
do the laundry	make progress
do your hair	make up your mind
do (brush) your teeth	make (cook) a meal
do (write) a paper	make (build) a house
do the right thing	make mistakes
do someone a favor	make a speech
do good deeds	make a living
do away with	make arrangements

FAULTY   I have to *make the homework* before I can *do a speech.*

REVISED   I have to *do the homework* before I can *make a speech.*

- *Tell* and *say* do *not* mean the same thing in English.

tell time	say a prayer
tell a story or a joke	say hello
tell me	say that we should go
tell the difference	say, "Let's go!"

FAULTY   say me; tell hello; say a joke

REVISED   tell me; say hello; tell a joke

Articles: *a, an,* and *the*

- Use *a* before words that begin with consonant sounds and *an* before words that begin with vowels.
    1. *A* and *an* mean the same as *one* or *each:* I want *an* ice cream cone. [*Just one*]
    2. *A* and *an* go with an unidentified member of a class: *A* small dog came toward her, *a* bone in its mouth. [*Some unknown dog, some unknown bone*]
    3. *A* and *an* go with a representative member of a class: You can tell by the way he talks that he is *a* politician.
    4. *A* and *an* go with a noun that places an idea in a larger class: The car is *a* four-wheeled vehicle.

    See "Cue Words That Identify Number" on pages 300–303 in Chapter 16, "Working with Nouns."

- *The* serves many functions.
    1. *The* modifies known people, objects, or ideas: *the* mother of *the* bride, *the* head of *the* household in which he stayed, *the* Copernican theory

2. *The* goes with superlatives: *the* best, *the* least
3. *The* goes with rank: *the* first book, *the* third child with this problem
4. *The* goes with *of* phrases: the way *of the* world
5. *The* goes with adjective phrases or clauses that limit or identify the noun: *the* topic being discussed
6. *The* refers to a class as a whole: *The* giraffe is an African animal.
7. *The* goes with the names of familiar objects (*the* store) and the names of newspapers *(The Wall Street Journal),* but not with the names of most magazines *(Time).*
8. *The* goes with the names of historical periods (*the* French Revolution), of legislative acts (*the* Missouri Compromise), political parties (*the* Green Party), the branches of government (*the* executive branch), official titles (*the* president), government bodies (*the* Navy), and organizations (*the* Girl Scouts).
9. *The* goes with rivers (but not lakes), canals, oceans, channels, gulfs, peninsulas, swamps, groups of islands, mountain ranges, hotels, libraries, museums, and geographic regions: *the* Panama Canal, *the* Mississippi River, *the* Okefenokee Swamp, *the* Hilton, *the* Smithsonian, *the* South.

FAULTY   According to *Philadelphia Inquirer,* the Lake Victoria is one of most beautiful lakes in world.

REVISED   According to the *Philadelphia Inquirer,* Lake Victoria is one of *the* most beautiful lakes in *the* world.

Spelling

- Watch for these common spelling errors:
  1. Leaving *h* out of *wh* words: *which,* not *wich*
  2. Adding an *e* to words that start with *s: stupid,* not *estupid*
  3. Confusing words that sound alike in English but have different meanings and different spellings:

his/he's (he is)	which/witch	there/their
whether/weather	here/hear	through/threw
advice/advise (noun/verb)	too/to/two	though/thought

  4. Confusing grammatical functions because of familiar sound combinations: *whose* or *who's* (who is), not *who his*
  5. Confusing words that sound similar using your native language's pronunciation patterns but have different meanings and different sounds in English:

this (singular)/these (plural)	chair/share
read/lead	boat/vote
heat/hit	

For more on dealing with these kinds of words, see Chapter 20, "Mastering Spelling."

Other Common Grammar Problems

Double Negatives

- Never use a double negative. As in mathematics, two negatives in the same subject–verb unit in English equal a positive.

FAULTY
$$(-) \quad + \quad (-) = +$$
I do*n't* have *no* money. [*Meaning becomes positive*]

REVISED
$$(-) \quad + \quad (-) = +$$
I do*n't* have *any* money. [*Meaning remains negative*]

See "Double Negatives" on pages 344–346 in Chapter 18, "Working with Adjectives and Adverbs: Using Modifiers Effectively."

Confusing Words

- *Too* does not have the same meaning as *very*. *Very* is an intensifier; it emphasizes quantity. *Too* is often negative and critical. It is sometimes attached to a word that goes with an infinitive (*to* + verb) to emphasize negative effects.

EXAMPLES
It is *very* cold, but we can walk to the restaurant. [*Very* = *intensely*]

It is *too* cold to walk, so we should take a taxi. [*Too* = *negative*]

FAULTY
He is *very* fat to play on the soccer team.

REVISED
He is *too* fat to play on the soccer team. [*He cannot play soccer because he is so heavy.*]

- *Hard* can be an adjective or an adverb, but *hardly* is generally an adverb meaning *barely, almost none,* or *almost not at all.*

EXAMPLES
adjective noun
He learned a *hard* lesson. [*A difficult lesson*]

verb adverb
He worked *hard*. [*With great effort*]

adverb verb
He *hardly* worked. [*Barely, almost not at all*]

adverb pronoun
Hardly anyone watches black-and-white television. [*Almost no one*]

- *A few* (count) and *a little* (noncount) mean *some,* while *few* and *little* mean *almost none.* The difference is between a positive attitude and a negative attitude.

EXAMPLES

I have *a little* money, so I can lend you some. [*Some, so positive*]

I have *little* money, so I can't lend you any. [*Almost none, so negative*]

A few students came, so we were pleased. [*Some, so positive*]

Few students came, so we were disappointed. [*Almost none, so negative*]

- *Some* and *any* both mean an indefinite amount. However, *some* is used in positive statements while *any* is used in negative statements.

EXAMPLES

I have *some* money. [*Positive*]

I don't have *any* money. [*Negative*]

- *Well* is usually an adverb, whereas *good* is an adjective. However, *well* can sometimes be an adjective referring to health.

EXAMPLES

noun   adjective
The *boy* is *good*. [*Well-behaved*]

verb   adverb
He doesn't feel *well*. [*Poor health*]

noun   adjective
The *boy* is *well*. [*Healthy, not sick*]

For more on working with confusing pairs of words, see "Irregular and Confusing Modifier Pairs" on pages 341–344 in Chapter 18, "Working with Adjectives and Adverbs: Using Modifiers Effectively."

Prepositions

- Use *on* when one thing touches the surface of another and *in* when one thing encloses another: *on* the desk (on top), *in* the desk (inside a drawer). Also, use *on* if you must step up to board (get *on* a motorcycle/bus/train/large ship) but *in* if you must step down (get *in* a small boat/car).

- *Since* goes with a specific initial time (*since* 3 P.M.; *since* July 3); *for* goes with duration, a length or period of time (*for* two hours; *for* ten days).

Punctuation and Capitalization

- All sentences have an ending punctuation mark. Statements end with a period (.). Exclamations end with an exclamation point (!). Questions end with a question mark (?). Statements, exclamations, and questions end with *only* one mark. Avoid multiple punctuation marks at the end of sentences.

For more on the use of end punctuation, see "Periods, Question Marks, and Exclamation Points" on pages 419–422 in Chapter 22, "Using Punctuation Properly."